Tina Thoburn
Virginia Arnold
Rita Schlatterbeck
Ann Terry

Macmillan English

SERIES E®

Macmillan Publishing Co., Inc.
New York

Collier Macmillan Publishers
London

ACKNOWLEDGMENTS

The publisher gratefully acknowledges permission to reprint the following copyrighted material:

"Fulton's Folly" by Steven Otfinoski © 1982 by Macmillan Publishing Co., Inc.

"Marian Anderson" adapted from *Marian Anderson* by Tobi Tobias. Copyright © 1972 by Tobi Tobias. By permission of Thomas Y. Crowell.

"Casey Jones," a ballad.

"Prairie Blizzard" by Louise Budde De Laurentis. Copyright © 1975 by Louise Budde DeLaurentis. Permission courtesy of the author.

"Call It Courage" from *Call It Courage* by Armstrong Sperry reprinted with permission of Macmillan Publishing Co., Inc. Copyright © 1940 by Macmillan Publishing Co., Inc., renewed 1968 by Armstrong Sperry. *The Boy Who Was Afraid (Call It Courage)*, by Armstrong Sperry, is published in the United Kingdom by The Bodley Head.

"Rumors" from *Jataka Tales* by Nancy DeRoin. Copyright © 1975 by Nancy DeRoin. Reprinted by permission of Houghton Mifflin Company.

"A Giant Firefly" from *An Introduction to Haiku* by Harold G. Henderson. Copyright © 1958 by Harold G. Henderson. Reprinted by permission of Doubleday & Company , Inc.

"Stillness," "Grasshopper," "The moon is in the water," and "The bat," translation of haiku from *Haiku* Vols. 1–4 by R. H. Blyth, copyright © 1949–52 R. H. Blyth, reprinted by permission of The Hokuseido Press, Tokyo.

"Dear Ranger Rick" by Kristen Wood. Reprinted from *Ranger Rick's Nature Magazine*, © April 1979, by permission of the publisher, the National Wildlife Federation.

"Voyager I Visits Saturn" by Meisha Goldish © 1982 by Macmillan Publishing Co., Inc.

Cover design: Nadja Furlan

Illustration Credits:
Konrad Hack, Rosemarie Karen, Ken Longtemps, Pat Merrell, Hima Pamoedjo, Larry Raymond, Frank Riccio, Charles Shaw, Joel Snyder, Yasemin Tomakan, Lloyd Kenneth Townsend, Michaele Trumel, Johann Wechter, Ed Young

Photography Credits:
Clara Aich; Black Star, ©Planet News Ltd.; ©Brown Brothers; ©Culver Pictures, Inc.; ©Sergio Dorantes; ©Lawrence Frank; ©Ingbert Gruttner; ©Henson Associates, Inc. 1978 (reprinted by permission); Courtesy of Hurok Attractions; ©Robert Lee II; Monkmeyer Press Photo Service, ©Freda Leinwand, ©Walter Ward; ©NASA; *Photo Researchers, Inc.*, ©George Holton, ©Richard Hutchings, ©Tom McHugh, ©Michael Philip Manheim, ©Larry Mulvehill, ©Tom Myers, ©Porterfield-Chickering, ©Bucky Reeves, ©Bruce Roberts, Rapho Div., ©R. Rowan, ©Quantas Airlines; *Shostal Associates,* ©Ernest Bernard, ©Clyde Martin, ©C. Uhlhorn; Stock, Boston, Inc., ©Donald Dietz; The Stock Market, ©Ed Goldfarb; © United Press International

Parts of this work were published in earlier editions of SERIES E: Macmillan English.

Macmillan Publishing Co., Inc.
866 Third Avenue, New York, New York 10022
Collier Macmillan Canada, Inc.

Printed in the United States of America
ISBN 0-02-247140-5
9 8 7 6 5 4 3 2 1

TABLE OF CONTENTS

Unit 1

Grammar and Related Language Skills • Sentences I . . . . 2 - 17

Sentences 2
Four Kinds of Sentences 4
Capitalizing and Punctuating Sentences 6
Skills Review 8
Subject Parts and Predicate Parts 10
Building Sentences 12
Using Commas 14
Skills Review 16

Practical Communication • Time-Order Paragraph . . . . 18 - 27

Study and Reference Skills
Parts of a Book 18
Putting Ideas in Order 20
Time Order in Paragraphs 22

Composition
A Class Paragraph 24
Practicing a Time-Order Paragraph 25
How to Edit Your Work 26
Independent Writing 27

Unit Review . . . . 28 - 29

Creative Expression . . . . 30 - 33

A Fable 30
"Rumors" 30
Creative Activities 33

Unit 2

Grammar and Related Language Skills • Nouns . . . . 36 - 55

Nouns 36
Plural Nouns 38
More About Plural Nouns 40
Compound Nouns 42
Skills Review 44
Common and Proper Nouns 46
Abbreviations 48
Possessive Nouns 50
Suffixes 52
Skills Review 54

Practical Communication • Descriptive Paragraph . . . . 56 - 65

Study and Reference Skills
Using the Dictionary 56

Composition
Words That Describe Senses 58
Descriptive Paragraphs 60
A Descriptive Paragraph in a Friendly Letter 62
Practicing a Descriptive Paragraph in a Friendly Letter 64
Independent Writing 65

Unit Review . . . . 66 - 67

Creative Expression . . . . 68 - 69

Haiku 68
Creative Activities 69

Unit 3

Grammar and Related Language Skills • Verbs I .... 72 - 95

Action Verbs 72
Objects of Verbs 74
Verb Tenses 76
Using the Present Tense 78
Using the Past Tense 80
Skills Review 82
Present and Past of *Have* 84
Past Tense with *Have* 86
Irregular Verbs 88
More Irregular Verbs 90
Prefixes 92
Skills Review 94

Practical Communication • Factual Paragraph .... 96 - 105

Study and Reference Skills
Using the Library 96
Reading Graphs and Tables 98
Composition
Facts in Paragraphs 100
A Factual Paragraph in a Business Letter 102
Practicing a Factual Paragraph in a Business Letter 104
Independent Writing 105

Unit Review .... 106 - 107

Creative Expression .... 108 - 109

A Letter 108
Dear Ranger Rick by Kristen Wood 108
Creative Activities 109

Unit 4

Grammar and Related Language Skills • Pronouns ...... 112 - 129

Pronouns 112
Pronouns as Subjects 114
Pronouns as Objects 116
Using Subject and Object Pronouns 118
Skills Review 120
Possessive Pronouns 122
Subject-Verb Agreement 124
Words Often Confused 126
Skills Review 128

Practical Communication • Persuasive Paragraph .... 130 - 139

Study and Reference Skills
Parts of a Newspaper 130
Fact and Opinion 132
Composition
Reasons in a Persuasive Paragraph 134
A Persuasive Paragraph in an Editorial 136
Practicing a Persuasive Paragraph in an Editorial 138
Independent Writing 139

Unit Review .... 140 - 141

Creative Expression .... 142 - 145

A Photo Essay 142

Voyager I Visits Saturn by Meisha Goldish 142

Creative Activities 145

Mid-Year Review .... *146 -149*

Unit 5

Grammar and Related Language Skills • Sentences II .... 152 - 173

Reviewing Sentences 152

Simple Subjects 154

Simple Predicates 156

Compound Subjects 158

Compound Predicates 160

Skills Review 162

Agreement of Verbs with Compound Subjects 164

Building Sentences 166

Using Commas in Writing 168

Punctuating Conversation 170

Skills Review 172

Practical Communication • Conversation .... 174 - 181

Study and Reference Skills

Using Test-Taking Skills 174

Listening and Speaking Skills 176

Composition

A Class Conversation 178

Practicing a Conversation 180

Independent Writing 181

Unit Review .... *182 - 183*

Creative Expression .... 184 - 189

A Play 184

Fulton's Folly by Stevan Otfinoski 185

Creative Activities 189

Unit 6

Grammar and Related Language Skills • Adjectives .... 192 - 207

Adjectives 192

Adjectives That Compare 194

Using *More* and *Most* to Compare 196

Skills Review 198

Spelling Adjectives 200

Proper Adjectives 201

Prefixes and Suffixes 202

Adjective Synonyms 204

Skills Review 206

Practical Communication • Summary Paragraph .... 208 - 215

Study and Reference Skills

Using Reference Works 208

Composition

Reviewing Paragraphs 210

Interviews and Surveys 212

Practicing a Summary Paragraph 214

Independent Writing 215

Unit Review . . . . *216 - 217*

Creative Expression . . . . **218 - 223**

A Biography 218
Marian Anderson by Tobi Tobias 218
Creative Activities 223

Unit 7

Grammar and Related Language Skills • Verbs II . . . . **226 - 243**

Linking Verbs 226
Nouns and Adjectives After Linking Verbs 228
Using Linking Verbs in the Present Tense 230
Using Linking Verbs in the Past Tense 231
Verb Antonyms 232
Skills Review 234
Verbs Ending in *-ing* 236
Using Apostrophes in Possessives and in Contractions 238
Verb Synonyms 240
Skills Review 242

Practical Communication • Two-Paragraph Report . . . . . . **244 - 251**

Study and Reference Skills
Using Note-Taking Skills 244
Composition
Two-Paragraph Reports 246
A Class Report 248
Practicing a Two-Paragraph Report 250
Independent Writing 251

Unit Review . . . . *252 - 253*

Creative Expression . . . . **254 - 257**

A Ballad 254
Casey Jones 255
Creative Activities 257

Unit 8

Grammar and Related Language Skills • Adverbs . . . . . . **260 - 277**

Adverbs 260
Using Adverbs to Compare 262
Forming Adverbs from Adjectives 264
Skills Review 266
Reviewing Capitalization 268
Homographs 270
Understanding Words from Context 272
Levels of Usage 274
Skills Review 276

Practical Communication • News Report . . . . 278 - 285

Study and Reference Skills
Developing a Two-Part Outline 278
Composition
Outlining a Two-Paragraph Report 280
A Class Outline 282
Practicing a Two-Paragraph Report 284
Independent Writing 285

Unit Review . . . . *286 - 287*

Creative Expression . . . . 288 - 293

A True Story 288
Prairie Blizzard by
Louise Budde DeLaurentis 288
Creative Activities 293

Unit 9

Grammar and Related Language Skills • Sentences III . . . 296 - 313

Reviewing Compound Subjects and Predicates 296
Compound Sentences 298
Building Compound Sentences 300
Skills Review 302
Prepositions and Prepositional Phrases 304
Parts of Speech in Sentences 306
Reviewing Commas 308
The History of Language 310
Skills Review 312

Practical Communication • Stories . . . . 314 - 321

Study and Reference Skills
Reviewing Dictionary Skills 314
Composition
A Story 316
Practicing a Story 318
Independent Writing 319
Writing a Book Report 320

Unit Review . . . . *322 - 323*

Creative Expression . . . . 324 - 329

A Story 324
Call It Courage by Armstrong Sperry 325
Creative Activities 329

End-of-Year Review . . . . *330 - 335*

Handbook . . . . 336 - 357
More Practice . . . . 358 - 376
Workbook . . . . 377 - 446
Index . . . . 447 - 455

EMPTY HOUSE NEAR GRAND ISLAND, NEBRASKA

Grammar and Related Language Skills

Four Kinds of Sentences
Punctuation of Sentences
Subject Parts and Predicate Parts
Using Commas

Practical Communication

STUDY AND REFERENCE SKILLS
Understanding Paragraph Structure
COMPOSITION
Writing a Time-Order Paragraph

Creative Expression

A Fable

1

What would the inside of a large old house be like? What would make it look or sound mysterious? Many people enjoy investigating mysterious places and events. People who try to solve mysteries are called detectives. What listening skills might help a detective solve a mystery? What writing skills might a detective need?

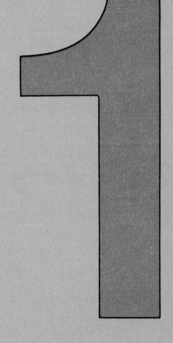

Reviewing Sentences

Some groups of words state a complete idea. Other groups of words may suggest part of an idea. Such groups of words are not sentences.

> A **sentence** is a group of words that state a complete idea.

- Look at the groups of words in the box.

The telephone.	The telephone rings under the bed.
The detective.	The detective opens the drawer.
The detective.	The detective searches for his glasses.

The groups of words on the left name a person or a thing. They do not say what action the person or thing does. The groups of words on the left are *not* sentences.

- Now look at the groups of words on the right. They name a person or a thing. They say what action the person or thing does. These groups of words are sentences.

Every sentence has two parts. Each part states only half an idea. You need both parts to state a complete idea.

- Read this sentence. Look carefully at its two parts.

The detective | searches for his glasses.

Notice that the first part of the sentence names whom the sentence is about. The sentence is about the detective. The second part of the sentence tells what action the first part is doing. What action is the detective doing?

Suppose you want to know if a group of words is a sentence. You have to answer the following questions:

> Whom or what does the group of words name?
> What action does that person or thing do?

Talk About It

Tell whether or not each group of words is a sentence. Give reasons for your answers.

1. A clown visits the detective.
2. A circus mystery.
3. The clown saws a box in half.
4. Loses half the box.
5. A missing part.
6. The bottom of the box.

Skills Practice

Some of the groups of words below are sentences. Other groups are not. Write each group of words that is a sentence. If a group of words is not a sentence, write **not a sentence.**

1. Needs the missing part.
2. The detective searches.
3. Looks for clues.
4. Peeks into animal cages.
5. Hears strange noises.
6. The detective sees footprints.
7. The detective finds a clue.
8. Opens the trunk.
9. The detective opens the trunk.
10. The clown lifts the lid.
11. Looks inside.
12. Finds the bottom of the box.

Sample Answers 1. not a sentence **2.** The detective searches.

Four Kinds of Sentences

You know that a sentence states a complete idea. Did you know that there are different kinds of sentences? Some sentences tell something. Other sentences ask something.

A **declarative sentence** is a sentence that makes a statement or tells something.

- Look at the picture. Find two sentences in the picture that are declarative sentences.

An **interrogative sentence** is a sentence that asks something.

- Look at the picture again. Find two sentences that are interrogative sentences.

Some sentences tell someone to do something. Other sentences show excitement or strong feeling.

An **imperative sentence** is a sentence that tells or asks someone to do something.

- Look in the box. Find two sentences that are imperative sentences.

Do not touch the furniture.	What a lot of dust there is!
Are there more footprints?	I will open the window.
Look for other clues.	How scared I am!

An **exclamatory sentence** is a sentence that shows excitement or strong feeling.

- Look in the box. Find two exclamatory sentences.

Some exclamations are not complete sentences. They are called *interjections*. An interjection shows strong feeling and is followed by an exclamation mark.

Wow! Ouch! Whew!

Talk About It

Tell what kind of sentence each one is. Give reasons for your answers.

1. The football disappeared.
2. Who took it?
3. A person ran away.
4. Did she climb out the window?
5. What a strange sight that was!
6. Call the detective.
7. She will solve the mystery.
8. What a detective she is!

Skills Practice

Write each sentence. Write whether each sentence is **declarative, interrogative, imperative,** or **exclamatory.**

1. Do you know Mr. Holmes?
2. I see him on Baker Street.
3. He is a great detective.
4. How smart he is!
5. Tell me about him.
6. He works with Dr. Watson.
7. He finds clues everywhere.
8. How does he solve his cases?
9. He plays the violin and thinks.
10. What a person he is!
11. Has he solved the mystery?
12. Ask the police.

Sample Answer 1. Do you know Mr. Holmes? interrogative

Capitalizing and Punctuating Sentences

Traffic lights tell a driver or a walker when to start and when to stop. A green light means *go*. A red light means *stop*. When you write sentences, you use special signals. They tell the reader where your sentences begin and where they end.

- Look at each sentence in the box. What kind of letter is at the beginning of each sentence?

The island was quite small.	What a strange building it is!
We stand on the beach.	Does someone still live here?
Who made the hut?	Look around.

Use a **capital letter** to begin the first word of every sentence.

- Look again at each sentence in the box. Then look at the definitions on page 4. What signal, or punctuation mark, is used at the end of each sentence in the box?

Use a **period** (**.**) at the end of a declarative or an imperative sentence.

Use a **question mark** (**?**) at the end of an interrogative sentence.

Use an **exclamation mark** (**!**) at the end of an exclamatory sentence or an interjection.

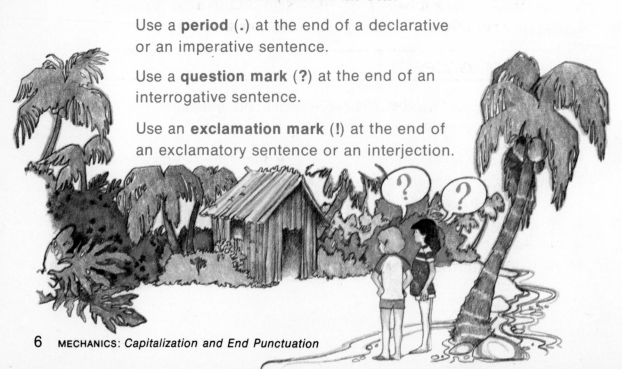

Talk About It

Read each sentence. What punctuation mark should you use at the end of each one? Give reasons for your answers.

1. A fire burned in the fireplace
2. We saw a potato baking
3. Who could have cooked it
4. What a strange place this is
5. Look in the other room
6. Is there butter for the potato

Skills Practice

Write each of the following sentences. Begin each sentence with a capital letter. End each sentence with the correct punctuation mark.

1. have you heard about Bigfoot
2. what is that
3. it is a big creature
4. what a strange beast that is
5. how does it walk
6. it walks like a person
7. what big footprints it has
8. have you seen the creature
9. no one has caught it
10. people are looking for it
11. what a catch that would be
12. i would like to see it
13. the creature is furry
14. what color is its fur
15. its fur is brown
16. look how thick it is

Writing Sentences

Imagine you are a detective. All the lights in your house just went out.

1. Write two declarative sentences. Tell how you would feel.
2. Write one imperative sentence. Tell someone to do something.
3. Write two interrogative sentences. Ask someone two questions.
4. Write one exclamatory sentence that shows your excitement.

Sample Answer 1. Have you heard about Bigfoot?

Skills Review

Some of the groups of words below are sentences. Other groups are not. Write **sentence** if the group of words is a sentence. If a group of words is not a sentence, write **not a sentence.**

1. A mystery story on TV.
2. Two girls went hiking together.
3. The beach.
4. The girls heard scary noises.
5. A dark cave.
6. Returned with a flashlight.
7. The girls entered the cave.
8. Pat led Sandy through the dark.
9. A strange sound.
10. Pat slipped on a rock.
11. The flashlight.
12. Fell on the ground.
13. The girls saw mysterious lights.
14. Pat stood very still.
15. Sandy peeked through a hole.
16. Friends sat around a campfire.

Read each of these sentences. Write whether each sentence is **declarative, imperative, interrogative,** or **exclamatory.**

17. Did you see that mystery story about the cave on TV?
18. What an exciting show it was!
19. Would you be afraid to go into the cave?
20. Pat and Sandy climbed on the big round rocks.
21. Look at the large waves pounding the shore.
22. The water from each wave went into the cave.
23. Did Pat and Sandy get their feet wet in the cave?
24. They dried their shoes by the campfire.
25. We went to the town dump yesterday.

26. What a lot of old furniture we saw there!
27. Please take me there today.
28. Why do you want to go there?
29. I want to find a table and a chair.
30. Why do you need a table and a chair?
31. I want to put them in my hideout.
32. Take a shortcut through the woods.
33. What a long way it is!

Write each of the following sentences. Begin each sentence with a capital letter. End each sentence with the correct punctuation mark.

34. what a great place this is
35. help me look for the dishes
36. do you see the dishes over there
37. what a lot of cups there are
38. will you help me carry this
39. let's put these in the wagon
40. what else can we get
41. the glasses will fit too

Careers

Some writers have become famous as authors of mystery stories. Dame Agatha Christie is a well known author of mystery stories. Two famous detectives, Hercule Poirot and Miss Jane Marple, appear in many of her stories. But the best-known author of mystery stories may be Sir Arthur Conan Doyle. His most famous character is Sherlock Holmes. *The Hound of the Baskervilles* is one of the most famous novels about this detective and his friend, Dr. Watson. Both writers were British and wrote many short stories, novels, and plays.

Subject Parts and Predicate Parts

Every sentence has two parts. Each part has a special job. One part names whom or what the sentence is about. This part is the *subject part*. The other part names what action the subject part does. This part is the *predicate part*. You need both parts to state a complete idea.

The **subject part** of a sentence names whom or what the sentence is about. The subject part may have one word or more than one word.

- Look at the following sentence. What is the sentence about?

A bright light | flashes in the sky.

The sentence is about a bright light. *A bright light* is the subject part of the sentence.

The **predicate part** of a sentence tells what action the subject part does. The predicate part may have one word or more than one word.

- Look at this sentence again. What action does the subject part do?

A bright light | flashes in the sky.

The subject part is *A bright light*. The bright light *flashes in the sky*. The predicate part of the sentence is *flashes in the sky*.

The subject part of a sentence is usually stated, but in an imperative sentence the subject *you* often is not stated.

Stop that. Look at the sky.

Talk About It

Look at the group of words in each box. Point out the subject part and the predicate part. Give reasons for your answers.

1. Many people | see the light.
2. Television sets | break.
3. Cars | stop.
4. A light | flashes.

Skills Practice

Write each sentence. Draw a line between the subject part and the predicate part. Draw one line under the subject part. Draw two lines under the predicate part.

1. Juanita Lopez reads a book.
2. Juanita hears a noise.
3. Taro goes to the door.
4. Taro sees an object.
5. The object floats overhead.
6. Green lights blink on and off.
7. The object stands still.
8. The noise stops suddenly.

Writing Sentences

You see something in the sky. It has flashing lights and makes noise. You are not sure what it is.

1. Write two sentences that tell about the object. Use these subject parts in your sentences.
   a. The flashing lights **b.** The loud noise
2. Write two more sentences that tell about what you see or hear. Use these predicate parts in your sentences.
   a. hear something **b.** see flashing lights

Sample Answer 1. Juanita Lopez | reads a book.

Building Sentences

You know that every sentence has a subject part and a predicate part. You have probably noticed that some telling sentences are very short.

- Read these sentences.

A farmer disappeared. The people searched.

These are complete sentences. Both sentences have a subject part and a predicate part. But you can make these sentences tell more by adding words to describe the subject part.

A kind farmer disappeared. A generous farmer disappeared.

The words *kind* and *generous* tel! more about the *farmer*. They help to build a more interesting subject part.

Sometimes you can add words and phrases to the predicate part. These words or phrases can help your sentence tell more.

- Read each sentence. What is added to the predicate part in each sentence? How does each predicate part help the sentence to tell more?

The people searched the village.

The people searched anxiously.

The people searched around the mountain.

Talk About It

Read each sentence. Add more words to the subject part to make a good sentence.

1. A man imagined.
2. The author wrote.
3. People read.
4. The mystery amused.

Add more words to the predicate part to make a good sentence.

5. Washington Irving told.
6. Rip Van Winkle disappeared.
7. Soldiers fought.
8. Colonists won.

Skills Practice

Add words to the subject part of each sentence. Write the sentence.

1. The farmer wandered.
2. The journey continued.
3. The river flowed.
4. The traveler rested.
5. The sun set.
6. A voice called.
7. The man listened.
8. A figure appeared.

Add words to the predicate part of each sentence. Write the sentence.

9. Strangers gathered.
10. The farmer sipped.
11. Years passed.
12. The town folk wondered.
13. The country flourished.
14. The man awakened.
15. The story amazed.
16. Everyone listened.

Writing Sentences

Imagine that you have written a mystery story. Here's what happened.

(1) The friends read. (2) A friend guesses. (3) The ending amazes. (4) A publisher enjoys. (5) The critics applaud.

Add words or phrases that describe to each sentence to tell more about the experience. Use as many as you can.

Sample Answer 1. The jolly farmer wandered.

Using Commas

Commas take the place of pauses. Commas help your reader to understand exactly what you mean.

Commas are used to set off words that interrupt a sentence.

> Use a **comma** (,) to set off words such as *yes, no,* and *well* when they begin a sentence.

Yes, I have heard of the Abominable Snowman.
No, it is still a mystery to me. Well, let's read more about it.

> Use a **comma** (,) to set off the name of a person who is spoken to directly in a sentence.

Ralph, have you any information on the subject?
There was an article in the paper, Betty.

The items in dates and addresses are separated by commas.

> Use a **comma** (,) to separate the day from the date and the date from the year.

James presented his report on Friday, January 6, 1984.

> Use a **comma** (,) after the year when it appears with the date in the middle of a sentence.

The class invited a reporter to speak on February 6, 1984, about the Abominable Snowman.

> Use a **comma** (,) to separate the name of a city and state.

My friend lives in Fairbanks, Alaska.

> Use a **comma** (,) after the name of a state when it appears with a city name in the middle of a sentence.

He collects articles in Fairbanks, Alaska, about the mystery of the Abominable Snowman.

Talk About It

Read each sentence. Tell how you would use commas.

1. Explorers left England on Wednesday April 19 1956 for Kathmandu Nepal to find the snowman.
2. What did they find out Dr. Hall?
3. Well they didn't really find anything new.

Skills Practice

Write each sentence. Use commas where necessary.

1. Howard have you read the *Legend of Sleepy Hollow?*
2. Yes it was a very mysterious book.
3. Well can you tell us about the "Headless Horseman"?
4. No my report is not ready yet.
5. Can you report on March 8 1984 in the afternoon Howard?
6. Do you have any information for him Brad?
7. Yes the story takes place in Sleepy Hollow New York on the Hudson River.
8. Well is there anyone who can share a mystery with us on Friday March 9 1984?

Writing Sentences

Imagine you are writing a news report on the legend of the Abominable Snowman. Write four sentences about it.

1. Begin one sentence with *yes, no,* or *well.*
2. Address a friend directly in one sentence.
3. Include a day, a date, and a year set in the middle of one sentence.
4. Include the name of a city and its state in the middle of one sentence.

Sample Answer 1. Howard, have you read the *Legend of Sleepy Hollow?*

Skills Review

Write the subject part of each sentence.

1. An alarm sounds in the police station.
2. People jump up from their desks.
3. Police officers rush out the door.
4. The officers race to their cars.
5. The cars leave the parking lot.
6. The sirens make noise.
7. The police drive to the building.
8. Police cars turn the corner.
9. A detective drives into the driveway.

Write the predicate part of each sentence.

10. Officers surround the building.
11. Some officers enter the dark building.
12. The officers climb the stairs.
13. The officers stomp on the wooden floors.
14. A box falls in a room.
15. The police officers turn on their flashlights.
16. Officer Conway opens the door to the room.
17. A ragged cat comes out of the room.
18. The cat looks up at the officers.

Add words to the subject part in each sentence to make the sentences more descriptive. Write each new sentence.

19. The cat walks.
20. The officers look.
21. The cat jumps down.
22. A man locks the door.
23. The police go back.
24. The cars leave.

Add words or phrases to the predicate part in each sentence to make the sentences more descriptive. Write each sentence.

25. The cat runs.
26. The dog rushes.
27. The cat jumps up.
28. It sees a hole.
29. The cat enters.
30. The alarm rings.

Write each sentence. Then add commas where they are needed.

31. My parents drove to Buffalo New York in the spring.
32. They left home on April 10 1984 in the morning.
33. Dad called us from Buffalo New York on April 15 1984.
34. Well why is that a mystery David?
35. Yes there is a mystery Jane because they should have been there two days earlier.
36. No you must be kidding David.
37. I think they went to Niagara Falls Canada on April 13 1984.
38. David how do you know that?
39. I got a post card dated April 14 1984 from Niagara Falls Canada from them.

You have learned that language is always changing. One way you can change the meaning of a word is to add another word to it.

For example, how does the word that is added change the meaning of ship?

steamship airship spaceship starship

How does the addition of the word sea change the meaning of each of these words?

seaweed seafood seaplane seashell

Exploring Language

Parts of a Book

The books you use in school are often reference books or textbooks. The books you read outside of school may contain stories or plays. Both types of books are organized so you can learn about their contents easily. Knowing how to use this organization will help you to save time.

Almost every book has a title page at the front of the book. The *title page* usually shows the name of the book, the author, the publisher, and the place of publication.

A copyright date is on the back of the title page. The *copyright date* tells when a book was published. It is useful to know how long ago a book was published. It is important that information be recent.

The table of contents comes next in most books. The *table of contents* lists the names of the chapters or units. It tells on which page each chapter or unit begins. The table of contents can tell you if a book has the kind of information you need.

The main part of a book is called the *body* of the book. In school books this part is made up of chapters or units of information. In other books it is the story, play, or poems.

How To Be a Detective
R. F. Lancer

Limon Publishing Co.
Chicago

TITLE PAGE

Copyright © 1975
Limon Publishing Co.
All rights reserved.

COPYRIGHT PAGE

Contents

1. Training of a Detective 3
2. What a Detective Does 17
3. Working with the Law 32
4. True Adventures 58

TABLE OF CONTENTS

School books often have special information sections at the back, such as a handbook and an index.

A *handbook* lists the important rules or facts from the body of the book. These rules or facts are organized so that you can refer to them quickly and easily.

An *index* is an alphabetical list. It tells on what page you can find a certain subject or name.

A **sentence** is a group of words that state a complete idea.

The Alberts prepared to go on a picnic.
James searched everywhere for his sneakers.

HANDBOOK

Pronouns, 50–58
defined, 50
list of, 52
correct usage of, 56

INDEX

Talk About It

Use this English book to discuss the following:

1. Name the publisher and the copyright date.
2. Tell on what page Unit 7 begins.
3. Tell where in the handbook you can find the definition of a noun.
4. Use the index to tell the pages that tell about adverbs.
5. How many units are in the body of this book?

Skills Practice

Look at the sample pages on the opposite page. Write the answers to these questions about the parts of a book. Identify the part of the book in which you found the answer.

1. What is the title of the book and name of the author?
2. Who is the publisher?
3. In what city was the book published?
4. What is the copyright date?

Putting Ideas in Order

You have lots of ideas. Everyone does. You can express your ideas in sentences and paragraphs. But you would confuse people if you wrote like this:

The telephone rang. I ate bananas for breakfast. My favorite TV show is *News 47*. I visited friends in Texas last summer. I love to go swimming.

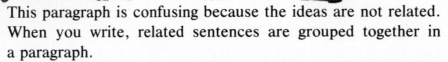

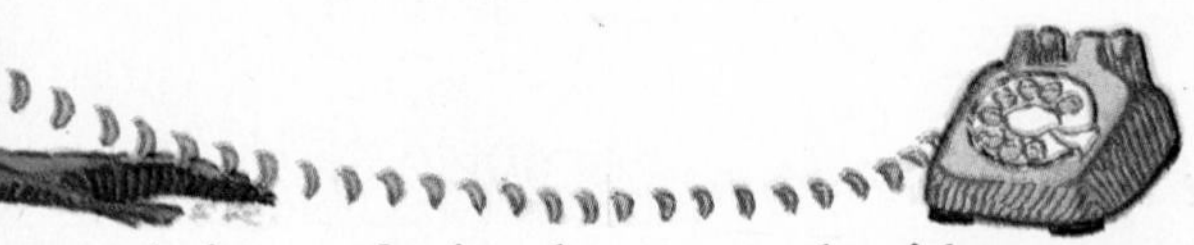

This paragraph is confusing because the ideas are not related. When you write, related sentences are grouped together in a paragraph.

Your paragraph should have a main idea. The sentence that states this main idea is called a *topic sentence*. The topic sentence is often the first sentence in the paragraph. The other sentences in the paragraph are called *detail sentences* because they give details to tell more about the main idea. Here is an example of a topic sentence and two detail sentences.

Topic Sentence: Sherlock Holmes solved cases that stumped Scotland Yard.

Detail 1: He sometimes used a bloodhound to help him find clues.

Detail 2: Sherlock Holmes was a brilliant thinker.

Sentences in a paragraph sometimes tell about things in the order in which they happen. Some time-order words that help you follow the action are *first, next, then, finally,* and *at last*.

Here is an example of how a group of sentences in a paragraph work together. Notice that the topic sentence comes first and that the detail sentences begin with the time-order words.

Topic Sentence: Rob discovered his shoes were missing.
Detail 1: *First* he looked upstairs for them.
Detail 2: *Next* he searched the downstairs.
Detail 3: *Then* he looked in one last place.
Detail 4: *Finally* he found them in the puppy's bed.

Talk About It

Read these sentences. Find the topic sentence first. Then tell how to put the other sentences in the correct order. Use the time-order words to help you.

1. Next she questioned her neighbor who was a detective.
2. Finally she decided to study to be a police officer.
3. Marin wanted to be a detective.
4. First she read many books about detectives.
5. Then she thought about the problems of the job.

Skills Practice

Read the group of sentences below. Write the topic sentence first. Write the detail sentences in the correct order after the topic sentence. Use the time-order words to help you.

1. First Larry and Marin checked the valve.
2. Larry's bike had a flat tire every day.
3. Finally the mystery was solved.
4. Next they questioned the neighborhood children.
5. Then they discovered a box of tacks on the floor.

Now write this group of sentences in the correct order.

6. Next she called the paper girl.
7. Mrs. Flynn's newspaper disappeared Sunday morning.
8. First she called the newspaper dealer.
9. Finally a newspaper was recovered.
10. Then she looked in the doghouse.

Time Order in Paragraphs

Thinking About Paragraphs

When you have an idea for a story, you can always talk about it. Sometimes you might want to write about your idea so others can read it. You can write a paragraph. A good way to begin writing is to organize your paragraph. Remember that a paragraph can be made up of a topic sentence and detail sentences. The *topic sentence* states the main idea of the paragraph. The *detail sentences* in the paragraph tell more about the main idea.

There are different ways to arrange sentences in a paragraph. One good way is to use *time order*. First you write the topic sentence. Then you order, or arrange, the detail sentences according to *time*. You tell what happened first and what happened next until you get to the last detail of what happened.

Words that show time can help you know how to order your sentences. Look for these time-order words at the beginning of detail sentences:

First	*Now*	*To begin with*	*Last*	*Next*	*Finally*

Can you think of more words that might signal time order?

You should also notice that the first line of a paragraph looks different from the other sentences. It is important to remember to *indent* the first word. Indenting means leaving a little space. It signals your reader that you are starting a new topic or paragraph.

●Read the paragraph below.

Michael followed clues to find his friends in the woods. First he saw the broken ends of the bushes. Next he found some marshmallow sticks left over from their campfire. Finally he found his friends asleep behind a group of trees.

Talking About Paragraphs

1. Find the topic sentence in the paragraph about Michael. It is the first sentence of the paragraph: *Michael followed clues to find his friends in the woods.*
2. Read the detail sentences. What are the time-order words in the detail sentences?

Writing a Paragraph

Read the sentences below.

1. Then it searched the tabletop.
2. First it looked in its food dish.
3. Finally it opened the refrigerator.
4. The cat was trying to find food.

Find the topic sentence. Write it on your paper. Now write the three detail sentences in the order that they happened. You have just written a time-order paragraph!

A Class Paragraph

Thinking About Your Class Paragraph

Your class is going to write a time-order paragraph together. The pictures will help you. You will use time order to arrange the sentences in your paragraph.

Writing Your Class Paragraph

1. Start your paragraph with this topic sentence: *The girl went swimming on a cold morning.* You or your teacher should write all the sentences on the board.
2. Think of a detail sentence that tells about the first picture. Choose a time-order word to begin your detail sentence.
3. Think of detail sentences that tell about the next three pictures. The topic sentence and the four detail sentences will make up your class paragraph.
4. Copy the paragraph on your paper. Remember to indent the first word.

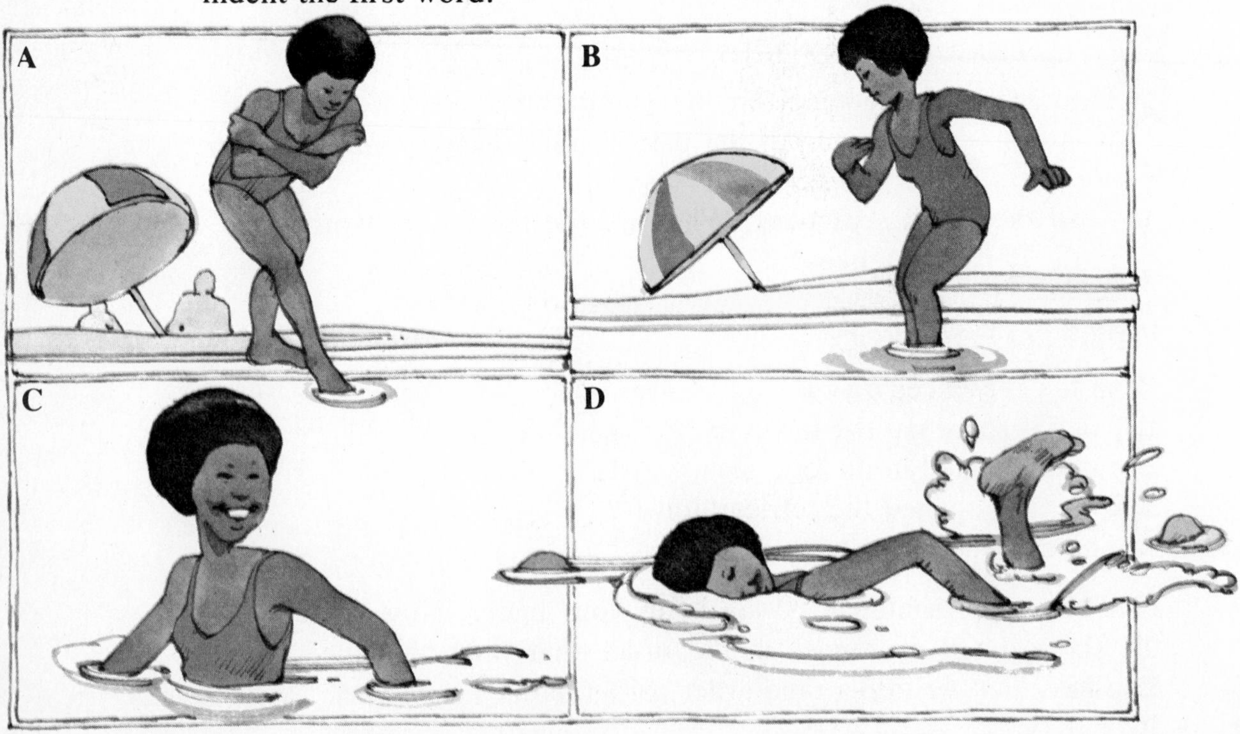

Practicing a Time-Order Paragraph

Thinking About Your Paragraph

Now you are ready to write your own paragraph. The pictures will help you. The Word Bank shows how to spell some of the words you may want to use.

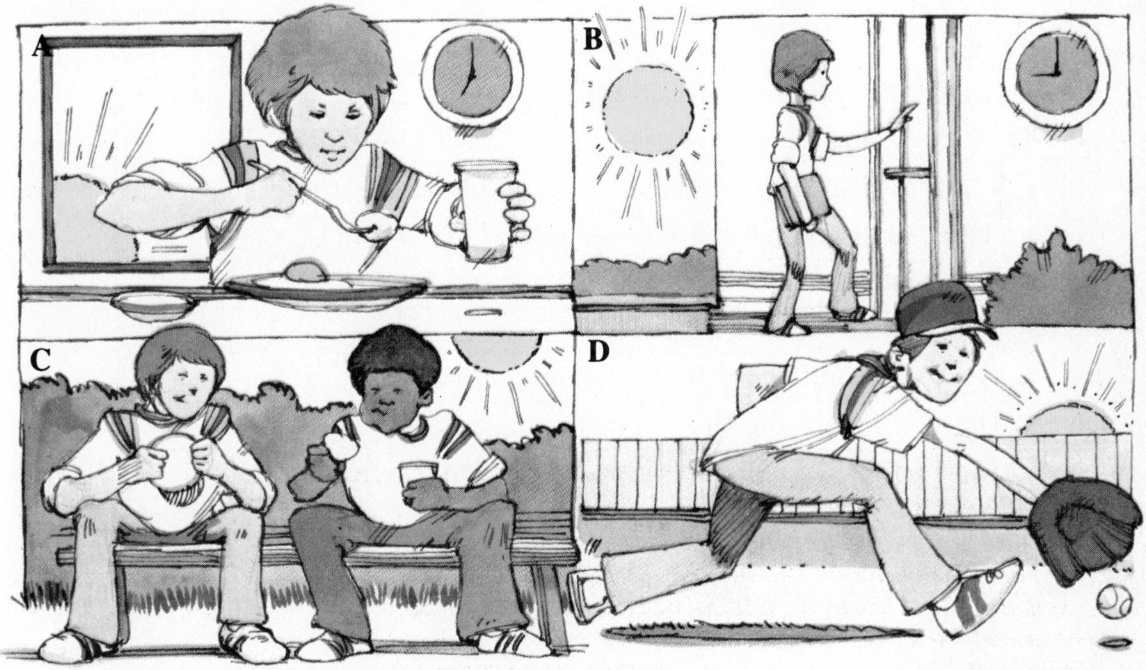

Writing Your Own Paragraph

1. Begin your paragraph with this topic sentence: *John had a very busy day.* If you wish, use your own topic sentence. Write the topic sentence on your paper. Remember to indent the first word.
2. Look at the four pictures. They are arranged in time order.
3. Write a detail sentence that tells about each picture. Remember to use the time-order words to show the order of the pictures.
4. Use the Word Bank to help you spell your words.
5. Save your paragraph.

Word Bank

next
baseball
friend
later
finally
school
reading
then
breakfast

How to Edit Your Work

Have you ever wanted to change something in a paragraph or work you have written? You may decide that you need to improve it or to correct mistakes. This important step in writing is called *editing*. It means you must read your work carefully and look for certain things that could be wrong or improved.

Read the time-order paragraph you wrote about John's day again. Check your work using these editing questions:

1. Look at the topic sentence. Does it tell what all the detail sentences are about?
2. Are your detail sentences in the correct time order?
3. Did you use time-order words?
4. Does each sentence state a complete idea?
5. Did you indent the first word?
6. Did you start each sentence with a capital letter?
7. Did you end each sentence with the correct punctuation?
8. Did you spell all the words correctly?
9. Do you need to recopy your work neatly?

Look at the time-order paragraph below. The writer made some mistakes. But the mistakes have been corrected.

¶Nadia was looking for her new bracelet.
First she looked under the bed. Next ^(she looked) on her
dresser. ~~t~~(T)hird she looked in her ~~her~~ closet.
~~Finly~~ (Finally) she found ^(it) in her ~~pockt~~ (pocket).

Editing Symbols

≡ capitalize
¶ indent
℘ take out
^ add

Look at the way the paragraph is corrected. The writer used marks called *editing symbols* to correct mistakes.

¶ —This symbol means to indent the first word in a paragraph.

≡ —These lines mean to make a capital letter.

∧ —A caret means something has been left out or is being corrected. You add missing letters or words above the correction.

ℊ —Delete means to take out something.

- Look for the carets in the edited paragraph. What words were left out? What words were misspelled? Which word needs a capital letter?

Now use the nine editing questions to check your paragraph. Use the editing symbols if you need them.

INDEPENDENT WRITING

A Time-Order Paragraph

Prewriting Writing accurate directions is an important skill. Directions for science experiments are usually written in time order. Think of a simple science experiment that you have done or would like to do. Look for ideas in your science book or in the library. Think about the purpose of the experiment. What materials are needed? What steps will you use for the directions? Jot down notes to help you remember the answers.

Writing Write a paragraph explaining the directions for a simple science experiment. First write a main-idea sentence that tells the purpose of the experiment. The detail sentences will list materials and state the directions for the experiment.

Editing Use the check questions on page 26 to edit your paragraph.

Unit Review

Some of the groups of words below are sentences. Other groups are not. Write **sentence** if the group of words is a sentence. If a group of words is not a sentence, write **not a sentence.** *pages 2–3*

1. Arnold hears a noise.
2. Calls his sister.
3. Doris looks under the bed.
4. Arnold walks to the closet.
5. Opens the closet door.
6. Doris walks to the window.
7. A branch.
8. Brushes against the window.
9. Sees the tree branch.
10. Doris smiles.

Read each sentence. Write whether each sentence is **declarative, interrogative, imperative,** or **exclamatory.** *pages 4–5*

11. The flower grows in a crack in the sidewalk.
12. What a mystery it is!
13. Did someone plant a seed?
14. Smell the flower.
15. How pretty it is!

Write each of the following sentences. Begin each sentence with a capital letter. End each sentence with the correct punctuation mark. *pages 6–7*

16. dinosaurs disappeared millions of years ago
17. how do people know what they looked like
18. people found dinosaur bones
19. how large they are
20. why did dinosaurs disappear
21. did it get too cold for them
22. some people think dinosaurs got sick

Write the subject part of each sentence. *pages 10–11*

23. Stephanie goes to the store.
24. The money falls out of her hand.
25. The sad girl looks on the sidewalk.

Write the predicate part of each sentence. *pages 10–11*

26. Then Stephanie looks under the cars.
27. Finally the girl finds her money.
28. Stephanie buys some food.

Add words to the subject part in each sentence to make the sentences more descriptive. Write each sentence. *pages 10–11*

29. The spaceship landed.
30. A visitor emerged.
31. The animals watched.
32. The astronaut walked.

Add words or phrases to the predicate part in each sentence to make the sentences more descriptive. Write each sentence. *pages 12–13*

33. The visitor collected.
34. The bags filled.
35. The animals waited.
36. The spaceship blasted off.

Write each sentence. Then add commas where they are needed. *pages 14–15*

37. The strange man landed near Fresno California on July 12 1983 in a spaceship.
38. No I don't believe it Pam.
39. Well I saw it George myself.

Read each set of sentences. Find each topic sentence. Then put the detail sentences in the right time order. Write the paragraphs. *pages 20–23*

40. **a.** Next he put all his books and games on the shelf.
b. First he made his bed.
c. Paul straightened his room today.
d. Finally he hung his clothes neatly in the closet.

41. **a.** Last she stands straight again.
b. Then she tucks her head between her legs.
c. Jessica can do a perfect somersault.
d. First she puts her hands flat on the ground.
e. Next she pushes with her feet and rolls over.

A Fable

Fables are short stories that try to explain why people act in certain ways. Writers of fables use animals as the main characters in their story. One way you can always know a fable is by looking at the last line. The last line usually states a proverb. A proverb tells an idea about how people can live together more happily and wisely.

This fable is about a series of misunderstandings. One misunderstanding leads to another. Read the fable. Why do you think the title is "Rumors"?

RUMORS

Once upon a time when Brahmadatta ruled, a little hare lived near the Western Ocean in a grove of palm and vilva trees. One day, as he was sitting under a vilva tree, the little hare suddenly thought:

"I have heard that sometimes there are earthquakes. The great earth shakes and starts to break into pieces. If an earthquake should start, what would I do" As he was worrying about this, a vilva fruit fell out of the tree and landed on the ground with a loud THUD!

Jumping up in terror, the hare cried, "Oh, my; Oh, dear; it's happening. The earth is breaking apart!" And he started running toward the ocean.

Another hare saw him rushing off, half frightened to death, and asked what was the matter.

The first hare cried, without stopping, "The earth is breaking apart!" Hearing this, the second hare began to run, too. And so, first one, then another hare joined in until 100,000 hares were all racing toward the ocean.

They were seen by a deer, a boar, an elk, a buffalo, a wild ox, a rhinoceros, a tiger, and an elephant. When these animals, in turn, heard that the earth was breaking apart, they too started to run.

And so, one by one, the number grew and grew until the earth seemed covered with running, terrified animals.

A young lion who was asleep in his cave high on the hillside was awakened by the thundering of so many feet. He looked out of his cave and was amazed to see the headlong flight of so many thousands of animals.

"Why," he said, "they are all running toward the ocean. If I don't do something, they will all drown themselves."

So, bounding down from the mountain, the lion ran in front of the stampeding animals and gave the mightiest roar ever heard before or since. The animals, paralyzed with fright, stopped dead in their tracks.

"What is the matter here?" the lion demanded.

"The earth is breaking apart," they cried, all together.

The lion thought, "The earth does not seem to me to be breaking apart," and he began asking questions starting with the largest animals. "Why are you running?" he asked the elephants.

"The earth is breaking apart," trumpeted the elephants.

"Who saw it breaking apart?" the lion asked.

"The tigers know all about it," the elephants replied.

The tigers said, "The rhinoceroses know."

The rhinoceroses said, "The oxen know."

The oxen said, "The buffaloes know."

The buffaloes said, "The elks know."

The elk said, "The boars."

The boars said, "The deer."

The deer said, "The hares."

When the hares were questioned, they pointed to the little hare and said, "He told us."

The young lion said to the hare, "Is it true, sir, that the earth is breaking apart?"

"Oh, yes, sir," the little hare replied, "I heard it with my own ears!"

"Where?" the lion asked.

Where I live, sir, a grove of palm and vilva trees. I was lying beneath a vilva tree when I heard the earth start to break apart."

The lion turned to the animals and said, "All of you, wait here. I myself will go to the very spot and see if this is true. Then I will come back and tell you."

Placing the hare on his back, the lion sprang forward with great speed and soon arrived at the palm and vilva grove. "Come," said the lion, "show me the place where the earth is breaking apart."

The hare jumped off his back, not daring to go too near the vilva tree and pointed. "Over there, sir, is where I heard the awful sound."

The lion went to the place and found the ripe vilva fruit that had fallen to the ground. Picking it up, he said, "Here, sir, is your world breaking apart—no more than a ripe fruit that fell upon the ground." Then, putting the hare on his back once more, the lion raced back to the frightened herd of animals and said:

"Do not be afraid any longer. You are perfectly safe. The world is not breaking apart. This hare only heard a ripe vilva fruit fall upon the ground." Then he said:

One foolish creature starts a rumor;
Ask yourself who is the worst:
He who takes it for the truth,
Or he who started it at first?

Creative Activities

1. Think about how the animals acted in the story. How did the rumors get started? What does the proverb at the end of the story tell you about rumors? Try playing this game. Six or more people can play. The first person should write a sentence and then whisper it to a second person very quickly. The second person whispers quickly what is heard to the third person. Keep whispering the sentence to each person until you reach the last player. The last player says the sentence aloud. See if the sentence is the same one the first player said.

2. **Creative Writing** A famous storyteller named Aesop told a great many fables. Go to the library and try to find a book of his fables. After you read more fables, try writing your own. Decide on the proverb for your fable first, such as "honesty is the best policy" or "little by little does the trick." If you still need ideas, you may wish to recall the story of "The Hare and the Tortoise" or "Chicken Little." Once you have chosen a proverb, make up a fable that shows how your proverb is true. Write the events of your story in time order, and remember to write the proverb at the end.

3. This fable, "Rumors," is fun to read aloud. Pick a person to read the story. That person will be called the narrator. Choose a person to read what each animal said. The narrator could read the proverb. Remember that the animals become more and more excited. Your voices should show you are becoming more and more excited, too. You might practice your fable, tape-record it, and share it with another class. Maybe you could even add background music to your tape.

WILDFLOWERS AT KERN RIVER, CALIFORNIA

2

Grammar and Related Language Skills

Nouns
Singular and Plural Nouns
Common and Proper Nouns
Possessive Nouns

Practical Communication

STUDY AND REFERENCE SKILLS
Using the Dictionary

COMPOSITION
Writing a Descriptive Paragraph
Writing a Friendly Letter

Creative Expression

Haiku

Have you ever seen a flower called bird of paradise? This flower grows on the Hawaiian Islands. How many flowers, plants, and trees can you identify? People who study flowers, plants, and trees are called botanists. Botany is a science. If you were a botanist, what speaking and writing skills would you need for your studies?

Nouns

Imagine living in a world where there were no people, places, or things. There would be no lawyers, no kings, no kitchens, no zoos, no ballparks, no money, no kites. The world would be a pretty dull place. But the real world does have lots of people, places, and things. We call words that name people, places, and things *nouns*.

- Look at the picture of the Grand Canyon.

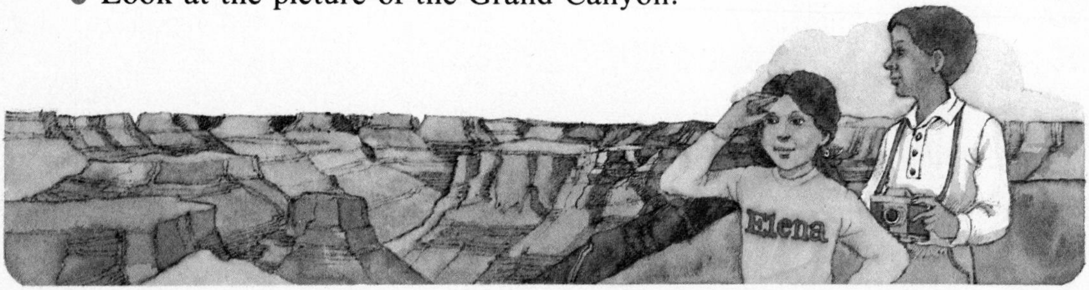

Notice the people, places, and things in the picture. The words that name them are nouns. *Elena* is a noun that names a special person. *Boy* is also a noun that names a person. *Trail* is a noun that names a place. *Camera* is a noun that names a thing.

- Think of some nouns that name other people, places, or things you see in the picture.

You can see and touch people, places, and things. But some nouns name things you cannot see or touch. They name ideas. *Anger, pain, peace,* and *love* are examples of nouns that name ideas that you cannot see or touch.

- Look at the underlined word in each sentence.

> A trip to the Grand Canyon brings joy to people.
> Do pictures give the same pleasure ?

The underlined words are nouns that name ideas.

> A **noun** is a word that names a person, place, thing, or idea.

Talk About It

Find each noun. Tell whether it names a person, place, thing, or idea.

1. Elliot pointed to a river.
2. Sarah walked to the water.
3. Angelo rented canoes.
4. Ed liked the beauty of the river.

Skills Practice

Write each sentence. Write each noun. After each noun, write whether it names a **person, place, thing,** or **idea.**

1. Nina paddled the canoe.
2. The canoe hit a rock.
3. Elliot waded into the water.
4. Elliot fixed the canoe.
5. Nina paddled quickly.
6. Rita stayed behind with Elliot.
7. The children chose mules.
8. The riders rode horses.
9. Sarah looked for a cave.
10. Sarah wanted peace and quiet.

Add a noun to fill each blank. Write each sentence. Make sure that the sentence makes sense.

11. We walked into a dark ___.
12. ___ saw a mole on a ledge.
13. A beaver gnawed the ___.
14. The boys walked past a ___.

Writing Sentences

Imagine that you and your friend went camping near a lake in the mountains. Write five sentences about what you see and do. Underline the nouns in each sentence.

Sample Answer 1. Nina paddled the canoe. Nina, person; canoe, thing

Plural Nouns

The child eats an apple on the beach.
The children eat apples on the beaches.

The nouns in the first sentence name only one person, place, and thing. Only one child eats one apple on one beach. These nouns are called *singular nouns*.

A **singular noun** is a noun that names one person, place, thing, or idea.

The nouns in the second sentence name more than one person, place, and thing. More than one child eats more than one apple on more than one beach. These nouns are called *plural nouns*.

A **plural noun** is a noun that names more than one person, place, thing, or idea.

- Look at each noun below.

thought → thoughts　　forest → forests
beach → beaches　　fox → foxes

What has been added to the singular nouns *thought* and *forest* to make them plural?

To make most singular nouns plural, add **-s.**

What has been added to the singular nouns *beach* and *fox* to make them plural?

If a singular noun ends with **s, ss, x, ch, sh,** or **z,** add **-es** to form the plural.

Some singular nouns form the plural in a different way.

child → children　　man → men
mouse → mice　　woman → women
goose → geese　　foot → feet
tooth → teeth　　ox → oxen

Talk About It

Read each sentence. Look at each underlined word. Tell how each plural was formed.

1. The children visited a forest.
2. The women talked to Sally.
3. Some geese flew overhead.
4. The man looked at three mice.

Skills Practice

Write each sentence. Write each noun in each sentence. Then write **singular** if the noun is singular. Write **plural** if the noun is plural.

1. The children went to a park.
2. Squirrels roamed freely.
3. Two squirrels climbed a pine.
4. Virgil climbed a tree.
5. Virgil perched on a branch.
6. Jo looked at the feet of Virgil.
7. Susan spotted the lake.
8. Waves pounded the shore.
9. Sally tied knots in a rope.
10. Lucia made hamburgers.

Write the plural form of each noun.

11. box
12. person
13. tree
14. bus
15. blanket
16. church
17. foot
18. ash
19. toe
20. girl
21. child
22. peach
23. button
24. march
25. farm
26. man

Writing Sentences

Suppose you are visiting a place that has many animals. The place might be a farm, a forest, or a zoo.

1. Write three sentences telling about things you see. Use only singular nouns in your sentences.
2. Write three sentences telling about things you do. Use only plural nouns in your sentences.

Sample Answers **1.** The children went to a park. children, plural; park, singular **11.** boxes

More About Plural Nouns

Not all singular nouns can be made plural in the same way. Here are some other ways you can form plural nouns.

Singular nouns that end in *y* form the plural in two different ways. Some nouns that end in *y* are like *sky*. *Sky* ends in a consonant and *y*.

> If a singular noun ends with a consonant and **y**, change the **y** to **i** and add **-es** to form the plural.

sky⟶skies   fly⟶flies

Some nouns that end in *y* are like *toy*. *Toy* ends in a vowel and *y*.

> If a singular noun ends in a vowel and **y**, add **-s** to form the plural.

toy⟶toys   boy⟶boys

● Look at each noun.

valley	dairies
baby	holidays
tray	territories
colony	ways

How would you change each noun in the left column to the plural form? *Valleys, babies, trays,* and *colonies* are the plurals. How were the nouns in the right column changed from the singular to the plural form? *Dairies* and *territories* were made plural by changing the *y* to *i* and adding *-es*. *Holidays* and *ways* were made plural by adding *-s*.

Many singular nouns ending in *f* or *fe* add *-s* to form the plural in the usual way.

roof → roofs   safe → safes   cliff → cliffs

For some singular nouns that end in *f* or *fe*, change the *f* to *v* and add *-s* or *-es* to form the plural.

knife	knives	shelf	shelves	half	halves
life	lives	leaf	leaves	loaf	loaves
		thief	thieves		

Talk About It

Spell the plural form of each noun.

1. alley **2.** army **3.** body **4.** reply **5.** navy **6.** half **7.** cliff **8.** shelf

Skills Practice

Write the plural form of each noun.

1. penny **2.** birthday **3.** factory **4.** spray **5.** life **6.** reef **7.** city **8.** belly **9.** boy **10.** thief **11.** leaf **12.** safe

Write each sentence with the plural form of the noun.

13. On ___ the children go to the zoo. (Sunday)
14. The goats eat ___ from the plants. (leaf)
15. The monkeys climbed on the ___ of the buildings. (roof)
16. Sophie laughed at two ___ on the rope. (monkey)
17. Evan stared at the fat ___. (turkey)
18. Phyllis and Adam saw a mother lamb with ___. (baby)
19. Ira and Debby rode two ___. (donkey)
20. Laura was as tall as the knees of the ___. (giraffe)

Sample Answers 1. pennies 13. On Sundays the children go to the zoo.

Compound Nouns

Sometimes new nouns are made by joining two or more words together. A *compound noun* is a noun made up of two or more other words. You can usually figure out the meaning of a compound noun if you know the meanings of the smaller words that form it.

- Look at these compound nouns.

spaceship   liftoff   splashdown

The words *space* and *ship* make up the compound noun *spaceship*. *Spaceship* means a *ship* that moves in *space*. *Liftoff* means the *lift* up *off* the ground. *Splashdown* means coming *down* in the water with a *splash*.

Sometimes compound nouns can help you say things in a short way.

- Look at each sentence.

Don saw a <u>ground for making</u> a camp.	Don saw a <u>campground</u>.
Kim gathered <u>wood for a fire</u>.	Kim gathered <u>firewood</u>.
Lu ate by <u>the light of the moon</u>.	Lu ate by <u>moonlight</u>.

The underlined words in each sentence show both a long and a short way to say the same thing.

Talk About It

Think of a compound noun to replace the underlined words in each sentence.

1. The trip started in the time after 12 o'clock noon.
2. The children saw falls of water at Yellowstone Park.
3. Suddenly a storm of rain started.
4. The children ran back to the ground where people camp.

Skills Practice

Write the compound noun in each sentence. Draw a line between the two words that make up each compound. Then write what each compound noun means.

1. Maria walked up the hillside on Tuesday.
2. Andy collected wood for a campfire.
3. Andy got a terrible backache.
4. Inés ate blueberries.
5. Roy made a fruitcake.

Write a compound noun to replace each group of underlined words.

6. Andy fed a deer by the side of the river.
7. Roy walked to the side of the lake.
8. Roy heard a snake that rattled.
9. Debbie climbed to the top of a tree.
10. The climb gave Debbie an awful ache in the head.

Writing Sentences

You are hiking through the woods. Write five sentences about what you see and do. Use one of the following compound nouns in each sentence: earthworm, wildflowers, hummingbird, footprints, sunset.

Sample Answers **1.** hill/side, the side of a hill **6.** riverside

Skills Review

Write each noun in each sentence. After each noun, write whether it names a **person, place, thing,** or **idea.**

1. The friends went to camp together.
2. The campers lived in cabins.
3. The children had fun.
4. The children explored the mountains.
5. Miko found a golden rock near a cave.
6. The surprised girl ran down the hill.
7. Angela approached the place.
8. Nina saw golden rocks on the ground.
9. Elliot found many strange stones.
10. Then Angela discovered a can of golden paint.

Write each noun. Then write **singular** if the noun is singular. Write **plural** if the noun is plural.

11. The campers swim in a large lake.
12. The children play near the shore.
13. The campers paddle the canoes.
14. Virgil stays near the beach.
15. Tony jumps in the waves.
16. A friend swims near an island.
17. Trees cover the island.
18. Randy swims across the lake.
19. Sally climbs into the boat.
20. A boy rows the boat.
21. A lifeguard watches the children.
22. A girl dives off the raft.

Write the plural form of each noun.

23. ability	27. tooth	31. monkey	35. bush
24. man	28. lady	32. girl	36. chief
25. bench	29. fox	33. knife	37. beach
26. delivery	30. cliff	34. shelf	38. horse

Write the compound noun in each sentence. Draw a line between the two words that make up each compound. Then write what each compound means.

39. Joe and Tina play basketball.
40. They like to play outside.
41. They play in the backyard.
42. The babysitter watches them play.
43. They hear a watchdog bark.

Write a compound noun to replace the underlined words in each sentence.

44. Animals in the <u>house on the farm</u> ran away.
45. Hens scampered through the <u>fields of corn</u>.
46. The hens scared the <u>insects that hop in the grass</u>.
47. A <u>figure used to scare the crows away</u> fell down.
48. The <u>soil on the top</u> of the land washed away.

Careers

Public health is concerned with protecting the cleanliness and safety of food, liquids, and air. People who work in public health test food that is eaten in public places such as hospitals, schools, or restaurants. Others test air and water samples for pollution. Another word for the protection of public health is *sanitation.*

People who work to remove garbage are often called *sanitation workers.* *Sanitation engineers* design plants to treat sewage, which is water containing waste matter.

Common and Proper Nouns

- Look at the sentence below.

A young woman liked a building in her town.

Find the nouns. The nouns in this sentence are *woman, building,* and *town*. These nouns are called *common nouns* because they name any person, place, and thing.

> A **common noun** is a noun that names any person, place, thing or idea.

- Now look at this sentence.

Samantha Carlsen liked the Sears Tower in Chicago, Illinois.

The nouns in this sentence are *Samantha Carlsen, Sears Tower, Chicago,* and *Illinois*. These nouns are called *proper nouns* because they name a special person, place, and thing.

> A **proper noun** is a noun that names a special person, place, thing, or idea. A proper noun can be one word or more than one word.

- Look at the nouns below. How does each proper noun begin?

George Washington Bridge	the bridge
Ritz Theater	the theater
Museum of the American Indian	the museum

Each proper noun begins with a capital letter. If a proper noun has more than one word, each important word begins with a capital letter.

Talk About It

Find the nouns in each sentence. Tell whether each noun is a common noun or a proper noun. Give reasons for your answers.

1. Henry Thoreau lived in the woods.
2. Thoreau lived near Walden Pond.
3. Walden Pond is in Massachusetts.
4. Thoreau studied plants.
5. Thoreau wrote a book.
6. The book is called *Walden*.

Skills Practice

Write each sentence. Write each noun. After each noun write whether it is **common** or **proper.**

1. The class went to Bear Mountain Park.
2. Frank Perez rented the bus.
3. The bus driver drove over the George Washington Bridge.
4. The group traveled along the Hudson River.
5. Amy pointed out a farm.
6. The class saw chickens, horses, and cows.
7. A big dog barked.
8. The children saw many towns.
9. The children liked Montrose.

Writing Sentences

Imagine that your friends lost their dog when they went to the store.

1. Write three sentences to tell how they lost their dog. Underline the common nouns in the sentences.
2. Write three sentences to tell how your friends found their dog. Underline the proper nouns in the sentences.

Sample Answer 1. The class went to Bear Mountain Park.
class, common; Bear Mountain Park , proper

Abbreviations

Sometimes people use shortened words to write the names of people, places, or things. These shortened words are called *abbreviations*.

Abbreviations are often used in writing. You use *Mr.* and *Mrs.* with names. *Miss* and *Ms.* are also used with names. *Miss* is written before the name of an unmarried woman. *Ms.* is used before the name of either a married or an unmarried woman.

Some abbreviations are used only in addresses and lists. We write *Ave.* on an envelope, but we write *Avenue* in a sentence.

Here are some common abbreviations. Notice that you must put a period after an abbreviation.

Abbreviations Used in Writing	Title Stands for	Abbreviations Used in Addresses, Lists	Stands for
Mr.	a man	Ave.	Avenue
Dr.	Doctor	Blvd.	Boulevard
Rev.	Reverend	Dr.	Drive
Sr.	Senior	Rd.	Road
Jr.	Junior	Rte.	Route
Mrs.	a married woman	St.	Street
		Co.	Company
		Inc.	Incorporated

• Look at the address that appears on the envelope.

In the address, *Mr.* stands for *Mister. Jr.* is short for *Junior. St.* is an abbreviation for *Street.* A comma (,) is placed between the name of a city and the name of a state.

Calendars often use abbreviations for the days and months.

DAYS: Sun. Mon. Tues. Wed. Thurs. Fri. Sat.
MONTHS: Jan. Feb. Mar. Apr. Aug. Sept. Oct. Nov. Dec.

The words *May, June,* and *July* are not usually abbreviated.

The abbreviation A.M. stands for the Latin words *ante meridiem.* Ante meridiem means "before noon." The abbreviation P.M. stands for *post meridiem.* It means "after noon." Are you in school at 11 A.M. or 11 P.M.? Are you sleeping at 4 A.M. or 4 P.M.?

Talk About It

Find the abbreviations in these phrases. Tell what each abbreviation stands for.

1. Dr. Anna Lopez
2. 487 Jackson Blvd.
3. Mrs. Hannah Bell
4. 6470 Jones Ave.
5. Mon., Aug. 12
6. 12:30 P.M.

Skills Practice

Change each underlined word to an abbreviation. Write the new phrase.

1. Route 66
2. Lakeville Boulevard
3. Friday, October 31
4. 98765 Twist Road
5. Fifth Avenue
6. 1:45 ante meridiem
7. Reverend Stan Nichols
8. 420 Bradley Drive
9. Pet Food Company, Incorporated
10. Doctor Jason Benton, Junior
11. Thursday, January 11
12. 2:30 post meridiem

Sample Answer 1. Rte. 66

Possessive Nouns

If you own a bicycle, you possess it. *Possess* means the same thing as *have* or *own.* Nouns can be used to show *possession.* Nouns that show possession are called *possessive nouns.*

- Look at each sentence.

> Jay found the bicycle of the boy. Jay found the boy's bicycle.

The underlined words in the first sentence show that the bicycle belongs to the boy. The underlined word in the second sentence is a *possessive noun.* It shows that the bicycle belongs to the boy.

> A **possessive noun** is a noun that names who or what has something.

- Look again at the second sentence in the box above. The noun *boy* is singular. An *apostrophe* and an *-s* have been added to the singular noun *boy* to form the possessive.

> Add an **apostrophe** and **s** (**'s**) to form the possessive of most singular nouns.

Form the possessive of singular proper nouns in the same way.

John—John's Ross—Ross's Sally—Sally's

- Look at each sentence.

The pet of the villagers escaped. The villagers' pet escaped.

> Add an **apostrophe** (') to form the possessive of plural nouns that end with **s.**

Form the possessive of plural proper nouns in the same way.

the Bernsteins	the Bernsteins' pet
the Rileys	the Rileys' pet

The plural forms of certain nouns do not end in *s*. For example, the plural form of the noun *child* is *children*.

- Look at each sentence.

The wagons <u>of the children</u> move quickly.
The <u>children's</u> wagons move quickly.

> Add an **apostrophe** and **s** (**'s**) to form the possessive of plural nouns that do not end with **s.**

Talk About It

Read each sentence. Use the possessive form of the noun at the end of the sentence. Spell the possessive noun.

1. Several ___ children played together. (neighbors)
2. The ___ fathers played, too. (children)
3. The children played in the ___ yard. (Leibers)
4. Mom found the ___ bicycle. (girl)
5. ___ parents served lunch. (Gerry)

Skills Practice

Change each word at the end of the sentence to make a possessive noun. Write each sentence.

1. The ___ children walked to the zoo. (neighbor)
2. A ___ eyes winked hello. (monkey)
3. The ___ meat fell to the floor. (lion)
4. The ___ mother paced back and forth. (cubs)
5. The ___ roars frightened the cubs. (elephants)
6. The ___ feet clattered on the rocks. (buffalo)
7. The zoo keeper pointed to the ___ cage. (snake)
8. The children fed lettuce to the ___ baby. (camel)
9. The ___ paws splashed water. (bear)

Sample Answer 1. The neighbor's children walked to the zoo.

Suffixes

A new word can sometimes be made by adding one or more letters to the end of a word. The added letters give a new meaning to the old word.

A suffix is one or more letters added to the end of a word.

- Look at each sentence.

Nellie Bly, a famous reporter, flew around the world.
The inventor Thomas Edison created a light bulb.

The underlined word in each sentence has a suffix added to it. What is the suffix in each word? The first suffix is *-er*. The second is *-or*. The suffixes *-er* or *-or* mean *a person who*. A *reporter* is a person who reports. An *inventor* is a person who invents. Most words use the suffix *-er* instead of *-or*. Some common words with the *-or* suffix are *actor, governor, director,* and *sailor*.

- Read the sentence below.

The girls found their way in the darkness.

Can you find the suffix in the underlined word? The suffix *-ness* means *the state of being*. *Darkness* means the state of being dark. *Coldness* means the state of being cold.

- Read each sentence.

Many people were helpless for days.
Sal spent a cheerless winter in the mountains.

What suffix is in each underlined word? The suffix *-less* means *without*. *Helpless* means without help. *Cheerless* means without cheer.

Suffix	Meaning	Example
-er	one who	printer (one who prints)
-or	one who	sailor (one who sails)
-ness	the state of being	happiness (state of being happy)
-less	without	senseless (without sense)

Talk About It

In each sentence find the word that has the suffix **-or, -er, -ness,** or **-less.** Tell what the word means.

1. The rain pleased the farmer.
2. The rain brought gladness to our town.
3. Green grass grew from the colorless ground.
4. The governor came to the town.

Skills Practice

In each sentence find the word that has the suffix **-er, -or, -ness,** or **-less.** Write the word and then write what it means.

1. The wetness of the rain cleaned the streets.
2. The street sweeper swept the rubbish.
3. A shoeless boy planted a garden.
4. The traffic director watched.

Add the suffix **-er, -or, -ness,** or **-less** to the incomplete word in each sentence. Then write each sentence.

5. The people lost their fond___ for rain.
6. A store own___ pumped water from his basement.
7. A sail___ fixed boats.
8. The fear___ people climbed the mountain.

Sample Answers **1.** wetness, state of being wet. **5.** fondness

Skills Review

Write the nouns in each sentence. After each noun write whether it is **common** or **proper.**

1. The family visited Carlsbad Caverns.
2. Karla explored the cavern in New Mexico.
3. A cowboy named Jim White discovered the cave.
4. Jim saw bats in the cave.
5. Betsy explored the large rooms.
6. The family saw some statues.
7. One room contained carvings.
8. Jim saw walls of limestone.
9. Guides took people through the caverns.
10. Mike took pictures with a new camera.
11. Jim tripped on a rock.
12. Many people from the United States visited the caverns.

Change each underlined word to an abbreviation. Write the new phrase.

13. Wednesday, January 11
14. State Street
15. 463 Rocky Road
16. Mister Arthur Green
17. 2:30 post meridiem
18. 79 Norton Drive
19. Doctor Lynn Stanton
20. John Fox, Senior
21. Route 21
22. 4:29 ante meridiem
23. Colfax Avenue
24. White Paper Company
25. Thursday, November 2
26. 21104 Bay Avenue
27. Car Wreckers, Incorporated
28. Northern Boulevard
29. February 18, 1950
30. Mister Mel Practice, Junior
31. Reverend Summers
32. Baker Street
33. Doctor Anna Washington
34. Zip Company, Incorporated

Change the word at the end of the sentence to make a possessive noun. Write the possessive noun.

35. The ___ smiles showed happiness. (children)
36. Tara saw the ___ cages. (bears)
37. The ___ mother protected her children. (goats)
38. One bear ate a ___ hat. (stranger)
39. Tara counted the ___ stripes. (raccoon)
40. The children laughed at the ___ tricks. (monkeys)

In each sentence find the word that has the suffix **-er, -or, -ness,** or **-less.** Write the word and then write what it means.

41. A climber went up Mount Rainier.
42. The breathless woman sat down.
43. The coldness of the wind caused the woman pain.
44. A visitor waved from the ground.
45. The fearless woman smiled.
46. The lifeless mountain glowed in the sunset.
47. At the top the woman met a hiker.
48. The woman laughed with happiness.
49. The stranger took the dullness out of the climb.

Have you ever wondered how the months and days got their names? Here are some names that some months and days come from.

1. January—Janus, Roman god of gates and beginnings and endings.
2. August—Augustus Caesar, a Roman emperor
3. Thursday—Thor, the Norse god of Thunder
4. June—Juno, Roman queen of the gods
5. March—Mars, Roman god of war

Exploring Language

Using the Dictionary

A dictionary is an important reference book. It is helpful to you in reading, writing, spelling, and speaking. A dictionary is really a long list of words. Each word in the list is called an *entry word*. Entry words are arranged alphabetically.

- Look at the dictionary sample page below.

dobbin/doctor

dob·bin (dob′in) *n.* a horse, especially a gentle, plodding one.

Do·ber·man pin·scher (dō′bər mən pin′shər) *n.* a dog belonging to a breed developed in Germany, having a long

head, slender legs, and usually a sleek, black or brown coat. [From Ludwig *Doberman,* a nineteenth-century German dog breeder.]

dock[1] (dok) *n.* a structure built along the shore; wharf.

dock[2] (dok) *n.* the solid, fleshy part of an animal's tail. *-v.t.* to cut the end off or shorten: *to dock a horse's tail.*

dock[3] (dok) *n.* the place in a criminal court where the defendant stands or sits during a trial. [Flemish *dok* cage.]

dock[4] (dok) *n.* any group of plants related to buckwheat. [Old English *docce.*]

doctor (dok′tər) *n.* **1.** a person who is licensed to practice medicine, such as pediatrics. **2.** a person who is licensed to practice any of various related sciences, such as dentistry. **3.** a person who holds the highest graduate degree given by a university.

Notice that the word **dobbin** is the first entry word on the sample page. At the top of the sample page there are two words printed in dark type: **dobbin/doctor.** These words are called *guide words*. The guide words are the first and last word on a particular dictionary page. Notice that **dobbin** is the first word and that **doctor** is the last word on the sample page. All the entry words on this page began with **dob** or **doc.**

You can use a dictionary to help you find the meaning of words that you do not know. Entry words usually have more than one meaning.

1. Often the meanings of a word are related. They are usually numbered after the entry word. Look at the word **doctor** on the sample page. Three related meanings are listed.
2. Sometimes a word has two or more unrelated meanings. Then there is more than one entry for the same word. Look at the word *dock*. The word *dock* is spelled and pronounced the same way four times, but the meanings are different. The numbers above the last letter of *dock* show the four unrelated meanings.
3. A part of a sentence or a sample sentence will sometimes show how the entry word is used. Look at the second meaning of *dock* to see how you could use it in a sentence.

Talk About It

Use the sample dictionary page to answer these questions.

1. What are the guide words?
2. Which word has the most related meanings? How do you know?
3. Which words have only one meaning in the dictionary?

Skills Practice

Below are guide words on two pages of a dictionary.

acceptable/accomplishment	7	**eyeball/Ezra**	341

On which page would you find each of these entry words?

1. accompany **2.** eyetooth **3.** accident **4.** eyebrow

Look at the sample dictionary page.

5. What is the third meaning of *dock*?
6. What is a synonym of the first meaning of *dock*?
7. What is a *dobbin*?
8. What is the third meaning of *doctor*?

Sample Answer 1. Page 7

Words That Describe

Thinking About Words That Describe

Our five senses, seeing, hearing, smelling, tasting, and touching, help us to know and understand the world around us. Using words that describe how things look, sound, smell, taste, or feel can make your writing more vivid and exciting.

Notice how these sentences appeal to the senses.

Yosemite Falls plunges down the huge, jagged cliffs.
Visitors sniff the sweet grasses in Yosemite Valley.
Tourists devour the crunchy, delicious nuts.
We went wading in the cool, rippling stream.
The Merced River flows quietly through the valley.

You can also create vivid mental pictures by comparing one thing to something else.

The snowcaps looked like whipped cream topping.

What are the *snowcaps* compared to in this sentence? Notice that the word *like* is used to compare two things. A comparison that uses *like* or *as* is called a *simile*.

> A **simile** is a comparison of two different things with the use of *like* or *as*.

- Now read this sentence.

The trees are an assembly of giants.

What are the *trees* compared to in this sentence? Does this comparison help you to imagine how the massed trees looked? Notice that the word *like* or *as* is not used to compare. This kind of comparison is called a *metaphor*.

> A **metaphor** is a comparison of two different things without the use of *like* or *as*.

Another way to create a strong image is to use words that make things and animals seem human.

The sunlight dances along the cliffs.

Sunlight is treated like a person who can dance. This use of words is called *personification.*

> **Personification** is the use of words to give things and animals human qualities.

Talking About Words That Describe

Use a **simile, metaphor,** or **personification** in each sentence.

1. The chilly cabin was ___ .
2. The fog hovered around our heads like ___ .
3. Are balsam trees as fragrant as ___ ?
4. The tall trees were ___ .

Identify the **simile, metaphor,** or **personification** in each sentence.

1. The clouds frolic above the hikers.
2. Cliffs border the canyon like great stone walls.
3. Fireflies are stars that live on Earth.
4. The clear lake is a mirror for the bordering trees.

Writing Words That Describe

Add describing words to finish these sentences. Then write whether each sentence is a **simile, metaphor,** or **personification.**

1. Rocks surrounded the lake like a ___ .
2. The juice of the wild berries was as sweet as ___ .
3. Have you ever eaten anything as bitter as ___ ?
4. As the sun rose, the shadows were ___ .
5. Sunflowers are ___ .
6. The taller trees were ___ .

Writing Sentences with Words That Describe

Write five sentences that tell about a place you visited. Describe how something looked, smelled, tasted, felt, or sounded in three sentences. Use a metaphor or a simile in one sentence. Use personification in one sentence.

Sample Answers: **1.** Rocks surrounded the lake like a stone fence.

Descriptive Paragraphs

Thinking About Paragraphs

Writing is one way to help you say clearly what you think or how you feel about an idea. A painter uses colors to make a picture. A writer paints pictures with words. As a writer, you must choose words that help you tell about or describe your idea. You could say, "It was windy today." It is more interesting to say, "A breezy wind laughed in my ear all day." A good description helps your reader to picture exactly what you have in mind.

● Read this paragraph. Can you picture what the writer is describing?

One morning I saw snow lightly falling outside my window. I left my warm bed and tiptoed to the window. I peered out on a world that in the night had become a magical place. The huge oak was wrapped in white and the evergreen trees drooped with white frosting. Houses and streets were covered with a thick, white blanket.

These are ways you can describe an idea.

1. Use words that describe how things look, smell, taste, sound, or feel. (The *huge* oak was wrapped in *white* and the evergreen trees drooped with *white frosting*.)
2. Use action words that describe what someone is doing or how something acts. (I left my warm bed and *tiptoed* to the window.)
3. Use a dictionary to find new words. Avoid using words over and over again, such as nice, terrible, awful, and wonderful.

Talking About Paragraphs

Read the paragraph about the snow again.

1. Find the topic sentence.
2. Read the detail sentences. What detail words are used to describe the snow?
3. What action words are used? You should have noticed the words *tiptoed, wrapped,* and *drooped.*
4. What word in the paragraph means the same thing as the word *looked*?

Writing a Paragraph

1. Look at the pictures above. Think of detail words and action words to describe each picture. Write this topic sentence: *The grassy meadow is a home for many animals.*
2. Write each of the following detail sentences after the topic sentence. Fill in the blank spaces with words that describe the pictures.
   The ___, ___ pony ___ across the ___ meadow.
   The ___, ___ rabbit felt ___ and ___.
   The ___ hawk ___ through the ___ sky looking for food.

A Descriptive Paragraph in a Friendly Letter

Thinking About a Letter

Sometimes you might want to write a letter to a friend. You could share an experience by describing what happened to you. When you write to a friend, you would use a special form of writing called a friendly letter. Study the letter below. The five parts in a friendly letter are listed on the left. Notice where each part is placed on the page.

Heading →

63 Barrow Street
Boston, Massachusetts
68102
January 14, 19__

Greeting →

Dear Kenny,

Body →

We had a lot of fun in the snow last week. A howling blizzard swept through our town on Monday. Jo Ann, Tommy, Amy, and I built a huge snow fort with a wall that was five feet high. It had a long, dark tunnel, too. Mom gave us delicious sandwiches and a thermos of hot, creamy chocolate for a picnic. Later we had an exciting snowball fight, but the dog kept catching the snowballs! I wish you could have been with us.

Closing →

Your friend,

Signature →

Charles

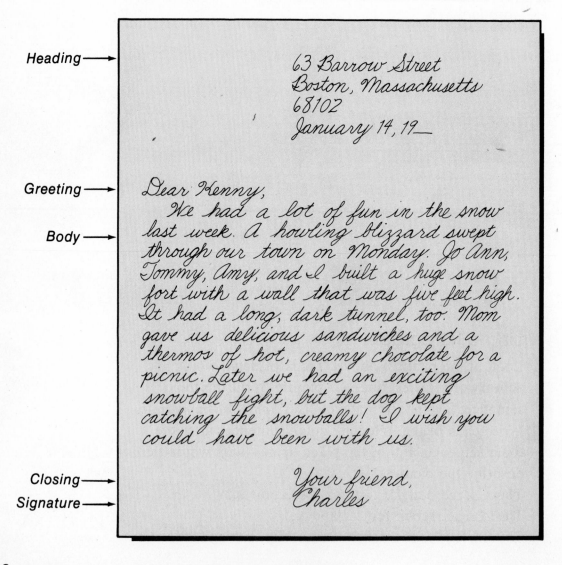

Think about the different parts of a friendly letter.

1. **Heading.** The heading is your address. It is placed in the upper right corner. The date should be the day you write the letter. Leave a space between the heading and the greeting.
2. **Greeting.** The greeting is your "hello" to the person to whom you are writing. The person's name is followed by a comma.
3. **Body.** The body is your message to the person to whom you are writing. Remember to indent all paragraphs and to use complete sentences.
4. **Closing.** The closing is your "good-by" to the friend. Place it under the body of the letter to the right and directly under the heading. Follow the closing with a comma.
5. **Signature.** Write your name directly under the closing. Use your first name in a friendly letter.

Talking About a Letter

Study the friendly letter that Charles wrote.

1. What information is found in the heading?
2. Why do you think the first name of a person is used with a friendly letter?
3. Look at the body of the letter.
   a. What is the topic sentence of the paragraph?
   b. How many detail sentences are there?
   c. What detail word describes the blizzard? What action word describes what the blizzard did?
4. What other words could you use in the closing?

Practicing a Descriptive Paragraph in a Friendly Letter

Thinking About Your Letter

Have you ever written a friendly letter? One way to make a new friend is to write a friendly letter to a pen pal. A pen pal is a person (pal) to whom you write (pen) letters. Probably you won't actually meet your pen pal, but your letters may help you to become friends. It is a good way to learn about new and interesting people. Choose one of these imaginary people to be your pen pal:

Ann-Marie Chapman; London, England; age 10
Jim Tucker; Honolulu, Hawaii; age 11
Carlos Martinez; San Rafael, California; age 9
Barbara Homes; Washington, D.C.; age 10

Writing Your Letter

1. Write the heading in the correct place. Remember that your address always needs a ZIP code. Use today's date.
2. Write the greeting. Remember that you use the first name of the pen pal in a friendly letter.
3. Write the message to your pen pal in the body of the letter. Use this topic sentence: My name is ___ and I am ___ years old. Fill in the blanks with your name and age.

   Remember to indent the first word in your paragraph. You might include the following information in the detail sentences:

   a. Describe what you look like. Remember to use details.
   b. Describe what you like to do. Use action words if possible.
   c. Describe a pet or a favorite animal.
4. Write the closing.
5. Write your signature. Use your first name only.

Edit Your Letter

Read your friendly letter and check it with these editing questions. Use the editing symbols to correct your work. If you need to, write your letter again.

1. Did your topic sentence tell the main idea?
2. Did each detail sentence state a complete idea?
3. Did you use vivid describing words in your sentences?
4. Did you use clear action words to state your details?
5. Did you follow the letter form correctly?
6. Did you indent the first word of the paragraph?
7. Did you capitalize the proper nouns and the first word in each sentence?
8. Did you use the correct end punctuation?
9. Did you check your spelling?

Editing Symbols

≡ capitalize
¶ indent
ᕍ take out
∧ add

INDEPENDENT WRITING

A Descriptive Paragraph in a Friendly Letter

Prewriting Writers try very hard to write clear, descriptive paragraphs. Imagine you saw a UFO, an unidentified flying object, or spotted a strange serpent-like creature in a lake or river. Describe your discovery in a letter to your cousin. Think about these questions and write short answers for them: What was the thing? Where was it? How big was it? What color was it? What other information might you include in your description?

Writing Write a letter to your cousin. The body of your letter will be a paragraph that describes the UFO or the creature. Try to choose interesting words to make your description clear.

Editing Use the check questions and the editing symbols above to edit your letter.

Unit Review

Write each noun in each sentence. After each noun, write whether it names a **person, place, thing,** or **idea.** Then write **singular** if the noun is singular and **plural** if the noun is plural.

pages 36–39

1. The people stayed on an island.
2. The families lived in huts.
3. Kim liked adventure.
4. The children explored the land.
5. Nick saw flowers near a cave.

Write the plural form of each noun. *pages 40–41*

6. daisy
7. ribbon
8. dress
9. dish
10. tie
11. journey
12. foot
13. woman
14. leaf

Write the compound noun in each sentence. Draw a line between the two words that make up each compound. Then write what each compound word means. *pages 42–43*

15. The children traveled to a playground.
16. The sunshine beamed brightly.
17. Marsha saw a mountaintop.

Write each noun in each sentence. After each noun write whether it is **common** or **proper.** *pages 46–47*

18. Ben Rogers visited the museum.
19. Lisa Rogers liked the Whitney Museum.
20. A guide pointed to a statue.

Change each underlined word to an abbreviation. *pages 48–49*

21. Friday, March 25
22. Doctor Rudolph Poe
23. 77 Oak Drive
24. Route 66
25. Quick Dry Company
26. December 25

Change the word at the end of the sentence to make a possessive noun. Write the possessive noun. *pages 50–51*

27. The children rode ___ trolleys. (San Francisco)
28. Charlie watched the ___ faces. (people)
29. Yoko painted ___ faces. (strangers)
30. The children loved ___ art. (Yoko)

In each sentence find each word that has the suffix **-er, -or, -ness,** or **-less.** Write each word and then write what it means. *pages 52–53*

31. A traveler goes many places.
32. A sailor travels on the sea.
33. A fearless man faces danger.
34. The darkness brings gloom.

Add describing words to finish these sentences. Write the sentences and then write whether each is a **simile,** a **metaphor,** or **personification.** *pages 58–59*

35. The icy pond was ___ .
36. Ashes flew about like ___ .
37. The moon was ___ .
38. Otters slid over the ice like ___ .

Below are the parts of a friendly letter. They are not in the right order. Put the parts in their proper order. Then write the letter. Be sure to use the correct punctuation. *pages 62–65*

1. Phyllis
2. I am busy making plans for summer camp. First I am deciding what clothes to take with me. I am sure I am going to need a new bathing suit. Then I have to sew labels with my name and address onto all my clothes. Last year I lost a swimming cap and my favorite hat.
3. 1601 15th Street
Auburn Montana
June 8 19__
4. Dear Sue
5. Your friend

Haiku

Haiku is a form of poetry which describes things in nature such as birds, butterflies, the sun, the moon, or even the seasons of the year. Haiku comes from Japan. Each haiku has three lines. The number of words may differ in each haiku. In Japanese the haiku always has seventeen syllables. However the haiku may not have that number when it is written in English.

Read the following haiku slowly and thoughtfully. Try to picture in your mind what the poet is describing.

Stillness:
The sound of petals
Sifting down together
—Chora

The bat
Lives hidden
Under the broken umbrella.
—Bushon

Grasshopper,
Do not trample to pieces
The pearls of bright dew.
—Issa

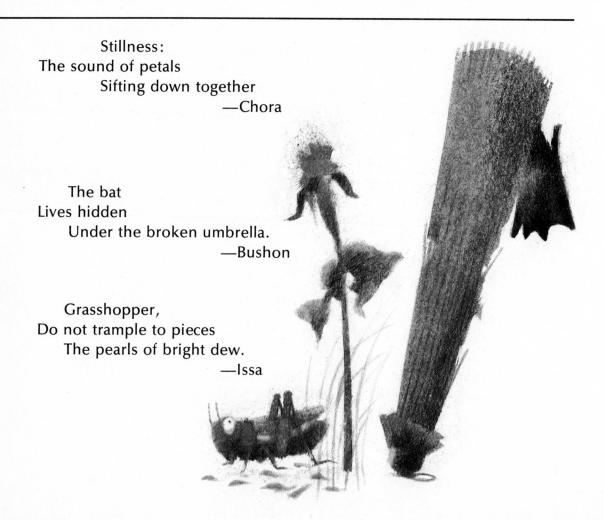

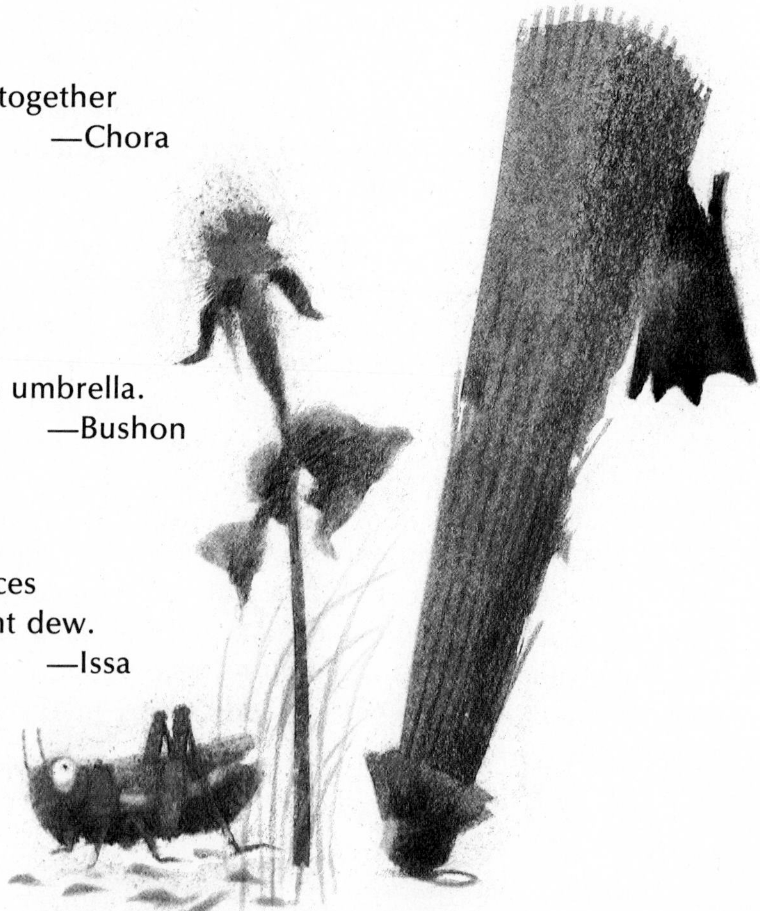

The moon is in the water
Turned a somersault
and floated away.
—Ryôta

A giant firefly:
that way, this way, that way, this—
and it passes by.
—Issa

Creative Activities

1. **Creative Writing** Choose something in nature that you would like to describe. Here are some suggestions:

   a lake   a snowflake   a rainbow   a bee

   Think about the colors, sounds, and movements of your chosen object. Write the important words that describe these things. Then write your own haiku about the object. Try to use five syllables in your first line, seven syllables in your second line, and five syllables in your third line.
2. **Creative Writing** The tanka is another form of poetry like the haiku. A tanka has five lines. The first line has five syllables. The second line has seven syllables. The third line has five syllables, the fourth line, seven syllables, and the fifth line, seven syllables. Try writing a tanka. This first line may help you begin:

   Snowflakes falling down . . .

HOCKEY PLAYER

3

Grammar and Related Language Skills

Verbs
Objects of Verbs
Tenses of Verbs
Irregular Verbs

Practical Communications

STUDY AND REFERENCE SKILLS
Using the Library

COMPOSITION
Writing a Paragraph with Facts
Writing a Business Letter

Creative Expression

A Letter

People who help athletes play sports well are called coaches. Coaches must be able to explain clearly the skills and rules needed to play a sport. They sometimes keep a daily record of an athlete's abilities. What writing skills would a coach need? What speaking skills would help a coach teach an athlete a sport?

Action Verbs

A sentence has two parts, the *subject part* and the *predicate part*. The *subject part* names whom or what the sentence is about. The *predicate part* tells what action the subject part does. The word in the predicate that names an action is called the *action verb*. Words like *run, jump, fly, eat, talk,* and *sing* show action. Can you think of some others?

- Look at this picture. What action do you see in it? What words could you use to tell about the action?

An **action verb** is a word that names an action. It may contain more than one word. It may have a main verb and a helping verb.

- Read each sentence below. The underlined word names an action. The underlined word is a verb.

A player <u>runs</u> with the ball.
Runners <u>grab</u> his leg.
The player <u>falls</u> down.
Another player <u>stumbles</u>.

- Which word names the action in each of the following sentences?

One runner carries the ball.
His shoe flies in the air.
The player throws the ball.
His teammate catches the ball.

Talk About It

What is the action verb in each of the following sentences?

1. The children play flag football.
2. Cindy takes a cloth.
3. Miko ties the knot.
4. Cindy carries the cloth.
5. The knot hangs down.
6. Cindy runs with the ball.
7. Althea grabs for the cloth.
8. Cindy drops the ball.
9. The ball bounces.
10. Jack catches the ball.

Skills Practice

Write each sentence. Underline the action verb.

1. Al saw a football game.
2. The Bears played the Colts.
3. Al drove to the stadium.
4. Al sat in the last row.
5. The teams came on the field.
6. The captains met.
7. The official tossed a coin.
8. The Colts kicked the ball.
9. The Bears caught the football.
10. The carrier ran down the field.
11. The Bears reached the goal.
12. The Colts defended their goal.
13. The Colts got the ball.
14. The teams played well.
15. The Colts scored a touchdown.
16. The teams rested.

Write an action verb to complete each of the following sentences. Write the complete sentence.

17. The player ___ the ball.
18. The fans ___ loudly.
19. One runner ___ on the field.
20. Both teams ___ well.
21. The ball ___ in the air.
22. The game ___ in a tie.

Writing Sentences

Think of a game you like to play with your friends. Write five sentences telling about the game. Use one of these action verbs in each sentence: run, throw, catch, play, win.

Sample Answer **1.** Al saw a football game.

Objects of Verbs

The verb in a sentence names an action. Sometimes there is a person or thing that receives the action. The person or thing that receives the action of the verb is called the *object* of the verb.

> The **object** of a verb receives the action of the verb. It answers the question *whom*? or *what*? after an action verb.

- Look at these sentences.

Nina bumps Nancy. Magda guards Nina.

The verb in the first sentence is *bumps*. Whom does Nina bump? She bumps Nancy. Therefore Nancy is the object of the verb. Who is the object of the verb in the second sentence?

- Now read these sentences.

Nina shoots the ball.
The ball hits the hoop.

The verb in the first sentence is *shoots*. What does Nina shoot? Nina shoots the ball. Therefore *ball* is the object of the verb. The object is often a noun. What is the object of the verb in the second sentence?

Sometimes there is no object of a verb in a sentence.

- Look at these sentences.

Verbs with No Objects	**Verbs with Objects**
The ball bounces.	Lois bounces the ball.
The team scores.	Nina scores two points.

The sentences on the left are complete as they are. The sentences on the right use objects to tell more about the action.

Talk About It

Read each sentence. Name the verb. Name the object of the verb.

1. Nina throws the ball.
2. The ball hits the wall.
3. Joanne pushes Magda.
4. Magda loses her shoe.
5. Her shoe hits the basket.
6. Lois catches the shoe.

Skills Practice

Read each sentence. Write the verb. Then write the object of the verb.

1. The fans filled the gym.
2. Ali and Bob found seats.
3. Children sold peanuts.
4. The coaches shook hands.
5. The referee blew a whistle.
6. The team missed a basket.
7. Magda raced Nina.
8. Nina grabbed the ball.
9. Nina passed the ball.
10. Joanne scored two points.
11. The fans cheered Joanne.
12. The team won the game.

Choose an object for the verb in each sentence. Write the sentence. Make sure that the word you use is a noun.

13. Nancy passed ___.
14. Magda threw ___.
15. Magda missed ___.
16. Lois lost ___.
17. Nancy scored ___.
18. The fans cheered ___.

Sample Answers **1.** filled, gym

Verb Tenses

A verb names an action. A verb also tells when an action happens. The *tense* of a verb shows when the action in a sentence takes place.

- Look at the verbs in these sentences.

The runners race around a track. A boy throws a heavy ball.

In these sentences each verb shows an action that happens now. These actions all take place at the present time.

> The **present tense** of a verb names an action that happens now.

- Look at the verbs in these sentences.

Tracy pitched for the Tigers. The rain ended the game.

Each verb shows an action that already happened. These verbs are in the past tense.

> The **past tense** of a verb names an action that already happened.

Verbs in the past tense have a special form. Most verbs that show action in the past end in *-ed*. The verbs end in *-ed* when the subject is either singular or plural.

The pitcher start*ed* the game. The players want*ed* a run.

- Look at the verbs in these sentences.

The teams will race tomorrow. Rita will run in the race.

In these sentences each verb shows an action that will happen at a future time. These verbs are in the future tense.

> The **future tense** of a verb names an action that will take place in the future.

Verbs that show action in the future have a main verb and the helping verb *will* or *shall*. A helping verb helps the main verb name an action.

Talk About It

Find the verb in each sentence. Then tell whether the verb is in the **present, past,** or **future** tense.

1. John raced to the finish line.
2. The race will start at noon.
3. The coach smiles at John.
4. Terry finished first.

Skills Practice

Write each sentence. Write the verb that appears in each sentence. Then write whether each verb is in the **present, past,** or **future** tense.

1. Mike will run in the race.
2. Anita runs very well.
3. Sally sits on the bench.
4. The best team will win.
5. The fans cheered the winner.
6. Bill runs on the track.
7. The coach watched the clock.
8. Raul will wear a number.
9. The race ended early.
10. They ride home together.

Sample Answer 1. Mike will run in the race. will run, future

Using the Present Tense

You already know that verbs can show time. A verb in the *present tense* names an action that happens now.

- Look at the verbs in the sentences in the box. Notice how the verbs end.

Jon wins the race.	The jumpers rest.
He breaks the tape.	I give you a heavy ball.
The coach cheers.	You throw the ball.

Verbs in the present tense have certain forms. In the sentences in the box, notice that an *-s* is added to the end of each verb in the first column. When the subject is a singular noun or *he, she,* or *it,* add an *-s* to form the present tense of a verb. Notice the verbs in the second column. When the subject is a plural noun or *I, you, we,* or *they* the verb doesn't change in the present tense.

You already know how to add *-es* to words that end in *s, ss, x, ch, sh,* or *z.*

- Notice the endings of the verbs in these sentences.

Anne crosses the finish line. The racers cross the finish line.

Sometimes you change the spelling before you add *-es* to a verb with a singular subject.

- Look at each pair of verbs. How is the spelling changed?

tidy	bury	carry
tidies	buries	carries

If a verb ends with a consonant and *y,* change the *y* to *i* and add *-es* to make the correct form of the present tense.

- Now look at each pair of verbs below. How is the spelling changed?

stay	obey	destroy
stays	obeys	destroys

If a verb ends with a vowel and *y*, add *s* to make the correct form of the present tense.

Talk About It

Complete each sentence with the correct form of the verb in the present tense.

1. Steve ___ the race. (watch)
2. The van ___ the fans. (carry)
3. Sue ___ the winner. (guess)
4. Terry ___ a number. (wear)
5. Terry ___ up the shoes. (mix)
6. The pole ___ in the wind. (sway)

Skills Practice

Write each sentence. Use the correct form of the verb in the present tense.

1. Molly ___ over the bar. (jump)
2. Molly ___ the bar. (miss)
3. The team ___ again. (try)
4. A runner ___ a stick. (pass)
5. Eva ___ for a win. (wish)
6. She ___ to the track. (hurry)
7. Richard ___ at home. (stay)
8. Luisa ___ her arm. (stretch)
9. A runner ___ the line. (cross)
10. A new race ___. (begin)
11. Rain ___ the field. (destroy)
12. Eva ___ the shoes. (carry)

Writing Sentences

Imagine that you are at a race. Write five sentences telling about what you see there. Use verbs in the present tense in your sentences.

Sample Answer 1. Molly jumps over the bar.

Using the Past Tense

A verb in the present tense names an action that happens now. A verb in the *past tense* names an action that ended before now.

- Look at the verbs in these sentences.

Sue played softball with the team last week.
The Lions wanted a home run. The fans cheered.

Each verb shows an action that already happened. These verbs are in the past tense. Most verbs that show action in past end in *-ed*. The verbs end in *-ed* when the subject is either singular or plural.

- Now look at the past tense of these verbs.

PRESENT	compare	race
PAST	compared	raced

Remember that verbs that already end in *e* drop the *e* and add *-ed* to form the past tense.

With some verbs you change the spelling before adding *ed*.

- Look at each pair of verbs. How is the spelling changed?

PRESENT	reply	study
PAST	replied	studied

If a verb ends in a consonant and *y*, change the *y* to *i* and add *-ed* to form the past tense.

If a verb ends in a vowel and *y*, add *-ed* to form the past tense.

The sick player stayed in bed.

- Now look at each pair of verbs below. How is the spelling changed to form the past tense?

PRESENT	clap	beg	bat	fan
PAST	clapped	begged	batted	fanned

If a verb ends in a consonant, vowel, consonant, double the last consonant and add *-ed* to form the past tense.

Talk About It

Find the verb in each sentence and change it to the past tense.

1. The teams play baseball.
2. The Tigers start the game.
3. The fans clap.
4. Tracy bats the ball.
5. The catcher misses the ball.
6. The runner races to second.

Skills Practice

Write each sentence with the verb in the past tense.

1. Baseball amuses the fans.
2. The fans compare the players.
3. The players tidy the lockers.
4. The game starts on time.
5. The umpire needs a nap.
6. Tracy obeys the coach.
7. Ming grabs the bat.
8. The players join the coach.
9. Tracy finishes the inning.
10. The rain destroys the grass.

Writing Sentences

Imagine that you played baseball with two famous ball players. They can be real or make-believe players. Write five sentences using verbs in the past tense.

1. Write a sentence telling what two famous pitchers did.
2. Write two sentences telling what two different batters did.
3. Write two sentences telling what one player did.

Sample Answer 1. Baseball amused the fans.

Skills Review

Read each sentence. Write the action verb.

1. Sam played ping-pong with Susie.
2. Sam beat Susie in each game.
3. Sam slammed the ball hard across the table.
4. The ball flew by Susie too quickly.
5. Now Susie tries harder.
6. Susie holds her paddle tightly.
7. Sam hits the ball very hard to Susie.
8. This time Susie returns the ball.
9. Sam yells in surprise.
10. Susie laughs at the look on his face.

Read each sentence. Write the verb. Then write the object of the verb.

11. Hugo coaches the racers.
12. The teams sail boats.
13. Hugo blows the whistle.
14. One boat races the other.
15. The sails catch the wind.
16. The wind fills the sails.
17. Hugo watches the winner.
18. The boat crosses the line.

Read each sentence. Write the verb. Then write whether each verb is in the **present, past,** or **future** tense.

19. Jim will play with Maria.
20. Jim plays with a new racket.
21. Maria uses her old racket.
22. She hits the ball very hard.
23. Their friends cheered.
24. Jim missed the ball.
25. Maria scored a point.
26. Now Jim will try harder.

Write the correct form of each verb in the present tense.

27. The class ___ funny games in gym. (play)
28. Mrs. Williams ___ the games to the class. (teach)

29. She ___ a sack around the legs of each student. (tie)
30. Each student ___ reaching the finish line first. (try)
31. The principal ___ the silly race. (watch)
32. He ___ at the humorous sight. (laugh)

Write the correct form of each verb in the past tense.

33. Emily races Craig.
34. She hurries past him.
35. Craig tries catching up.
36. Their friends cheer loudly.
37. Everyone claps at the end of the race.
38. Each runner stops to sit on the bench.

Careers

There are many different kinds of jobs in a small business. A business must have an *owner* who makes decisions about the way the business is run. Also two or more people could be responsible for the business and form a *partnership.* The owner needs other people to help run the store. A *clerk* helps people find what they want in the store. A *stock clerk* orders and takes care of the products that the store sells. A *bookkeeper* or *accountant* keeps records of sales and expenses.

Present and Past of Have

The verb *have* is a special verb. *Have* forms the present and past tense in a different way from most verbs.

- Look at these sentences. The verb *have* is in the present tense in each sentence.

Manuel has a checkers game.	The children have a game.
It has rules.	You have the rules.
He has a friend, Marina.	I have the scorecard.
She has the red checkers.	We have a good time.
The game has two players.	They have fun, too.

When the subject is a singular noun or *he, she,* or *it,* the present tense form of this verb is *has.* When the subject is a plural noun or *I, you, we,* or *they,* the form is *have.*

- Look at these sentences. The verb *have* is in the past tense in each sentence.

He had a good day yesterday.	They had a good game.
The children had fun.	Marina had three checkers.

The past tense of the verb *have* is always *had.*

Talk About It

Complete each sentence. Use the correct form of the verb *have*.

1. Today Marina ___ good luck. (present)
2. The table ___ a flat top. (past)
3. Manuel ___ the black checkers. (past)
4. The players ___ twelve pieces. (present)
5. You ___ all the checkers. (present)
6. Marina ___ fun today. (present)
7. Yesterday they ___ a good time. (past)

Skills Practice

Write each sentence. Use the correct form of the verb *have*.

1. The friends ___ a new hobby now. (present)
2. They ___ a small puppy. (present)
3. It ___ the name "Dinky." (present)
4. The puppy ___ brown eyes and soft fur. (present)
5. The friends ___ a lot of fun with Dinky. (present)
6. Marina ___ some unusual pets. (past)
7. She ___ a pair of hamsters last summer. (past)
8. The hamsters ___ a family. (past)
9. They ___ six baby hamsters. (past)
10. The hamsters ___ a great time inside their cage. (past)

Writing Sentences

Write five sentences telling about games you have at home that you play. Use the present tense of *have* in three of the sentences. Use the past tense of *have* in two of the sentences.

Sample Answer 1. The friends have a new hobby now.

Past Tense with Have

There is a special way of talking about the past. Sometimes you want to tell about an action that began in the past and is still going on. Sometimes you want to talk about an action that did not happen at a definite time in the past.

The rain has started. (still going on)
The teams have played many games. (not at a definite time)

The underlined verbs are examples of the *past tense with have*. They have a main verb, and they use the helping verb *have* or *has*. The main verb is in the past tense. Notice how the past tense with *have* is formed.

Verb	Past tense with *have*
race	has or have raced
play	has or have played
ask	has or have asked
move	has or have moved

- Find the verbs that are examples of the *past tense with have*.

  Irene has played first base this season.
  Tom has pitched well.
  The outfielders have received much praise.

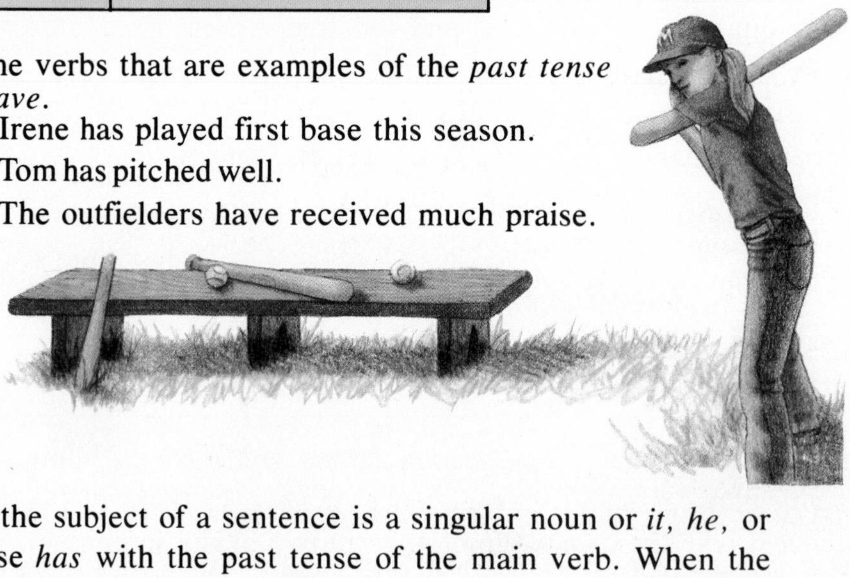

When the subject of a sentence is a singular noun or *it, he,* or *she,* use *has* with the past tense of the main verb. When the subject of a sentence is plural or *I, you, we* or *they,* use *have* with the past tense of the main verb.

Talk About It

Complete each sentence. Use the correct form of the verb in the past tense with *have* or *has*.

1. The game ___. (has started, have started)
2. The coach ___ the weather. (has checked, have checked)
3. The players ___ well this year. (has played, have played)
4. Practice ___. (has helped, have helped)

Complete each sentence. Use the correct form of the verb in the past tense.

5. The coach has ___ hard. (work)
6. The team has ___ all season. (practice)
7. The players have ___. (improve)

Skills Practice

Write each sentence. Complete each sentence by using the correct form of the verb in the past tense with *have* or *has*.

1. The stadium ___. (has filled, have filled)
2. The fans ___. (has arrived, have arrived)
3. The cheers ___. (has started, have started)
4. The umpire ___. (has appeared, have appeared)
5. The teams ___ for the game. (has dressed, have dressed)

Write each sentence. Complete each sentence by using the correct form of the verb in the past tense.

6. Sam has ___ many Green Sox games. (watch)
7. The players have ___ Sam. (notice)
8. Sam has ___ the dugout. (share)
9. The players have ___ a ball for Sam. (sign)
10. Sam has ___ the ball on his bookshelf. (place)

Sample Answers 1. The stadium has filled.
6. Sam has watched many Green Sox games.

Irregular Verbs

The past tense of some verbs is not formed in the regular way. These verbs do not change to past tense by adding *ed*. They have special forms that do not follow any rules. You must learn these special forms.

Verb	Past Tense	Past Tense with Have
begin	began	has, have begun
blow	blew	has, have blown
break	broke	has, have broken
choose	chose	has, have chosen
come	came	has, have come
do	did	has, have done
draw	drew	has, have drawn
drink	drank	has, have drunk
fly	flew	has, have flown
give	gave	has, have given
go	went	has, have gone
grow	grew	has, have grown
know	knew	has, have known
lose	lost	has, have lost
run	ran	has, have run
see	saw	has, have seen
sing	sang	has, have sung
sit	sat	has, have sat
swim	swam	has, have swum
write	wrote	has, have written

- Study the sentences below. Notice how the verb changes in a special way from present to past tense and then to past tense with *have*.

The team loses every game.
The team lost every game.
The team has lost every game.

They break all records for losing.
They broke all records for losing.
They have broken all records for losing.

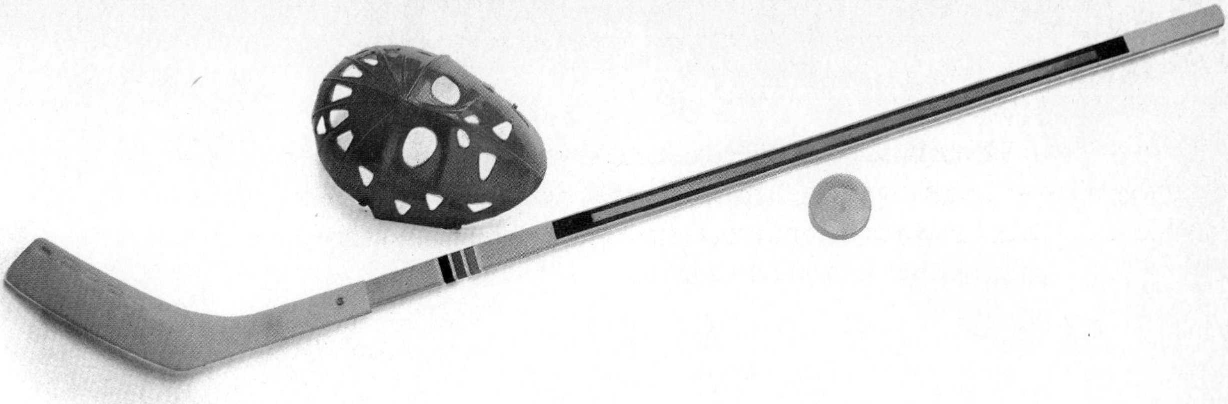

Remember that this special past tense with *have* tells about action that started in the past and is still continuing. It also tells about action that did not happen at a particular time.

Talk About It

Use the correct form of the verb in the past tense.

1. Yesterday the team ___. (lose)
2. The team has ___ again. (lose)
3. Fans have ___ to cry. (begin)
4. Last week Bob ___. (run)
5. The players have ___ home. (fly)
6. Bob has ___ up hockey. (give)

Skills Practice

Write each sentence. Use the correct form of the verb in the past tense.

1. Ali ___ taller last year. (grow)
2. Ali has ___ taller. (grow)
3. The fans have ___ down. (sit)
4. The puck ___ over the ice. (fly)
5. Bob ___ away his stick. (give)
6. Amy has ___ her stick. (break)
7. Guy has ___ some water. (drink)
8. Bob has ___ away. (run)
9. The coach ___ down. (sit)
10. Maya ___ a song. (begin)
11. Maya has ___ well. (do)
12. Goalies ___ badly. (do)
13. Fans ___ soda. (drink)
14. Jill ___ her toe. (break)
15. The coach ___ a horn. (blow)
16. The fans ___ to go. (choose)
17. Guy has ___ the score. (write)
18. The team has ___ home. (go)
19. The players ___ fast. (run)
20. Maria ___ the game. (see)
21. Fans have ___ early. (come)
22. Maya ___ the players. (know)

Sample Answer 1. Ali grew taller last year.

More Irregular Verbs

You know that there are no rules for forming the past tense of some verbs. The only way you can learn these special forms is to memorize them. Here are some more past tense forms that you need to learn.

Verb	Past Tense	Past Tense with Have
bring	brought	has, have brought
drive	drove	has, have driven
eat	ate	has, have eaten
fall	fell	has, have fallen
feel	felt	has, have felt
freeze	froze	has, have frozen
have	had	has, have had
lay	laid	has, have laid
leave	left	has, have left
let	let	has, have let
lie	lay	has, have lain
ride	rode	has, have ridden
ring	rang	has, have rung
rise	rose	has, have risen
say	said	has, have said
set	set	has, have set
speak	spoke	has, have spoken
steal	stole	has, have stolen
take	took	has, have taken
teach	taught	has, have taught
think	thought	has, have thought
throw	threw	has, have thrown
wear	wore	has, have worn

- Study the sentences below. Notice how the verb changes from present to past tense and then to past tense with *have*.

He takes a nap. He took a nap. He has taken a nap.

Talk About It

Read each sentence using the correct past tense form of the verb in parentheses.

1. The Olympics ___ place in 1980. (take)
2. Coaches have ___ Nadia. (teach)
3. They ___ her practice. (let)
4. Nadia has ___ a medal. (wear)
5. The fans ___ up. (rise)
6. The judges ___ she won. (say)
7. The old record has ___. (fall)
8. Nadia ___ proud. (feel)

Skills Practice

Write each sentence. Use the correct past tense form of the verb in parentheses.

1. Jim Thorpe ___ proud. (feel)
2. He has ___ a record. (set)
3. We ___ about Jim. (think)
4. We ___ to the games. (drive)
5. Greeks ___ to Olympia. (ride)
6. Greece has ___ a long history. (have)
7. Many games ___ place. (take)
8. He has ___ the torch. (bring)
9. Bob Garrett ___ up. (rise)
10. He has ___ a discus. (throw)
11. He has ___ the show. (steal)
12. They have ___ in chariots. (ride)
13. The race has ___ place. (take)
14. Two skiers have ___. (fall)
15. The winners ___ medals. (wear)
16. The coach ___. (speak)
17. He has ___ quietly. (speak)
18. He has never ___ a hat. (wear)
19. The lake has ___. (freeze)
20. We have ___ lunch. (eat)
21. Who ___ the goal? (set)
22. Fans ___ peanuts. (eat)
23. We have ___ happy. (feel)
24. The team has ___. (leave)

Writing Sentences

Write four sentences about a rodeo. Use past tense forms of these verbs.

ring throw ride fall

Sample Answer 1. Jim Thorpe felt proud.

Prefixes

A *prefix* is a letter or a group of letters added to the beginning of a word. Adding a prefix changes the meaning of the word.

- Look at the underlined words in these sentences. What prefix can you find in each word?

Jack misuses the equipment.
Jack misbehaves on the golf course.

The prefix added to these verbs is *mis-*. *Mis-* means "badly" or "in the wrong way."

Our language has many other prefixes. Here are four of the most common prefixes used with action verbs:

Prefix	Meaning	Example
mis-	badly, in the wrong way	Did you know you misspelled my name?
re-	again	Please rewrite my name.
un-	opposite of	Jack untied his shoelaces.
pre-	before	Sally premixed the cake batter.

- Look at these sentences. Let the prefixes help you understand the meaning of the verbs.

Jack misplaces his golf ball.
Jack reopens his locker.
Jack unzips the pocket of his jacket.
Jack preplans his game.

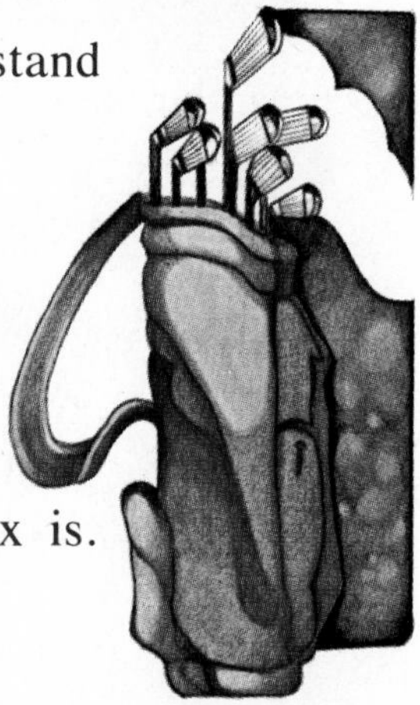

- Look at these sentences. Notice how helpful the prefix is.

Jack does the opposite of pack his lunch.
Jack unpacks his lunch.

Talk About It

Tell what the underlined word means in each sentence.

1. Jack misjudges the ball.
2. The workers replace the grass.
3. Jack prelocks the door.
4. Jack unbuttons his shirt.

Skills Practice

Find the verb that has a prefix in each sentence. Write the verb. Then write what the verb means.

1. Jack misplaced his golf clubs one morning.
2. Jack unlocked his locker to look there.
3. He rechecked his locker in the afternoon.
4. He prepacked the clubs that night.

Write each sentence. Change each group of underlined words to one word that has a prefix.

5. Jack understands in the wrong way the game of golf.
6. Jack does the opposite of cover his equipment in the rain.
7. Jack plans before his hard shots.
8. Jack reads again his book on playing golf.

Writing Sentences

Imagine that you are playing a game.

1. Write a sentence using an action verb with the prefix *mis-*.
2. Write a sentence using an action verb with the prefix *re-*.
3. Write a sentence using an action verb with the prefix *un-*.
4. Write a sentence using an action verb with the prefix *pre-*.

Sample Answers 1. misplaced, placed wrongly
5. Jack misunderstands the game of golf.

Skills Review

Read each sentence. Use the correct form of the verb *have*.

1. Two teams ___ a tug-of-war. (present)
2. Our team ___ strong pullers. (present)
3. The other team ___ luck. (present)
4. Last year we ___ a tie. (past)
5. We ___ a line between us. (present)
6. Last time I ___ the rope end. (past)

Read each sentence. Write the correct form of the verb in the past tense with *have* or *has*.

7. The team ___ a goal. (has scored, have scored)
8. The fans ___. (has cheered, have cheered)
9. One player ___ the puck. (has chased, have chased)
10. Another player ___ the goal. (has blocked, have blocked)
11. Both teams ___ well. (has skated, have skated)

Read each sentence. Write the correct past tense form of each verb in parentheses.

12. The sun ___ through the clouds. (break)
13. The captains have ___ their teams. (choose)
14. The coach has ___ the game. (begin)
15. Ali ___ to first base. (go)
16. The ball has ___ over the fence. (fly)
17. Two players ___ across home plate. (come)
18. The score has ___ quickly. (grow)
19. The visitors ___ the game. (lose)
20. The fans have ___ down. (sit)
21. We have ___ an exciting game. (see)
22. Who ___ him out at first base? (throw)
23. The cold air has ___ my feet and hands. (freeze)
24. The players ___ over each other. (fall)
25. The coach ___ to the umpire. (speak)

26. Who has ___ Jim to field the ball? (teach)
27. The doctor ___ there were no injuries. (say)
28. The boys ___ sandwiches to the park. (bring)
29. They have ___ all their food. (eat)
30. I ___ to the game with Connie. (ride)

Find the verb that has a prefix in each sentence. Write the verb first. Then write what the verb means.

31. Jean prewrapped her team jacket.
32. The company misspelled her name on the jacket.
33. Jean rewrapped her jacket sadly.
34. The company worker unfolded the jacket.
35. The worker reprinted her name the right way.

Write the following sentences. Change each group of underlined words to one word that has a prefix.

36. The Pirates <u>did the opposite of pack</u> their uniforms.
37. The Pirates <u>judged in the wrong way</u> the Rockets.
38. The Pirates will <u>play again</u> the Rockets next year.
39. The Rockets <u>planned before</u> their game with the Pirates.
40. The Pirates' coach had <u>handled badly</u> his team.

Have you ever wondered . . .

If the past of grow is *grew,*
Why isn't the past of snow *snew?*
If the past of give is *gave,*
Why isn't the past of live *lave?*
If the past of sit is *sat,*
Why isn't the past of hit *hat?*

Can you think of other questions like these?

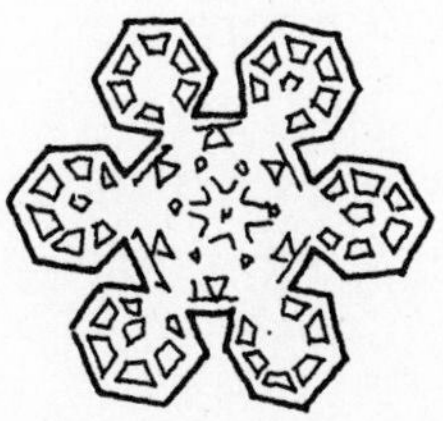

Exploring Language

Using the Library

The library is a good place to find interesting books and magazines to read. It is also a good place to find information

Books in libraries are organized by categories, such as fiction, nonfiction, or biography. Each category occupies a different section of the library. For instance, all fiction books are grouped together in one section and are arranged alphabetically by the authors' last names. So, if you wanted to find the story of *Robinson Crusoe* by Daniel Defoe, you would look in the fiction section under the **D's.**

Nonfiction books are in another section of the library. Nonfiction books are classified and arranged according to their subjects, such as history, literature, science, or language.

Biographies, books about peoples' lives, are in yet another section of the library. Biographies of different people are arranged alphabetically by the last names of the persons written about. Thus all the books about Abraham Lincoln are placed together. The separate biographies of Lincoln are then arranged alphabetically by each different author.

The books you might use to find information about a particular subject or for a report are called *reference works*.

An encyclopedia is one of the most useful reference works to use when gathering facts for a report. An *encyclopedia* is a book or set of books that gives information about many subjects. All the subjects in an encyclopedia are arranged in alphabetical order. There are pictures or photographs in encyclopedias that can help you, too. An encyclopedia often has an index in a separate book to help you find all the references to your subject.

Another good reference work is an almanac. An *almanac* is a single book that gives you the latest figures about many subjects. Almanacs list facts about important records, events, and people in your country or in the world. Almanacs are printed every year.

If you are looking for a book, but do not know the name of the author or the title, you should use the *card catalog*.

Every library has a card catalog to help you find books. There are three cards for every book. The number in the upper left corner shows where you find the book.

523
B
What the moon is like
Branley, Franklyn M.

TITLE CARD

523
B
Branley, Franklyn M.
What the moon is like

AUTHOR CARD

523
B
MOON
Branley, Franklyn M.
What the moon is like

SUBJECT CARD

Look at these sample cards:

1. The **author card** lists the name of the author and the title of the book. The author's last name is first.
2. The **title card** gives the name of the book and the author.
3. The **subject card** states the topic of the book and lists the author and title.

Talk About It

Look at the cards above and answer these questions.

1. What is the subject on the subject card?
2. What information is on every card?
3. What number would you give a librarian to find the book?

Skills Practice

Write the answers to these questions.

1. How are fiction books arranged in a library?
2. How would you find a biography of Thomas Jefferson?
3. Where would you find a list of volcanoes in the world?
4. Where would you find facts about how peanuts grow?
5. Where would you look for facts on Native Americans?
6. Where would you find facts about your state's rainfall?
7. Where would you find a list of space flights?

Sample Answer 1. Fiction books are arranged alphabetically by authors' last names.

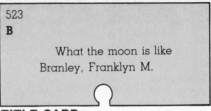

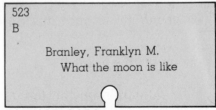

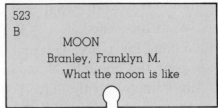

Reading Graphs and Tables

When you write a report, you will often look up information or facts in reference works. Some information is presented in paragraphs. Other information may be given in graphs. A *graph* shows information in picture form.

- Look at this graph.

The numerals on the left tell the number of medals. The words on the bottom tell what countries won bronze medals. Look at the column for USA. Go up to the top of the column. Now look at the numeral on the left. You can see that the United States won 25 bronze medals.

BRONZE MEDALS—1976 SUMMER OLYMPICS

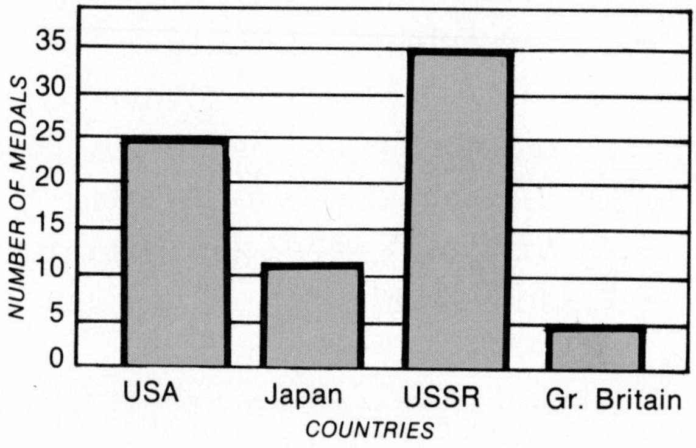

- Look at the graph. Which country won the most bronze medals in the 1976 Olympics? How many did Great Britain win?

Another way that information may be presented is in a table. Writers often use tables to give information that involves facts and numbers. A *table* is made up of columns and rows. The heading at the top of each column explains the facts in the column.

This table shows where the Summer Olympic Games were held in three different years and how many countries took part in the games.

SUMMER OLYMPIC GAMES

YEAR	PLACE	COUNTRIES
1968	Mexico City, Mexico	109
1972	Munich, West Germany	121
1976	Montreal, Canada	89

- Look at the table above. How many countries took part in the Summer Olympic Games in 1976? Where were the games held that year?

Talk About It

Graph A

BASKETBALL GAMES WON IN 1978

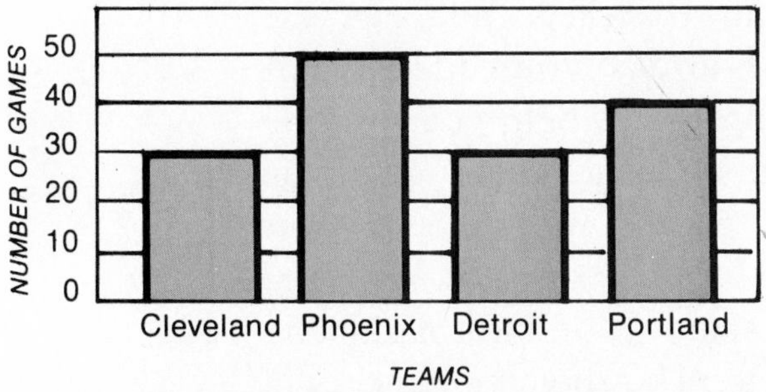

Table B

BASEBALL HALL OF FAME

NAME	POSITION	YEAR ELECTED
Joe DiMaggio	Outfielder	1955
Whitey Ford	Pitcher	1974
Lou Gehrig	First baseman	1939
Jackie Robinson	Second baseman	1962

Answer these questions about *Graph A*.

1. What do the numerals on the left side tell?
2. How many games did Portland win?

Answer these questions about *Table B*.

3. What kind of information does the table show?
4. Who was elected to the Hall of Fame in 1974?

Skills Practice

Answer these questions about *Graph A*. Write your answers.

1. How many games did Cleveland win?
2. Which team won the most games?
3. Which two teams won the same number of games?

Answer these questions about *Table B*. Write your answers.

4. Who was elected to the Hall of Fame in 1962?
5. Who was elected to the Hall of Fame first?
6. What position did Joe DiMaggio play?

Sample Answer 1. Cleveland won thirty games.

Facts in Paragraphs

Thinking About Paragraphs

Writing is a good way to share information with others. One place to find information is in a library. You can use reference works to gather facts about your ideas. For example, you might use an encyclopedia to help you to write about a person in history. Or an almanac could give you information about the number of people who live in your state. Ask questions such as *who, what, where, when,* and *how* to find facts. You can then share your information by writing a paragraph using your facts. The topic sentence will state the main idea. Each detail sentence should give specific facts which support the main idea.

● Read the paragraph below. Look for facts about the main idea:

> Tennis is an old sport that is played all over the world. Tennis began in France in the twelfth century. It was called the "game of the palm." The players batted the ball over the net with the palms of their hands. In 1873, the English introduced "lawn tennis." It was played on grass courts. Now the sport is known by the name "tennis."

Talking About Paragraphs

1. The topic sentence tells you that tennis is an old sport. What did you expect the paragraph to be about?
2. Read the detail sentences. The facts in the paragraph should help you answer the following questions: Where and when did tennis begin? Why was it called the "game of the palm"? When was tennis introduced in England?

Writing a Paragraph

Facts tell you something specific about a main idea. Look at the picture below. A list of facts beside the picture tells about a great moment in sports.

Date: April 8, 1974
Time: 9:06 P.M.
Place: Atlanta Stadium
Teams: game between the Atlanta Braves and the Los Angeles Dodgers
Record: Hank Aaron's 715th home run
Hit on Al Downing's second pitch

1. Think about how to arrange the facts in the paragraph. You can arrange the facts by using the answers to the questions: *who, what, where, when,* and *how*.
   a. Write this topic sentence on your paper: *Hank Aaron broke Babe Ruth's home-run record.*
   b. Write a detail sentence from the list of facts that gives information about *when* the event happened. Use the date and time.
   c. Write a detail sentence about *where* it happened. Use the place.
   d. Write a detail sentence about *who* was there. Use the names of the teams.
   e. Write a detail sentence about *what* and *how* it happened. Tell about the record.

A Factual Paragraph in a Business Letter

Thinking About a Letter

A business letter is different from a friendly letter. It is a serious *letter* often written to a business to ask for information or to order something. A paragraph in a business letter should use facts to explain the purpose of the letter.

The greeting in a letter tells to whom the letter is written. In a business letter the greeting is often the name of a company or a department.

Read the advertisement on the right.

> SALE! Warm-Up Suits $20
> red with blue stripes
> green with yellow stripes
> Sizes: small, medium, large
> Order from: Brown's Sporting Goods.
> 472 Ocean Avenue;
> Johnson, New York 11005

The following business letter was written to Brown's Sporting Goods. How is this letter different from the friendly letter?

Heading →

130 Hugh Street
Omaha, Nebraska 58412
May 17, 19__

Inside Address →

Brown's Sporting Goods
472 Ocean Avenue
Johnson, New York 11005

Greeting →

Dear Brown's Sporting Goods:

Body →

I want to order a warm-up suit. I read your ad about the sale in this morning's newspaper. I want a suit that is red with blue stripes. My size is small. I am sending a check for the sale price of $20.00.

Closing →

Yours truly,

Signature →

Jan L. Hanson
Jan L. Hanson

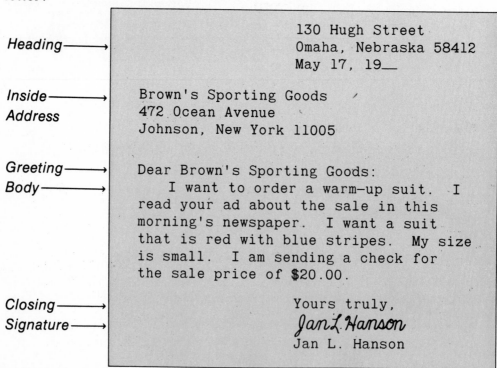

Look at the business letter written to Brown's Sporting Goods. Notice that it has six parts.

1. **Heading.** The heading is in the upper right corner of the letter. It gives your address and the date. Notice that there is a comma between the city and state and the date and the year.
2. **Inside address.** The inside address starts at the left margin. This part is not found in a friendly letter. It is the address of the person or business receiving your letter.
3. **Greeting.** The greeting begins in the left margin and ends with a punctuation mark called a colon.
4. **Body.** The body of the letter states why you are writing the letter. It should be polite and short with all needed facts.
5. **Closing.** The closing comes after the body, directly under the heading. Write: "Yours truly," or "Sincerely."
6. **Signature.** Use your full name directly under the closing. Many business letters are typed. If so, you leave a space between the closing and the signature and write in your name.

Talking About a Letter

Study the business letter that Jan wrote. Use it to answer these questions.

1. How would Brown's Sporting Goods know where to send the warm-up suit? The correct address with a ZIP code in the heading is very important in a business letter.
2. What information is written in the inside address?
3. Notice that the greeting gives the full name of the business. What other kind of greeting could you use?
4. Look at the body of the letter.
   a. What is the topic sentence of the paragraph?
   b. What facts are in your detail sentences? Notice that the facts answer the questions where, when, and what.
5. What last two parts are needed in a business letter?

Practicing a Factual Paragraph in a Business Letter

Thinking About Your Letter

Read the business letter to Brown's Sporting Goods in the last lesson. Imagine that you ordered a warm-up suit from the store. When you received it, you found that something was wrong with it. Now you want to return it and get your money back. Think of some reasons for returning the suit. For example, give facts such as the colors faded when you washed it, or the zipper was broken when you received it.

Writing Your Letter

Read again the business letter that Jan wrote. Write a letter to Brown's Sporting Goods saying that you want to return the warm-up suit. Follow the directions below. If you prefer, choose your own topic for a similar business letter.

1. Write your heading with today's date.
2. Write to this inside address: Brown's Sporting Goods; 472 Ocean Avenue; Johnson, New York 11005.
3. Write the greeting. Use a colon in a business letter.
4. Use facts in the body of the business letter.
   a. Write this topic sentence: *I am returning a warm-up suit.*
   b. Use detail sentences to give the facts clearly and briefly. Tell the store why you are returning the suit and ask for your money back. Try to arrange your sentences according to: *When* you ordered it.
      Where you read about it.
      What is wrong.
      What you want them to do.
   Remember that even though you may feel angry about returning the suit, it is important to be polite in a business letter.
   c. Be sure to indent the first sentence.

Word Bank

advertised
ordered
problem
unhappy
wrong
style
money

Edit Your Letter

Read your business letter and check it with these editing questions. Use the editing symbols to correct your work. If you need to, write your letter again.

1. Did you write a good topic sentence?
2. Did your detail sentences state facts clearly?
3. Did all your sentences express a complete idea?
4. Did you use clear action words in your paragraph?
5. Did you indent the first word of the paragraph?
6. Did you follow the business letter form correctly?
7. Did you check the spelling of your words?
8. Did you use capitals to start every sentence?
9. Did you use commas correctly in your heading? Did you use a colon in your greeting?

Editing Symbols

- ≡ capitalize
- ¶ indent
- ℘ take out
- ∧ add

Help Wanted

Young person to help elderly couple with chores on weekends. Duties include mowing lawn, tending garden, and house cleaning. Write to John Marshall, 14 Pinewood Acres, Jackson, N.J. 08527

INDEPENDENT WRITING

A Factual Paragraph in a Business Letter

Prewriting Study this help-wanted ad. A person answering any kind of job-related ad must be truthful. It is important to be able to organize and write a factual paragraph about your ability and experience. Jot down ideas that you might include in a letter of reply to this ad.

Writing Write a business letter with a factual paragraph in which you describe your qualifications for this job. Tell your age and what kinds of chores you do at home that might be similar to what this job demands. List any other jobs that you have done in or outside your home.

Editing Use the check questions above and the editing symbols to edit your letter.

Unit Review

Read each sentence. Write the action verb. *pages 72–73*

1. The player catches the ball.
2. Diane shoots the basketball through the hoop.
3. Diane scores two points for her team.

Read each sentence. Write the verb and the object of the verb. *pages 74–75*

4. Ché hit the ball.
5. Andrea grabbed the flag.
6. The judge blew her whistle.
7. Fans filled the stadium.

Write the verb in each sentence. Write whether the verb is in the **present, past,** or **future** tense. *pages 76–77*

8. They will play a game.
9. She holds the bat.
10. She missed the ball.
11. She will try again.

Write the correct form of the verb in the present tense. *pages 78–79*

12. She ___ an egg. (toss)
13. He ___ the egg. (catch)
14. He ___ the egg. (throw)
15. She ___ the egg. (drop)
16. A judge ___ the contest. (watch)
17. The judge ___ him the winner. (call)

Read each sentence. Write the verb in the past tense. *pages 80–81*

18. They begin the game over.
19. This time she tries harder.
20. The egg almost flies.
21. The judge declares her the winner.
22. She skips down the street.
23. The dog wags its tail.

Read each sentence. Write the correct form of the verb *have*. *pages 84–85*

24. Once I ___ a bird. (past)
25. It ___ three eggs. (past)
26. Now the bird ___ a nest. (present)
27. The birds ___ a family. (present)

Read each sentence. Write the correct past tense form of each verb in parentheses. *pages 86–89*

28. The coach has ___ the whistle. (blow)

29. The winners have ___ a song. (sing)
30. The players have ___ bags. (pack)
31. Two players ___ home. (run)
32. Many fans have ___ to the game. (come)
33. Who has ___ with you? (go)
34. We have ___ to listen to the radio. (choose)
35. My grandparents have ___ to Pittsburgh. (drive)
36. Will you ___ me pay the bill? (let)
37. The union has ___ the matter aside. (lay)

Write the following sentences. Change each group of underlined words to one word that has a prefix. *pages 92–94*

38. The Tigers <u>did the opposite of fasten</u> their sails.
39. The Bears <u>handled wrongly</u> their boat.
40. The captain <u>arranged again</u> the sails.
41. The teams <u>cooked ahead</u> their meals.

Below are the parts of a business letter. They are not in the right order. Put the parts in their proper order. Then write the letter. Be sure to use the correct punctuation in each part *pages 100–105*

1. Yours truly
2. Camp Rodeo
   70 Oak Lane
   Pine Bluffs Utah 33601
3. Helen Swartz
4. I would like to spend two weeks at your rodeo camp this summer. I need to know how much it costs and what kinds of activities you offer. Also, could I have my own pinto pony to ride? Please send all your information to the address above.
5. Dear Camp Rodeo
6. 601 West Orange Avenue
   Phoenix Arizona 68315
   May 5 19 ___

A Letter

People write letters to communicate with others. Writers of business letters usually ask for information or order something. People who write friendly letters often describe personal experiences.

This selection is a friendly letter. The writer describes being on a whale-watching trip. The letter reports the events and reveals the author's thoughts and feelings. As you read the letter, try to imagine being a part of the action.

Dear Ranger Rick:

Last spring my family and I went whale watching off Cape Cod near Provincetown, Massachusetts. We went on a ninety-foot boat named *Dolphin III,* skippered by Captain Al Avellar.

When everyone was aboard, a biologist told us about the whales we might see. He showed us baleen, the comblike stuff that some whales strain their food through. He also played some humpback whale sounds on a tape. They were real funny, all kinds of squeaks and howls.

An hour after we left the pier we saw the first whale, a humpback nearly forty feet long!

For the next two hours we watched a pair of the giant mammals as they fed near the boat. Most of the time they surfaced between fifty and a hundred feet from us. Once one came so close that he sprayed us when he blew!

Just before we headed back, it started to rain. Once we got under way the rain stopped, but it got so rough that I had to hold onto the rail to stand up. The spray coming over the side of the boat got me soaked. It was still worth it! Just before we got into the harbor, I climbed up to the ship's bridge and rode the rest of the way in to the pier with the captain.

Kristen Wood
Chester Depot, VT

Creative Activities

1. **Creative Writing** Imagine you were on a sea voyage. During the trip you met with a strange sea creature. Write a letter to a friend that describes the creature. Tell what happened during your encounter. Add enough details so the reader can picture the scene. Describe your thoughts and feelings at the time.
2. Use the encyclopedia and other books to find more facts about whales or other sea animals. Share the facts with the class.

TELEVISION CONTROL ROOM

Grammar and Related Language Skills

Pronouns
Subject and Object Pronouns
Possessive Pronouns
Pronoun Usage

Practical Communication

STUDY AND REFERENCE SKILLS
Learning About Facts and Opinions
COMPOSITION
Writing an Editorial

Creative Expression

A Photo Essay

4

Many people with different skills work together to produce a television program. A control room director helps decide what images will appear on the screen. The director must organize and manage the people in the control room. What listening and speaking skills does this person need? How is television a valuable means of communication?

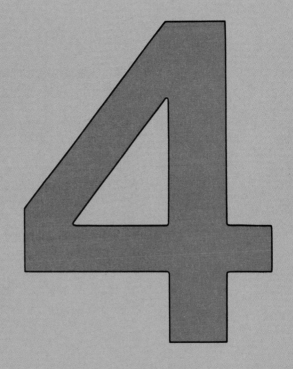

Pronouns

Think of how odd it would sound to repeat the same nouns again and again. A *noun* is a word that names a person, place, thing, or idea. Special words can be used to replace these nouns. These words are called *pronouns*.

> A **pronoun** is a word that takes the place of one or more nouns.

Suppose your name were Lisa. Without pronouns, you would have to speak about yourself like this:

> Lisa watches television often.
> Television teaches Lisa about many new things.

- Try saying the above sentences using your own name. Don't they sound strange?

- Now read the same sentences below. This time there is one difference.

> I watch television often.
> Television teaches <u>me</u> about many new things.

In the sentences above the pronouns *I* and *me* are used to take the place of the noun *Lisa*.

- Look at the word list in the box below. These are some pronouns that are often used.

I	me
you	you
she, he, it	her, him
we	us
they	them

Talk About It

Read each pair of sentences. The second sentence in each pair has one or more pronouns. Name each pronoun. Then tell the noun or nouns each pronoun replaces.

1. The United States has three main television networks. They show the programs Americans watch.
2. Many viewers like news programs. They watch them daily.
3. Miguel watches funny programs. They make him laugh.

Skills Practice

Read each pair of sentences. The second sentence in each pair has one or more pronouns. Write the second sentence. Then draw a line under each pronoun. Write the noun or nouns each pronoun replaces.

1. Paul watches nature programs. They give him facts about plant and animal life.
2. One nature program described how bees live. It told how they build hives.
3. Maria came from Mexico to visit Paul. During the visit she watched American television with him.
4. Maria liked American television. She found it very different from Mexican television.
5. Maria watched a lot of television with Paul. He helped her with some of the language.
6. Maria saw a program about snakes. It described how they get new skin.
7. Maria and Paul watched a very funny show. It made them laugh for hours.
8. In America Maria learned a lot of English. She remembered it for many years.

Sample Answer 1. They give him facts about plant and animal life. programs, Paul

Pronouns as Subjects

The *subject part* of a sentence names whom or what the sentence is about. Look at the subject part in these sentences.

Pablo reads nature magazines. He enjoys stories about animals.

In the first sentence the subject part is the noun *Pablo*. In the second sentence the subject part is the pronoun *He*. *He* replaces the noun *Pablo*.

Only certain pronouns can replace nouns in the subject part of a sentence. These pronouns are *I, you, he, she, it, we,* and *they*. They are called *subject pronouns*.

A **subject pronoun** is a pronoun that is used as the subject of a sentence.

It is important to choose the correct subject pronoun.

- Read each pair of sentences below. Notice that the pronouns and the nouns they replace are underlined.

<u>Lisa</u> and <u>Roberto</u> read the newspaper. <u>They</u> learn many interesting facts.

<u>Roberto</u> reads the sports pages. <u>He</u> discovers which teams win.

A subject pronoun can also replace a noun and a pronoun that work together. Read the following pair of sentences. In the second sentence, the pronoun *we* replaces the noun *Roberto* and the pronoun *I*.

Roberto and I buy a newspaper. We read the weather report.

These sentences tell you how to choose a subject pronoun.

Use *I* to talk about yourself.

Use *you* to talk directly to one or more people.

Use *he* to talk about one male.

Use *she* to talk about one female.

Use *it* to talk about one thing.

Use *we* to talk about yourself and at least one other person.

Use *they* to talk about two or more people or things.

Talk About It

In the second sentence of each pair, some words are underlined. Tell which subject pronouns can be used in place of the underlined words.

1. Mr. and Mrs. Mason work for a newspaper.
   Mr. and Mrs. Mason work for *The Sun*.
2. *The Sun* prints a great many facts.
   The Sun gives information about the world.
3. Chris and I read about foreign places.
   Chris and I read about nearby places, too.
4. Anna likes to read the comics.
   Anna likes to read the want-ads, also.

Skills Practice

Read each pair of sentences. Write the second sentence. Use the correct subject pronoun in place of the underlined words.

1. Lisa and I read articles about dogs.
   Lisa and I raise dogs.
2. One article describes correct puppy care.
   Puppies need very special attention.
3. Lisa knows the puppies like soft food.
   Lisa feeds the puppies puppy meal.
4. One puppy eats no meal.
   The puppy only drinks milk.
5. Chuck loves the puppies.
   Chuck plays with the puppies every day.
6. Puppies need exercise.
   The puppies play outdoors for two hours.
7. Does Lisa clean the litter boxes?
   No, Lisa doesn't.

Sample Answer 1. We raise dogs.

Pronouns as Objects

The *object of a verb* receives the action of the verb. It answers the question *whom*? or *what*? It comes after an action verb. What is the object of the verb in each of these sentences?

> Brian showed an ad to Diana.
> Then Diana showed it to Adam.

In the first sentence the object of the verb is the noun *ad*. In the second sentence the object of the verb is the pronoun *it*. *It* replaces the noun *ad*.

Special pronouns can be used as the object of a verb. These pronouns are *me, you, him, her, it, us,* and *them*. They are called *object pronouns*.

> An **object pronoun** is a pronoun that is used as the object of a verb.

It is important to choose the correct object pronoun.

- Read each pair of sentences below.

Teddy read a news story to Juan.
Then Juan read it to Carol.
Paula gave some presents to Patti.
Patti showed them to Joan.

The pronouns and the nouns they replace are underlined.

An object pronoun can also replace a noun and a pronoun.

- Read the following pair of sentences.

The children taught Maggie and me about interviews.
Then the teacher taught us about newspapers.

In the second sentence the pronoun *us* replaces the noun *Maggie* and the pronoun *me*.

Talk About It

Read each pair of sentences. In the second sentence of each pair, some words are underlined. Tell which object pronouns can be used in place of the underlined words.

1. Pat Brown's father works for a movie company.
   One day Pat and Joey visited Pat's father at work.
2. The company just finished a movie.
   The company completed the movie in two months.
3. Pat and Joey looked all around the movie lot.
   Mr. Brown took Pat and Joey to every location.

Skills Practice

Read each pair of sentences. In the second sentence of each pair, some nouns are underlined. Write the second sentence. Use the correct object pronoun in place of the underlined words.

1. Gino Palma listens to the radio a lot.
   Gino plays the radio early in the morning.
2. Gino's mother bought a clock radio.
   Gino thanked Gino's mother.
3. Gino listens to the sports report.
   The report gives Gino facts about the city teams.
4. Gino and I heard that the Bullets won the basketball game.
   This news pleased Gino and me.
5. Gino listens to the weather report in the morning.
   The report tells Gino about today's weather.
6. Today Gino bought a CB radio.
   Gino put the CB radio in the car.

Sample Answer 1. Gino plays it early in the morning.

Using Subject and Object Pronouns

A *subject pronoun* is a pronoun that is used as the subject of a sentence. It tells who or what does the action. An *object pronoun* is a pronoun that is used as the object of a verb. It comes after an action verb.

It is important to know when to use a subject pronoun and when to use an object pronoun.

- Read the pair of sentences below. Which pronoun would you use to fill in the blank space?

  Benny ordered a sports magazine.
  ___ ordered the magazine by mail. (He, Him)

Ask yourself whether the pronoun is in the subject part of the sentence or whether it is the object of the verb. In the second sentence above, the pronoun is in the subject part of the sentence. It tells who is doing the action. The subject pronoun *He* must be used.

- Now read the pair of sentences below. Which pronoun would you choose this time?

  Benny called Karen on the phone.
  Benny called ___ twice a day. (she, her)

In the second sentence above, the pronoun comes after the action verb. It is the object of the verb. The object pronoun *her* must be used here.

- Read this list. It tells you the subject and object pronouns.

Subject Pronouns		**Object Pronouns**	
I	we	me	us
you	you	you	you
she, he, it	they	her, him, it	them

Talk About It

Read each sentence. Name the pronoun that belongs in each blank space. Explain your answers.

1. Mrs. Wilson said, "Sometimes ___ speak without words." (I, me)
2. Then Mrs. Wilson showed ___ how. (we, us)
3. ___ walked over to Kenny. (She, Her)
4. Mrs. Wilson patted ___ on the shoulder. (he, him)
5. ___ smiled at Kenny, too. (She, Her)

Skills Practice

Write each sentence, using the correct pronoun.

1. "___ just spoke to Kenny," Mrs. Wilson said. (I, Me)
2. Kenny said, "___ heard nothing at all." (I, Me)
3. Mrs. Wilson explained, "___ smiled at Kenny." (I, Me)
4. "My smile tells ___ about my feelings." (he, him)
5. "A pat on the shoulder tells ___ about the same thing." (he, him)
6. "___ used a silent language called body language." (I, Me)
7. "People tell ___ about their feelings with body language." (we, us)
8. "___ show feeling with body language." (They, Them)

Writing Sentences

You can use parts of your body other than your voice to say something. You raise your eyebrows to show surprise. You shrug your shoulders when you don't know. You nod your head when you agree. Using parts of the body to say something is called *body language*.

Write four sentences. Describe a different example of body language in each sentence. Tell what each kind of body language is saying. Use subject and object pronouns.

Sample Answer 1. "I just spoke to Kenny," Mrs. Wilson said.

Skills Review

Read each pair of sentences. The second sentence in each pair has one or more pronouns. Write each pronoun. Then write the noun or nouns each pronoun replaces.

1. Paula reads a sports magazine.
   It tells her about the players.
2. Paula reads about basketball.
   She likes it better than baseball.
3. Paula reads about some new basketball shots.
   She tries them with friends.
4. The magazine has many ads.
   Paula reads them carefully.
5. Paula sees an ad for special sneakers.
   She orders them by mail.

Read each pair of sentences. Write the subject pronoun that can be used in place of the underlined words.

6. Esther wrote a report.
   <u>The report</u> told about fish.
7. First Esther read lots of articles.
   <u>Esther</u> found the articles in the library.
8. Jimmy found some facts for Esther.
   <u>Jimmy</u> discovered the facts in a nature magazine.
9. Mr. Carbera, our teacher, read the report.
   <u>Mr. Carbera</u> gave the report an *A*.

Read each pair of sentences. In the second sentence some words are underlined. Write the object pronoun that can be used in place of the underlined words.

10. The children made a simple telephone.
    The children made <u>the telephone</u> from cups and wire.

11. Paul found two good paper cups.
Paul tied the cups to a long wire.

12. Anne talked softly into one cup.
Paul heard Anne through the other cup.

13. Then Paul answered Anne.
Anne heard Paul very clearly.

Read each pair of sentences. Write the pronoun that belongs in each blank space.

14. Dave sent a telegram to Mary.
Dave sent ___ for Mary's birthday. (her, it)

15. Dave used only a few words in the telegram.
Dave chose ___ carefully. (they, them)

16. Mary enjoyed Dave's telegram.
Mary called ___ on the telephone. (he, him)

17. Mary spoke to Dave.
Mary thanked ___ for the nice birthday message. (he, him)

The pronoun *you* once had a close relative. This word was *thou. Thou* had the same meaning as *you. Thou* was used for talking with friends and family. Now *thou* has disappeared from our language. Think of other words that have disappeared.

Exploring Language

Possessive Pronouns

You have learned that possessive nouns show who or what has something. Words like *Emma's* or *boys'* are possessive nouns. Special pronouns are also used to show who or what has something. They are called *possessive pronouns*.

> A **possessive pronoun** is a pronoun that names who or what has something.

There are two kinds of possessive pronouns. The first kind must be used in front of nouns. These pronouns are *my, your, his, her, its, our,* and *their*. They take the place of the name of the person or thing that has something.

• Look at this example.

> Rita's ads have words and pictures.
> Her ads appear in several newspapers.

Rita is one female. The possessive pronoun that takes the place of one female is *her*. *Her* tells what Rita has.

The second kind of possessive pronoun is not used in front of nouns. These pronouns stand alone in a sentence. They are *mine, yours, his, hers, ours,* and *theirs*. Notice that *his* is used both ways.

• Now look at this example.

> Karen writes articles about birds.
> The articles in this magazine are hers.

In the second sentence above, the possessive pronoun *hers* takes the place of *Karen's articles*.

• Look at each possessive pronoun in these sentences. Is it used in front of a noun or does it stand alone?

What noun does each possessive pronoun replace?

> Joel finished his report in two hours.
> The report on the table is his.

In the first sentence above, *his* is used in front of the noun *report*. *His* takes the place of *Joel's*. In the second sentence, *his* stands alone. *His* takes the place of *Joel's report*.

Talk About It

Read each sentence. Tell the possessive pronoun that fits in each blank space. Explain your choice.

1. ___ sister writes magazine ads. (My, Mine)
2. ___ ads appear in many magazines. (Her, Hers)
3. All of the ads on the wall are ___. (her, hers)
4. One of ___ school reports hangs on the wall. (my, mine)
5. The report near the door is ___. (my, mine)

Skills Practice

Write each sentence. Use the correct possessive pronoun for each blank space.

1. Ed and Pam write articles for ___ newspaper. (their, theirs)
2. Most of the sports articles are ___. (their, theirs)
3. Some of ___ articles appear in the newspaper. (our, ours)
4. Some of the nature articles are ___. (our, ours)
5. Some of the nature articles are ___. (your, yours)
6. One of ___ articles tells about snakes. (your, yours)
7. The article tells about ___ unusual habits. (their, theirs)
8. Many of the news articles are ___. (your, yours)
9. Some of the news articles are ___. (their, theirs)
10. One of ___ articles was about the mayor. (our, ours)

Sample Answer 1. Ed and Pam write articles for their newspaper.

Subject-Verb Agreement

Every sentence has a subject part and a predicate part. The subject part has a noun or a pronoun. The predicate part has a verb. You know that subject nouns must work together with verbs in a sentence. The subject noun and the verb *agree*.

- Read these sentences.

  Debbie writes science articles.
  Other girls write science articles, too.

In the first sentence the verb *writes* agrees with the subject noun *Debbie*. In the second sentence the verb *write* agrees with the subject noun *girls*. In both sentences the verbs agree with the subject nouns. *Write* and *writes* are verbs in the present tense. Verbs in the present tense tell what is happening *now*.

A subject pronoun can take the place of one or more nouns in a sentence. The pronouns *I, you, he, she, it, we* and *they* are subject pronouns. Verbs must agree with subject pronouns, too.

- Look at the following sentences.

  He watches television each night.
  She listens to the radio.
  It plays for hours.

Notice that the verb changes to agree with the subject. The verbs end in *s* or *es*.

- Look at the following sentences.

I read the newspaper each day. We study science articles.
You like magazines better. They tell interesting facts.

The verbs in the sentences above do not change. No *-s* or *-es* is added to the verbs when the subject is *I, you, we,* or *they*.

Remember these rules when you are adding endings for agreement to verbs in the present tense. Add *-es* to verbs that end in *s, ss, ch, sh,* or *x*. Add *-s* to most other verbs.

Talk About It

Read each pair of sentences. Tell the correct form of the verb in the present tense that belongs in each blank space.

1. Nan makes movies.
   She ___ movies for television. (make)
2. Nan uses a movie camera.
   It ___ good pictures. (take)
3. Nan's movies tell about many different things.
   She ___ for interesting subjects. (watch)

Skills Practice

Read each pair of sentences. Write the second sentence. Use the correct form of the verb in the present tense.

1. Juan often helps Nan.
   He ___ to many places.
   (travel)
2. Juan films unusual people.
   He ___ a special camera.
   (use)
3. Nan and Juan plan many films.
   They ___ down ideas. (write)
4. Nan's brain works hard.
   It ___ of new ideas. (think)
5. Juan's brain works hard, too.
   It ___ of places to go.
   (dream)
6. Nan travels to many cities.
   She ___ for new faces.
   (look)
7. Nan and Juan work together.
   They ___ many films. (study)
8. Nan travels to cities.
   She ___ her cameras. (bring)

Writing Sentences

Suppose you work with two friends at a radio station. Write five sentences that tell about the jobs you do. Include any of these pronouns in your sentences: I, he, she, it, we, they. Use at least one pronoun in each sentence.

Sample Answer 1. He travels to many places.

Words Often Confused

Some possessive pronouns sound exactly like other words. Although they sound alike, they are different in other ways.

- Read the following sentences.

  Jane and Eddie wrote their report.
  Now they're finished with the typing.
  The children put the report over there.

How are the underlined words different? *Their, they're* and *there* are different in two ways. They have different spellings and different meanings.

Their shows what two people have. It is a possessive pronoun.
They're is a short way of writing they are.
There means in that place.
Words like their, they're, and there are homonyms.

Homonyms are words that sound alike but have different spellings and different meanings.

- Read the following sentences.

  Is this your magazine?
  You're welcome to read it.

Do the sentences give you a clue to their meanings? *Your* shows what you have. It is a possessive pronoun. *You're* is a short way of writing *you are.*

- Now read these sentences.

  This television has its own antenna.
  But it's broken.

In the first sentence above, *its* means *belonging to it.* In the second sentence *it's* is a short way of writing *it is.*

Talk About It

Complete each sentence with the correct word for each blank space. Explain your answers.

1. The magazine is on the table over ___ . (their, there, they're)
2. ___ welcome to look at it. (Your, You're)
3. Look at ___ table of contents. (its, it's)
4. ___ full of articles about sports. (It's, Its)
5. Reading will increase ___ word power. (your, you're)
6. Have the children returned ___ books? (they're, their, there)

Skills Practice

Write the sentences correctly, adding one of the words in parentheses.

1. ___ friends read many magazines. (Your, You're)
2. Magazines have ads throughout ___ pages. (there, their, they're)
3. ___ filled with items for sale. (There, They're, Their)
4. "___ easy to order by mail," Bonnie says. (It's, Its)
5. Soon, ___ packages arrived in the mail. (their, they're, there)
6. "___ poorly wrapped," says Bonnie. (There, Their, They're)
7. "___ address label has been lost." (It's, Its)
8. "I'll put it over ___", says Bonnie. (there, their, they're)
9. "This is not ___ book." (your, you're)
10. Was ___ enough postage on the letter? (they're, there, their)
11. ___ hard to read the address. (It's, Its)
12. ___ going to tell the postman, aren't you? (Your, You're)

Writing Sentences

Imagine that you are writing an advertisement for your favorite television program. Write five sentences telling people why they should watch that program. Use these words in your sentences: *their, they're, there, your, you're, its, it's.*

Sample Answer 1. Your friends read many magazines.

Skills Review

Read each sentence. Write the correct possessive pronoun for each blank space.

1. Many people understand ___ pets. (theirs, their)
2. Gloria talks with ___ all the time. (her, hers)
3. She understands ___ special language. (their, theirs)
4. I understand ___ cat very clearly. (my, mine)
5. Sarah understands ___ cat, too. (her, hers)
6. Sarah's cat often plays with ___. (my, mine)
7. Perhaps they talk about ___ owners. (their, theirs)
8. Do you understand ___ pets? (your, yours)

Read each pair of sentences. Write the correct form of the present tense of the verb.

9. Brian and Alice work for a newspaper.
They ___ articles. (write)

10. Alice writes sports articles.
She ___ many games. (attend)

11. Alice likes hockey games best.
She ___ the players very carefully. (watch)

12. The players move easily across the ice.
They ___ very well. (skate)

13. Brian writes human interest stories.
They ___ about people's lives. (tell)

14. Brian tells about helpful people.
He ___ brave people, too. (describe)

15. Brian waits for unusual happenings.
He ___ for interesting events. (wish)

16. One woman calls on the telephone.
She ___ about an unusual event. (whisper)

17. Brian leaves in a hurry.
He ___ out of the office. (dash)

Write the sentences correctly, adding one of the words in parentheses.

18. "Are those ___ magazines?" asked Maggie. (your, you're)
19. "No," answered Ricky. "The magazines over ___ belong to Lenny and John." (there, their, they're)
20. "___ reading the magazines for your report?" (Your, You're)
21. "Yes, ___ for my report." (their, there, they're)
22. "Many of ___ articles describe plants." (their, there, they're)
23. "___ is an article about house plants." (Their, There, They're)
24. "___ filled with wonderful information." (Its, It's)
25. "May I look through ___ table of contents?" (its, it's)

Careers

A person who has a job writing about the news is called a *journalist.* Journalists work on newspapers and magazines or at radio and television stations. Some journalists have college degrees. Others receive their experience by working at a newspaper office or at a television station. Some journalists write stories about news events that happen anywhere in the world. Others write about sports, entertainment, or business. Journalists must first find the facts before they write news articles. To gather their facts they ask people questions, use reference works, and observe news stories as they happen. Almost all journalists think that students should work on school newspapers if they are interested in a career in journalism.

Parts of a Newspaper

Almost every city or town has at least one newspaper. All newspapers try to give information to their readers. They also have many parts in common.

Newspapers usually contain news articles. *News articles* give information. Some tell about world events, national events, or local events. Other articles deal with sports, business, or entertainment. A news article usually starts with a headline. A *headline* is printed in bigger, darker type. It often states the main idea of a news article.

THE GAZETTE

TOWN WINS AWARD

The mayor of Auburn happily accepted the award on Tuesday night for the cleanest city in the entire United States.

NEWS ARTICLE

● Look at these other parts of a newspaper. What kind of information would you find in each part?

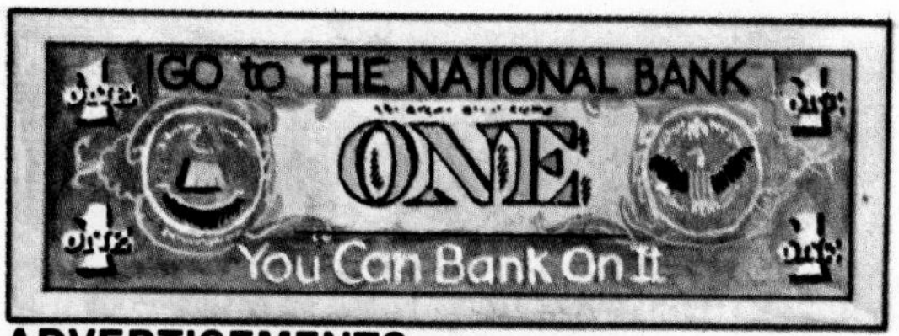
GO to THE NATIONAL BANK
ONE
You Can Bank On It
ADVERTISEMENTS

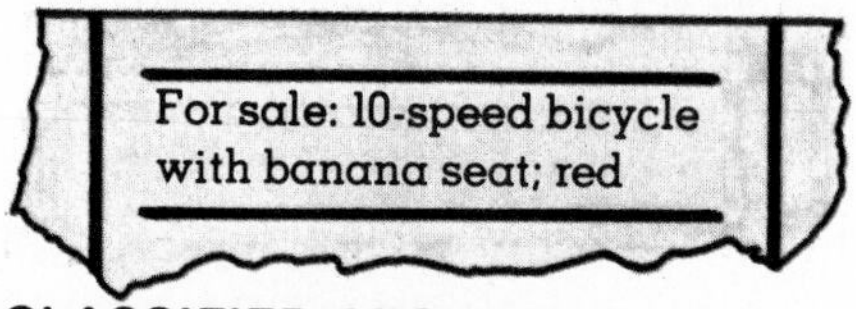
For sale: 10-speed bicycle
with banana seat; red
CLASSIFIED ADS

T.V. TONIGHT
7:00 P.M.-Newscast
8:00 P.M.-The Comedy Hour
9:00 P.M.-Movie of the Week
ENTERTAINMENT

Clear tonight. Cloudy tomorrow. Rain by noon.
WEATHER REPORTS

CARTOON/COMICS

Often editors of newspapers write about certain subjects. Their written opinions are called *editorials*. They express the point of view of the editorial board of the newspaper. Editorials usually appear on the editorial page. Sometimes readers write letters giving their opinions. Most newspapers publish some of these letters under the title of "Letters to the Editor."

THE EDITOR SPEAKS

This newspaper thinks the city park needs new tennis courts.

EDITORIAL

Talk About It

Look at the newspaper parts again. Tell which part would help you answer the following questions.

1. Which part would tell you if it will be cold tomorrow?
2. Which part would help you plan your evening?
3. Which part could make you laugh?
4. Which part would help you choose a bank?
5. Which part tries to sell you something?
6. Which section is your favorite part of the newspaper?

Skills Practice

Look at the parts of a newspaper again. Write in which part you would find the following information.

1. Vote for a new school building
2. For rent: 5 rm. apt. Near park
3. President visits Mexico City
4. Temperature drops 5°. Rain
5. Daffy Dill buys a Duckmobile
6. News about the governor's visit
7. The time a TV show begins
8. Reasons to vote for a new pool
9. An ad for a summer job
10. Weather for the weekend

Sample Answer 1. In an editorial

Fact and Opinion

News articles report the facts in a newspaper. Opinions are given in editorials or letters to the editor. You will find facts and opinions in many places besides newspapers. It is important to learn the difference between a fact and an opinion.

A fact is a statement which can be checked to find out if it is true. For example, the following statement is a fact:

A new school gym was built last year on Ridge Road.

You can check this fact by looking at records, newspaper articles, or by checking the area yourself.

An opinion is what a person believes or thinks is true. For example, the following statement is an opinion:

The Rocky Mountains are the most beautiful in the world.

There are many mountains in the world that people might think are beautiful. It is an opinion that the Rocky Mountains are the *most* beautiful.

People often mix facts with opinions when they talk about various subjects. You form many of your opinions from the ideas of others. If you are able to recognize the difference between fact and opinion, you can form your own opinions in a careful and fair way.

- Decide which of the following are facts and which are opinions. How do you know the difference?

Summer is the best season of the year.
The swimming pool opened last week.
Swimming is lots of fun.

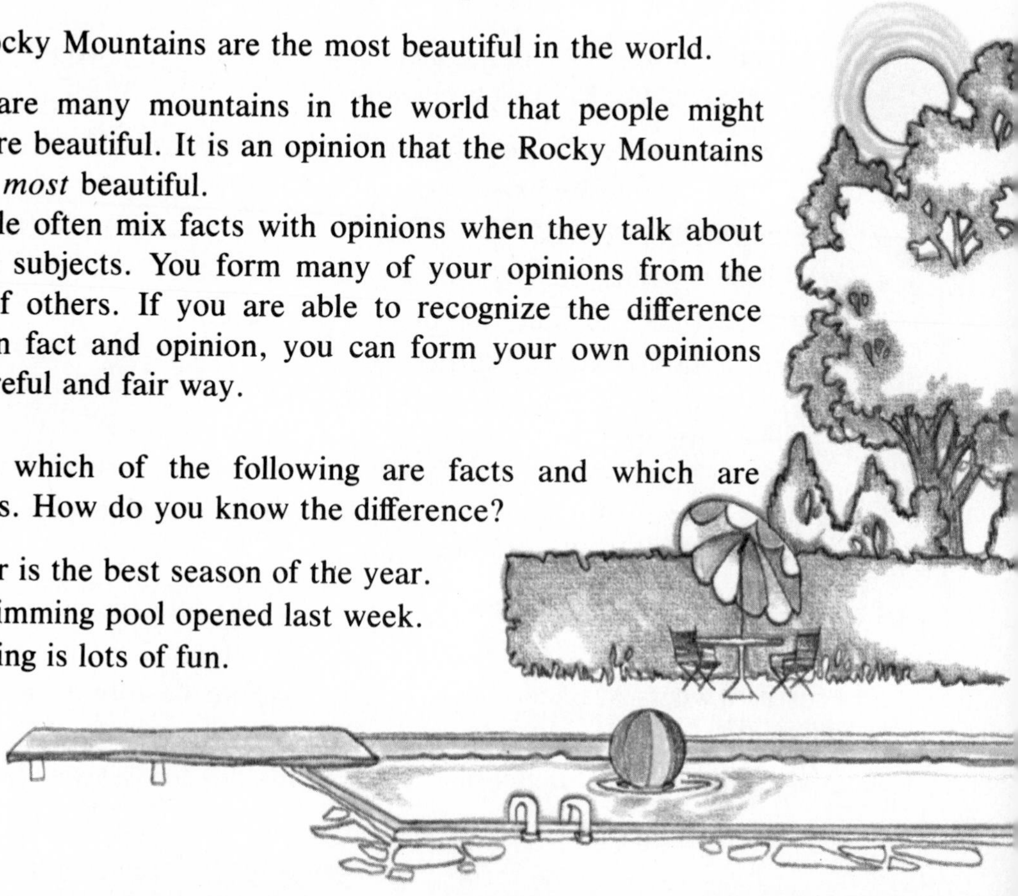

Talk About It

Tell which of the following sentences are facts and which are opinions.

1. George Washington was the first President of the United States.
2. He was the best President, too.
3. His picture is in many schools and office buildings.
4. A president today should look good on television.
5. A president should write all of his or her own speeches.

Skills Practice

Read each of the following sentences. Write **fact** for those that state facts. Be sure that they can be checked. Write **opinion** for those that give opinions.

1. Most schools in the United States close in the summer.
2. Schools should stay open all year round.
3. Some schools offer summer programs.
4. Some students go to summer camps.
5. All summer camps are about the same.
6. Many camps offer swimming lessons.
7. Every student should swim during the summer.
8. Some birds cannot fly.
9. Penguins are the prettiest birds.
10. All people should have birds as pets.
11. Birds eat insects that attack crops.
12. Ducks and geese fly in flocks.
13. The cuckoo makes the funniest noise.
14. Parakeets make the best pets.
15. Some parakeets can repeat words.

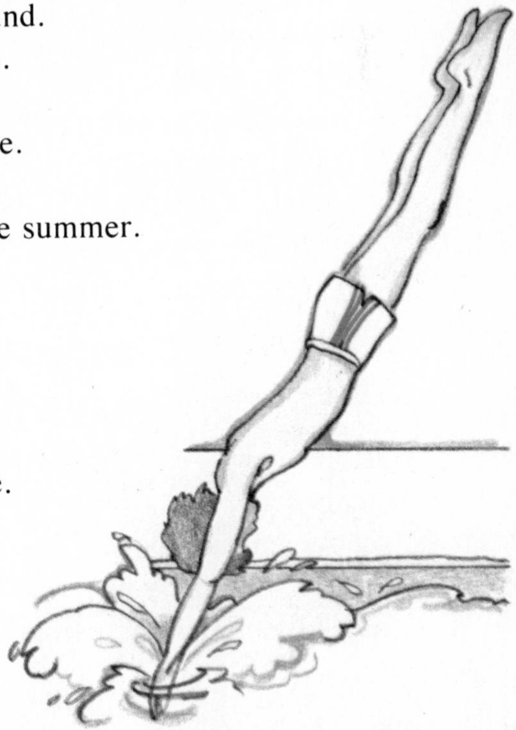

Sample Answer 1. Fact

Reasons in a Persuasive Paragraph

Thinking About Persuasive Paragraphs

You know how to write a paragraph that uses facts in the detail sentences. But that is not the only way to use facts in a paragraph. Suppose, for example, that you want to persuade your student council that your school needs a new media center. You might write a topic sentence that states your point of view:

Our school needs a media center.

A fact is a statement which can be checked to find out if it is true. An opinion is what a person believes or thinks is true. The topic sentence above states an opinion. An opinion should have facts to support it. In this kind of persuasive paragraph, you would use facts in your detail sentences. The facts are the reasons for the opinion.

- Read this paragraph. What reasons support the topic sentence?

> Our school needs a media center. We use media such as books, newspapers, tapes, and records every day. We also use film strips, films, and television. Next year students will use computers for individual study. This material is now kept in different classrooms. Such media would be easier to use if they were all in one place. We should change our library into a media center for the whole school.

Talking About Persuasive Paragraphs

Look for facts and reasons in the detail sentences.

1. How many reasons does the writer give to support the topic sentence? Are the reasons based on facts? How could you find out?
2. Which one do you think is the strongest reason? Where does it come in the paragraph?

3. Can you think of other reasons why a school would need a media center? Can you think of any reasons not to do as the writer suggests?

Writing a Persuasive Paragraph

Each topic sentence below states an opinion. Write a paragraph about one of the following opinions. Give three reasons in your detail sentences to support the topic sentence.

a. Our school needs more after-school activities.
b. I would like to have an unusual pet.
c. All team sports should be made up of girls and boys.

A Persuasive Paragraph in an Editorial

Thinking About Editorials

A newspaper has many parts. You can read news articles about world events, sports, business, or entertainment. All news articles must have facts. You can also read a special report called an *editorial.* It is written by the editor of the newspaper to persuade readers to share his or her opinion about important news events. Readers can also write letters to the newspaper about what they think about certain news events. The letters and the editorial appear on the *editorial page.*

School newspapers may also have editorials. Read this letter that a fifth grade class wrote to their school newspaper:

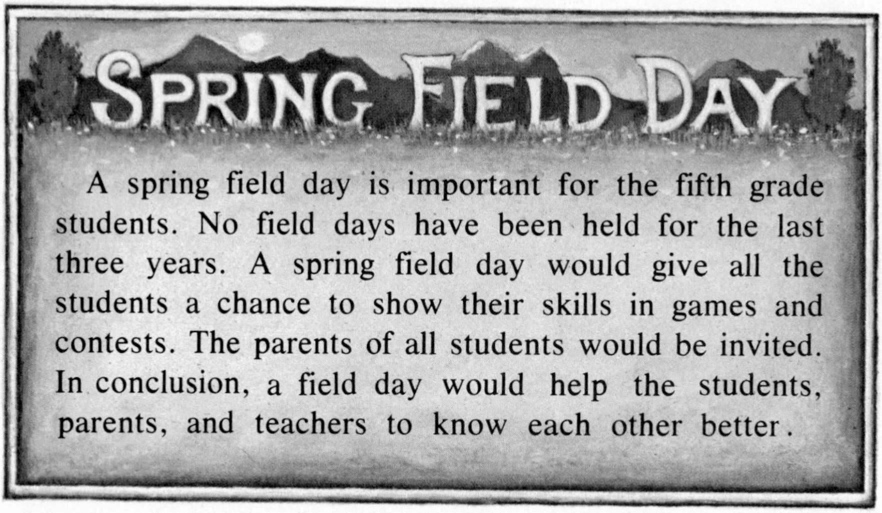

SPRING FIELD DAY

A spring field day is important for the fifth grade students. No field days have been held for the last three years. A spring field day would give all the students a chance to show their skills in games and contests. The parents of all students would be invited. In conclusion, a field day would help the students, parents, and teachers to know each other better.

Sometimes editorials are broadcast on radio or TV news programs. Before the editorial is delivered, an announcement is made that the following is an editorial. In this way, listeners know that the announcer is giving an opinion.

An editorial should have a *topic sentence* that states the opinion of the writer or speaker. *Detail sentences* must state facts that support the opinion. The editorial may end with a *concluding sentence* that states the opinion in the topic sentence but in a different way.

Talking About Editorials

Look at the editorial about the spring field day. The students might picture their spring day as in the drawing below.

- Read the editorial again.

1. What is the topic sentence of the news article?
2. Is the topic sentence an opinion or a fact? How can you tell?
3. What do students do on a spring field day?
4. Read this sentence: *No field days have been held for the last three years.* Why is it an important reason?
5. What reason do they give for wanting to play games?
6. What fact is given about parents?
7. What is the strongest reason given? Notice that it is the last reason so that you remember it best.
8. What is the concluding sentence?

Practicing a Persuasive Paragraph in an Editorial

Thinking About Your Editorial

Imagine that you are a television news announcer. You have been asked to write an editorial to persuade the viewers to share your opinion. Remember that an editorial states an opinion supported by reasons.

You are going to write an editorial about city parks. A park can be fun for children and adults. Think about all the things you can do in a park. If you have a dog, it might also like to play in a park. When many people use a park, it can get very dirty. Look what happened to the City Park in the picture below. If you do not want to write about the City Park, choose another topic for your editorial.

Word Bank

litter
flowers
bench
grass
mow
sign

Writing Your Editorial

1. Write this topic sentence: *Our city park needs to be cleaned.* If you choose another topic, make up your own topic sentence.
2. Write 3 or 4 detail sentences that give reasons to persuade people to share your opinion. Look at the picture again. What could be done to clean that park?
3. Use the Word Bank to help you spell words that you might like to use.
4. Read your paragraph aloud as if you were a television news announcer.

Edit Your Editorial

Read your editorial. Check it carefully with these editing questions. Use the editing symbols to correct your work. If you need to, write your editorial again.

1. Did your topic sentence tell your opinion?
2. Did your detail sentences state reasons based on facts?
3. If you used pronouns, did you write them correctly?
4. Did you indent the first word?
5. Did you capitalize the first word in each sentence?
6. Did you end each sentence with the correct punctuation?
7. Did you check over your spelling?

Editing Symbols

- ≡ capitalize
- ¶ indent
- ꝭ take out
- ∧ add

INDEPENDENT WRITING

A Persuasive Paragraph

Prewriting The entertainment section of the newspaper often has reviews of television programs. These reviews discuss the content, characters, and the reviewer's opinion of the program. In the review the reporter tries to persuade the viewer to agree with his or her opinion about the program. Of course, you may not agree with that opinion.

Read some television reviews. Then plan to review a television program yourself. Choose a show and jot down the title, date, and time of the program. As you watch the show, write notes to describe the characters and events in the story. What are your reactions to the characters and the story line?

Writing Write a television review in a persuasive paragraph. Begin your review with the title, date, time, and a brief description of the show. Then state your opinion of the program, and give specific reasons why you liked or disliked the story and characters in the program.

Editing Use the check questions and the editing symbols above to edit your television review.

Unit Review

Read each pair of sentences. In the second sentence some of the nouns are underlined. Write the subject pronoun that can be used in place of the underlined nouns. *pages 114–115*

1. Many people make long distance phone calls.
   People call friends in other countries.
2. Most places have an area code.
   The area code connects the phone call to another place.
3. Maria called her friend in Chicago.
   Maria spoke to her friend for three minutes.

Read each pair of sentences. In the second sentence some nouns are underlined. Write the object pronoun that can be used in place of the underlined nouns. *pages 116–117*

4. Peggy called Paul in Iowa.
   Peggy called Paul on Sunday.
5. Peggy spoke to Paul awhile.
   Paul heard Peggy very clearly.
6. Peggy asked about the family.
   Did Paul know about the family?
7. The phone fell to the floor.
   Was the phone broken?

Read each sentence. Write the correct pronoun. *pages 118–119*

8. Karen beat ___ at tennis. (I, me)
9. Then ___ beat Kevin. (I, me)
10. I beat ___ two times. (he, him)
11. Have ___ played today? (they, them)
12. Louisa and ___ teamed up. (I, we)
13. Kevin watches ___ play. (we, us)

Read each sentence. Write the correct possessive pronoun. *pages 122–123*

14. Gina and Judy write articles for ___ nature club. (their, theirs)
15. The nature article in last week's newspaper is ___. (their, theirs)
16. The article describes how a queen bee lives ___ life. (her, hers)
17. How can you tell if the article is ___, Gina? (your, yours)

Read each pair of sentences. Write the correct form of the present tense of the verb. *pages 124–125*

18. David carries the mail in all kinds of weather.
    He ___ the mail by truck. (deliver)

19. David sorts the mail quickly.
    He ___ from mailbox to mailbox. (rush)

20. The mail arrives quickly.
    It only ___ two or three days. (take)

Read each sentence. Write the correct word. *pages 126–127*

21. "Is ___ science report ready?" (you're, your)
22. "Yes, ___ all finished." (its, it's)
23. "I hope ___ not late with it." (you're, your)
24. "Joe and Sam finished ___ report quickly." (their, there)
25. "Leave the report over ___." (there, they're)

Here is the topic sentence for a paragraph of reasons: *Our school needs to build a new gymnasium.* Decide which seven sentences below belong in the paragraph. Write the paragraph using the topic sentence and the detail sentences that you have chosen. *pages 134–139*

a. The walls of the old gym are cracking.
b. The floor of the old gym is sinking in certain spots.
c. Our basketball court isn't big enough to hold the crowds.
d. Basketball is an exciting sport to watch.
e. The old ceiling leaks in several places.
f. The paint is peeling off the walls of the shower room.
g. It is fun to swim during the summer.
h. I got two new bathing suits last week.
i. Half the showers in the old shower room are broken.
j. The electrical wiring in our old gym is not safe.

A Photo Essay

A *photo essay* is a group of pictures that tell a story or explain facts. One or more introductory paragraphs may discuss the main idea of the essay. In addition, each picture may have a *caption* beneath it that further explains the picture.

This photo essay contains some interesting facts about science. It tells about the trip that a spacecraft took to the planet Saturn. Look at the material. Do the pictures help you understand the idea of the essay?

For hundreds of years scientists have studied our solar system. At first only simple telescopes were used to examine the planets. Today we explore the universe with more complex instruments. Spaceships soar through the galaxy. They supply new information about the planets.

In November, 1977, a two-ton spacecraft called *Voyager 1* was launched at Cape Canaveral, Florida. It flew near the planet Saturn. It sent back information that surprised scientists. Pictures from *Voyager 1* revealed rings and moons around Saturn that no one knew existed. The photos on the next pages help explain the story of *Voyager 1*.

VOYAGER I VISITS SATURN

This photo shows the Jet Propulsion Lab in Pasadena, California. Giant screens display the pictures sent by *Voyager 1*. Two screens show pictures of Saturn's rings. A lab computer enlarged the pictures so they could be studied more closely. The other screens show a map and a chart used to track the spacecraft.

Voyager 1 traveled 38 months in space before flying by Saturn. Moving 56,000 miles per hour, the TV cameras took pictures of the planet for two days. The spacecraft went behind some of Saturn's rings and through others. The pictures were transmitted a billion miles back to earth. After *Voyager 1* completed its job, it headed into empty space.

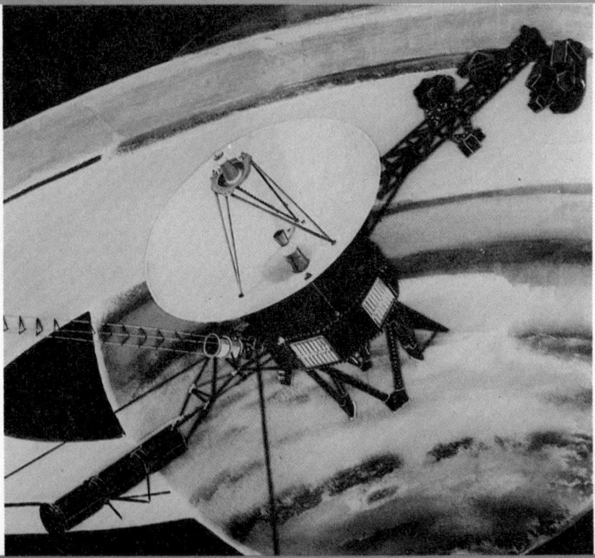

Voyager 1, about the size of a compact car, carried ten scientific instruments. They measured planet temperatures and studied the atmosphere. They also sent radio signals back to earth. The two TV cameras could point in any direction. Scientists built a computer on the craft to command all activities. It kept *Voyager 1* on course and made repairs. The equipment was powered by a nuclear generator beneath the spacecraft.

Before *Voyager 1*'s journey, astronomers thought Saturn had only six rings. This picture taken by *Voyager 1* shows there are actually hundreds of small rings close together. They look like the grooves in a phonograph record. Scientists cannot understand how the rings manage to stay together. They seem to defy the laws of space.

Voyager 1 made many discoveries about Saturn's moons. It now seems that Titan, Saturn's biggest and brightest moon, is wrapped in nitrogen. Scientists had thought it was methane. This is a picture of Titan enveloped in the chemical, shown in blue. Other photos from *Voyager 1* revealed three moons that scientists never knew existed. —*Meisha Goldish*

Creative Activities

1. In a photo essay, both the written information and the pictures are important. Give reasons why both parts are necessary for the essay to be understood clearly. Tell what might happen if either the written explanations or the pictures were not provided.
2. **Creative Writing** Prepare a photo essay on a topic of your choice. It might tell about a recent event in the news, or it might explain how something works. Find pictures in magazines, or use pictures you already have. Write a paragraph that introduces the topic of the photo essay. Also, under each picture write one or two sentences that tell about the photo.

Mid-Year Review

Some of the groups of words below are sentences. Write **sentence** if the group of words is a sentence. If a group of words is not a sentence, write **not a sentence.** *pages 2–3*

1. A shadow.
2. A candle burned in the dark.
3. Opened a squeaky door.
4. A dog howled.
5. A detective.
6. The moonless night.

Write whether each sentence is **declarative, interrogative, imperative,** or **exclamatory.** *pages 4–5*

7. What a scary place this is!
8. Did you see a shadow?
9. My friend and I walk slowly.
10. Blow out the candle.
11. Can you see anything?
12. How dark the room is!
13. Come with me.
14. The house is empty.

Write each sentence. Begin each sentence with a capital letter. End each sentence with the correct punctuation mark. *pages 6–7*

15. a fierce wind blew open a door
16. is someone behind the curtain
17. get a flashlight
18. how frightening this is
19. who will help us
20. watch your step
21. what a big house this is
22. do you hear a noise
23. my friend is brave

Write each sentence below. Draw a line between the subject part and the predicate part. Draw one line under the subject part. Draw two lines under the predicate part. *pages 10–11*

24. The dog crawled under the bed.
25. Joe hid in a closet.
26. Mai searched for clues.
27. Tamu found footprints.

Write each noun in each sentence. After each noun, write whether it names a **person, place, thing,** or **idea.** *pages 36–37*

28. Joel walked by a stream in the mountains.
29. Lana loved the quiet of the river.

30. Jeff studied the beauty of the trees.
31. Diane photographed a wildflower beside a rock.

Write the plural form of each noun. *pages 38–39*

32. class	34. loaf	36. dish	38. leaf	40. sky
33. toy	35. box	37. tree	39. roof	41. woman

Write each compound noun. Draw a line between the two words. Then write what each compound means. *pages 42–43*

42. The townspeople enjoy camping in the woods.
43. They sing songs around a campfire.
44. They get up at daybreak.

Write each noun. Write whether it is common or proper. *pages 46–47*

45. The train arrived in Chicago.
46. Mrs. Ruiz was the engineer of the train.
47. The conductor collected a ticket from Dr. Geer.

Write each underlined word as an abbreviation. *pages 48–49*

48. <u>Monday</u>, <u>August</u> 23 49. Oak <u>Street</u> 50. <u>Mister</u> Lee

Change the word at the end of the sentence to make a possessive noun. Write the possessive noun. *pages 50–51*

51. The ___ bark woke the children. (dog)
52. The ___ cat ran away. (woman)
53. Many ___ children joined the search. (neighbors)
54. Several ___ friends helped. (boys)

Write each action verb. Then write the object of the verb. *pages 72–75*

55. Santos played a game.
56. Henry lost his cap.
57. Santos swung the bat.
58. Henry finished the game.

Mid-Year Review

Write the verb in each sentence. Write whether the verb is in the **present, past,** or **future** tense. *pages 76–77*

59. A sick player stayed home.
60. Minoru carries the ball.
61. Mary will finish soon.
62. Rosa bats the ball.
63. Fans clapped for Rosa.
64. Henry will catch the ball.

Read each sentence. Write the correct form of the verb in the present tense. *pages 78–79*

65. Meg ___ tennis. (play)
66. Meg ___ tennis lessons. (take)
67. Joanna ___ tennis. (teach)
68. A player ___ a game. (watch)
69. Joanna ___ the ball. (hit)
70. Meg ___ again. (try)

Read each sentence. Write the verb in the past tense. *pages 80–81, 88–91*

71. Many fans hurry to the field.
72. We stop for ice cream.
73. Rain delays the game.
74. The game begins at noon.
75. He runs to third base.
76. The pitcher chases the ball.

Read each sentence. Write the correct form of the verb *have*. *pages 84–85*

77. She ___ new tennis shoes. (present)
78. They ___ new uniforms. (present)
79. You ___ a new tennis racket. (present)
80. You ___ an old tennis racket. (past)
81. They ___ ragged uniforms. (past)

Write the correct form of each verb in the past tense with *have* or *has*. *pages 86–87, 88–89*

82. They have ___ hard. (practice)
83. He has ___ in many races. (run)
84. The boys have ___ the race. (lose)
85. He has ___ before. (race)
86. It has ___ dark. (grow)
87. The bus has ___. (return)

Read each pair of sentences. Write the subject pronoun that can be used in place of the underlined words. *pages 112–115*

88. Jeff wrote a letter to mother.
Jeff sent the letter special delivery.

89. Jeff and Jules read a mystery story.
Did Jeff and Jules enjoy the story?

90. Mother and I went to the bookstore.
Mother and I love mysteries.

91. Mother counted the money.
Mother put the money away.

Read each pair of sentences. Write the object pronoun that can be used in place of the underlined words. *pages 116–119*

92. Alicia wrote a short story. Ivan read the story.

93. Ivan praised Alicia. Ivan told Alicia to write more.

94. Alicia wrote Jeff. Alicia thanked Jeff for his letter.

95. Did you bring the children? I brought the children by bus.

Write the correct possessive pronoun for each blank. *pages 122–123*

96. Carol writes articles about pets.
The articles on the desk are ___. (her, hers)

97. You have two pets.
Those two puppies are ___. (your, yours)

98. Carol and Karl have a canary.
The canary is ___ pet. (their, theirs)

99. Ivan and I have two beautiful horses.
The horses are ___. (our, ours)

100. I bought a mule.
The brown mule is ___. (my, mine)

COMPUTER CIRCUITRY

5

Grammar and Related Language Skills

Review of Sentences
Simple Subjects and Predicates
Compound Subjects and Predicates
Commas in Writing

Practical Communication

STUDY AND REFERENCE SKILLS
Listening and Speaking Skills
COMPOSITION
Writing a Conversation

Creative Expression

A Play

New inventions excite people. How do new inventions change people's lives? Most inventors work carefully and record their findings. If you were an inventor, what would you like to invent? What listening, speaking, and writing skills would help you in your work?

Reviewing Sentences

A *sentence* is a group of words that state a complete idea. Every sentence has a subject part and a predicate part. Remember:

> The **subject part** of a sentence names whom or what the sentence is about. The subject part may have one word or more than one word.
>
> The **predicate part** of a sentence tells what action the subject part does. The predicate part may have one word or more than one word.

- Look at the sentences below.

An Indian chief | invented potato chips in 1853.

His tall cap | fell on the floor.

In the first sentence *An Indian chief* is the subject part. These words tell *whom* the sentence is about. The predicate part of this sentence is *invented potato chips in 1853.* These words tell what action the subject did. In the second sentence

His tall cap is the subject part. These words tell *what* the sentence is about. The predicate part of this sentence is *fell on the floor*. These words tell what action the subject did.

Talk About It

Tell what the subject part and predicate part are in each of these sentences.

1. Chief George Crum cooked at a hotel in New York.
2. A visitor came from Paris.
3. The visitor ordered French fried potatoes.
4. Chief Crum prepared them in the kitchen.
5. The visitor saw the potatoes.
6. The visitor sent a message to the cook.
7. This impossible man wanted thinner potatoes.

Skills Practice

Write each sentence. Draw a line under the subject part of each sentence.

1. The chief cut the potatoes thinner.
2. The unhappy visitor looked at them.
3. This impatient person sent another message to the chief.
4. The visitor wanted even thinner potatoes.
5. Chief Crum checked his knife.

Write each sentence. Draw a line under the predicate part of each sentence.

6. The chief cut the potatoes into very thin pieces.
7. The angry cook dipped the pieces quickly into hot fat.
8. The brown pieces of potato curled up.
9. Cook Crum put salt on them.
10. The Indian chief marched into the dining room.

Sample Answers **1.** The chief cut the potatoes thinner. **6.** The chief cut the potatoes into very thin pieces.

Simple Subjects

The *subject part* of a sentence names whom or what the sentence is about. The subject part may have one word or more than one word.

- Look at these sentences.

Some girls invented a weather machine.

Girls in our class invented a weather machine.

Two girls in our class invented a weather machine.

In each sentence the subject part is in a blue box. However there is one word in each subject part that is more important than the other words. That word is *girls*. The word *girls* is called the *simple subject*.

> The **simple subject** of a sentence is the main word in the subject part.

- Read each sentence below. The subject part is in a blue box. The simple subject, *machine,* is the main word of the subject part. The word *machine* is more important than the other words in the subject part.

The machine tells the weather.

The large machine tells the weather.

The large blue machine tells the weather.

Talk About It

Find the subject part of each sentence below. Then find the simple subject. Explain your answer.

1. Our science teacher taught the class about the weather.
2. Two girls found an idea in a book.
3. The eager girls built a special machine.
4. This amazing machine records the weather each day.

Skills Practice

Write each of the following sentences. Draw one line under the subject. Draw two lines under the simple subject.

1. The large machine has an arrow in the middle.
2. The long arrow points to different boxes.
3. Each box names a certain kind of weather.
4. The girls show their invention.
5. The judges gather around the machine.
6. The judges at the fair watch the machine.
7. The sharp arrow points to "Snowy."

Writing Sentences

Suppose you just saw a wonderful new machine. These sentences are from an article you wrote about it.

1. The machine has flashing lights.
2. Buttons are on the front.
3. People come to see it.
4. The motor runs smoothly.

Add details to the underlined subject in each sentence above to make the sentences more interesting. Write the new sentences.

Sample Answer 1. The large machine has an arrow in the middle.

Simple Predicates

The *predicate part* of a sentence tells what action the subject part does. The predicate part may have one word or more than one word.

● Look at these sentences.

Elisha Otis worked.

Elisha Otis worked hard.

Elisha Otis worked hard every day.

In each sentence the predicate part is in a red box. However there is one word in each predicate part that is the most important because it names the action. The word is *worked*. The word *worked* is called the verb or *simple predicate*.

The **simple predicate** is the main word or group of the words in the predicate part.

● Read each sentence below.

Otis invented.

Otis invented the elevator.

Otis invented the elevator in 1852.

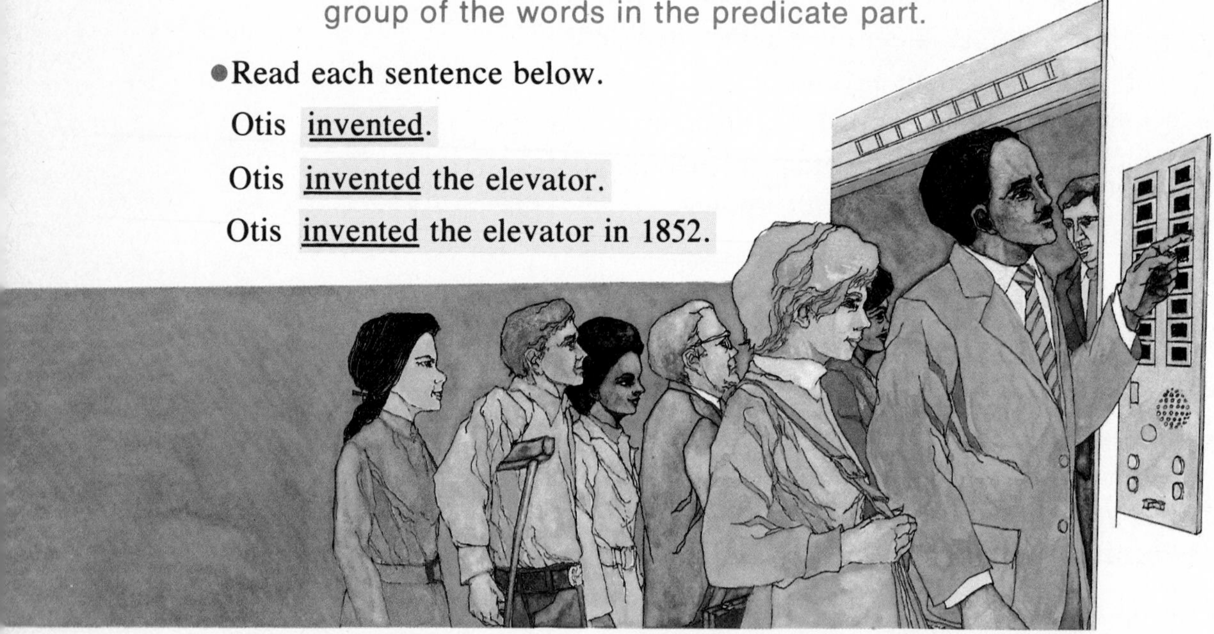

In each sentence the predicate part is in a red box. The simple predicate, *invented*, is the main word of the predicate part. The word *invented* is the most important word because it names the action.

Talk About It

Find the predicate part of each sentence below. Then find the simple predicate. Explain your answer.

1. People used platforms for years.
2. Platforms lifted things to high places.
3. Sometimes the platforms crashed to the ground.
4. Elisha Otis built safe platforms.

Skills Practice

Write each of the following sentences. Draw one line under the predicate. Draw two lines under the simple predicate.

1. Otis worked his platform carefully.
2. The inventor raised beds on the platform.
3. Otis showed his elevator to many people.
4. Otis rode to the top floor.
5. Other people used the elevator too.
6. Hotel owners bought the elevator.
7. People built many skyscrapers.

Writing Sentences

You are writing a letter to a friend about something that you invented. You might use the following sentences.

1. I gathered. **2.** I used. **3.** I worked. **4.** I put.

You can add to the underlined predicates by telling more about the actions. For example:

1. I gathered many materials.

Add to the underlined predicates in sentences 2, 3, and 4, and write the new sentences.

Sample Answer 1. Otis worked his platform carefully.

Compound Subjects

The *simple subject* of a sentence is the most important word in the subject part. It names whom or what the sentence is about. Sometimes there are two important words in the subject part.

- Look at the following sentences.

Jan built a robot.	Jan and Molly built a robot.
The robot walked.	The robot and Molly walked.
The lights worked.	The bright lights and bells worked.

In each sentence on the left, the subject part has only one important word. That word is the simple subject. In each sentence on the right, the subject part has two simple subjects that are joined by *and*. Both simple subjects have the same predicate. The sentences on the right have *compound subjects*.

> A **compound subject** has two or more simple subjects that have the same predicate. The subjects are joined by **and**.

- Now look at these sentences.

She and Molly tested the robot. Consuelo and I watched.

Each of these sentences has a pronoun in the subject part. The pronouns that may appear in the subject part are *I*, *you*,

he, she, it, we, and *they.* When the pronoun *I* is part of a compound subject, it always comes last in the subject.

Talk About It

Name the subject part in each sentence. Tell which sentences have compound subjects.

1. Jan and Molly finished their robot.
2. The giant robot has four arms.
3. Batteries and electric power move the robot.
4. Its arms and legs move in all directions.
5. The robot cleaned Molly's room this morning.
6. Her mother and father know nothing about the robot.
7. They thanked Molly for her work.
8. Molly and the robot winked at each other.

Skills Practice

Write each of the sentences. Underline the subject part of the sentence. If the subject is compound, write **compound.**

1. Jan and her sister played with the robot.
2. The robot brought them breakfast in bed.
3. Glasses and bowls rested on two arms.
4. The robot held the forks.
5. The girls and the robot ate breakfast.
6. Jan thought of other jobs for the robot.
7. She and Carmen rode to school on the robot.
8. Teachers and friends stared at the invention.
9. Many boys and girls ran away.
10. The robot went to classes with Jan.
11. It took a test in science class.
12. Jan and the robot finished the test.

Sample Answer 1. <u>Jan and her sister</u> played with the robot. compound

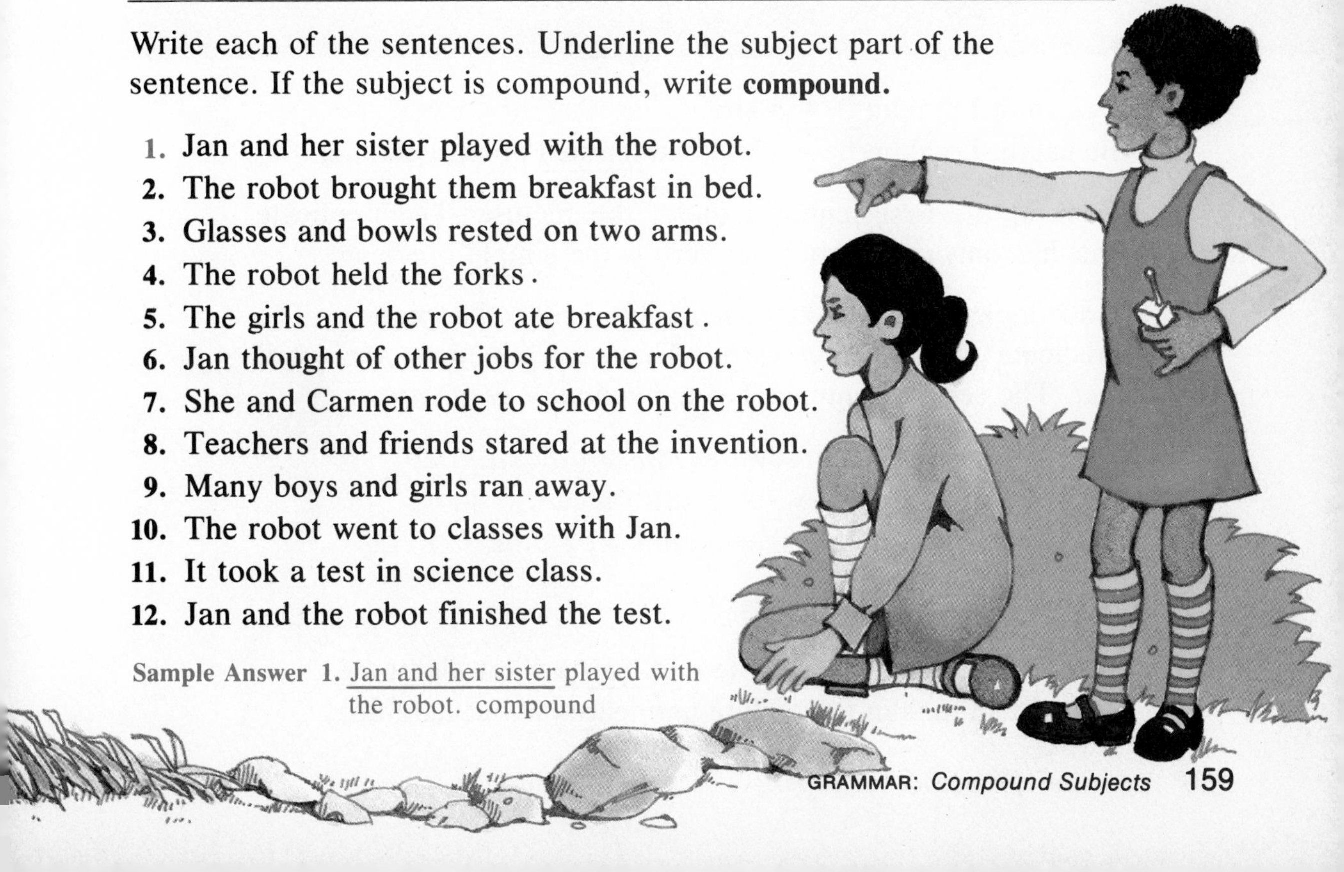

Compound Predicates

The *predicate part* of a sentence tells what action the subject part does. The *simple predicate* is the main word or group of words in the predicate part. Sometimes the predicate part names more than one action.

Benjamin Franklin <u>flew</u> a kite.
Benjamin Franklin <u>flew</u> a kite and <u>learned</u> about lightning.

- Look at the first sentence under the picture. The predicate part has only *one* verb. That verb is the simple predicate.
- Now look at the second sentence under the picture. The predicate part has *two* verbs. They are joined by the word *and*. The second sentence has a *compound predicate*.

> A **compound predicate** is a predicate that has two or more verbs that have the same subject. The verbs are joined by **and**.

- Now look at these sentences.

RIGHT: Franklin <u>flies</u> a kite and <u>learns</u> about lightning.
WRONG: Franklin <u>flew</u> a kite and <u>learns</u> about lightning.

In the first sentence both verbs in the compound predicate are in the present tense. They both name an action that happens now. This sentence is right because both verbs in the compound predicate must be in the same tense. In the second sentence *flew* is in the past tense and *learns* is in the present tense. This sentence is wrong because the verbs in the compound predicate are not in the same tense.

Talk About It

Name the predicate part in each sentence. Tell which sentences have compound predicates.

1. Benjamin Franklin studied and experimented with lightning.
2. Franklin made a kite and used some string.
3. Franklin found a key and tied it to the string.
4. Franklin flew the kite on a stormy night.
5. A bolt of lightning hit the key.

Skills Practice

Write each sentence. Underline the predicate part of the sentence. If the predicate is compound, write **compound.**

1. Benjamin Franklin invented and discovered many things.
2. Franklin invented a special pair of glasses.
3. People look through one part and see things nearby.
4. People look through another part and see things far away.
5. Franklin invented and built a new kind of stove.
6. Franklin invented lightning rods also.
7. The rods carry lightning away and protect buildings.
8. Franklin made a special stick.
9. People lift things and put things on high shelves with it.
10. Benjamin Franklin shared his ideas with the world.

Sample Answer 1. Benjamin Franklin invented and discovered many things. compound

Skills Review

Write the subject part of each of the following sentences.

1. Many people invent unusual things.
2. Samuel Applegate made a different kind of clock.
3. This alarm clock has special parts.
4. The parts fall on a person's face at wake-up time.
5. The person sits up in bed.
6. The clock's parts do a good job.

Write the predicate part of each of the following sentences.

7. A man from Chicago made another kind of alarm clock.
8. The person fills a cup of water at night.
9. The alarm clock pushes the cup over.
10. Water spills on the person's face.
11. Many people buy alarm clocks with bells.

Write the subject part in each of the following sentences. Draw a line under the simple subject.

12. Thomas Jefferson invented many things.
13. Most people do not know this.
14. President Jefferson invented a turning chair.
15. Many office workers sit on turning chairs today.
16. Mr. Jefferson made a seven-day alarm clock.

Write the predicate part in each of the following sentences. Draw a line under the simple predicate.

17. Mr. Jefferson put the clock in his home.
18. Thomas Jefferson made other machines, too.
19. This scientist tried all kinds of experiments.
20. Mr. Jefferson planted one of the finest gardens.
21. Thomas Jefferson helped many farmers.

Read each of the following sentences. Write the subject part of the sentence. If the subject is compound, write **compound.**

22. The Wright brothers invented the airplane.
23. Orville and Wilbur lived in North Carolina.
24. Orville and his brother built their own flying machine.
25. Many men and women laughed at the Wright brothers.
26. Their first trip and second trip lasted thirty seconds.
27. Many people fly in airplanes and helicopters today.

Write the predicate part of the sentence. If the predicate is compound, write **compound.**

28. Some people invent and make clever things.
29. Eoina Nudelman made and sold "Hungry Piggy."
30. A toy pig sat at the breakfast table.
31. The pig hooked on a plate and opened its mouth.
32. A child ate one bite of food and gave one bite to the pig.
33. The pig's food slipped back and returned to the plate.

Some words in the English language come from the names of inventors.

For example:

Antoine Joseph Sax worked for his father in a music store in Brussels. He invented the *saxophone*. (The suffix phone means *making sound.*)

Louis Braille lost his sight in an accident at the age of three. He invented a special way for people without sight to read. They run their fingers over raised dots on paper. This kind of raised printing is called *braille*.

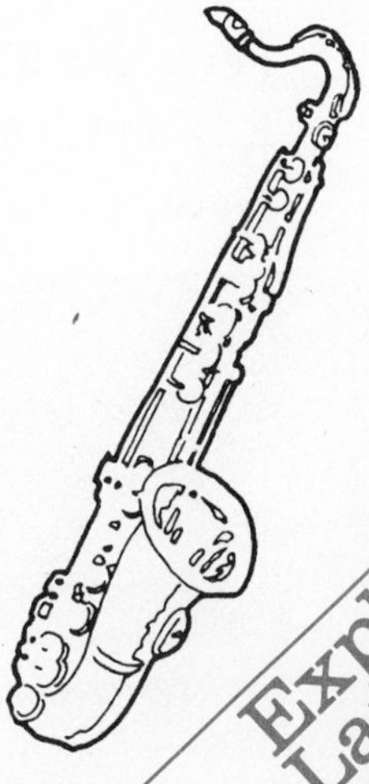

Exploring Language

Agreement of Verbs with Compound Subjects

The simple subject in a sentence works together with the verb. In other words they agree with each other. Here are two examples.

invent | The girls invent things at home. (Plural subject)
invent | Sara invents things at home. (Singular subject)

When the subject is plural, the main verb does not change. When the subject is singular, an *-s* is usually added to the main verb.

In a sentence with a compound subject, the verb must also agree with the subject. A compound subject with *and* names two or more people or things. It is like a plural subject. Here are two examples.

invent | Sara and Lenore invent things at home.
draw | Lenore and her brothers draw pictures of the things.

The verbs *invent* and *draw* agree with the compound subjects.

• Find the compound subjects in these examples. Check to see that the verbs agree.

Peter and his friends buy old bicycle parts.
Roy and Jennifer put the parts together.
Kathy and Inés sell the parts from their garage.

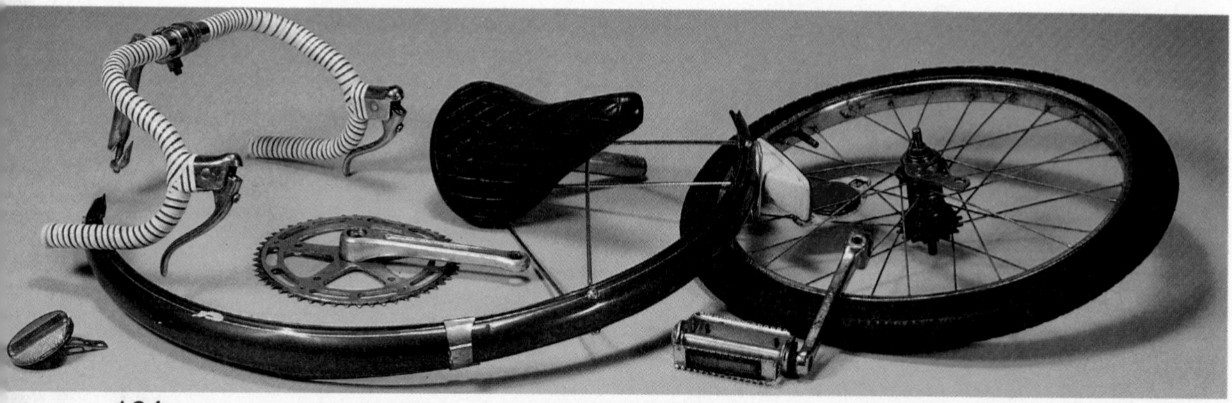

Talk About It

Complete each sentence. Use the correct form of each verb in the present tense.

1. Anthony ___ tree houses. (make)
2. Ruth ___ tree houses. (make)
3. Anthony and Ruth ___ tree houses. (make)
4. Joel ___ dog houses. (build)
5. His sisters ___ dog houses. (build)
6. Joel and his sisters ___ dog houses. (build)

Skills Practice

Write each sentence. Use the correct form of the verb in the present tense.

1. Juan ___ the dog houses. (paint)
2. Cindy ___ the dog houses. (paint)
3. Juan and Cindy ___ the dog houses. (paint)
4. The twins ___ the neighbors. (call)
5. Barbara ___ the neighbors, too. (call)
6. Barbara and the twins ___ the neighbors. (call)
7. The neighbors ___ dog houses. (buy)
8. The relatives ___ dog houses. (buy)
9. The neighbors and the relatives ___ dog houses. (buy)

Writing Sentences

Imagine that you and your best friend are inventors who have made something new. Write about your invention.

1. Write two sentences with compound subjects.
2. Write two sentences with compound predicates.

Sample Answer 1. Juan paints the dog houses.

Building Sentences

When you are writing about one subject, sometimes you may notice that your sentences are short. Some of your sentences may repeat the same words. Then you should study your sentences and rewrite them. See if you can combine two short sentences to make one more interesting, longer sentence.

You can build an interesting sentence by combining the subject parts of different sentences.

- Look at these sentences. The subject part in the two sentences are different, but the predicate parts are the same.

Joseph Henry | experimented with electricity.

Samuel Morse | experimented with electricity.

- Now read this sentence. Notice how the subject parts have been combined to form one longer sentence. The new sentence does not repeat any words.

Joseph Henry and Samuel Morse | experimented with electricity.

Another way to build a sentences is to combine the predicate parts of different sentences.

- Look at these sentences. In these sentences the subject parts are the same, but the predicate parts are different.

Alexander Bell | traveled to Brazil. Alexander Bell | met the judge.

- Now read this sentence. The predicate parts have been combined to form one sentence.

Alexander Bell | traveled to Brazil and met the judges.

Talk About It

Read each set of sentences. Tell how to combine the sentences to form one sentence.

1. Alexander Bell had an idea. Alexander Bell invented the telephone.
2. Bell shouted to Watson. Bell sent sound over a wire.
3. Bell talked into the machine. Watson talked into the machine.

Skills Practice

Combine each pair of sentences to make one longer sentence.

1. News traveled over land. Messages traveled over land.
2. Joseph Henry built magnets. Michael Faraday built magnets.
3. Electric charges flowed. Electric charges sparked.
4. Galvani experimented with frogs. Galvani wrote about it.
5. Volta stacked several cells. Volta formed the first battery.
6. Samuel Morse studied. Samuel Morse learned about electricity.
7. Robert Fulton built two steamboats. Robert Fulton built two ferries.
8. Ships sailed across the ocean. People sailed across the ocean.
9. Ships carried the telegraph cables. Ships laid them across the ocean.
10. Robert Fulton used mathematics in his studies. Robert Fulton used chemistry in his studies.

Sample Answer 1. News and messages traveled over land.

Using Commas in Writing

You use commas in your writing to tell the reader when to pause in a sentence.

Use a **comma** (,) to set off words such as *yes, no,* and *well* when they begin a sentence.

Yes, Carver invented many useful things.
No, he did not invent the telephone.

Use a **comma** (,) to set off the name of a person who is spoken to directly in a sentence.

Rita, here is a book about George Washington Carver.
Carver became famous for his inventions, Elena.

Use a **comma** (,) to separate the name of the day from the date, and the date from the year.
Use a **comma** (,) after the year when it appears with the date in the middle of a sentence.

My friend met me on Friday, May 15, 1980, in Chicago.

Use a **comma** (,) to separate the name of a city and state.

George Washington Carver was born near Diamond, Missouri.

Use a **comma** (,) after the name of a state when it appears with a city name in the middle of a sentence.

Walter went camping in High Point, New York, last year.

Use a **comma** (,) to separate each noun in a series of three or more nouns.

Aaron, Henry, and George carried backpacks.

Use a **comma** (,) to separate each verb in a series of three or more verbs.

The hikers walked, swam, and rested.

Talk About It

Tell where the commas should go in each of these sentences.

1. Carver worked struggled and traveled for his schooling.
2. Was life hard for Carver Alice?
3. He worked in school to pay for his room food and books.
4. Well Carver painted in his youth.
5. Carver the other students and the teachers worked hard.

Skills Practice

Write these sentences. Add commas where they are needed.

1. Carver studied tested and experimented with peanuts.
2. He used peanuts to make oil milk and other foods.
3. Yes he also made coffee and rubber from peanuts.
4. Other scientists thanked honored and rewarded Carver.
5. Well Carver accomplished great things in his lifetime.
6. He even made shoe polish from sweet potatoes Sarah.
7. Carver was born near Diamond Missouri in 1864.
8. He found many uses for peanuts sweet potatoes and soybeans.
9. Carver died on Friday January 5 1943 in Tuskegee Alabama.
10. He created a research center in Tuskegee Alabama in 1940.

Writing Sentences

Write two sentences with lists of three or more nouns telling about your two favorite foods. Write two more sentences with three or more verbs telling how you prepare your favorite foods. Write one sentence telling a friend about your favorite snacks. Address the friend directly in the sentence.

Sample Answer 1. Carver studied, tested, and experimented with peanuts.

Punctuating Conversation

One important way to make a story lively and fun to read is to use conversation or dialogue. In 1877 Thomas Edison and a worker in his shop might have had this conversation.

The worker asked, "Mr. Edison, what is this thing?"

"This machine is going to talk," Mr. Edison said. He spoke loudly into a special opening.

"Mary had a little lamb," he shouted. He played with the machine for a moment.

"Mary," the machine said, "had a little lamb."

"I don't believe it," the worker whispered. Mr. Edison had invented the phonograph or record player.

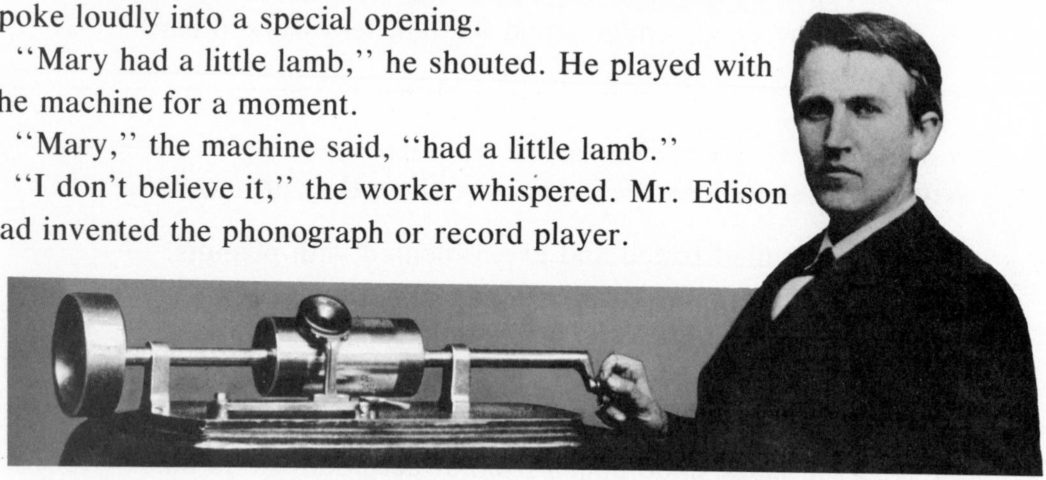

Remember these rules for punctuating a conversation.

1. Use **quotation marks** (" ") to show the exact words of a speaker. They show where the conversation starts and stops.
   "This machine is going to talk," Mr. Edison said.
2. Indent the first word of each new speaker's conversation.
   →"This machine is going to talk," Mr. Edison said.
3. Use conversation words such as *asked, shouted,* and *cried* to show how a person is speaking. Use a **comma** (,) to divide the spoken words from the person who is saying them. It always comes before the quotation marks.
   "This machine is going to talk," Mr. Edison said.
   The worker asked, "Mr. Edison, what is this thing?"
4. If the speaker asks a question, use a **question mark** (?) instead of a comma before the end quotation marks.
   "Mr. Edison, what is this thing?" the worker asked.

5. Capitalize the first word of a quotation as in any sentence.
   Mr. Edison said, "This machine is going to talk."
6. When the conversation words and the speaker's name follow the quotation, do not capitalize the first word after the quotation. Always capitalize proper nouns.
   "Mary had a little lamb," he shouted.
7. When the speaker's name and conversation words come in the middle of the quotation, use commas to divide the spoken words from the speaker's name.
   "Mary," the machine said, "had a little lamb."
8. Use a **period** (.) to end a complete quotation or sentence.
   "Mary had a little lamb," he shouted.

Talk About It

Tell how each sentence should be punctuated and if any words should be capitalized.

1. The manager smiled and asked may I help you
2. Do you sell record players asked the customer
3. Mr. Wilson said the manager will show you the phonographs
4. Mr. Wilson replied come this way please

Skills Practice

Write each sentence with the correct punctuation and capitalization.

1. My son wants his own phonograph said Mr. Bono
2. How old is your son asked Mr. Wilson
3. He's ten years old said Mr. Bono
4. Then Mr. Bono added we have a very good stereo in the den
5. Well said Mr. Wilson how about one of these portable ones
6. This looks like a good model replied Mr. Bono
7. It would be a very special gift said Mr. Wilson

Sample Answer: 1. "My son wants his own phonograph," said Mr. Bono.

Skills Review

Write each sentence. Use the correct form of each verb in the present tense.

1. Wilma ___ papers every morning. (deliver)
2. Judy ___ papers every morning. (deliver)
3. Wilma and Judy ___ papers every morning. (deliver)
4. Dan ___ lawns in the summer. (mow)
5. His brothers ___ lawns in the summer. (mow)
6. Dan and his brothers ___ lawns in the summer. (mow)
7. Maria and Sue ___ garages. (clean)
8. Gail and Doug ___ dogs. (walk)

Combine each set of sentences to make one longer sentence.

9. Men are creative inventors. Women are creative inventors.
10. Inventors recognize problems. Inventors think of solutions.
11. People create things. People invent ways of using things.
12. Morse invented practical solutions to problems. Carver invented practical solutions to problems.
13. Eli Whitney invented changeable parts. Eli Whitney developed the assembly line.
14. Henry Ford was an early car manufacturer. Ransom Olds was an early car manufacturer.
15. Edison invented the incandescent light bulb. Edison invented the phonograph.

Write each sentence. Add commas where they are needed.

16. Well my whole family likes to play baseball.
17. My brother sister and mother invented a new rule.
18. You hit kick and throw the ball during a game.
19. Yes sometimes we get very excited at a game.
20. Betty show us how you play.
21. It works on sand grass and water.
22. On Monday July 4 1984 we played a good game.

23. The game included many runs hits and errors.
24. Our family went to Saratoga New York for a holiday.
25. Yes we played the game while there.
26. Do you remember what happened Don?

Write each sentence. Then add the correct punctuation or capitalization.

27. The store manager said hello
28. Mother replied good morning
29. Do you have any fresh plums Mother asked
30. They arrived this morning a clerk replied
31. Tommy spoke up can I have an apple
32. Find the apples Mother said and we'll look at them
33. We just got some fresh peaches from Georgia the manager said
34. They're rather expensive said Mother
35. Come here said the clerk and have a taste
36. If Tommy likes the peaches said Mother we'll take a few

You have already learned about words that come from names of inventors. Here are some more:

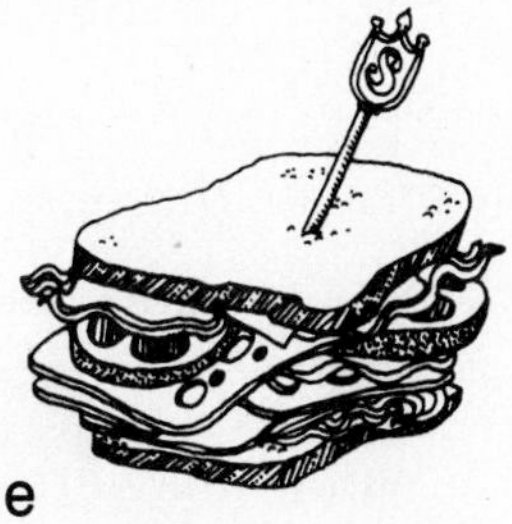

Rudolf Diesel was a German engineer who invented a special engine that runs on a kind of oil. It is called the *diesel engine.*

Joseph Montagu, the fourth Earl of Sandwich, liked to take a piece of meat and put it between two pieces of bread. Today we call this invention a *sandwich.*

Exploring Language

Using Test-Taking Skills

Most people do not really like to take tests, but tests can be a helpful measure of how well you have learned something. You can often help yourself do better on a test by following a few common-sense guidelines.

1. Follow directions carefully. This step is the first and most important guideline.
    a. Listen closely if the directions are *spoken*.
    b. Read all of the directions before you begin to answer any questions if the directions are *written*.
    c. Look for the main idea in the directions.
    d. Look also for important details.
    e. Ask your teacher about any directions you don't understand.
2. Be sure to have pens, pencils, ruler, paper, or any other materials you need for the test.
3. If the test is short, read all the questions in a section before you answer any questions. Often one question contains information that can help you answer another question.
4. First answer the questions that you know. Go back to work on the more difficult questions if you have the time.
5. Write your answers neatly and clearly. Be sure to write your answers where the directions tell you. Try not to erase or to make any extra marks on your paper.

Talk About It

Below is a test on test-taking. Review the guidelines for test-taking and take the test on your own paper.

1. Read items 2 through 6 before you begin to write.
2. Write your name at the top left part of your paper.
3. Write the date at the top right.
4. Number 1 to 15 on the left side of your paper.
5. Draw a line down the middle of your paper.
6. Do not write anything on your paper. Ignore items 2 through 5.

You did not follow the directions if you wrote on your paper.

Skills Practice

Read the test paper below.

Read each sentence carefully. Choose the answer that completes the sentence correctly. Fill in the circle for the correct answer in the answer column. Do not write on the test paper.	Name April 18, 19 Date J. R. Samuels Answer Column
1. The correct plural for mouse is mice A. mouses B. mousse C. mice D. mousies	**1.** A B C D ○ ● ● ○
2. The opposite of hot is _______ A. warm B. rapid C. cold D. exciting	**2.** A B C D ○ ○ ● ○
3. A synonym for shiny is bright A. bright B. dull C. slow D. funny	**3.** A B C D ○ ○ ○ ○

1. What is wrong with the name and date?
2. What mistakes can you find on the answer sheet and test paper?

Listening and Speaking Skills

Every day you receive a great deal of information by listening. You may even start your day by listening to the radio. Listening to directions and reports are part of your daily school work.

You may be surprised to learn that listening skills are very much like reading skills. When you listen to a talk or speech you listen for the main idea. You also listen for important details that tell about or explain the main idea. You must practice to become a good listener just as you practice to become a good reader.

Here are some rules to help you become a good listener.

1. Look directly at the speaker.
2. Do not talk to others while you are listening.
3. Try to think only about what the speaker is saying.
4. Listen for the main idea. The speaker usually states the subject at the beginning of the speech.
5. Try to remember at least two important details that the speaker gives.
6. When the speaker is finished, take notes by writing the main idea and details immediately.
7. Ask questions about what you can't remember or don't understand.

Sometimes you may be the speaker rather than the listener. You may have to give a speech in class or in a club. When you speak to a group, you have to choose your words carefully so that everyone can understand you. It is important to organize your thoughts before you speak. It is also important to speak clearly.

Here are some rules to help you become a good speaker.

1. Plan what you want to say. Outline your main points.
2. Practice giving your speech in front of someone before you give it for a group.
3. Look directly at your audience while you talk.
4. Speak in a loud, clear voice that all can hear.
5. Speak slowly and pronounce your words carefully.

Talk About It

Listen carefully as your teacher or classmate reads this paragraph. Name the main idea. Name the important details.

A bloodhound is a kind of hunting dog. It hunts by scent alone. It can even follow scent when there are not any tracks. Many police departments use bloodhounds to locate criminals.

Skills Practice

1. Listen as your teacher or classmate reads this paragraph. After you have listened to the paragraph, write a sentence telling the main idea. Write one or two sentences which tell about important details.

   Camels are good desert animals. Their bodies can store food and water. They store food in their humps. Their stomachs have pouches. Camels store water in each pouch.

2. Think about what you do on a school day. Prepare a short talk to give to your classmates. Write an outline of your main points. You might want to tell the class how you get ready for school and what you do after school.

A Class Conversation

Thinking About a Conversation

Your class is going to write a conversation together. The pictures below will help you. It will be about an invention.

There have been many inventions in the 20th century. How many can you name? Television, automobiles, and refrigerators are very important to us. But there have been inventions made by people for thousands of years. Think about what some early inventions might have been. Someone had to invent the first candle or sheet of paper.

People have always tried to invent things to make traveling easier. First they walked and carried their belongings on their backs, and then they used animals. Next someone had animals pull a sled that would slide on the ground. But it made the animals tired, and the sled was a problem over rocky ground. Someone else invented the first wheel to make traveling easier. That may seem like a simple invention, but remember no one had ever seen a wheel before.

- Look at the pictures below. What are Ogg and Blogg inventing?

Writing a Conversation

Think about the conversation that the cavepeople might be having. Ogg is the caveman with the long hair, sitting on the ground. Blogg is his wife, and the cave is their home. Blogg is watching Ogg invent the first wheel. In the first picture they might be having this conversation:

"What are you doing?" asked Blogg.
"I am inventing a wheel for the wagon," answered Ogg.

1. Think about what conversation might be taking place in the second picture. Blogg could say something about how she feels about the new wheel. Ogg could answer her. Write all the sentences on the board. Check to be sure you use the correct punctuation marks and capitals in the conversation.
2. Think about the conversation in the third picture. Suggest two sentences that describe their conversation. Blogg could ask Ogg a question. Ogg could say how he feels about the wheel.
3. Think of two sentences that describe the conversation in the last picture.
4. Together all the sentences make a long conversation. Check the board to be sure that you have used the correct capitals and punctuation marks in the conversation.

Practicing a Conversation

Thinking About a Conversation

Now you are ready to write a conversation. The pictures will help you. The Word Bank shows you how to spell some of the words you may want to use.

Gayle and Marilyn are friends. They meet each other one day as they are walking down the street. Look at the pictures below. Think about the conversation Gayle could be having with her friend Marilyn. In a drawing, a conversation balloon above a character's head is used to show who is speaking.

Writing a Conversation

Look at the conversation between Gayle and Marilyn again.

1. Begin your conversation with the first picture. Write:

   ''Hello, Gayle,'' said Marilyn happily.

2. Write what each girl might be saying to the other in the five pictures. Check the conversation rules on pages 170 and 171. Use the Word Bank.

Word Bank

buy
store
window
wind
blowing
caught

Edit a Conversation

Read the conversation and check it with these editing questions. Use the editing symbols to correct your work. If you need to, write your conversation again.

1. Did you use different conversation words for each speaker?
2. Did you put quotation marks around a person's exact words?
3. Did you indent the first word each time a quotation began with a new speaker?
4. Did you capitalize the first word in the quotation?
5. Did you use the correct punctuation marks in a quotation and at the end of the sentence?
6. Did you check your spelling?

Editing Symbols

≡ capitalize
¶ indent
ℯ take out
∧ add

INDEPENDENT WRITING

Writing a Conversation

Prewriting Suppose you met your favorite television performer, sportsperson, or recording star. Imagine a conversation with that person. What would you say? What might the person reply? Jot down some conversation notes.

Writing Write the conversation with the famous person.

Editing Use the check questions and editing symbols to edit your conversation.

Unit Review

Write the subject part of each of the following sentences. Draw a line under the simple subject. *pages 152–153*

1. Leonardo da Vinci lived in Italy long ago.
2. This famous man kept many notebooks.
3. Maria reads Leonardo's ideas in these notebooks.
4. This man covered page after page with drawings.
5. The drawings show many inventions.

Write the predicate part of each of the following sentences. Draw a line under the simple predicate. *pages 156–157*

6. Leonardo painted pictures.
7. His paintings hang in museums all over the world.
8. People see drawings of airplanes in his notebooks.
9. Leonardo watched birds during the day.
10. The inventor had ideas for helicopters.

Read each sentence. Write the subject part of the sentence. If the subject is compound, write **compound.** *pages 158–159*

11. Leonardo da Vinci and the Duke of Milan lived in Italy.
12. Leonardo worked for the Duke.
13. The man painted pictures and designed costumes.
14. The Duke and his friends listened to Leonardo sing.
15. This famous inventor moved to France in 1516.

Read each sentence. Write the predicate part of the sentence. If the predicate is compound, write **compound.** *pages 160–162*

16. Leonardo drew and painted.
17. Leonardo invented things and tested them.
18. The man wrote with both hands.
19. Da Vinci read his notes in a mirror.

Write the correct form of each verb in the present tense. *pages 164–165*

20. Scientists and teachers still ___ Leonardo's notebooks. (study)
21. Lili ___ about his ideas in the notebooks. (read)
22. Inventors and engineers ___ from his work. (learn)

Combine each pair of sentences to make one longer sentence. *pages 166–167*

23. Francois Appert invented a way to preserve food. Clarence Birdseye invented a way to preserve food.
24. Louis Daguerre made one of the first cameras. Louis Daguerre perfected a photographic process.
25. Jethro Tull invented a kind of farm machinery. Eli Whitney invented a kind of farm machinery.

Write the following sentences. Add commas where they are needed. *pages 168–169*

26. Yes Leonardo Da Vinci enjoyed his work.
27. Da Vinci drew painted and invented.
28. He sketched planes helicopters and parachutes.
29. Leonardo painted many pictures Bill.
30. On Friday October 18 1503 he completed a portrait.
31. Well Leonardo wrote his ideas in notebooks.
32. He lived in Milan Italy for many years.

Write each sentence in the conversation. Then add the correct punctuation or capitalization. *pages 170–171*

33. Mel what do you know about Marie Curie asked Norma
34. Well said Mel I remember she won a Nobel Prize
35. Norma replied no actually Marie Curie got two Nobel Prizes.
36. she must have been a very intelligent woman answered Mel

A Play

Plays are fun to read, to watch, to act in, and to write. Plays tell stories by having the characters speak to each other. This speech is called *dialogue*. You learn about the characters by the way that they talk to each other. Besides dialogue, a play has *stage directions*. These directions are written in parentheses. Sometimes they tell the actors and actresses where to move on stage. The characters do not read these stage directions aloud. They just do what the directions say to do.

Now you will read a play called *Fulton's Folly*. It tells about Robert Fulton, an American inventor. He developed the first steamboat that carried passengers. The play begins when Robert is just a child.

You might read the dialogue aloud with other classmates. Also read the stage directions to yourself. Think about how the characters would talk and act. How would they be dressed? Would their voices sound different? Why do you think the characters acted as they did?

FULTN'S FOLLY

Characters:

NARRATORS 1 AND 2
ROBERT FULTON
MARK, A CHILDHOOD FRIEND
ALICE, MARK'S SISTER
A NEWSPAPER REPORTER
THE GOVERNOR OF NEW YORK
CITY OFFICIALS 1 AND 2
A MAN
A WOMAN
A FEMALE PASSENGER ON "THE STEAMBOAT"

NARRATOR 1: The year is 1779. Fourteen-year-old Robert Fulton is trying out a new invention on his boat. Two friends pass by.

MARK: *(He points to a wheel on the boat.)* What are you doing to your fishing boat, Robert? Trying to sink it with that thing?

ROBERT: No, Mark, not at all. This "thing" should help propel my boat through the water. It's called a paddle wheel.

ALICE: A paddle *what*?

ROBERT: A paddle wheel, Alice. It's turned by the force of the water. It makes the boat go forward.

MARK: A wheel to do your paddling! I've never heard of anything so crazy!

ROBERT: What's so crazy about trying to do something better and faster?

ALICE: Next you'll be saying that little paddle wheel can take you upstream against the current.

ROBERT: No, I'd need another source of power to do that. But I'll find it.

MARK: You're a dreamer, Robert Fulton!

ROBERT: Maybe so. I can't talk any longer. The fish are waiting.

(With a push, Robert leaves the shore. His little boat paddles quickly across the water. The two young people stare after it in amazement.)

ALICE: Do you think he'd build a paddle wheel for our boat if we asked him?

NARRATOR 1: The years passed. Robert Fulton continued to dream about a large boat that could travel upstream.

NARRATOR 2: Several inventors found the answer to the problem — a boat powered by steam. But the boat couldn't carry passengers.

NARRATOR 1: Then, in 1807, Fulton built a new steamboat. He used an efficient engine made by James Watt, an English inventor.

NARRATOR 2: Fulton appropriately called his ship "The Steamboat." He decided to run it 150 miles up New York's Hudson River to Albany.

(A large crowd gathers at the dock in New York City to see Fulton off. A reporter interviews people.)

REPORTER: Excuse me, sir, but will you be a passenger on Mr. Fulton's first voyage?

MAN: Certainly not! If I wanted to go to Albany, I'd ride in a carriage or go horseback like any *normal* human being!

REPORTER: It sounds as if you don't think much of "The Steamboat."

WOMAN: "Steamboat"? That's what *he* calls it. To me, it's "Fulton's Folly." And it will surely come to folly when it hits that downstream current!

(Robert Fulton comes above deck and suddenly sees two old friends.)

ROBERT: Mark! Alice! What are you doing here?

ALICE: We came to see you off, old friend.

ROBERT: Well, welcome aboard "Fulton's Folly." You know, many people say I'll never make it to Albany.

MARK: Just like *we* said your paddle wheel would never work, remember?

ROBERT: Yes, but this time it's much more important that I succeed.

ALICE: Your boat doesn't look much different from a sailing ship, Robert.

ROBERT: No, except for the smokestack and the paddle wheel. Well, I think it's time I started the engine.

MARK: Good luck!

MAN: He'll need more than that!

(The next day in Albany an anxious group of people are waiting on the banks of the Hudson.)

GOVERNOR: Where can he be? He left New York 32 hours ago.

CITY OFFICIAL 1: There's no point in waiting any longer. He'll never make it. Imagine! Trying to run a boat on hot air! Steam should be kept where it belongs — inside a tea kettle!

CITY OFFICIAL 2: Did you just hear that sound?

CITY OFFICIAL 1: It sounded like a whistle.

GOVERNOR: And it's no tea kettle either! Look!

CITY OFFICIAL 1: I don't believe it!

CITY OFFICIAL 2: It's coming around the river bend!

ALL THREE: FULTON'S FOLLY!

(Fulton's boat pulls up to the dock and the crowd rushes to greet him.)

GOVERNOR: Congratulations, Fulton! I must say, you had us worried there for a while.

ROBERT: Sorry if I'm a bit behind schedule, Governor. But I stopped off in Clermont.

GOVERNOR: Well, it was worth the wait. Fulton, you can begin regular passenger service between New York and Albany at once.

CITY OFFICIAL 1: This steamboat is going to be the biggest thing since the horse and buggy!

CITY OFFICIAL 2: *And* the tea kettle?

CITY OFFICIAL 1: Anyone can be wrong once, can't they?

(The passengers begin to leave the boat.)

ROBERT: What did you think of our trip?

PASSENGER: Quite pleasant. But could I ask a favor of you, Mr. Fulton?

ROBERT: Of course.

PASSENGER: On the ride back to New York, could you go a little slower? Five miles an hour is faster than I care to travel on water!

NARRATOR 1: Later, Robert Fulton renamed his steamboat "The Clermont." It ran people and goods up and down the Hudson for years to come.

NARRATOR 2: More important, the steamboat conquered the mighty Mississippi and other large American waterways. It remained a major means of transportation for over half a century.

—Steven Otfinoski

Creative Activities

1. Peform the play ***Fulton's Folly*** for your class or for other classes. You will need twelve people in your group. Decide which part each person will take. Practice reading your lines. You do not have to memorize them, but you should be able to read them well. Also practice where you will move on stage. Decide what costumes each character will wear. Your group can also paint scenery on large sheets of paper and hang them on the wall. Practice the play several times before performing it for a group.
2. **Creative Writing** Imagine you invented a time machine that could send you to any time in the past or future. Choose a time you would like to live in. Write a play that tells how you travel in the machine to that time period. Tell what happens when you get there. A friend can help you with the dialogue. Also include stage directions. You might perform your play for the class.

DRUMS ON PARADE

Grammar and Related Language Skills

Adjectives
Adjectives That Compare
Spelling Adjectives
Prefixes and Suffixes

Practical Communication

STUDY AND REFERENCE SKILLS
Using Reference Works

COMPOSITION
Writing a Summary Paragraph

Creative Expression

A Biography

6

Do you know how to play a musical instrument? Have you ever attended a concert? The person who leads the musicians in a band or an orchestra is called the conductor. The conductor gives special instructions throughout a musical composition. Do you know the names of any famous conductors? What communication skills does a conductor need?

Adjectives

Take a look around you. Suppose you were asked to tell about everything you see. You would need to use words that describe people, places, and things. You would need to use *adjectives*. Adjectives describe in two ways. They can tell *how many* or *what kind*.

- Look at these three sentences that tell about the picture.

  Three children play in a band.
  The leader holds a red stick.
  The children sing a pretty song.

In the first sentence the word *three* describes *children*. It tells how many children. In the second sentence the word *red* describes *stick*. It tells what kind of stick. In the third sentence the word *pretty* describes *song*. It tells what kind of song. *Three, red,* and *pretty* are adjectives.

An **adjective** is a word that describes a noun or a pronoun.

Talk About It

Read each sentence. Then look at each underlined adjective. Tell what noun it describes.

1. The <u>small</u> band practices for <u>two</u> hours.
2. A <u>white</u> dog with <u>black</u> spots makes <u>funny</u> faces.
3. The <u>happy</u> musicians sit on the <u>hard</u> chairs.
4. The band gives a <u>beautiful</u> concert.

Skills Practice

Write each sentence. Write each adjective. After each adjective, write the noun it describes.

1. Large crowds of people drive to the park.
2. They spread colorful blankets on the green grass.
3. The musicians walk onto the high stage.
4. Tiny bugs crawl on the bright lights.
5. The tall leader turns to the quiet audience.
6. She has a deep voice and a serious look.
7. She lifts her wooden stick.
8. The three musicians take a deep breath.
9. Heavy rain falls from the dark sky.
10. The happy musicians smile at the beautiful rain.

Writing Sentences

Think about a concert or a movie you have attended. Write five sentences about it. Use five of these adjectives.

long	two	funny	serious
beautiful	happy	small	dark

Sample Answer 1. Large crowds of people drive to the park. large, crowds

Adjectives That Compare

Adjectives are words that describe. One way to describe a thing is by comparing it with something else. Adjectives that compare often end in *-er* or *-est*.

*Toby plays a **long** horn.*

*Carla's horn is a **longer** horn than Toby's.*

*José's horn is the **longest** horn of all.*

- Look at the picture on the left. What adjective describes the horn?
- Now look at the picture in the middle. Two horns are compared. What adjective describes Carla's horn?
- Look at the picture on the right. Three horns are compared. What adjective describes José's horn?

An **adjective** ending in **-er** compares two nouns. An adjective ending in **-est** compares more than two nouns.

- Note how the form of the adjective changes in each of these groups of words.

bright	cool	neat
bright|er	cool|er	neat|er
bright|est	cool|est	neat|est

- Notice how the form changes in these adjectives.

large	pale	safe
larg|er	pal|er	saf|er
larg|est	pal|est	saf|est

If an adjective ends in **e,** drop the **e** and add **-er** or **-est** to make the correct form of the adjective.

Talk About It

Tell what form of the adjective goes in each sentence.

1. Myra is the ___ player in the whole band. (loud)
2. Her horn is ___ than mine. (large)
3. She plays a ___ note than I can. (high)

Skills Practice

Write each sentence with the correct form of the adjective.

1. The ___ member of the band plays the drum. (short)
2. His drum makes a ___ sound than my horn. (dull)
3. The flute player is the ___ person of all. (smart)
4. Her flute is ___ than my horn. (light)
5. It is also a ___ instrument than mine. (simple)
6. It makes ___ music than the horn. (soft)
7. She even plays on the ___ day of the year. (cold)

Sample Answer 1. The shortest member of the band plays the drum.

Using More and Most to Compare

Many adjectives have an *-er* or *-est* ending when they compare two or more things. However most adjectives with two or more syllables do not use the *-er* or *-est* endings. Instead these adjectives have a different form for comparing.

Carmen is a more interesting musician than Paul

Susan is the most interesting musician of all.

- Look at the sentence under the picture on the left. The adjective *interesting* has four syllables. Since two people are compared, the form of the adjective is **more interesting.**
- Now look at the sentence under the picture on the right. In this case, more than two people are compared. Therefore the form of the adjective is **most interesting.**

Do not use *more* or *most* before adjectives that already have *-er* or *-est* added to them.

WRONG: Carmen plays a more louder horn than Paul.
RIGHT: Carmen plays a louder horn than Paul.

WRONG: Susan plays the most loudest horn of all.
RIGHT: Susan plays the loudest horn of all.

Talk About It

Tell which form of the adjective goes in each sentence.

1. Carmen plays ___ music than Paul. (more beautiful, most beautiful)
2. Susan is the ___ player in the group. (more careful, most careful)
3. She has the ___ job of all. (more difficult, most difficult)

Skills Practice

Write each sentence. Use the correct form of the adjective that goes in each sentence.

1. Susan is the ___ person in the whole band. (more wonderful, most wonderful)
2. She makes a ___ sound than Paul does. (more powerful, most powerful)
3. Juan plays the ___ music of all. (more beautiful, most beautiful)
4. He is also a ___ person than Paul. (more polite, most polite)
5. Ming is the ___ musician I know. (more pleasant, most pleasant)
6. Paul is the ___ student of all the group. (more curious, most curious)

Writing Sentences

What is your favorite kind of music? Write four sentences comparing it with other music. Use one adjective in each sentence. Use *more* before the adjective in two sentences. Use *most* before the adjective in the other two sentences.

Sample Answer 1. Susan is the most wonderful person in the whole band.

Skills Review

Write each adjective that appears in each sentence. After each adjective, write the noun it describes.

1. The three musicians play on a new stage.
2. The new place has many seats.
3. Many people buy tickets.
4. A clear sky covers the entire city.
5. Happy people arrive at the large building.
6. The nervous leader peeks through the gold curtain.
7. People rush to the empty seats.
8. The unhappy musicians give the leader a late message.
9. They forgot the new instruments.
10. The sad leader has a pale face.
11. She walks on the wide stage.
12. She faces the bright lights.

Read each sentence. Write the correct form of the adjective.

13. It is the ___ audience of all. (large)
14. She has a ___ face than she did five minutes ago. (pale)
15. She speaks in a ___ voice than last time. (soft)
16. This is the ___ problem she has ever had. (great)
17. It seems like the ___ moment in her life. (long)
18. Then the ___ voice of all shouts, "Come outside for free food!" (loud)
19. They leave the ___ way they can. (quick)
20. The musicians are the ___ runners of all. (fast)
21. People exit in a ___ time than last time. (short)

Read each sentence. Write the correct form of the adjective that goes in each sentence.

22. Which instrument makes the ___ music in the world? (more beautiful, most beautiful)

23. Some people think a violin makes the ___ sound of all.
(more delicate, most delicate)
24. A piano is ___ than a violin to some people.
(more interesting, most interesting)
25. The violin is the ___ instrument in the orchestra.
(more common, most common)
26. A violin is ___ than a piano to play.
(more difficult, most difficult)
27. I think a flute has a ___ sound than a piano.
(more exciting, most exciting)
28. A drum has the ___ sound I can think of.
(more powerful, most powerful)
29. A horn is the ___ instrument I know.
(more joyful, most joyful)
30. Some people say it is the ___ instrument of all to play.
(more difficult, most difficult)

Have you ever wondered what the longest and shortest words are in the English language? The shortest words, of course are, *a* and *I*. They have only one letter each.

The longest word, believe it or not, has 3,600 letters! It is the name of a certain chemical. (Would you like that word on your next spelling test?)

A long word is called a *sesquiped* (se'kwi ped'). Here are two sesquipeds and their meanings: **abecedarian** (ā'bē sē der'ē ən), simple, elementary. **triskaidekaphobia** (tris'kī dek' ə fo' bē ə), fear of the number 13.

Some people say the longest word is *smiles*, because there is a *mile* between the first and last letters.

Exploring Language

Spelling Adjectives

You already know that *-er* or *-est* is added to an adjective when two or more things are compared. Sometimes you must change the spelling of the adjective before adding *-er* or *-est*.

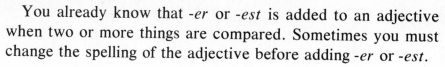

If an adjective ends with a consonant and *y*, change the *y* to *i* and add **-er** or **-est** to make the correct form of the adjective.

heavy → heavy̸ (i) + er = heavier
A piano is a heavier instrument than a violin.

heavy → heavy̸ (i) + est = heaviest
A piano is the heaviest instrument in the band.

Some adjectives change in another way before *-er* or *-est* is added to them.

If a one-syllable adjective ends with consonant, vowel, consonant, double the last consonant and add **-er** or **-est** to make the correct form of the adjective.

Adjectives that end in *w*, *x*, or *y* are exceptions to this rule.

big → big + g + er = bigger
She plays a bigger drum than I do.

big → big + g + est = biggest
He plays the biggest drum of all.

Talk About It

Spell each adjective with **-er.** Then spell each with **-est.**

1. happy	**3.** juicy	**5.** roomy	**7.** hot
2. gloomy	**4.** noisy	**6.** fat	**8.** thin

Skills Practice

Write each adjective with **-er.** Then write each with **-est.**

1. pretty	**3.** windy	**5.** busy	**7.** funny	**9.** rosy	**11.** tiny
2. dim	**4.** wet	**6.** flat	**8.** red	**10.** slim	**12.** mad

Sample Answer 1. prettier, prettiest

Capitalizing Proper Adjectives

You learned that a *proper noun* is a noun that names a special person, place, thing, or idea. Some proper nouns can be used as adjectives.

a Brahms lullaby a Georgia peach the Greenwich time

Some proper adjectives are formed by adding endings to proper nouns.

a Chinese silk an Icelandic sweater a Swedish architect

A **proper adjective** is an adjective formed from a proper noun. Begin a proper adjective with a capital letter.

Talk About It

Name the proper adjectives. Tell why each should be capitalized.

1. At the party we danced to a beatles recording.
2. We first listened to some lovely strauss waltzes.
3. Someone tried to play the scottish bagpipes.
4. Then we listened to some mexican folk songs.

Skills Practice

Write each sentence. Capitalize the proper adjective.

1. Does your german stereo play well?
2. Have you ever listened to spanish guitar music?
3. My favorite station plays american jazz.
4. I heard the broadcast of a philadelphia orchestra.
5. My mother listens to old italian serenades.
6. We heard a chorus of russian singers give a concert.
7. The family gathered to hear a mozart opera.

Sample Answer **1.** Does your German stereo play well?

Prefixes and Suffixes

Sometimes new words are made by adding groups of letters to words.

A **prefix** is one or more letters added to the beginning of a word.

A **suffix** is one or more letters added to the end of a word.

- Look at these sentences.

Ira plays an unusual instrument. Ira is unaware of the noise.

The prefix *un-* before an adjective means *not. Unusual* means *not usual.* What does *unaware* mean?

- Now look at these sentences.

Rose is a thirsty girl. She drinks the chilly water.

The suffix *-y* means *having. Thirsty* means *having a thirst.* What does *chilly* mean?

- Read these two sentences.

Ira is a careful musician. Ira has played a cheerful song.

The suffix *-ful* means *full of. Careful* means *full of care.* What does *cheerful* mean?

- Now read these sentences.

Rose played a harmless joke. She wouldn't hurt a helpless person.

The suffix *-less* means *without. Harmless* means *without harm.* What does *helpless* mean?

		Meaning	Example
Prefix	*un-*	not	unusual (not usual)
Suffix	*-y* *-ful* *-less*	having full of without	thirsty (having thirst) careful (full of care) harmless (without harm)

Talk About It

Tell what each underlined word means.

1. You must be a skillful musician to play the bottles.
2. Most musicians use colorless bottles.
3. Fill the bottles with unequal amounts of water.
4. Make sure you do not have any leaky bottles.

Skills Practice

Write each underlined word. Then write the meaning of the word.

1. Take an unbroken pencil or a spoon.
2. Give a powerful tap on each bottle.
3. A lucky person will not break the bottles.
4. A careless musician spills the bottles.
5. We enjoy this noisy music.
6. The musicians are hopeful about the music.

Write one word to replace each group of underlined words.

7. It is not wise to hit the bottles too hard.
8. A player who is having luck hits each note correctly.
9. Bottle music can be full of joy.
10. A player who is without thought hits the wrong notes.
11. That kind of music is not bearable.

Sample Answers **1.** unbroken, not broken. **7.** unwise.

Adjective Synonyms

Suppose everyone in your class were asked to describe the same person, place, or thing. All the students probably would not use the same adjectives. There are many adjectives that have similar meanings.

A **synonym** is a word that has nearly the same meaning as another word.

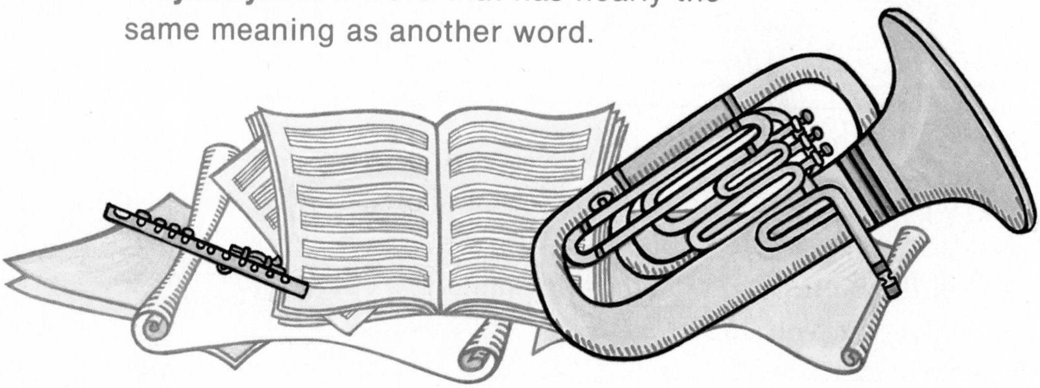

- Look at the instrument on the left side of the picture. You might describe it as a *small* instrument, but *small* is not the only adjective you can use. Five synonyms for the word *small* are:

little tiny short thin narrow

Any of these words could be used to describe the flute, but they do not all mean exactly the same thing. When you are writing, use words that most clearly say what you mean.

- Now look at the instrument on the right. You can describe it as a *big* instrument. But *big* is not the only adjective you can use. Here are five synonyms for the word *big:*

huge enormous giant grand large

Any of these words can also be used to describe the instrument on the right. The synonyms *huge* and *enormous* are the words that best describe the tuba.

Talk About It

Read each sentence. Read the words after each sentence. Which of these words is a synonym for the underlined word?

1. It was a peaceful night. (calm, dark, cold)
2. A happy audience filled the hall. (brave, large, cheerful)
3. They came to hear pleasant music. (costly, lovely, loud)

Skills Practice

Read each sentence. Read the words after each sentence. Write the word that is a synonym for the underlined word.

1. The nervous musicians waited. (bitter, scared, eager)
2. They had done a silly thing. (different, old, foolish)
3. They had brought the wrong music. (sad, true, incorrect)
4. The noisy crowd became silent. (anxious, loud, angry)
5. The lights went out in the whole room. (crowded, entire, dark)

Replace each underlined word with a synonym. Write the sentence with the word you have chosen.

6. The cautious audience walked in the darkness.
7. They looked for a fast way to leave the room.
8. The musician walked through the long hall.
9. The unhappy people went home without a concert.

Writing Sentences

1. Write two sentences that describe music you like. Use synonyms for these words in your sentences.
   a. great **b.** nice
2. Write two sentences that describe music you don't like. Use synonyms for these words in your sentences.
   a. silly **b.** loud

Sample Answers 1. scared **6.** The careful audience walked in the darkness.

Skills Review

Write each adjective with **-er.** Then write each with **-est.**

1. ripe
2. tiny
3. red
4. slim
5. deep
6. tasty
7. sad
8. sleepy
9. small
10. wet
11. windy
12. dizzy
13. heavy
14. big
15. noisy

Write the sentences. Capitalize the proper adjectives.

16. Mozart was an austrian composer.
17. He performed for the viennese empress at the age of 6.
18. Mozart traveled to many european cities.
19. His italian opera *Don Giovanni* is a masterpiece.
20. His german opera *The Magic Flute* still delights audiences.
21. Some mozart serenades are performed outdoors.
22. Young american musicians study his works.
23. A new york music festival is held each summer to honor him.

Write each underlined word. Then write the meaning of the word.

24. I am unable to carry a tune.
25. My singing is hopeless.
26. My friend has a powerful voice.
27. She can break a frosty glass with her high notes.

Write one word to replace each group of underlined words.

28. I once had singing lessons that were not pleasant.
29. I was full of hope that voice lessons would improve my singing.
30. When I sang, my teacher was without speech.
31. I was having luck to have such a good teacher.

Read each sentence. Read the words after each sentence. Write the word that is a synonym for the underlined word.

32. The musicians prepared for a final concert. (best, last, single)
33. They brought the entire music. (right, proper, complete)
34. They remembered their usual instruments. (regular, odd, old)
35. The frightened musicians appeared. (sleepy, nervous, angry)
36. Their leader entered the large hall. (enormous, crowded, new)
37. The musicians played a difficult song. (long, familiar, hard)
38. They did a perfect job. (fair, excellent, awful)
39. The cheerful audience clapped at the end. (sad, happy, dull)
40. The astonished musicians fainted from surprise. (red, amazed, tired)

Have you ever played "Think Pink?" All you have to do is think of an adjective and a noun that rhyme. Then make up a question for someone else to answer. For example:

—What do you call a sneaky insect? (a sly fly)

You also can play the game with two-syllable words.

—What do you call an empty gulp?

(a hollow swallow)

How many "Think Pinks" can you make up?

Exploring Language

Using Reference Works

You know that a library is a place where you can borrow books on many subjects. A card catalog can help you find the books you need. Remember that there are three cards you can use: the author card, title card, and subject card.

Reference works in a library can help you with reports.

WORLD ATLAS

ROAD MAP

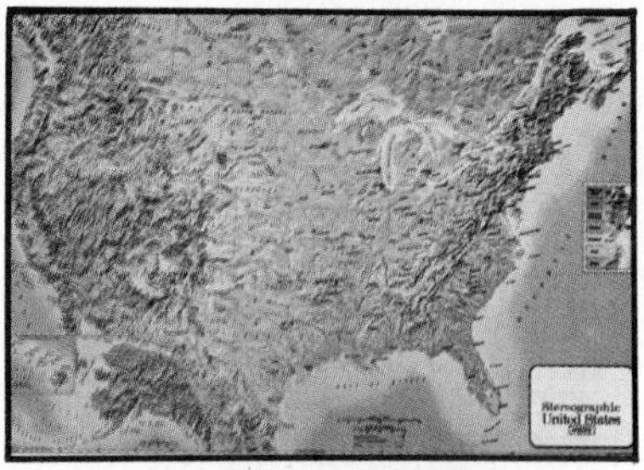

RELIEF MAP

1. The *encyclopedia* gives information about many subjects.
2. The *almanac* gives the latest facts and figures.
3. An *atlas* is a book of maps. It has a table of contents and an index to help you find the map you need. The most complete kind of atlas is a *world atlas* that contains maps of separate countries and the world. There are also other kinds of maps. A *road map* can help you plan an automobile trip. A *relief map* shows you what the land in an area looks like with mountains, valleys, and bodies of water.
4. *Periodicals* are magazines or newspapers that are published at certain periods of time. Most magazines are printed weekly or monthly. You can find magazines about hobbies, news, and many other subjects.

● Look at the chart on the next page. It shows you how most libraries are organized.

LIBRARY ORGANIZATION	
1. Fiction books (books of stories)	Arranged alphabetically by the authors' last name.
2. Nonfiction books (books about subjects based on fact)	Arranged numerically by subject
3. Reference works (encyclopedia, almanac, atlas)	Arranged in a reference section
4. Magazines, newspapers, records	Arranged in a special section
5. Children's books	Arranged in a special room.

Talk About It

Tell where you would find the following information in a library. Use the library organization chart above.

1. A book on American history
2. A book of children's poems
3. A detective story for an adult
4. A map of China
5. A children's book of stories
6. An encyclopedia article on Africa.

Skills Practice

Write whether you would use an encyclopedia, almanac, atlas, newspaper, or magazine to find information about each of the following.

1. The lowest temperature recorded in Texas
2. Road maps of the Western states
3. Facts about Mexico
4. Last week's baseball scores
5. Information about Native Americans

Write one sentence about what you might look for in each of the following reference works.

6. An encyclopedia **7.** An atlas **8.** An almanac **9.** A magazine

Sample Answer 1. almanac

Reviewing Paragraphs

Thinking About Paragraphs

You have learned that most paragraphs have two types of sentences. The topic sentence states the main idea of the paragraph. Detail sentences give more information about the main idea or topic sentence.

You have learned how to write four different types of paragraphs, depending on the kind of detail sentences you want to use. These are the different types of detail sentences.

1. time order **2.** description **3.** facts **4.** reasons

The kind of paragraphs you use depends on what you are writing. For example, you would put your details in *time order* if you write to a friend about an exciting trip you took. But you would use details that *describe* if you write about the view from a mountaintop in Vermont. You will need *facts* to explain your topic sentences when you write a report in school. And you will need *reasons* for your opinions when you write to convince people of your point of view.

Talking About Paragraphs

Read these paragraphs. What type of paragraph is each of the following? Give reasons for your answers. Remember that there are four types of paragraphs.

1. The concert was about to begin. First the lights grew dim. Next the audience grew quiet. Then the conductor stepped on stage. She turned to the musicians. At last she lowered her baton.
2. Our band needs uniforms. Band members would have more pride if they wore uniforms. Other bands wear coats or sweaters with their school colors. We need uniforms to wear at band contests.
3. The concert was held outdoors high on a hill. The setting sun turned the river far below a fiery orange. Stars soon crowded the sky as though they, too, had come to listen. Music filled the sky.
4. Our marching band won the state contest last year. We have 70 members, and we practice every day after school. The school bought us new uniforms for the contest. We are putting the prize in the front hall.

Writing Paragraphs

Write two detail sentences for each of the topic sentences below. Notice the kind of paragraph that would be written. Be sure that you write complete sentences.

1. Our band is raising money for a trip to Mexico. Write a paragraph using facts.
2. My sister's rock band practices in our basement. Write a paragraph that uses words that describe.
3. Music is a language everyone in the world loves and understands. Write an opinion paragraph with reasons.
4. We left for the spring concert an hour early. Write a time order paragraph about the trip.

Interviews and Surveys

Thinking About Interviews and Surveys

The first step in writing any type of paragraph is to think of an idea. Next you find information to help explain your idea clearly. One way to find information is by using reference works in the library. Other ways to get information are by interviewing a person and by taking a survey.

In an interview, you direct questions to someone who knows information about the subject of your paragraph. First, however, you must prepare for the interview. Try to read about the subject so you can ask good questions. Then decide what questions to ask. Finally, call or write the person to set up a date and time for the interview.

At the interview itself, be sure to arrive on time. After you ask each question, listen carefully to the answer and take notes. Have the person repeat or explain an answer if you do not understand it. Soon after the interview is over, reread your notes and correct any mistakes.

In a survey, you ask many people the same question or questions. The questions may be shorter than those you ask in an interview. After your survey is completed, you can write the results in a graph or table. Here are the results of a survey that asked students this question:

What career would you like to enter when you finish school?

500 students were surveyed
40% said "guidance counselor"
30% said "teacher"
20% said "lawyer"
10% said "police officer"

Based on the results of the survey, a student decided to interview the school guidance counselor. Read the interview questions and notes on the next page.

Interview Questions

1. What does a guidance counselor do?
2. How could you help a fifth grade student?
3. Why do you give tests?

Interview Notes

Marcia Gerdes. October 30, 19__
A counselor helps people make decisions about their lives. She could help a student who is having problems in school, or she could help a person decide what after-school activities to choose. She gives tests to get more information about students so she can better help them.

Talking About Interviews and Surveys

Look again at the survey results and the interview.

1. What career was second most popular among the students? What career was least popular?
2. What information is found in the first line of the interview notes? Why?
3. Why are the interview notes taken in the order of the questions?
4. Can you think of other questions you would ask a counselor?

Doing an Interview

Now you are ready to try an interview. First choose a partner. Decide who should be interviewed first. Then switch parts. Imagine you are one of these people being interviewed.

1. A character in one of your favorite books
2. A character in a television series
3. A sports hero

Before you begin, think about what information you want to know. Then write your questions. Take notes on your partner's answers. Save your notes for the next lesson.

Practicing a Summary Paragraph

Thinking About Paragraphs

You have learned about many types of paragraphs. Another important type is called a summary paragraph. A *summary paragraph* summarizes or briefly states only the most important facts or ideas you have learned. These facts may include those you gathered while doing interviews or surveys. A summary paragraph has a topic sentence and detail sentences like other paragraphs.

When you write a summary paragraph, you must ask yourself some questions about your information.

1. What facts are the most important?
2. What facts could be combined or put together?
3. What facts are interesting but are not about the main idea?

- Read the information below. It was gathered from an interview with a scientist who studies desert life.

Interview Questions

1. What desert animals have you studied?
2. Where do they live?
3. How do they get water?

Interview Notes

Geraldo Ramos. March 3, 19__.
He has studied kangaroo rats and gila monsters. Most animals go without water for days. They live under stones or dig in the sand. The gila monster gets water by eating other animals. The kangaroo rat eats plants to get water. They also eat seeds. They have small bodies.

Think about how the interview notes could be used in a summary paragraph. Read the paragraph that follows, page 215.

Gila monsters and kangaroo rats are desert animals. They avoid the sun by living under stones or by digging a hole in the sand. These animals can go without water for days. The gila monster gets water by eating other animals. The kangaroo rat gets water from plants and seeds.

Writing a Summary Paragraph

Write a summary paragraph. Read the notes you made when you interviewed your partner in the last lesson.

1. Think about the main idea for your topic sentence.
2. Study your interview notes and questions. Use the questions on page 214 to help you select your facts.
3. Write your topic sentence. Write factual detail sentences.

Edit Your Paragraph

Read your summary paragraph again. Check it with the following questions. Use the editing symbols.

1. Are all the facts in the paragraph about the main idea?
2. Do your adjectives express your meaning clearly?
3. Did you punctuate and capitalize correctly?
4. Did you spell words correctly?

Editing Symbols

≡	capitalize
¶	indent
℘	take out
∧	add

INDEPENDENT WRITING

A Weather Summary

Prewriting You are going to write a summary paragraph about today's weather. A weather report is a summary of weather information. Check the weather today. What facts are reported? Write notes to include in your report.

Writing Write a paragraph to provide a summary weather report. Follow the steps above in writing your summary.

Editing Use the check questions and the editing symbols to edit your summary paragraph.

Unit Review

Write each adjective that appears in each sentence. After each adjective write the noun it describes. *pages 192–193*

1. The ten children wait to go to the concert.
2. The anxious friends talk about the concert.
3. One boy talks about the lively songs.
4. The boy with the green cap talks about his favorite song.

Write the correct form of the adjective for each sentence. *pages 194–196*

5. The ___ girl in the class leads the group. (tall)
6. The theater is the ___ of all. (large)
7. The music sounds ___ than last week's music. (soft)

Read each sentence. Write the correct form of the adjective that goes in each sentence. *pages 196–197*

8. The band plays the ___ music of any band. (more lively, most lively)
9. Josie plays the ___ guitar music of anyone I know. (more beautiful, most beautiful)
10. I think Donald is the ___ musician in our school. (more famous, most famous)
11. I think a guitar makes ___ music than a drum. (more delightful, most delightful)

Write each adjective with **-er.** Then write each with **-est.** *page 200*

12. sad **13.** muddy **14.** crazy **15.** short **16.** low

Write each sentence. Capitalize the proper adjective. *page 201*

17. Edvard Grieg was a famous scandinavian artist.
18. I enjoy the music of Grieg, the norwegian composer.
19. His music has been performed at chicago concerts.
20. The grieg music for *Peer Gynt* is very popular.
21. Grieg composed a quartet on american themes.

Unit Review

Write each underlined word. Write the meaning of the word. *pages 202–203*

22. Tina has a healthy voice.
23. I was unaware of her desire to be a singer.
24. I hope her efforts are not hopeless.
25. Singing lessons are a wonderful idea.
26. Tina might make a delightful entertainer.

Read each sentence. Read the words after each sentence. Write the word that is a synonym for the underlined word. *pages 204–205*

27. I sang a jolly song at the party. (quiet, happy, sad)
28. Friends were amazed by my lovely voice. (pretty, loud, slow)
29. I sang a lively song. (slow, fast, funny)

Read the four paragraphs below. Each paragraph either gives directions in time order, describes something, explains facts, or states reasons. Label your paper from a to d. Write the kind of paragraph that each represents. *pages 210–215*

a. Bill cleaned his clothes today. First he put them in the washer. Next he added soap. Later he placed the clothes in the dryer. Then he folded them.

b. All drivers of cars should wear seat belts. Seat belts make driving much safer. They have saved many people's lives. The seat belts are easy to fasten and to remove.

c. The card catalog in a library helps you find books. Each card has the author and title of a book. It also has a special number that tells where the book is located.

d. I have a pet rabbit. Her ears are white. Her eyes are red. She hops around all day and makes a funny sound when eating. Her fur is soft.

A Biography

A *biography* is a story of someone's life. It tells about the events in that person's life. Marian Anderson is a famous black singer who worked very hard in her life to reach her goals. The following selection about her early life is from a biography about Marian Anderson.

Marian Anderson

In a small house in Philadelphia a three-year-old girl was singing. She sat at a little table that she liked to make believe was her piano. The walls of the room were covered with flowered paper. The child thought she saw friendly faces in the flowers, looking down at her as she played and sang. The child's name was Marian Anderson. When she grew up, she became one of the world's best-loved singers.

Marian was born on February 27, 1903. Her father, John Anderson, worked long hours delivering coal and ice. Her mother, Anna Anderson, had been a schoolteacher once. Now she was busy keeping the house comfortable for her husband and their three daughters: Marian, Alyce, and Ethel. The Anderson family did not have much money, but they cared about each other and had many happy times together.

As Marian grew older, her father took her to church with him every Sunday. The Union Baptist Church was important to the people in Marian's neighborhood. Often their lives were unhappy. Many of them were poor. Some of them had trouble getting jobs. In church they heard words and music that said to them: "Yes, you have troubles. We know that life can be hard. We must hope for good things to come."

Marian joined the children's choir of the church. As she sang with this group, the choirmaster noticed her beautiful voice. He asked her to practice a duet with her best friend, Viola Johnson. The next Sunday the two girls stood up to sing for the whole congregation. It was Marian's first public performance. She was six years old.

Marian was finding out about music in other ways, too. When she was eight, her father bought an old piano. But there was no money for music lessons. After weeks of trying, Marian taught herself to play simple tunes. She wished she could learn more.

Then one day she saw a used violin in a store window. She went in and asked the man how much it cost. "Three dollars and ninety-five cents," he said. "Is it a good violin?" Marian asked. She knew how hard it would be for her to get that much money. "Oh, it's a very fine instrument," the storekeeper said.

Marian went to work after school. She scrubbed steps for her neighbors and ran their errands. If someone gave her a few cents for candy, she put the money carefully away. At last she earned and saved enough nickels and pennies. Proudly she went back to the store and bought the violin. A friend of the family taught her to tune it and to play a few notes. But before long the strings snapped and the wood of the violin cracked. It was no good at all. Marian was sad and disappointed. She wanted so much to make music well.

Still she was never downhearted for long. She loved singing in the choir. Her full, rich voice poured through the church. The sound she made was so loud the choirmaster sometimes laughed and said, "Hold back a little there, Marian. We want

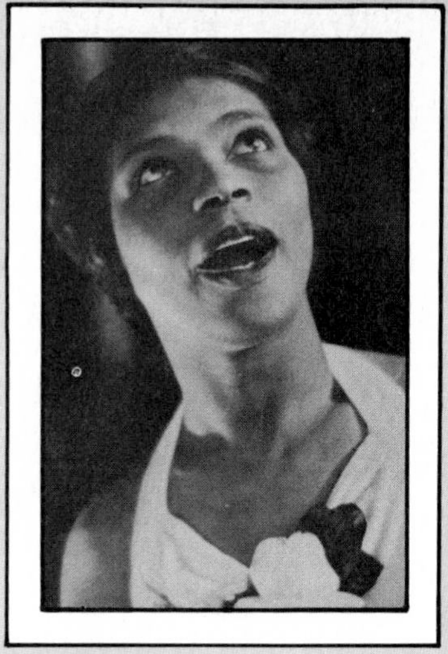

to hear the other singers, too." Friends and neighbors in the congregation, though, had nothing but praise for Marian.

Her voice was deep and velvety, the kind musicians called contralto. But she could reach up to the high soprano notes, too, and even down to the low music of the baritone. When the choir prepared a new song, Marian learned all the different parts, high and low, not just her own. Then, if a singer could not come to church on Sunday, she helped out by singing in his place. It made her happy to know the choir needed her, and she learned a lot about music this way. Secretly she dreamed of being a singer when she grew up.

But when Marian was twelve, her father died. Life changed then. Harder times began. Marian's mother had to go out to work. She got a job cleaning other people's houses and bringing their laundry home to wash and iron. Mrs. Anderson was a frail, gentle woman, but she had great spirit. She never complained and somehow she found the extra strength to make a good home for her children.

As the years went by, Marian began to realize how hard her mother worked to provide for her family. "I'm getting old enough now," she thought, "I must do something, too." When she entered high school she tried to study useful subjects, like typing. But all the time her heart was really set on singing.

If only she could earn enough money at it, she could make singing her life's work. Of course she was not paid for singing

in church. Ever since she was eight, though, she had been invited to sing in other churches, too. People all over Philadelphia got to know about her splendid voice. They began asking her to perform at their parties and club meetings. By the time Marian was in high school, she was getting $5.00 every time she sang at one of these gatherings.

This seemed like a lot of money to her. Yet she knew she was still a long way from being a professional singer. She had been born with a fine voice and she sang with deep feeling. But Marian saw how much she still had to learn. The best way, she decided, would be to have lessons, at a music school.

Early one morning she took the trolley car to a well-known school in uptown Philadelphia. She went into the building and got in line with a group of girls who were waiting to apply. When Marian's turn came, the pretty, blue-eyed woman in charge paid no attention to her. Marian stepped aside. After everyone else had been taken care of, the woman said, "What do *you* want?" in a sharp voice. "I'd like to arrange for lessons, please—" Marian began politely. "We don't take colored," said the woman coldly, and turned away.

Marion felt hurt and confused. She had often heard that white people sometimes behaved in this cruel, thoughtless way toward Negroes. But it had never really happened to her before. In her neighborhood black people and white people lived side by side. Most of the time they were comfortable and friendly with each other. True enough, their skins were different, Marian thought, but not their feelings.

Sadly she went home to tell her mother what happened at the school. "The way that woman spoke," she cried, "it bit into my soul." Was she wrong to think a Negro girl could become a singer? Marian asked.

Mrs. Anderson thought for a while. Then, in her calm, sure way, she said, "Of course you can become a singer, Marian. You must have faith. There will be another way for you to learn what you need to know."

And there was another way. The people at the Union Baptist Church believed in Marian's talent. These friends and neighbors planned a concert to help her. Every bit of money they got from the tickets was set aside to pay for private singing lessons for Marian.

Marian performed at the concert herself, but the main star was Roland Hayes. Mr. Hayes was the first Negro singer to become famous in the concert halls of America and Europe.

He sang the spirituals Marian and her people knew so well. These were powerful songs of sorrow, of joy, and of hope that the Negroes made up when they were slaves. Mr. Hayes also sang lieder, poems set to music by the great European composers. Marian could not understand the French or German languages they were sung in. Still she was quick to hear the beauty of the music. She longed to learn such songs herself.

Then, as she listened to Mr. Hayes's pure tenor voice, she suddenly realized, "His skin is dark, like mine. And he has gone so far. They say he has even sung for kings and queens. If he can, perhaps I can too." Slowly, from this time on, Marian's pride began to grow. It was never an angry pride, but full of faith and hope. Throughout her life, no matter what happened, it kept her strong.

Tobi Tobias

Creative Activities

1. **Creative Writing** Imagine that you were given the chance to interview Marian Anderson. What questions would you ask? How would she answer them? Here is one possible question and answer?
   YOU: What did you dream of when you were a child?
   MARIAN: I secretly dreamed of becoming a singer.
   Write four more questions that you would ask Marian Anderson. Also write her answers based on the information in her biography.
2. **Creative Writing** Imagine that someone wanted to write your biography. Think of the events in your life that would be most interesting or unusual. For example, did you ever move from another town? Did you ever get lost or lose something important? Have you ever won an award? Write three sentences that tell about three important events in your life.

DOG WALKER IN NEW YORK CITY

7

Grammar and Related Language Skills

Linking Verbs
Nouns and Adjectives After Linking Verbs
Linking Verbs in Present and Past Tense
Apostrophes in Possessives and Contractions

Practical Communication

STUDY AND REFERENCE SKILLS
Taking and Organizing Notes

COMPOSITION
Writing a Two-Paragraph Report

Creative Expression

A Ballad

Would you enjoy the job of walking many dogs? Some people clean chimneys. Some people become magicians and entertain at parties. Other people make and sell arrangements of colorful balloons for special occasions. Can you think of other unusual occupations? What writing and speaking skills would you need to advertise these special skills?

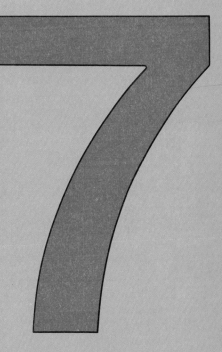

Linking Verbs

Every sentence has a verb. Some verbs name an action. Other verbs do not name an action. Instead, they connect the subject part with a noun or adjective in the predicate part.

An **action verb** is a word that names an action.

A **linking verb** is a verb that connects the subject part with a noun or adjective in the predicate part. It tells what the subject is or is like.

The most common linking verb is *be*. The chart shows the forms of *be* in the present tense and the past tense.

Present		Past	
I	**am**	I, She, He, It	**was**
She, He, It	**is**		
You, We, They	**are**	You, We, They	**were**

- Look at these two sentences.

Tracy works in a circus. She is a clown.

The verb *works* names an action. The verb *is* does not name an action. It connects the subject *she* with the noun *clown*. *She* and *clown* are the same person. *Is* is a linking verb.

- Now look at these two sentences.

Tracy went to a clown school. Her teachers were funny.

The verb *went* names an action. The verb *were* does not name an action. It connects the subject *teachers* with the adjective *funny*. *Funny* tells what the *teachers* were like.

Talk About It

Tell whether each underlined verb is an action verb or a linking verb.

1. She <u>is</u> a clown.
2. Her costume <u>is</u> colorful.
3. The buttons <u>are</u> special.
4. They <u>spray</u> people with water.

Skills Practice

Write each sentence. Underline each verb. If the verb names an action, write **action verb.** If the verb is a linking verb, write **linking verb.**

1. Tracy liked clown school.
2. Her teachers were clowns.
3. She paints her face today.
4. Her face is yellow.
5. Her nose is round and red.
6. Her shoes are very large.
7. Tracy chases other clowns.
8. The audience is happy.
9. Tracy travels with the circus.
10. She was sick once.

Writing Sentences

Imagine that you have a job in the circus. Write five sentences describing what you do. Use action verbs in two sentences. Use linking verbs in three sentences.

Sample Answer 1. Tracy <u>liked</u> clown school. action verb

Nouns and Adjectives After Linking Verbs

You know that a linking verb connects the subject part with a noun or adjective in the predicate part. It tells what the subject is or is like. A linking verb is usually followed by a noun or an adjective.

> A **noun** is a word that names a person, place, thing, or idea.
> An **adjective** is a word that describes a noun or pronoun.

A linking verb *connects,* or links, the subject with a noun or adjective that follows it.

- Read the sentences below.

Roberta is a shepherd. Her great-grandparents were ranchers.

In the first sentence the verb *is* connects the subject *Roberta* with the noun *shepherd.* (Do not count words such as *a, an, the, her, his,* or *their.*) *Roberta* and *shepherd* are the same person. In the second sentence the verb *were* connects the subject *great-grandparents* with *ranchers. Great-grandparents* and *ranchers* are the same people.

- Now look at these sentences.

Roberta was busy. Now she is happy.

In the first sentence the verb *was* connects the subject *Roberta* to the adjective *busy. Busy* tells what *Roberta* was like. In the second sentence the verb *is* connects the subject *she* to the adjective *happy. Happy* tells what *she* is like.

Talk About It

Tell whether a noun or an adjective follows each linking verb. Then tell the word to which the noun or adjective is connected.

1. Some jobs are difficult.
2. Roberto's job is unusual.
3. He is a shepherd.
4. His sheep are young.
5. His hours are long.
6. Roberto is sleepy.
7. His feet are sore.
8. His father is a farmer.

Skills Practice

Write each sentence. Underline the word that follows the linking verb. (Do not count words such as *a, an, the, his, her,* or *their.*) If the word is a noun, write **noun.** If the word is an adjective, write **adjective.** Then draw two lines under the word to which the noun or adjective is connected.

1. His boss is a rancher.
2. Shepherds are busy.
3. Their work is hard.
4. Coyotes are dangerous.
5. Roberto is careful.
6. The dog is a companion.
7. The sheep are noisy.
8. Their home is the pasture.
9. Some girls are shepherds.
10. The job is fun.
11. The life is different.
12. I am curious.
13. My dog is a shepherd.
14. She is tan.
15. She is lazy.
16. She is a pet.

Writing Sentences

Think about a job that you would like to have someday. Write five sentences telling about that job. Use at least one linking verb in each sentence. Use nouns after the linking verb in three sentences. Use adjectives after the linking verb in the other two sentences.

Sample Answer 1. His boss is a rancher. noun

Using Linking Verbs in the Present Tense

The subject of a sentence tells whom or what the sentence is about. The subject may be singular or plural.

- Notice how the subjects and the verbs work together.

I am a reporter.	Gary is a lawyer. He is a friend of Sue. She is a judge. The courtroom is huge. It is old.	You are innocent. We are happy. John and Ed are sad. They are angry. Our friends are joyful.

Each column shows a different form of the linking verb *be* in the present tense. Remember, use *am* when the subject is *I*. Use *is* when the subject is *she, he, it,* or a singular noun. Use *are* when the subject is *you, we, they,* a plural noun, or a compound subject.

Talk About It

Read each sentence. Tell which linking verb to use.

1. Ed ___ angry. (is, are)
2. He and John ___ upset. (is, are)
3. The coins ___ old. (is, are)
4. Ed's face ___ sad. (is, are)
5. The coins ___ rare. (is, are)
6. John ___ furious. (is, are)

Skills Practice

Write each sentence. Use the correct form of the linking verb.

1. The judge ___ wise. (is, are)
2. I ___ nervous. (is, am)
3. John ___ calm. (is, are)
4. The coins ___ old. (is, are)
5. The judge ___ smart. (is, are)
6. Her mind ___ quick. (is, are)
7. I ___ curious. (is, am)
8. The case ___ clear. (is, are)

Sample Answer 1. The judge is wise.

Using Linking Verbs in the Past Tense

In the present tense the linking verb in a sentence must agree with the subject part. The same is true of linking verbs in the past tense.

- Notice how the subjects and verbs work together.

I was a cook.	You were hungry.
Sam was a cook.	We were busy.
He was quick.	The children were happy.
Joyce was a customer.	They were playful.
She was hungry for lunch.	Toni and Sue were thirsty.

Each column shows a different form of the linking verb *be*. Use *was* when the subject is *I, she, he, it,* or a singular noun. Use *were* when the subject is *you, we, they,* a plural noun, or a compound subject.

Talk About It

Read each sentence. Tell which linking verb to use.

1. The day ___ hot. (was, were)
2. We ___ thirsty. (was, were)
3. Our mouths ___ dry (was, were)
4. Sam ___ busy. (was, were)
5. We ___ hungry. (was, were)
6. The meal ___ good. (was, were)

Skills Practice

Write each sentence. Use the correct form of the linking verb.

1. The day ___ strange. (was, were)
2. Sam ___ nervous. (was, were)
3. His hands ___ damp. (was, were)
4. His boss ___ angry. (was, were)
5. You ___ curious. (was, were)
6. The eggs ___ bad. (was, were)
7. We ___ angry. (was, were)
8. I ___ sick. (was, were)

Sample Answer 1. The day was strange.

Verb Antonyms

Some words have opposite meanings. These words are called *antonyms*.

Daniel enters his shop.

Daniel leaves his shop.

- Look at the two sentences that describe the pictures. The verb in the first sentence is *enters.* The verb in the second sentence is *leaves. Leaves* means the opposite of *enters.* The words *enter* and *leave* are antonyms.

> An **antonym** is a word that means the opposite of another word.

- Look at the words in the boxes. The two words in each box are antonyms.

win lose	live die	succeed fail

Not every word has an antonym. For example, the word *yawn* can be a verb, but there is not a verb that means the opposite of *yawn.* There is not a word that means the opposite of *tickle* or of *rhyme.* These words do not have antonyms.

Talk About It

Read each sentence. Tell which word is an antonym for the underlined word.

1. Daniel opens his barber shop. (designs, closes, measures)
2. He stands all day. (sits, cuts, plays)
3. A customer arrives early. (applies, leaves, smiles)
4. Daniel grins at him. (frowns, smiles, looks)

Skills Practice

Read each sentence. Write each sentence with the word that is an antonym for the underlined word.

1. The customer raises his chin. (lowers, rests, lifts)
2. He begins telling a story. (relates, finishes, starts)
3. The story bores Daniel. (interests, surprises, bothers)
4. He forgets his work. (speaks, outlines, remembers)
5. Daniel removes too much hair. (clips, replaces, brushes)
6. This upsets the customer. (calms, angers, awakens)
7. He yells at Daniel. (screams, whispers, sings)
8. Daniel watches the customer. (calms, ignores, scares)
9. Daniel dislikes his job sometimes. (enjoys, lives, succeeds)

Writing Sentences

So far in this unit you have read about a clown, a shepherd, a judge, a cook, and a barber. Now think about what these workers do in their jobs.

1. Write four sentences with action verbs that are antonyms. For example, you might write: The cook likes salad. The cook hates salad.
2. Write three sentences with linking verbs.

Sample Answer 1. The customer lowers his chin.

Skills Review

Write the verb in each sentence. If the verb names an action, write **action verb.** If the verb is a linking verb, write **linking verb.**

1. Ruth works in an unusual job.
2. She is a chimney cleaner.
3. She sweeps chimneys.
4. Her uniforms are always dirty.
5. She wears a special suit.
6. The color is black.
7. Her hat is also black.
8. Her boots are gray.
9. She uses brooms and brushes.
10. The equipment is important.
11. Ruth cleaned a chimney today.
12. Dust was heavy.
13. Dirt was grimy.
14. Ruth climbed the chimney.
15. Bats were black.
16. Ruth was calm.
17. They flew away.
18. Ruth watched from the roof.
19. Ruth's job is different.
20. I am curious about her job.

Write the word that follows the linking verb. (Do not count words such as *a, an,* or *the.*) If the word is a noun, write **noun.** If the word is an adjective, write **adjective.** Then write the word to which the noun or adjective is connected.

21. Consuelo is a banker.
22. Her work is pleasant.
23. The job is fun.
24. Friends are customers.
25. They are neighbors.
26. Consuelo is friendly.
27. She is helpful.
28. The customers are thankful.
29. I am happy.
30. The job was easy.
31. Consuelo was busy.
32. Two customers were nervous.
33. They were strangers.
34. The strangers were thieves.
35. Consuelo was alert.
36. The alarm was loud.
37. The police were quick.
38. Both strangers were sorry.

Read each sentence. Write the correct form of the linking verb.

39. Kay ___ a ranger. (is, are)
40. Her work ___ fun. (is, are)
41. She and Vi ___ busy. (is, are)
42. They ___ foresters. (is, are)
43. The area ___ clean. (is, are)
44. Fires ___ common. (is, are)

45. I ___ warm. (is, am)
46. We ___ curious. (was, were)
47. Smoke ___ heavy. (was, were)
48. The fire ___ small. (was, were)
49. It ___ strange. (was, were)
50. Vi ___ grateful. (was, were)

Write the word that is an antonym for the underlined word.

51. Otto repaired a watch in his shop. (studied, broke, lifted)
52. He scattered the parts on a table. (gathered, emptied, lost)
53. Then he lowered a bright lamp. (switched, clicked, raised)
54. Otto bent a piece of metal. (hammered, folded, straightened)
55. He hooked two springs. (unfastened, locked, tied)
56. The watch stopped ticking. (ended, began, decided)
57. The angry owner left. (arrived, ran, stepped)
58. Otto lost another customer. (pleased, bothered, found)

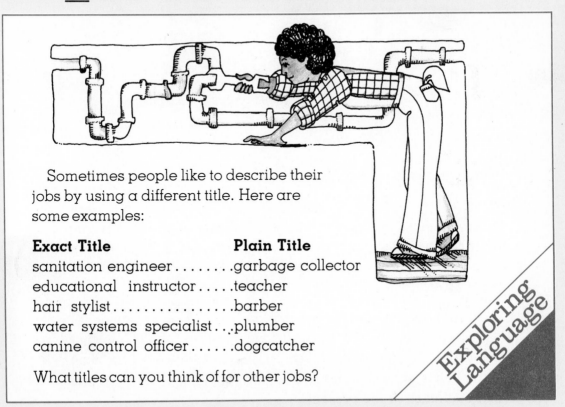

Exploring Language

Sometimes people like to describe their jobs by using a different title. Here are some examples:

Exact Title	**Plain Title**
sanitation engineer	garbage collector
educational instructor	teacher
hair stylist	barber
water systems specialist	plumber
canine control officer	dogcatcher

What titles can you think of for other jobs?

Verbs Ending in -ing

The form of a verb tells the time of the action. The *present tense* of a verb names an action that happens now. The *past tense* of a verb names an action that already happened. There is another form that tells when something happens. It tells that the action continues.

Jesse was selling ice before. Jesse is selling water now.

- Look at the sentence under the picture on the left. *Was selling* is the entire verb. *Was* is a helping verb. It tells you that the action happened in the past. *Selling* is the main verb. It has an *-ing* ending. The verb *was selling* shows action that began in the past and continued for a time.

- Now look at the sentence under the picture on the right. *Is selling* is the entire verb. *Is* is a helping verb. It tells you that the action is happening in the present. *Selling* is the main verb. It has an *-ing* ending. The verb *is selling* shows action that continues in the present.

When a verb ends in *-ing,* the helping verb is a form of *be*. Remember the forms of *be* in the present tense and past tense.

Present	I **am**, she, he, it **is**	You, we, they **are**
Past	I, she, he, it **was**	You, we, they **were**

Now you know other ways to talk about the present and the past. The present tense of the helping verb *be* (*am, is, are*) and a main verb ending with *-ing* name an action that continues in the present. The past tense of the helping verb *be* (*was, were*) and a main verb ending with *-ing* name an action that began in the past and continued for a time.

Talk About It

Read each sentence. Decide if each verb should be in the present or past tense. Tell the correct form of the verb *be*.

1. Jesse ___ selling ice on the street before. (was, is)
2. Many people ___ buying it three hours ago. (were, are)
3. The sun ___ melting all his ice now. (was, is)
4. Now people ___ going away. (is, are)

Skills Practice

Write each sentence. Decide if each verb should be in the present or past tense. Use the correct form of the verb *be*.

1. I ___ watching Jesse before. (am, was)
2. He ___ doing very well a while ago. (was, is)
3. His customers ___ asking for lots of ice before. (were, are)
4. They ___ calling for ice yesterday, too. (are, were)
5. Now the heat ___ hurting his business. (is, was)
6. The ice ___ turning into water now. (was, is)
7. I ___ helping Jesse at this moment. (am, was)
8. His customers ___ buying cold water now. (are, were)

Sample Answer 1. I was watching Jesse before.

Using Apostrophes in Possessives and in Contractions

An **apostrophe** (') is used to show possession and to show that two words have been joined to make a contraction.

- Read these sentences. Both sentences tell whose voice is very good. In the second sentence an apostrophe (') and an *s* are added to *Walter* to show possession.

The voice of Walter is very good. Walter's voice is very good.

> Add an **apostrophe** and **s** (**'s**) to form the possessive of most singular nouns.

- Look at these sentences. *Boys* is a plural noun ending in *s*. In the second sentence an apostrophe (') is added after the *s* of *boys* to show possession.

The voices of the boys are strong. The boys' voices are strong.

> Add an **apostrophe** (') to form the possessive of a plural noun that ends with **s**.

- Now read these sentences. The word *people* is a plural noun that does not end in *s*. In the second sentence an apostrophe (') and *s* are added to *people* to show possession.

The boys sing the words of people. The boys sing people's words.

> Add an **apostrophe** and **s** (**'s**) to form the possessive of a plural noun that does not end with **s**.

An apostrophe is also used to join two words to make one word. The new word with the apostrophe is called a *contraction*.

> A **contraction** is a word made up of two words. The words are joined to make one word.

The chart on the next page shows contractions of pronouns and verbs. The first section lists contractions of pronouns with the present tense of *be*. The second section shows contractions of pronouns with *have* and *has*. The third section lists contractions of pronouns with *had*.

Contraction	Short For	Contraction	Short For	Contraction	Short For
I'm	I am	I've	I have	I'd	I had
you're	you are	you've	you have	you'd	you had
he's	he is	he's	he has	he'd	he had
she's	she is	she's	she has	she'd	she had
it's	it is	it's	it has	it'd	it had
we're	we are	we've	we have	we'd	we had
they're	they are	they've	they have	they'd	they had

Now read these two sentences. In the first sentence *Walter's singing* shows that the singing belongs to Walter. In the second sentence *Walter's singing* is short for *Walter is singing*. *Walter's* is a contraction for *Walter* and *is*.

Walter's singing is beautiful. Walter's singing for our class now.

Talk About It

Tell whether the apostrophe in each word shows a possessive or a contraction. Then tell what each word means.

1. The group's work is hard.
2. They're helping each other.
3. The boys' jobs are important.
4. The choir's going on tour.
5. They've got to pay expenses.
6. All the boys' singing is great.

Skills Practice

Write each sentence. Add the apostrophe in the correct place. Then write what each possessive or contraction means.

1. My friends a travel agent.
2. My friends name is Lucy.
3. Lucy arranges peoples trips.
4. Lucy loves her customers trips.
5. Theyve always used her suggestions for traveling.
6. Im going on vacation.
7. Lucys arranged my trip.
8. The trips cost is expensive.
9. Its my first grand tour.
10. My vacation will not be like my many other friends trips.

Sample Answer 1. My friend's a travel agent. friend is

Verb Synonyms

Life would be dull if we used the same words over and over again. Words wear out. For this reason our language has different words that have similar meanings. A *synonym* is a word that has nearly the same meaning as another word.

- Look at the words below. All of them are synonyms. Each verb names almost the same action.

say talk speak mention tell

- Now look at each word below. Do all of these synonyms mean exactly the same thing?

laugh snicker giggle smile titter chuckle

Words may be synonyms even when they do not name exactly the same action.

Sometimes in your writing you may be able to think of more than one verb to tell about an action. When you have a choice, always use the verb that best names the action.

- Look at these sentences below. Each one tells about the picture.

Amy hits the ball.	Amy knocks the ball.
Amy taps the ball.	Amy strikes the ball.
Amy sends the ball.	Amy slams the ball.

The verbs in the six sentences are synonyms. The verbs mean nearly the same thing. But the verb *slams* most closely names the action. *Slams* is the only verb that tells how hard the ball is hit.

Talk About It

Each sentence is followed by two verbs that are synonyms. Either verb completes the sentence. Which verb most closely names the action? Give reasons for your answer.

1. Shawn ___ across the court in record time. (walked, sped)
2. The hard-hit ball ___ by. (whizzed, went)
3. Shawn ___ the ball as hard as he could. (slammed, tapped)
4. The other player ___ at the ball in surprise. (looked, stared)

Skills Practice

Choose the verb in parentheses that most closely names the action. Write each sentence with the verb you have chosen.

1. The big tennis match ___ the eager watchers. (pleased, thrilled)
2. Hundreds of fans ___ the small stadium. (jammed, filled)
3. Trina just barely ___ between two other people. (squeezed, sat)
4. The players ___ quickly to and fro. (ran, darted)
5. Jake ___ the ball as hard as he could. (hit, smacked)
6. Shawn's leg hurt. He ___ off the court. (limped, walked)
7. Busy reporters ___ to the telephones. (dashed, went)
8. Excited fans ___ up to see the action. (stood, jumped)

Writing Sentences

Imagine you are playing some kind of ball game. Use an action verb in each sentence.

1. Write a sentence using the action verb hit.
2. Write a sentence using a synonym for hit.
3. Write a sentence using the action verb run.
4. Write a sentence using a synonym for run.

Sample Answer 1. The big tennis match thrilled the eager watchers.

Skills Review

Write each sentence. Decide if each verb should be in the present or past tense. Use the form of the verb *be*.

1. Rick ___ working for the post office last week. (is, was)
2. Now he ___ resting from his accident. (was, is)
3. Last Friday we ___ waiting for our mail. (are, were)
4. That morning our cousin ___ visiting us. (was, is)
5. Her two dogs ___ running in our yard then. (were, are)
6. Rick ___ carrying a large sack of mail that time. (is, was)
7. The dogs ___ chasing him for an hour that day. (were, are)
8. I ___ delivering mail for Rick now. (am, was)
9. The dogs ___ playing at their own home now. (were, are)
10. At this moment we ___ sitting on the lawn. (were, are)
11. I ___ receiving a package today. (was, am)
12. No dogs ___ jumping at us now. (are, were)
13. Yesterday they ___ barking noisily at Rick. (were, are)

Write each sentence. Add apostrophes in the correct places. Then write what each possessive or contraction means.

14. Pauls hair falls in his eyes.
15. Pauls tried combing it back.
16. Im sure that he cannot see clearly.
17. Hes having trouble working as a waiter.
18. Paul gets all the customers orders.
19. One customers asking for more soup.
20. Paul loads the boys meals on a tray.
21. He does not like the swinging doors movements.
22. The swinging doors hit the waiters tray.
23. The trays contents fly through the air.
24. Hed better get a haircut.
25. Theyre saying things about him.
26. But weve always liked Paul.
27. The restaurants service is excellent.

Choose the verb in parentheses that most closely names the action. Write the verb you have chosen.

28. Our team ___ hard for the frisbee championship. (played, battled)
29. The frisbee ___ high in the air all day. (went, sailed)
30. Our team ___ down the field quickly. (rushed, moved)
31. The fans ___ loudly to the players. (spoke, cheered)
32. Arif ___ the frisbee to June. (tossed, gave)
33. June ___ the frisbee to win. (placed, heaved)
34. Jonathan ___ to greet the winning team. (ran, dashed)

Language often tells us something about the way people live. For example, for a long time in the United States, few jobs were held by women. Many jobs even had male titles such as *policeman, fireman,* and *chairman.*

Times are changing and the language is changing, too. As more women enter the work world, job titles are changing. *Policeman* has become *police officer, fireman* is now *firefighter,* and *chairman* is *chairperson* or *chair.*

What other job titles are changing with the times?

Exploring Language

Using Note-Taking Skills

To prepare a report, you gather information from different places. It is helpful to take notes on the important facts. Careful notes will help you write a well-organized report.

These steps are helpful to follow when taking notes.

1. Know the main subject of your report.
2. Think about the kinds of information in the library.
3. Read the information carefully.
4. Decide what facts are most important.
5. Write your notes in sentences or in groups of words called phrases.
6. Reread your notes and compare them with the sources. Make sure you have chosen the most important facts.

● Look at these examples of taking notes from a reference source.

> There are many kinds of ants. *Carpenter ants* chew holes in wood to make homes. *Army ants* make no nests at all but travel in large groups. *Pharaoh's ants* are smaller than this letter **a**. *Honey ants* live on sweet juices from flowers. *Amazon ants* capture ants from different groups to work for them.

Sentence Notes	**Phrase Notes**
Many types of ants exist.	—types of ants
Carpenter ants live in wood.	—*carpenter ants* (wood)
Army ants travel and have no home.	—*army ants* (travel)
Pharaoh's ants are tiny.	—*Pharaoh's ants* (tiny)
Honey ants collect juices.	—*honey ants* (juices)
Amazon ants have slaves.	—*Amazon ants* (slaves)

Talk About It

Look at the selection and notes about ants again.

1. What is the main idea of the selection?
2. What is the difference between the sentence notes and the selection?
3. What is the major difference between the two kinds of notes?
4. When would you want to use phrase notes rather than sentence notes?

Skills Practice

Review how to take notes. Take sentence notes on the first paragraph. Take phrase notes on the second paragraph.

1. Many people do not know that backgammon is a very old game. It was developed by the Persians long ago. The ancient Greeks and Romans played backgammon. Native Americans also played backgammon. Backgammon has become popular again.

2. The most important part of making bread is kneading the dough. To knead dough, first fold the dough toward you. Next, press the dough with the heel of your hands. Then turn it a little bit. Fold it and press it again. Keep kneading the dough until it is smooth.

Sample Answer 1. Backgammon is a very old game.

Two-Paragraph Reports

Thinking About Paragraphs

You have been learning how to write different types of paragraphs. Now you are going to use your skills to write a longer report. A two-paragraph report must have a main idea. Both paragraphs in the report should be about that main idea. Usually the first paragraph introduces the idea and tells about it in a general way. The second paragraph then uses more details and tells about the idea in a more specific way. Sometimes the report has a title. The title briefly states the main idea.

You can use any of the types of paragraphs you have learned to write in a two-paragraph report. The report could contain two paragraphs with facts or two paragraphs that describe. You can also mix the two paragraphs. The first paragraph could be an opinion paragraph with reasons that introduce the main idea. The second paragraph could use facts to prove the main idea.

- Read the two-paragraph report below that uses facts.

Oceanography

Oceanography is the study of the ocean or sea. The ocean needs to be studied because it covers over 70 per cent of the earth. Plants and fish may someday increase our food supply. Also oil and natural gas can be found in rocks under the ocean bottom.

An oceanographer can study the sea in many different ways. Some oceanographers draw the plants and animals for reports. Others study only certain parts of the sea such as rocks or shellfish. All oceanographers should be good sailors because they must study the sea on stormy as well as on calm days.

Talking About Paragraphs

Look at the report about oceanography.

1. What is the main idea of this two-paragraph report?
2. What kind of paragraphs are they?
3. What is the topic sentence of the first paragraph?
4. What is the topic sentence of the second paragraph?
5. What words are similar in each topic sentence?
6. How is the second paragraph different from the first?
7. What is the title of the report?

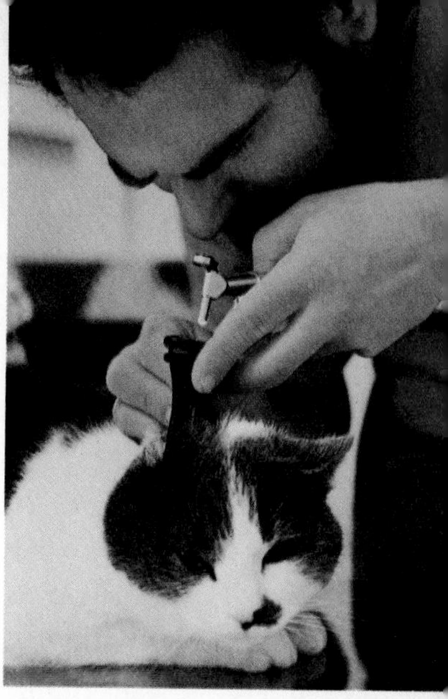

Writing Paragraphs

You are going to write a two-paragraph report based on the following topic sentences and detail sentences. Follow these directions carefully.

1. Use this topic sentence for the first paragraph: *Veterinary medicine is an interesting career.*
2. Use this topic sentence for the second paragraph: *A veterinarian is an animal doctor.*
3. Read the following detail sentences. Some of these detail sentences go with the first topic sentence, and some go with the second topic sentence. Decide which ones support the first topic sentence. Choose the ones that support the second topic sentence.
   - **a.** It deals with the health and care of animals.
   - **b.** In cities veterinarians take care of people's pets.
   - **c.** In the country they take care of farm animals.
   - **d.** People in veterinary medicine must like to work with animals.
   - **e.** There are hospitals for animals that have the same equipment that is used with human beings in hospitals.
   - **f.** Veterinarians also test meat and milk for diseases.
4. Write the report using the topic and detail sentences.
5. Write a title for the report.

A Class Report

Thinking About a Report

Your class can write a two-paragraph report together. Remember that the first step in preparing for report writing is to decide upon your main idea. Then you must gather information about the idea. You can use a card catalog in a library to find the reference works you need. Besides books you can use magazines to find the most up-to-date information. You can also use nonprint materials such as records, films, and filmstrips.

The main idea of your report will be clowns. Besides going to the library, you can also use notes from interviews. Imagine that you are going to interview a clown.

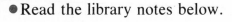

● Read the library notes below.

Library Notes

1. Clowns used to be called jesters.
2. Modern circuses started in England two hundred years ago.
3. Clowns have always been an important part of the circus.
4. Clowns make people laugh after scary acts like the high wire or trapeze artists.
5. Every clown has a special costume and make-up.

Next you would need to think of questions to ask the clown. Then you would use your library notes and the questions to do the actual interview with the clown.

Interview Questions	Interview Notes
1. What is your real name?	Jolly the Clown. August 4, 19__.
2. Why did you become a clown?	Her real name is Lisa Dunne.
3. How did you become a clown?	She likes to make people laugh.
4. How do you like the circus?	She went to a special clown school. She learned to walk on stilts there. She finds circus work hard but fun.

Writing a Report

Now you are ready to write the class report.

1. Choose one of the two topic sentences below for the beginning of the first paragraph. Remember that the first paragraph usually introduces the main idea in a general way.

a. Circuses have changed over the years.

b. Clowns have been entertaining people for hundreds of years.

2. Now choose a topic sentence for the second paragraph of your class report from the two sentences below. The second paragraph tells more about the main idea of the report. It usually has more specific information than in the the first paragraph.

a. A circus clown has to learn many things.

b. A clown needs to know how to walk on stilts.

3. Write your report on the board.

4. Write the topic sentence of the first paragraph.

5. Use the library and interview notes for information. Write the detail sentences for the first paragraph.

6. Write the topic sentence for the second paragraph. Then write the detail sentences.

7. Read the two paragraphs aloud. Check that all the sentences are about the main idea of clowns.

8. Write a title for the report.

Practicing a Two-Paragraph Report

Thinking About a Report

Now you are ready to write a two-paragraph report. Imagine that a Navy pilot came to speak at a school assembly. He is training to be an astronaut. You are to write a report for the school newspaper.

- Read these library notes about astronauts.

Library Notes

1. Astronauts are pilots or scientists.
2. They spend two or more years in training.
3. Much time is spent in classroom work.
4. They learn how rockets work.
5. They study many different sciences.
6. There are many tests for the body and the mind.

- Read the interview notes taken with the Navy pilot.

Interview Questions

1. How did you learn to fly?
2. Where do you live now?
3. What do you want to do?
4. Do you have any hobbies?

Interview Notes

John Knight. April, 19__. He served on an aircraft carrier. He was a test pilot, also. He now lives at The Space Center, Houston, Texas. He wants to explore other planets. His hobby is science fiction.

Writing a Report

1. Write a topic sentence for the first paragraph. The sentence should tell about the training of U.S. astronauts. Use the library notes to write detail sentences.
2. Write a topic sentence for the second paragraph. The sentence should tell about the interview with John Knight. Use the interview notes to write detail sentences.
3. Write a title for the report.

Edit Your Report

Use this check list to edit your two-paragraph report.

1. Do both paragraphs tell about the main idea of the report?
2. Do topic sentences state the main idea of the paragraph?
3. Do the detail sentences tell about each topic sentence?
4. Do the subject and verb in each sentence agree?
5. Did you capitalize and punctuate correctly?
6. Did you use correct punctuation for dates and place names?
7. Did you spell the words correctly?

Editing Symbols

≡ capitalize
¶ indent
ℓ take out
^ add

INDEPENDENT WRITING

Writing a Two-Paragraph Report

Prewriting Many pioneers traveled West in wagon trains. Find, read, and take notes about the facts concerning life on these cross-country trips. Write questions that you might ask in an imaginary interview with a pioneer from such a wagon train. Then jot down answers to your questions.

Writing Write a two-paragraph report about wagon train life. In the first paragraph tell facts about trail life. In the second paragraph write an interview summary.

Editing Use the check list and the editing symbols above to edit your two-paragraph report.

Unit Review

Write the verb in each sentence. If the verb names an action, write **action verb** after the verb. If the verb is a linking verb, write **linking verb** after the verb. *pages 226–227*

1. Gina works in a factory.
2. She is a machine operator.
3. They sell bread.
4. She twisted the dough.
5. It was sticky.
6. The bread is delicious.

Read each sentence. Write the word that follows the linking verb. (Do not count words such as *a, an, the, his, her,* or *their.*) If the word is a noun, write **noun.** If the word is an adjective, write **adjective.** Then write the word to which the noun or adjective is connected. *pages 228–229*

7. Bob is a secretary.
8. He is a typist.
9. Bob is happy.
10. Bob was busy.
11. The others were loud.
12. They were clerks.

Write the correct verb form of **is** or **are** for each sentence. *page 230*

13. Lee ___ a designer.
14. His customers ___ children.
15. Some clothes ___ fancy.
16. Some clothes ___ plain.
17. The shop ___ pretty.
18. Lee ___ a hard worker.

Write the word that is an antonym for the underlined word. *pages 232–233*

19. Carmen <u>placed</u> a sign in her window. (removed, repaired, put)
20. She <u>lowered</u> the curtains. (raised, shut, closed)
21. Then Carmen <u>locked</u> all the doors. (turned, opened, checked)
22. The next day she <u>began</u> her vacation. (started, left, ended)

Read each sentence in the story below. Decide if the verb should be in the present or past tense. Write the form of the verb **be** that belongs in each blank. *pages 236–237*

23. Bill ___ working as a page-turner now. (is, was)
24. He ___ washing dishes before. (is, was)
25. Bill ___ enjoying his new job now. (is, was)

Write each sentence. Add apostrophes in the correct place. Then write what each possessive or contraction means. *pages 238–239*

26. Rita directs the citys traffic.
27. Shes a good police officer.
28. She does not mind the many cars horns.
29. Weve seen her handle traffic jams.
30. The traffics running smoothly now.
31. Ritas job is an important one.
32. Janes an interpreter.
33. She interprets a speakers talk.
34. She gets many visitors attentions.
35. Theyre happy she is there.

Choose the verb in parentheses that most closely names the action. *pages 240–241*

36. Mickey quickly ___ each number in a row. (says, counts)
37. The other players ___ in all directions. (scatter, leave)
38. Mickey ___ the ball fast to Linda. (tosses, twirls)
39. The team ___ for the ball. (reaches, scrambles)

Write a two-paragraph report from the following topic sentences. *pages 246–251*

The topic sentence of the first paragraph: *My friends like to read different kinds of stories.* The topic sentence of the second paragraph: *It is important to be able to read.* Read these detail sentences. Write both paragraphs, using the topic and detail sentences you chose.

a. You may read an encyclopedia to learn different facts.
b. Four friends told me that they like books about animals.
c. Two friends like to read sports stories.
d. In a restaurant you need to read the menu.
e. One friend said he likes to read ghost stories.
f. Reading a newspaper tells you about world events.

A Ballad

One of the oldest forms of poetry is a ballad. A *ballad* is any story told in song. In the Middle Ages there were many poets who wandered through castles and villages singing ballads. Ballads usually introduce characters who are part of a situation. Often there is a problem to solve or some danger from which to escape. Because ballads tell a story and usually have a particular rhythm, they are also called *narrative poems*.

One of the most famous American ballads is *Casey Jones*. It tells the story of a man who made a brave sacrifice for others. The ballad was written in memory of a railroad engineer named John Luther Jones, better know as Casey Jones. In the spring of the year 1900, Casey saw that his mail train, called the *Cannonball,* was going to crash into two freight trains. He stayed on board to slow down the train. He gave his life to save the lives of his passengers.

Read the ballad about this brave man. Do you know the tune that goes with the poem?

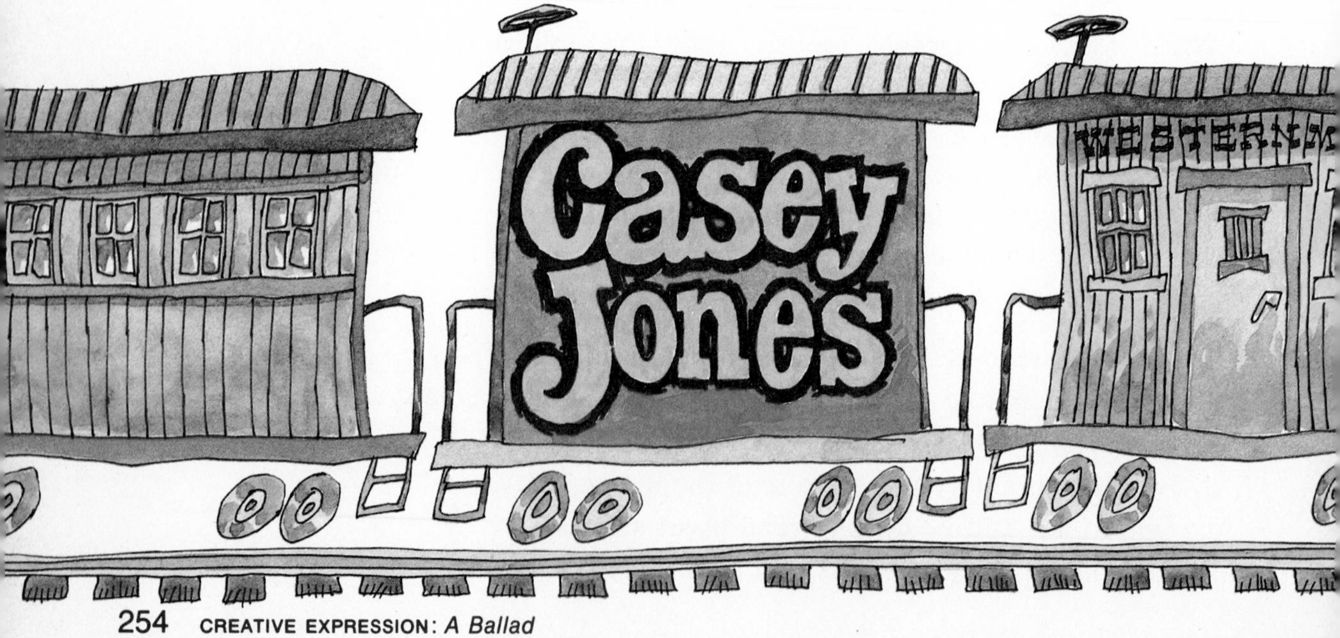

Come all you rounders if you want to hear
The story of a brave engineer;
Casey Jones was the hogger's name,
On a big eight-wheeler, boys, he won his fame.
Caller called Casey at half-past four,
He kissed his wife at the station door,
Mounted to the cabin with orders in his hand,
And took his farewell trip to the promised land.
Casey Jones, he mounted to the cabin,
Casey Jones, with his orders in his hand!
Casey Jones, he mounted to the cabin,
Took his farewell trip into the promised land.

"Put in your water and shovel in your coal,
Put your head out the window, watch the drivers roll,
I'll run her till she leaves the rail,
'Cause we're eight hours late with the Western Mail!"
He looked at his watch and his watch was slow,
Looked at the water and the water was low,
Turned to his fireboy and said,
"We'll get to 'Frisco, but we'll all be dead!"

Casey Jones, he mounted to the cabin,
Casey Jones, with his orders in his hand!
Casey Jones, he mounted to the cabin,
Took his farewell trip into the promised land.

Casey pulled up Reno Hill,
Tooted for the crossing with an awful shrill,
Snakes all knew by the engine's moans
That the hogger at the throttle was Casey Jones.
He pulled up short two miles from the place,
Number Four stared him right in the face,
Turned to his fireboy, said, "You'd better jump,
'Cause there's two locomotives that's going to bump."

Casey Jones, he mounted to the cabin,
Casey Jones, with his orders in his hand,
Casey Jones, he mounted to the cabin,
Took his farewell trip into the promised land.

Creative Activities

1. **Creative Writing** Imagine that you are a TV newscaster or a newspaper reporter. You are reporting the story of Casey Jones. Your report might start like this:

   > Yesterday near San Francisco tragedy struck on the railroad. John Luther Jones, better known as "Casey" to his friends, died in a train accident.

   Continue the rest of the news article. Add about six more sentences. Tell when, where, and how the accident occurred. Use the content of the ballad as information for your article. When you are finished, read the article to the class.
2. Read *Casey Jones* aloud as a choral reading. Three different class members can read the stanzas of eight lines each. The whole class can chant the refrain. The refrain is a group of lines that are repeated. Think about which lines could be read fast and which ones slower. Also think about which words should be read softly, and which ones should be read more forcefully.
3. Go to a library and find other ballads to read. *The Adventures of Robin Hood* is a famous ballad. You could also listen to ballads sung as songs on a record.
4. **Creative Writing** Choose a famous event from history. You might choose the discovery of America, the walk on the moon, or an historical character such as Joan of Arc. Think about who took part in the event. Also think about when, where, and how it happened. Try writing a ballad that tells the story. Introduce the characters and mention the most important details of the story. Later you can try to set your poem to music.

SOMEWHERE IN SPACE

8

Grammar and Related Language Skills

Adverbs
Adverbs That Compare
Formation of Adverbs
Review of Capital Letters

Practical Communication

STUDY AND REFERENCE SKILLS
Developing an Outline

COMPOSITION
Writing a News Story

Creative Expression

A True Story

Have you ever read a science fiction story about spaceships or imaginary satellites? People who decide what stories will be printed are called editors. Editors also correct and improve stories before they are printed. An editor often communicates with authors. What speaking skills does an editor need? What kinds of writing might an editor do?

Adverbs

Suppose someone asked you to tell about the things you do each day. You would need to use verbs to name the actions. You would also use words that describe the actions.

> An **adverb** is a word that describes an action.

An adverb may tell *how, when, where,* or *how often* an action is done.

- Look at these sentences. *Quickly* describes the action verb *worked,* and *slowly* describes the action verb *walked. Quickly* and *slowly* are adverbs. They tell *how* the action is done.

  Lucia worked quickly. The visitors walked slowly.

- Now read these sentences. *Early* describes the action verb *arrived. Later* describes the action verb *came. Early* and *later* are adverbs. They tell *when* the action is done.

  David Wang arrived early. Later the children came.

- Read these sentences. *Outdoors* describes the action verb *played. Nearby* describes *walked. Outdoors* and *nearby* are adverbs that tell *where* the action is done.

  The children played outdoors. Some adults walked nearby.

• Now read these sentences. In the first sentence *frequently* describes *shouted.* In the second sentence *once* describes *laughed. Frequently* and *once* tell *how often* the action is done. Both are adverbs.

The children frequently shouted. The adults laughed once.

Notice that many of the adverbs in the examples end in *-ly*. Look at the examples again. Which adverbs end in *-ly*?

Talk About It

What is the adverb in each sentence? Tell the word it describes.

1. David quietly disappeared.
2. The family clapped merrily.
3. The visitors talked excitedly.
4. They looked indoors.
5. They searched everywhere.
6. David often performs.

Skills Practice

Write each sentence. Underline each adverb. Then write the word it describes.

1. Neighbors came quickly.
2. They searched carefully.
3. Then Mr. Wang spoke.
4. A bell rang next.
5. Everyone listened curiously.
6. Mr. Wang softly whispered.
7. The baby smiled happily.
8. Mr. Brown phoned twice.
9. He arrived instantly.
10. The guests laughed merrily.
11. Nearby children played.
12. They called loudly.
13. He laughed happily.
14. The family called again.
15. David immediately returned.
16. Grandpa slept outdoors.
17. The rabbit sped away.
18. It rained regularly.
19. The people returned home.
20. My number came first.

Sample Answer 1. Neighbors came quickly. came

Using Adverbs to Compare

Sometimes you may describe an action by comparing it to another action. When you do, the adverb has a special form.

- Look at these sentences.

  Eddie walked <u>fast</u>.
  Susan walked <u>faster</u> than Eddie.
  Their mother walked <u>fastest</u> of all.

Add *-er* to one-syllable adverbs when comparing two actions. Add *-est* to one-syllable adverbs when comparing more than two actions.

- Look at these sentences.

  Eddie May ran <u>quickly</u> to the window.
  His sister ran <u>more quickly</u> than Eddie.
  Mrs. May ran <u>most quickly</u> of all.

In each sentence, *quickly* is an adverb describing the verb *ran*. The second sentence uses *more quickly* because two actions are compared. The third sentence uses *most quickly* because more than two actions are compared. Use *more* before most adverbs ending in *-ly* when comparing two actions. Use *most* before most adverbs ending in *-ly* when comparing more than two actions.

Remember that if an adverb already has an *-er* or *-est* ending, do NOT use *more* or *most* before the adverb.

RIGHT: Eddie went *nearer* to the UFO than Susan.
WRONG: Eddie went *more nearer* to the UFO than Susan.

RIGHT: Mrs. May went *nearest* of all to the UFO.
WRONG: Mrs. May went *most nearest* of all to the UFO.

Talk About It

Read each sentence. Use **-er, -est, more,** or **most** to make the correct form of the adverb.

1. I hid ___ in the grass than my friend. (low)
2. The blue creatures squealed the ___ of all. (loud)
3. The creatures walked ___ than I. (slowly)
4. The first UFO landed ___ than the second. (quickly)
5. The second UFO zoomed ___ than the others. (high)
6. The third UFO landed the ___ of all. (swiftly)

Skills Practice

Write each sentence below. Use **-er, -est, more,** or **most** to make the correct form of the adverb.

1. The first UFO dug ___ than the second. (deep)
2. The third UFO landed ___ to us. (near)
3. It braked ___ of them all. (late)
4. The second UFO bounced ___ than the first. (hard)
5. The red creatures walked ___ than the blue ones. (fast)
6. The creatures behaved ___ than the humans. (politely)
7. The second pilot acted ___ than the first pilot. (friendly)
8. The humans asked questions ___ than the creatures. (often)
9. I think I can run ___ than they can. (fast)
10. The third pilot whispered the ___ of all. (softly)

Writing Sentences

Suppose you saw a movie about a UFO. Describe what the creatures in the UFO might be doing.

1. Write two sentences with adverbs ending in *-er* or *-est*.
2. Write two sentences with *more* or *most* before the adverb.

Sample Answer 1. The first UFO dug deeper than the second.

Forming Adverbs from Adjectives

You know that an adjective describes a person, place, or thing. Some adjectives can be made into adverbs. The form of the adjective must be changed.

clever   clever + ly = cleverly
Albert Ostman escaped *cleverly* from strange animals.

Add **-ly** to some adjectives to form an adverb.

- Notice how these words change from adjectives to adverbs.

final	wild	main	thick
finally	wildly	mainly	thickly

Sometimes an adjective must be changed before *-ly* is added.

busy   busi + ly = busily
Ostman was searching *busily* for gold in Canada.

Change **y** to **i** and add **-ly** to form an adverb from an adjective that ends in **y**.

- Notice how these words change from adjectives to adverbs.

happy	heavy	jerky	tricky
happily	heavily	jerkily	trickily

Talk About It

Change each adjective to an adverb. Tell how the adverb is formed.

1. Albert Ostman was hunting ___ for gold in Canada. (eager)
2. A hairy thing called Sasquatch grabbed Ostman ___ in his sleep. (sudden)
3. The large animal carried his prize ___ in a sack. (easy)
4. Ostman kicked ___, but he could not escape. (wild)

Skills Practice

Change each adjective to an adverb. Write the new sentence.

1. Ostman rode ___ in the sack for a long time. (unhappy)
2. The Sasquatch ___ lowered the bag. (final)
3. Ostman looked ___ around him. (careful)
4. Four large Sasquatch stood ___ in the mountains. (excited)
5. They spoke ___ with one another. (loud)
6. Ostman searched ___ for the way out. (wild)
7. Ostman ___ found that he was trapped. (sad)
8. He lived ___ with the Sasquatch for a week. (helpless)
9. He waited ___ for a chance to escape. (patient)
10. One day they went ___ for water. (quick)
11. Ostman moved ___ from the camp. (hurried)
12. Ostman escaped ___ through the mountains. (merry)
13. Today some people search ___ for Sasquatch. (curious)

Writing Sentences

Imagine you are telling about your search for Sasquatch.

Write four sentences with adverbs ending in *-ly*.

Sample Answers 1. Ostman rode unhappily in the sack for a long time.
2. The Sasquatch finally lowered the bag.

Skills Review

Write the adverb in each sentence. Then write the word it describes.

1. The Bermuda Triangle frequently confuses people.
2. Airplanes disappear suddenly.
3. Five planes left smoothly on a trip.
4. They flew together.
5. The planes quickly traveled.
6. The pilots flew happily.
7. Then a strange thing happened.
8. The head pilot called wildly.
9. His sense of direction disappeared completely.
10. The plane acted crazily.

Read each sentence. Add **-er, -est, more,** or **most** to make the correct form of the adverb.

11. Our spaceship flew ___ than ever. (fast)
12. Jim and I drove ___ than before. (long)
13. Jim was nervous and spoke the ___ of all. (excitedly)
14. I whispered ___ than Jim. (quietly)
15. One planet shone the ___ of all. (bright)
16. The creatures there grew ___ than giants. (tall)
17. The creatures behaved ___ than lambs. (kindly)
18. One creature came ___ than the others. (near)
19. This creature reached out ___ than the people. (slowly)
20. It spoke the ___ of all the creatures. (loud)
21. My mind thought ___ than before. (calmly)
22. My heart beat ___ than ever. (quick)
23. Jim breathed the ___ of all. (hard)
24. The creature smiled the ___ of all. (friendly)
25. I wondered ___ of all about the future. (anxiously)

Change each adjective to an adverb. Write the new adverb.

26. On vacation we looked ___ for the Mystery Spot. (curious)
27. After a long drive we ___ found it. (final)
28. We ___ got out of the car. (happy)
29. The Mystery Spot snuggled ___ in the woods. (cozy)
30. A printed sign hung ___ overhead. (loose)
31. It told ___ the Mystery Spot's history. (plain)
32. Weird things occur ___ to people there. (mysterious)
33. Strange things ___ frightened us. (unexpected)
34. Vines and plants crept ___ over the paths. (wild)
35. Loud noises scared us ___. (sudden)
36. We shall ___ return to the Mystery Spot. (definite)
37. We will remember ___ our visit to the place. (fond)
38. Our decorated souvenirs remind us ___. (easy)

Have you ever written a Tom Swifty? What is it, you say? A Tom Swifty is a sentence in which the adverb makes a joke. Here are some examples:

"Where are all the sick people?" said the doctor *patiently.*
"I need to sharpen my pencil," said Linda *pointlessly.*
"Please buy me a pony," said Mary *hoarsely.*
Now try to think up your own Tom Swifties.

Exploring Language

Reviewing Capitalization

It is important to remember the special times when a word needs to be capitalized.

Use a **capital letter** to begin the first word of every sentence.

Have you heard about the giant animal?
Some people believe it lives in a lake.

Use a **capital letter** to begin each important word of a proper noun. A proper noun is a noun that names a special person, place, thing, or idea.

Mr. John Mackay lived on Fifth Avenue in New York City.
Mr. Mackay saw the giant animal in a large lake in Scotland.
The thing is called the Loch Ness Monster.
One was reported in the Lake of the Seven Glaciers.

Use a **capital letter** to begin the names of the months and days of the week.

John Mackay visited Scotland in May.
He camped by the lake on Monday and Tuesday.

Use a **capital letter** for each initial in a person's name. Use a **period** (.) after an initial.

Honey T. Williams read about this monster.

Use a **capital letter** to begin each important word in a book title. Always begin the first word of a title with a capital letter.

Luisa read a book called The Monster in the Lake.
Helen enjoyed the short story, "Strange Creature."

Words in a book title should be underlined when you write them. Words in the title of a short story or poem should be in quotation marks.

Talk About It

Tell each word in each sentence that should begin with a capital letter.

1. the lake in loch ness is twice as deep as the north sea.
2. a police officer says he saw the animal in 1933.
3. mr. john mackay saw it on a tuesday.
4. in july, some people from london saw the thing.

Skills Practice

Write each word in each sentence that should begin with a capital letter.

1. sir edward mountain took his camera to scotland.
2. the strange animal has been talked about often.
3. people on a bus saw the thing on a wednesday.
4. a fishing boat was crossing the lake in december.
5. in 1958, the loch ness monster made a noise.
6. a broadcasting company from britain heard it.
7. a group of scientists from japan studied the animal in 1974.
8. lieutenant commander t. r. gould thinks it is something from the early days of the world.
9. dr. m. barton wrote a book called the monster of loch ness.
10. dr. barton lives on first avenue.

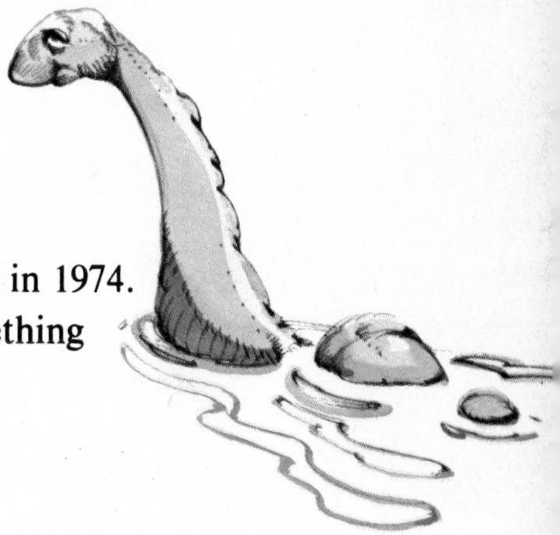

Writing Sentences

Decide which words should begin with a capital letter. Write each sentence correctly.

1. Write two sentences in which someone's name is capitalized.
2. Write two sentences in which the name of a place is capitalized.
3. Write two sentences in which a day or a month is capitalized.

Sample Answer **1.** Sir Edward Mountain took his camera to Scotland.

Homographs

Did you ever see twin brothers or sisters who dressed alike? They look the same, but the two people are still different in many ways. Words can also look alike and still be different. Sometimes two words can be spelled the same way, but the words have different meanings. Sometimes these words even have different pronunciations. They are called *homographs*.

- Read the sentences below. Notice the underlined words.

  The scientist took a rose from the garden.
  She rose from her chair and left.

Both sentences use the word *rose*. The words are spelled and pronounced the same way, but they have different meanings. In the first sentence *rose* means *a flower*. In the second sentence *rose* means *stood up*. You need to read the whole sentence to know which meaning is used.

- Now look at these sentences. Notice the underlined words.

  A strong wind blew out the fire.
  It is time for me to wind my watch.

Both sentences use the word *wind*. The words are spelled alike, but they are pronounced differently. They also have different meanings. *Wind* in the first sentence rhymes with *pinned*. It means *air that is moving*. *Wind* in the second sentence rhymes with *find*. It means *tighten the spring of*.

Talk About It

Read each sentence. Tell your answer to the questions that follow it.

1. The scientist turned on the **light** and lifted a **light** box.
   Which word means *not heavy*?
   Which word means *something that lets you see*?
2. Dr. Forbes will **lead** me to a piece of **lead**.
   Which word sounds like *need*? Which word sounds like *bed*?

Skills Practice

Two sentences with underlined words are followed by two meanings. Write the letter of the correct meaning next to each number.

1. Dr. Forbes lost her <u>left</u> shoe. **2.** The scientist <u>left</u> the room.
a. went out of **b.** the opposite of right

3. A lamp stood <u>close</u> to the door. **4.** Please <u>close</u> the door.
a. shut **b.** near

5. The child opened a <u>chest</u>. **6.** I put an apron over my <u>chest</u>.
a. trunk **b.** part of body

Read the sentences. Next to the number of each sentence, write the letter of the rhyme that matches the underlined word.

7. A <u>live</u> rabbit hopped from the chest. **8.** A box is a funny place to <u>live</u>.
a. sounds like dive **b.** sounds like give

9. The rabbit made a <u>tear</u> in my coat. **10.** A <u>tear</u> ran from my eye.
a. sounds like near **b.** sounds like care

11. The scientist put a <u>bow</u> on the rabbit.

12. The scientist tried to <u>bow</u> very low.
a. sounds like go **b.** sounds like now

Sample Answers 1. b **7.** a

Understanding Words from Context

The meaning of words is important when you read and write. To find the meaning of a word, you may do three things. You may ask someone. You may look up the word in a dictionary. You may figure out the meaning by thinking about the other words in the sentence.

- Read the following sentences.

> Workers put up a new traffic light. The light is at the intersection of Ash Street and Madison Avenue.

Suppose you do not know the meaning of *intersection.* Notice the words *traffic light* in the sentence. Where do you usually find a traffic light? You usually find it where two roads cross. Therefore, *intersection* means a place where two roads cross.

Sometimes the meaning of a new word is not clear. The other words in the sentence do not help you. Then you have to read the sentence that comes before or after. Sometimes you have to read several sentences. These sentences may help you understand the new word.

- Read the following sentences.

> Last year we painted our whole house. During the winter we painted the inside of the house. When the warm weather came, we painted the exterior.

Suppose the new word is *exterior.* The first sentence tells you that the whole house was painted. The second sentence tells you that the inside was painted. What part of the house was left to paint? You can figure out that *exterior* means *outside.*

Talk About It

Read each of the following sentences carefully. Try to figure out the meaning of each underlined word.

1. The snow and sleet made driving very hazardous.
2. The helicopter pilot took an aerial picture of the city.
3. Our team is in competition with two others for the prize.
4. The noise was a disturbance to the readers in the library.

Skills Practice

Write the underlined word in each sentence. Then write what you think each underlined word means.

1. I could see the luminous numbers on my watch in the dark.
2. We saw the moon emerge from behind the clouds.
3. The fragile glass broke even though she moved it carefully.
4. You need light, water, and soil to nourish plants and trees.
5. I grow all my own food. I do not depend on buying it at the market.
6. Dishes and furniture shook from the vibrations of the earthquake.
7. A garbage truck turned over and spread debris everywhere.
8. The library had too many books. It gave the surplus books away.

Writing Sentences

Use the dictionary to check the meanings of the underlined words in the Skills Practice activity. Then write your own sentence using each word. The other words in the sentence should give clues to the meaning of the word.

Sample Answer 1. luminous—glowing with light

Levels of Usage

When you speak or write, you have many ways to say the same thing. You must select words to fit certain situations. You might say to a friend:

"Want to eat chow at my house?"

However, suppose you are writing to ask your grandmother to dinner. Then you might write:

"Would you like to come to dinner at our house?"

When addressing friends in everyday situations, you often use everyday words. At other times you choose your words more carefully.

- Look at the pictures. Which picture shows a situation where you would use everyday language? Which picture shows a situation where you would want to choose words more carefully?

- Read the sentences. Which pair of sentences would you use in each of the situations pictured?

"Thank you very much. This is a great honor."
"Hey, thanks a lot. These are really super."

- Here are some other special kinds of situations when you may want to choose your words carefully:

  You are talking to some people at your mother's office.
  You are speaking to a judge to arrange a class visit to the city court.
  You are writing a letter to your town newspaper.
  You are applying for a job in your neighborhood.

Talk About It

Read the pairs of words and phrases below. Which might you hear on the school bus? Which might be used for more special situations?

1. Let's take off.
   It is time to leave.
2. This is a nice surprise!
   Wow! What a treat!
3. Have a seat.
   Please sit down.
4. Want to tag along?
   Would you like to join us?
5. What's the story?
   What happened?
6. Please call me.
   Give me a buzz.

Practice interviewing for a job. Choose the job you want:

newspaper delivery   salesperson   lawn mowing

Be sure to use the kind of language that will help you get the job. Which of the sentences below might you use in your speech? Which would you avoid?

My past experience qualifies me for this job.
Would you believe my experience?
I'm always right on top of things.
I have a good sense of responsibility.
Cheap rates.
My rates are reasonable.

Skills Review

Write the words in each sentence that should begin with a capital.

1. mr. ramirez told us about the bermuda triangle.
2. he said there were often strong winds near florida.
3. last july mr. ramirez and dr. baker visited miami beach.
4. captain lowell talked to the visitors in august.
5. the missing planes and boats might disappear in storms.
6. captain lowell sent me a book called the bermuda triangle.

Two sentences with underlined words are followed by two meanings. Write the letter of the correct meaning next to each number.

7. The inventor could not bear our picnic. **8.** A bear ate our lunch.
 a. a large animal **b.** put up with

9. A spoke on my bicycle broke. **10.** The inventor spoke angrily.
 a. part of a wheel **b.** talked

11. A bat flew into our cave. **12.** My bat hit the ball.
 a. baseball stick **b.** animal.

13. The date was June 26. **14.** The baker put a date in the dough.
 a. fruit **b.** time

15. The dog with us was mine. **16.** The dog visited an old gold mine.
 a. belongs to me **b.** place where gold is found

17. The brown bark fell off. **18.** Dogs bark all day.
 a. dog noises **b.** tree covering

19. The weather was fair. **20.** Later our group went to a fair.
 a. kind of market **b.** nice

Read each sentence. Write the underlined words. Then write what you think each underlined word means.

21. The flood did a lot of damage in our town. Many houses were ruined.
22. No one could make any sound. Retta put her hand to her mouth to stifle a laugh.

23. People who read a lot are enlightened on many subjects.
24. You always lag behind and are always the last one at school.
25. We watched the kite ascend high into the sky.
26. Kim was lost. She inquired how far the next town was.
27. Carlo could not find his missing gloves. He had to rummage through the closet until he found them.
28. How can you write with that pencil? The point is too blunt. You need to sharpen it.
29. Chris did not know what he would do the next day. He pondered the problem all night.
30. It is customary for us to spend the Fourth of July with our grandparents. It is unusual to spend this holiday alone.
31. We rent our house from the landlord.
32. Mr. Rivera stepped hard on the brakes. His car came to an abrupt stop.
33. Timmy does not go to school alone. His sister and brother accompany him.

Careers

Very few people will ever have an opportunity to travel in space. However, many *aerospace engineers* work to make space travel safe and successful. Engineers plan and develop space vehicles and land equipment. Engineers design living quarters for astronauts that are comfortable and efficient.

An *aerospace engineer* is one of many career opportunities in the field of *engineering*. Students who enjoy mathematics and science may find this a challenging career.

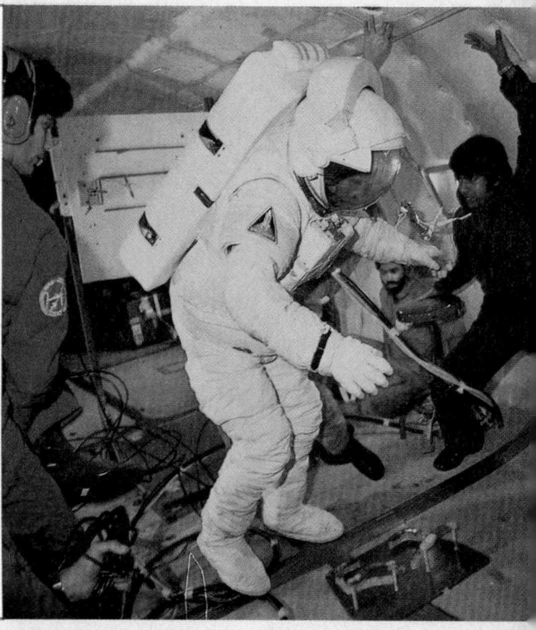

Developing a Two-Part Outline

A good report starts with careful planning. First you choose your main idea. Then you gather information and take notes. Finally you make an outline. The *outline* is your plan for arranging your ideas into paragraphs.

● Read this outline.

Fur Traders in America

I. Fur traders in the West
   A. Found new lands
   B. Found new routes for pioneers
II. Fur traders in the mountains
   A. Called mountain men
   B. Learned many Indian skills

● Look again at the parts of this outline.

1. The main idea is shown in the title.
2. Roman numerals identify the main headings of an outline. Develop these main headings into the topic sentences for your paragraph.

   Fur traders were the first explorers in the American West.

3. Put a period after the Roman numeral for each main heading.
4. Capital letters identify the subheadings of an outline. Develop these subheadings into the detail sentences for the paragraphs in your report.

   They found many new lands as they traveled west.

5. Put a period after the capital letter for each subheading.
6. Notice that the main headings and subheadings in this outline are written in phrases. Sentences can be used instead of phrases in an outline.

Talk About It

Read the outline again about fur traders.

1. What is the main idea of the report? How did you know?
2. What is the first heading? How are the subheadings related to the main heading?
3. What is the second heading? How are the subheadings related to the main heading?
4. Is the outline written in sentences or phrases?

Skills Practice

Read the following two-paragraph report.

The Moon

The moon is a natural satellite that travels around the earth. It has no light of its own. It seems to change as different parts are lighted by the sun. It appears to have no life.

The moon's surface is covered with craters. Scientists think there may be half a million craters that are over a mile wide. Some are called <u>ray craters</u> because they have light gray streaks known as rays. Others are called <u>secondary craters</u> because they were formed by rocks thrown out of the ray craters.

Review the parts to an outline. Write an outline for this report using the following steps:

1. Write the title of the outline.
2. Write this first heading and subheading:
   I. Travels around the earth
      A. No light of its own
3. Write two more subheadings after this first heading.
4. Write the second main heading.
5. Write two subheadings under the heading.

Outlining a Two-Paragraph Report

Thinking About Outlines

The key to writing a good report is *planning*. You prepare to write about your main idea by gathering information from reference works and from interviews. You should take notes about the important facts so that you can remember the information. Your notes should try to put the main ideas into your own words. You can use sentences or phrases. Then you can be sure that you understand the facts that you are writing.

After you have taken your notes, the next step is to write a plan for your report. The *outline* is your plan. It helps you arrange your ideas so that they make sense. When you write a two-paragraph outline, you must think about these questions:

1. What is the main idea of the two-paragraph report?
2. What are the main topics for each paragraph?
3. What information will be in the report?
4. How will you arrange that information?

● Read this outline for a report. Note that Roman numerals list the main headings, and the capital letters list the subheadings.

Unidentified Flying Object

I. UFO's as strange sights in the sky
    A. Saucer shapes
    B. Flying patterns of UFO's
    C. Strange effects on animals
II. Many reports on UFO's since World War II
    A. Air Force and 12,000 reports
    B. Unexplained reports
    C. Flying saucers and some groups

Talking About Outlines

Look again at the outline.

1. What is the main idea of the outline? How do you know?

2. What are the two main headings in the outline? How do you know that these are the main headings?
3. What subheadings are listed under each topic? Why are capital letters used? Why are these subheadings indented?

Using An Outline

Read the outline again. You are going to write a two-paragraph report using that outline. Read the sentences below. Match the sentences with the main heading and subheadings in the first part of the outline. Write the sentences in a paragraph.

1. UFO's are strange sights in the sky.
2. Most reports say that UFO's can fly very fast or float near the ground.
3. People claim UFO's make animals act strangely.
4. People report that they have saucer shapes and glow brightly.

Match these sentences with the main heading and subheadings in the second part of the outline. Write these sentences in a paragraph.

1. Thousands of people from many countries have reported seeing UFO's since World War II.
2. That study and others explained most, but not all, of the reports.
3. The Air Force *Project Blue Book* was a study of more than 12,000 UFO reports.
4. Some groups insist that flying saucers really exist.

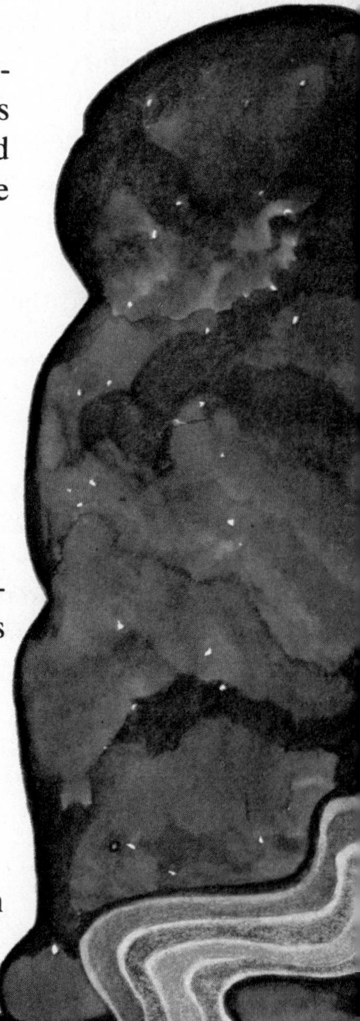

A Class Outline

Thinking About an Outline

Your class is going to write an outline together. The outline will help you to plan a two-paragraph report that will use facts. The report will be about science projects that could be shown at science fairs and school programs. First an encyclopedia will be used to research the main idea of a science project. Then a student will be interviewed about a science project. The notes from the reference work and from the interview will be used to make the outline.

- Read the notes taken in phrases about science projects.

Library Notes

-models and experiments done by students
-planning and doing can take days or months
-report prepared and project shown at science fair
-report must tell what was learned and how it was done

- Read the notes taken from an interview with a science student.

Interview Questions	*Interview Notes*
	Janet Katz. December 1, 19__
1. What is your science project about?	*- precipitation*
2. What are some different types of precipitation?	*-rain, snow, sleet, hailstones*
3. What will be in your report?	*-chart of types of water and the temperatures needed to make them*
4. What is your experiment?	*-to make rain in a jar*

Writing an Outline

Study the library and interview notes. Your class will use them to write a class outline. Your teacher or a student should write the headings and subheadings of the outline on the board.

1. The title of the report is "Science Projects." It is the main idea of the report. Write it at the top of the board.
2. Look at the library notes. The topic for the first main heading of your outline is: I. A science project
3. Read the library notes. Use the library notes for the subheadings in the first part of your outline. The first subheading could be: A. Activities for a science project.
4. Now your outline should look like this:

   I. A science project

   A. Activities for a science project
5. Use the library notes to write two more subheadings for this part of your outline. Remember to use only important facts and combine them when possible.
6. Look at the interview notes. The topic for the second main heading of your outline is: II. Janet Katz's science project.
7. Use the interview notes to write the subheadings in the second part of your outline. The first subheading could be: A. Topic of project.
8. Use the other interview notes to write two more subheadings. Remember to combine facts when possible.

Practicing a Two-Paragraph News Report

Thinking About News Reports

One kind of two-paragraph report is found in the newspaper. A news article is a report that gives information about a subject of current interest. A news reporter follows these steps in preparing a news article.

1. Chooses the main idea.
2. Gathers information from reference works and interviews.
3. Takes notes.
4. Makes an outline.
5. Writes the report.

Writing a News Report

Write a news article about science projects. Reread the library and interview notes in the last lesson. Look at your class outline. Use it to write a two-paragraph report.

1. Write a topic sentence using the first main heading from the outline. Then use the subheadings to write detail sentences about science projects in general.
2. Write a topic sentence using the second main heading from the outline. Then use the subheadings to write detail sentences about Janet Katz's specific project.

Edit Your Report

1. Do the paragraphs tell about the main idea of the report?
2. Is the topic sentence in each paragraph based on the main headings in the outline?
3. Are the detail sentences in each paragraph based on the subheadings in the outline?
4. Did you use interesting adverbs to describe actions?
5. Did you indent each paragraph?
6. Did you use correct punctuation and capitalization?
7. Did you spell the words correctly?

Editing Symbols

- ≡ capitalize
- ¶ indent
- ℘ take out
- ^ add

An Oral Report

Follow these steps in giving an oral report:

1. Write the report using your notes and outline.
2. Practice reading your report aloud in front of a mirror or read it to a friend. You could also tape-record the report.
3. Begin your report with an interesting sentence to capture the attention of your audience.
4. Use pictures, charts, or maps to add interest to the report.
5. Look directly at your audience.
6. Speak clearly and loudly enough to be heard by the audience. Use your voice to make the report interesting.
7. End with an interesting sentence.
8. Ask for questions from the audience.

INDEPENDENT WRITING

A Two-Paragraph Historical Report

Prewriting Information about people long ago can be interesting. Think of a famous event in the history of our country. Imagine you were there. Maybe you were a reporter at the Boston Tea Party. Perhaps you wrote an article about a slave escaping with Harriet Tubman. Plan a news report you might write about your adventure. Research information. Take notes. Then make an outline to use in writing paragraphs in your report.

Writing Write a two-paragraph report describing the famous historical event. Use your outline to write the body of your report. Check the report form on page 62.

Editing Use the check questions and editing symbols on page 284 to edit your letter.

Unit Review

Write the adverb in each sentence and the word it describes. *pages 260–261*

1. Della rode slowly.
2. She often sang.
3. She laughed once.
4. She looked carefully.
5. A light shone brightly.
6. It moved closer.
7. Della stood stiffly.
8. She watched silently.
9. The light traveled smoothly.
10. Soon it arrived.
11. Its beam shone everywhere.
12. People gathered around.
13. Then a voice spoke.
14. It talked softly.
15. The people listened gladly.
16. Della nodded happily.

Read each sentence. Use **-er, -est, more,** or **most** to make the correct form of the adverb. *pages 262–263*

17. Janet rode ___ than ever. (fast)
18. Her breath came ___ than before. (hard)
19. Pam drove ___ than Janet. (carefully)
20. Rita drove the car the ___ of all. (carefully)
21. Her car traveled the ___ of all. (slowly)
22. The horn on Pam's car blared the ___ of all the cars. (loud)
23. Her car's engine purred ___ than Rita's engine. (quietly)
24. Rita's car took ___ to start than Pam's. (long)
25. Even the bus travels ___ than Rita's car. (rapidly)
26. A train travels ___ than a bus. (rapidly)
27. Mike got started ___ than the others. (late)
28. He arrived ___ than he expected. (soon)
29. The children behaved ___ than the adults. (quietly)
30. Kim sat the ___ of all the children. (patiently)

Change each adjective to an adverb. Write the adverb. *pages 264–265*

31. Della talked ___. (curious)
32. She ate ___. (light)
33. She slept ___. (poor)
34. She woke ___. (lazy)
35. It arrived ___. (strange)
36. Its voice spoke ___. (nice)
37. It left ___. (quick)
38. Mike laughed ___. (happy)

Unit Review

Write each word or letter in each sentence that should begin with a capital letter. *pages 268–269*

39. della montelone and mike stevens told their story to dr. bean.
40. della spotted another light near talcott street in bloomsdale.
41. they read a book called strange airships from outer space.

Two sentences with underlined words are followed by two meanings. Write the letter of the correct meaning. *pages 270–271*

42. Leonardo worked fast. **43.** On Sundays there was a fast.
(a) quickly (b) time without food

44. The duke's page wore a cap. **45.** Leonardo drew on each page.
(a) part of a notebook (b) helper to carry messages

Read each sentence. Write the underlined word in each. Then write what you think each underlined word means. *pages 272–273*

46. Jan won a scholarship. Now she has money to go to school.
47. My brother is thrifty. He doesn't waste his money.
48. My sister knows monetary matters. She handles all questions about money.

Below on the left is the outline for a two-paragraph report. On the right are sentences for the report. The sentences are not in the right order. Put them in the correct order by following the outline. Then write both paragraphs. *pages 284–285*

I. Forms of energy	**1.** It lets us travel quickly.
A. Gas	**2.** Gas is one type of energy.
B. Coal	**3.** We also depend on the sun for energy.
C. Sun	**4.** It also gives us light to see.
II. Uses of energy	**5.** Energy comes in many forms.
A. Travel	**6.** Much of our energy is from coal.
B. Heat	**7.** Energy supplies the heat we need.
C. Light	**8.** Energy has many valuable uses.

A True Story

Writers often try to use experiences in their personal lives as ideas for stories. This story is true. The author remembers an experience as a child in Kansas in the 1930 s.

PRAIRIE BLIZZARD

When I was a child in western Kansas, there were no school buses. On windy wintery days, if Dad didn't have to work on the farm machinery, he drove me. On other days, I walked the mile and a half to the one-room schoolhouse.

Because there was no windmill nor well near the school, the fathers took turns hauling water. This was Dad's week. After he emptied the five gallon can into the school fountain, he said, "I don't like the looks of the weather. We may have a blizzard before dark."

A chill ran down my backbone, as I watched Dad's car move along the flat straight road toward town.

I walked into the school-house just in time to see Leroy pick up my lunch pail. Leroy was an eighth grader and the biggest boy in school. He had strong hands and a face that turned hard and ugly when he twisted someone's arms to make them do what he said. He probably wanted to hide my lunch, but when he saw me, he just grinned, said, "Hi, Georgia," and set the pail on a cupboard shelf.

Miss Talcott rang the bell to call her twelve pupils in from the first recess. By this time a northwind was howling around the building. She sent Leroy and then one of the Reece boys out with a bucket to get more coal for the big round stove. And she pulled down the window shades on the north side of the room to keep out some of the cold wind. This made it darker inside.

The clouds got thicker. Soon it started to snow. It was a fine stinging snow that burned and froze my face. The snow was blowing so hard that you couldn't even see the schoolhouse. Why couldn't there be at least a few trees to break the wind?

Miss Talcott said we weren't going to have an afternoon recess. Then she looked at her watch and out into the storm in a worried way. "To make up for no recess, I'll let school out early at a quarter to four."

The fire roared, but the schoolhouse was getting cold as the storm grew worse. Suddenly there was a loud pounding on the school door. Miss Talcott jumped, and so did the rest of us. No one had heard a car outside. Maybe it was a tramp.

The bigger Reece boy went to the window and peered into the storm. He said, "There ain't no car out there."

Miss Talcott didn't even bother to correct his speech. More pounding shook the door of the dim room. She went to the stove and picked up the iron poker. Then, in a strange voice, she said, "Leroy, come with me to the door."

In the past, Leroy's swagger had always made me feel scared. But now I was glad that he looked almost as strong as a man as he stomped to the back of the room after Miss Talcott and opened the door.

Mr. Reece, whose farm was about a half mile from school, came in stamping his feet and brushing snow off his red, wind-burned face. He took a big pack from his shoulders, got out some blankets, and said, "I walked up here to tell you kids that the blizzard's getting so bad nobody can see to drive. Georgia's dad called me on the phone. He barely made it home from town. He says you kids aren't supposed to try walking home. Most of you would have to walk against the wind. I had a hard enough time getting here with the wind at my back. You'll have to stay in the schoolhouse all night."

At three in the afternoon, it was almost dark. How could a blizzard of white snow make the day black?

Mr. Reece told Leroy and his two boys to put on their coats. Leroy picked up the coal bucket, and Mr. Reece and the boys went outside. Because of the howling storm, we couldn't see what they were doing. But Mr. Reece had said they would stand at arms' length from each other so that no one would get lost between the school building and the coal shed. By passing the bucket from hand to hand, they brought in a lot of coal and dumped it beside the stove. When the snow from the coal melted, dirty blobs of inky

water lay on the wood floor.

Mr. Reece said, "I'm going to take my boys home. Leroy, I want you to behave yourself and help Miss Talcott take care of the little kids. If the blizzard eases off after a while, Georgia's dad will come over on horseback and bring more blankets and something to eat."

A shaky feeling came around me when the door closed behind Mr. Reece and his two boys. I couldn't help thinking about what had happened last year along the road to town. Three children, the oldest in high school, had been driving home during a blizzard. Their car got stuck, and they tried to walk home—less than a mile. But the snow had drifted so deep and the wind blew so hard that finally they sank down exhausted.

Dad always said, "They ought to have stayed in the car. They could have sat close together to keep from freezing. Else they should have kept each other going. If you don't want to freeze to death in a blizzard, you've got to keep moving."

I squeezed closer to the big stove. My front got warm, but my back felt colder than ever.

Leroy put on his coat and said, "I'm going out and get some snow to melt, so we'll have something to drink."

He brought in a big heap of snow and put it in the pan Miss Talcott used for making her coffee at noon. The snow melted down into only a little bit of water. Leroy fought his way out into the storm and got more snow and still more. Bits of it clung to his face like soft fuzz.

Miss Talcott made as much coffee as she could in the small pan, putting in lots of sugar. Then she poured a trickle in each of our thermos bottle cups. I had never liked coffee, but drinking something warm made my stomach feel a little better.

Soon the coffee and the sugar were used up. Nothing warm was left to drink and nothing at all to eat. The winds howled louder. Never before had there been enough time for Miss Talcott to read as much from the Tom Swift book as we wanted to hear. Tonight there was too much time.

At last Miss Talcott said, "We'll put the blankets on the floor near the stove. The littlest children can lie down on them and cover up with their coats and go to sleep."

One of the first graders cried, "I want Mamma." He cried the words over and over until I almost felt like crying too.

Miss Talcott took him on her lap and told the rest of us to sing softly together. Finally he fell asleep, and Miss Talcott put him on one of the seats. We tried lying down on the floor but were soon shivering.

Leroy pushed some desk benches toward the stove, and we used them to lie on. I knew I would never be able to fall asleep. My coat wouldn't cover my shoulders and my feet at the same time. My stomach was a big empty cave, and my bones felt as though they were pushing down through my sore skin to touch the hard bench.

After a long while, I asked Miss Talcott what time it was. "Nine o'clock," she whispered.

The wind rattled the windows fiercely. The room was completely dark except for a little glow from the stove.

Suddenly there came a loud pounding on the door. I squeezed tight against the wooden bench until I heard my father's gruff voice outside. He had come to the schoolhouse on horseback, bringing a big can of chocolate milk with marshmallows

melted on top, three loaves of fresh bread, and some blankets.

Miss Talcott reheated the chocolate on the stove. Those of us who were still awake ate as much as we wanted. After that, we fell asleep.

I woke up to see sunlight streaming in the windows. I ran over and looked out. The whole country was white and wonderful, with drifts of snow glistening like silver stars all over the flat fields.

I climbed up on the horse behind Dad. We waved at Leroy and the others. Then we rode off over the fresh crunchy snow. I was so excited, I felt sure I could have walked all the way home without getting the least bit tired. Mother gave me a bearhug, and I gave Dick one. Breakfast smelled delicious. But before I sat down, I ran over to the window and looked out at the sparkling country again. Everything was so beautiful.

Louise Budde DeLaurentis

Creative Activities

1. ''Prairie Blizzard'' taught you many things about life in western Kansas in the 1930's. Here is one fact that you learned from the story: Some schools used a well or windmill to get their water. Compare this fact to your life today. Divide a paper into two parts. List on one side of your chart facts about life in the 1930's. On the other side compare the facts to your life now.
2. **Creative Writing** You can learn more about life in years past by interviewing your parents, grandparents, or other adults. Ask them to describe the biggest changes that they have seen since they were children. Write the answers you receive. Later you can read your interview to the class.

SIBERIAN TIGER

9

Grammar and Related Language Skills

Review of Compound Subjects and Predicates
Compound Sentences
Sentence Building
Prepositions and Prepositional Phrases

Practical Communication

STUDY AND REFERENCE SKILLS
Using the Dictionary

COMPOSITION
Writing a Story
Writing a Book Report

Creative Expression

A Story

Have you ever photographed a wild animal, such as a squirrel or a lizard? Some professional photographers travel around the world to take pictures of particular wild animals. What wild animals would you like to photograph? Where would you go to find the animals? What listening and speaking skills would help you succeed?

Reviewing Compound Subjects and Predicates

Every sentence has a subject part and a predicate part. The *subject part* names whom or what the sentence is about. The *predicate part* tells what action the subject does. Sometimes the predicate part tells what the subject is or is like.

Some sentences have a compound subject.

- Look at each of these sentences. The subject parts are in a blue box.

Maria and Zeb liked horses.

The children got a book about two horses at the library.

Muhammed and Zarif were special horses from Germany.

The second sentence has just one important word, or *simple subject*. The first and last sentences have two simple subjects joined by the word *and*. They have *compound subjects*.

A **compound subject** has two or more simple subjects that have the same predicate. The subjects are joined by **and.**

Some sentences have more than one simple predicate, or verb. Some have *compound predicates*.

- Look at each of these sentences. The predicate parts are in red boxes.

Muhammed and Zarif solved arithmetic problems.

They could add and subtract.

The two horses amazed the public and puzzled scientists.

The first sentence has just one verb, or *simple predicate*. There is just one action in the sentence.

The second and last sentences have compound predicates. Each sentence has two verbs joined by the word *and*.

A **compound predicate** is a predicate that has two or more verbs that have the same subject. The verbs are joined by **and.**

Talk About It

Which of these sentences have a compound subject? Which have a compound predicate?

1. The trainer and his pretty helper gave the questions.
2. Muhammed and Zarif answered with their feet.
3. The horses stamped their feet and tapped their hooves.
4. People looked for signals and watched for tricks.

Skills Practice

Write each sentence. If the predicate is compound, write **compound predicate.** If the subject is compound, write **compound subject.**

1. Kluge Hans and Berto were also smart horses.
2. Berto added numbers and gave the answers.
3. People stared and gasped in amazement.
4. Kluge Hans performed tricks and solved problems.
5. Many young people and some old people came.
6. They sat quietly and watched closely.
7. The girls and boys were thrilled.

Writing Sentences

Imagine you are at an aquarium.

1. Write two sentences with a compound subject.
2. Write two sentences with a compound predicate.

Sample Answer 1. Kluge Hans and Berto were also smart horses. compound subject

Compound Sentences

You know that a simple sentence expresses just one idea. Sometimes you may want to write a sentence that expresses more than one idea.

- Look at these sentences.

  Most alligators prefer fresh water.

  Most crocodiles like salt water.

Each of these sentences expresses one complete idea. They are simple sentences. A *simple sentence* has one subject part and one predicate part. Now read this sentence.

Most alligators prefer fresh water, and most crocodiles like salt water.

This sentence expresses two complete ideas. The two ideas are joined by the word *and.* This sentence is a *compound sentence.* The word *and* is called a *conjunction.* The two ideas in a compound sentence may also be joined by the conjunction *but.* Use a comma before a conjunction that joins the two ideas in a compound sentence.

A **compound sentence** is a sentence that contains two simple sentence joined by **and** or **but.**

You can check if a sentence is compound. If the sentence has the word *and* or *but,* cover it up and see if there are two complete sentences. If so, you have a compound sentence.

- Look at this sentence.

These reptiles live in swamps and hunt for fish.

Cover up the word *and.* You are not left with two complete sentences. *Hunt for fish* is not a whole idea because there is no subject. Therefore, the sentence is not a compound sentence. It is a simple sentence with a compound predicate.

- Now look at this sentence.

Alligators are black, but crocodiles are gray-green.

Cover up the word *but.* You are left with two complete sentences. Therefore, the sentence is a compound sentence.

Talk About It

Which sentences are compound sentences? Tell why.

1. They are closely related, and they are very much alike.
2. Alligators and crocodiles are reptiles.
3. Their legs are short, but they can move quickly.

Skills Practice

Write each compound sentence. If any sentence is not compound, write **not compound** on your paper.

1. Some alligators and crocodiles live in Florida.
2. They live in swamps and lie on river banks.
3. People fear them, but they fear people.
4. The alligators have broad heads, and their teeth are sharp.
5. Crocodiles can be vicious, and some have hurt people.

Write each pair of simple sentences as one compound sentence, using the conjunction. Place a comma where it belongs.

6. Some crocodiles live in Florida. Others live in Africa. (but)
7. Crocodiles have narrow heads. Their teeth are long. (and)
8. We saw some crocodiles in Florida. They were huge. (and)
9. Jan almost stepped on one. She saw it just in time. (but)
10. A young crocodile slept on the bank. An older one moved toward the water. (and)

Writing Sentences

Suppose you are a judge at a pet show. Write four compound sentences about the animals you see.

Sample Answers **1.** not compound **6.** Some crocodiles live in Florida, but other crocodiles live in Africa.

Building Compound Sentences

Many sentences that you write are simple sentences. They have one subject part and one predicate part.

- Look at these simple sentences.

  Giraffes are tall animals.

  They weigh less than elephants.

Sometimes you can make your writing more interesting by using a compound sentence instead of two simple sentences. In the compound sentence below, the two simple sentences have been joined by the conjunction *but*. Notice that a comma appears just before the conjunction.

  Giraffes are tall animals, but they weigh less than elephants.

You may join two simple sentences to form a compound sentence. However, do not join too many simple sentences together, or you will end up with a sentence that contains too many ideas. The ideas in a compound sentence should be related to each other in some way.

- Look at this sentence.

  Giraffes live in Africa and they roam in the grasslands and trees grow in these grasslands and giraffes eat their leaves, twigs, and fruit.

The sentence can be improved as follows:

  Giraffes live in Africa, and they roam in the grasslands. Trees grow in these grasslands, and the giraffes eat their leaves, twigs, and fruit.

Remember that the two simple sentences in a compound sentence are joined by the conjunction *and* or *but*. Each conjunction has a different meaning. The word *and* means "in addition." The word *but* is used to join contrasting, or opposite, ideas.

Talk About It

Read each pair of sentences. Tell how you could combine the sentences to make a compound sentence.

1. The giraffe has a brownish-yellow coat. The color protects the animal.
2. The giraffe stands in the shade of trees. The enemy cannot see the animal.
3. The elephant is a tall animal. The giraffe is even taller.

Skills Practice

Write each pair of sentences as a compound sentence.

1. The giraffe can make soft sounds. The animal seldom uses its voice.
2. Giraffes have good eyesight. Their hearing is excellent.
3. The length of the neck is long. The giraffe has only seven neck bones.
4. The giraffe has a short mane on its neck. Its tail ends in long, black hairs.
5. A male giraffe can weigh 2,000 pounds. A male African elephant can weigh six times as much.
6. The giraffe appears to be a slow and awkward animal. A giraffe can run up to 30 miles an hour when frightened.

Writing Sentences

Complete each sentence below to make a compound sentence. Write the new sentence.

1. A giraffe stands near a tall tree, and ___ .
2. A lion walks through the trees, but ___ .
3. A herd of giraffes runs quickly, but ___ .

Sample Answer **1.** The giraffe can make soft sounds, but the animal seldom uses its voice.

Skills Review

If the subject is compound, write **compound subject.** If the predicate is compound, write **compound predicate.**

1. Rudy and Elsie read books about dogs.
2. Chips helped the soldiers and attacked the enemy.
3. He captured one man and chased others.
4. Men and women got lost in the mountains in Switzerland.
5. The snow and ice created problems for them.
6. Chips left the Army in 1945 and returned to his owner.
7. Cold weather and strong winds were constant dangers.
8. Princess and other dogs helped the travelers.
9. The dog Chips lived and worked during World War II.
10. Rudy read and memorized poems about animals.
11. Rudy and his dog went to the library together.
12. The dog sat on the steps and waited there for Rudy.
13. Spot and Ginger were the family dogs.
14. The dogs played and ran in the yard.
15. Rudy and his sister make up stories about their dogs.

If a sentence is compound, write **compound.** If a sentence is not compound, write **not compound.**

16. I do not have a pet, but I love stories about them.
17. My brother and sister told me about a cat named Daisy.
18. She lived with a family, and the family had two homes.
19. Their country home was big, and it had a barn in back.
20. The family packed and returned to the city in the fall.
21. Daisy was going to have kittens, and she stayed behind.
22. Later she went to the city, but she got lost.
23. She looked for two days and finally found the family.
24. Daisy left later and returned with another kitten.
25. She made five trips, and each time she brought a kitten.

Write each pair of simple sentences as one compound sentence, using the conjunction. Place a comma where it belongs.

26. Mei bought our cat Boots at a pet store. Our home is no longer the same.
27. Boots has black fur. His feet are white.
28. We gave him cat food. He liked the milk better.
29. Mom chased him into the corner. Julia grabbed him.
30. Later we fed our new cat. He purred loudly.
31. Boots loves the backyard. He watches birds by the hour.
32. Last week he caught a bird. Mother got very angry.
33. We tried to train him. He still chases birds.
34. Boots likes mother's flowers. Sometimes he rolls over on them.
35. Mother picked up the broom. Boots dashed out of reach.
36. Boots likes roses. He will lie under a rosebush for hours.
37. Roses have a strong scent. Cats will use the scent of roses as protection.

Exploring Language

Sometimes when it is raining hard, people say it is "raining cats and dogs." How did this expression start?

No one knows for sure. Some say it may come from the Greek word *catadupa,* meaning "waterfall." Perhaps Greek people said *catadupa* when it rained hard. People who did not know Greek may have thought they were saying "cats and dogs."

Another reason might be this: in England many cats and dogs used to run wild in the streets. During storms many drowned. Some people may have seen the animals lying in the street. They may have imagined the storm had really "rained cats and dogs."

Prepositions and Prepositional Phrases

The words in a sentence work together to express an idea. One type of word may relate a noun or pronoun to another word in the sentence. This type of word is called a *preposition*.

- Read this sentence.

  Some penguins live on the ice.

The word *on* is a preposition. It shows the position of the noun *ice* in relation to the word *live*.

> A **preposition** is a word that relates a noun or pronoun to another word.

Here are some commonly used prepositions.

about	at	for	of	through
above	before	from	on	under
across	behind	in	onto	with
after	below	inside	to	without
around	by	near		

The noun or pronoun that follows the preposition is called the *object* of the preposition. Often words come between the preposition and its object. The preposition, object, and words in between are called a *prepositional phrase*.

> A **prepositional phrase** is a group of words that begins with a preposition and ends with a noun or pronoun.

- Look at these sentences. The prepositional phrase is underlined in each sentence.

  Some penguins live in Australia.
  The birds with thick feathers are penguins.

Talk About It

Read each sentence. Tell which group of words is the prepositional phrase. Then tell which word is the preposition and which word is its object.

1. The black and white penguins stand on short legs.
2. The birds walk with a clumsy waddle.
3. The penguins stay in southern areas.
4. They like the area below the equator.
5. The large penguin at the zoo swims well.

Skills Practice

Write each sentence. Draw one line under the prepositional phrase. Draw a second line under the preposition and its object.

1. Several penguins stand by the cold water.
2. One brave bird dives from a large rock.
3. The largest penguin inside the zoo stands four feet tall.
4. The birds near the water eat many fish.
5. One small penguin swims across the cold pond.
6. The baby penguin behind the rock has an orange neck.
7. Some penguins lay their eggs below the ground.
8. First the father cares for the baby.
9. The male penguin feeds the baby through its mouth.
10. Later the mother returns to the baby.

Sample Answer 1. Several penguins stand by the cold water.

Parts of Speech in Sentences

Words can be divided into groups according to the role they play in a sentence. You already know five word groups: *nouns, pronouns, verbs, adjectives,* and *adverbs*. These word groups are called *parts of speech*. Some parts of speech are more important in sentences than others. You cannot make a complete sentence without a verb. Most sentences have either a noun or a pronoun.

- Look at the first two words in this sentence.

Brave sailors cheered loudly.

Brave is an adjective. *Sailors* is a noun.

A **noun** is a word that names a person, place, thing, or idea.

An **adjective** is a word that describes a noun or a pronoun.

Brave and *sailors* make up the subject part of the sentence. Without the word *brave,* the sentence still makes sense. *Sailors cheered loudly* is a complete thought. Without the word *sailors,* the sentence no longer makes sense. *Cheered loudly* is not a complete thought. A subject part is needed.

- Look at the last part of the sentence.

Brave sailors cheered loudly.

Cheered is a verb. *Loudly* is an adverb.

A **verb** is a word that names an action.

An **adverb** is a word that describes an action.

Together *cheered* and *loudly* make up the predicate part of the sentence. Without the word *loudly,* the sentence still makes sense. *Brave sailors cheered* is a complete thought.

Without *cheered,* the sentence no longer makes sense. *Brave sailors* is not a complete thought. A verb is needed.

You can see that sentences need verbs. Sentences need nouns, too, or something to take the place of a noun.

> A **pronoun** is a word that takes the place of one or more nouns.

- Look at these sentences.

Brave sailors cheered loudly. They cheered loudly.

The word *they* is a pronoun. It takes the place of the word *sailors*. The pronoun *they* is the subject.

Talk About It

Read each sentence. Decide what part of speech each word is. Tell whether the underlined word is a **noun, pronoun, verb, adjective,** or **adverb.**

1. The sailors liked Sid the porpoise.
2. The smart porpoise lived in the ocean.
3. Sid often helped the sailors.
4. Sid swam in front of the ship.
5. He guided the sailors carefully.

Skills Practice

Write each sentence. Write whether the underlined word is a **noun, pronoun, verb, adjective,** or **adverb.**

1. The waves crashed fiercely.
2. The big ship tilted.
3. It missed the sharp rocks.
4. The sailors cheered loudly.
5. Many sailors cried with joy.
6. Sid leaped high in the air.
7. He helped other sailors.
8. A man hurt Sid.
9. The accident happened suddenly.
10. Sid healed quickly.

Sample Answer 1. The waves crashed fiercely. crashed, verb; fiercely, adverb

Reviewing Commas

You have learned that a comma tells the reader when to pause in a sentence. Review the rules below for using commas.

Use a **comma** (,) to set off words such as *yes, no,* and *well* when they begin a sentence. Use a **comma** (,) to set off the name of a person who is spoken to directly in a sentence.

Well, you know how it is. Have you been to the zoo, Norma?

Use a **comma** (,) to separate the name of the day from the date, and the date from the year. Use a **comma** (,) after the year when it appears with the date in the middle of a sentence.

Work will begin on the zoo on Monday, January 3, 1988, in New York.

Use a **comma** (,) to separate the name of a city and state. Use a **comma** (,) after the name of a state when it appears with a city name in the middle of a sentence.

I've visited the zoo in San Diego, California, often.

Use a **comma** (,) to separate each noun or verb in a series of three or more nouns or verbs.

Bears, dogs, and cats are mammals. Bears run fast, swim, and hunt.

Use a **comma** (,) before the conjunctions *and* or *but* in a compound sentence.

Pandas look like bears, but they belong to the raccoon family.

When writing conversation, use a **comma** (,) to separate the spoken words from the person who is saying them. Place the comma before the quotation marks.

"Some bears hibernate in the winter," said José.

If the speaker asks a question, use a **question mark** (?) instead of a comma before the end quotation marks.

"Where do bears live?" David asked.

If the speaker's name comes in the middle of the spoken words, use **commas** (,) to separate the spoken words from the speaker's name.

"Most bears," said Lisa, "live in forests."

Talk About It

Tell where commas belong in each of these sentences.

1. Brown bears live in Colorado Idaho Wyoming and Montana.
2. Bears dig climb and grip with their sharp claws.
3. Black bears brown bears and the Andean bears climb trees.
4. Bears have keen smell but their eyesight is poor.
5. "Bear cubs" said Tom "weigh very little at birth."

Skills Practice

Write each sentence. Add commas where they are needed.

1. Betty what do you know about pandas?
2. Well they are the cutest animals.
3. "Pandas look a bit like clowns" said Betty.
4. The red panda eats fruit leaves eggs and insects.
5. "Giant pandas" explained Bob "live in bamboo forests."
6. A zoo in Boise Idaho would like to have a panda.
7. On Friday March 12 1986 we will see the pandas.
8. Only a few zoos have pandas but most zoos have bears.
9. The Andean bear lives in a warmer climate finds food easily and does not hibernate.

Sample Answer 1. Betty, what do you know about pandas?

The History of Language

Linguists are people who study languages. Linguists are really language detectives. They gather clues that tell about the beginnings of languages. Their detective work makes a good story.

Long ago a group of people all spoke one language. It was called *Indo-European,* because the people lived between India and Europe. As time passed, small groups of people moved to new places. Slowly the language of each group changed a little as the people had new experiences. People added new words to describe new things. The sounds and spellings of words changed. In time Indo-European was no longer spoken. Each small group spoke its own language. Some languages that grew from Indo-European are French, Spanish, Italian, German, and Hindi.

Talk About It

English has *borrowed,* or taken, many words from other languages. Use each word in a sentence. Can you think of other words?

1. patio (Spanish)
2. veranda (Hindi)
3. sausage (French)
4. violin (Italian)
5. ranch (Spanish)
6. mosquito (Spanish)
7. spaghetti (Italian)
8. kindergarten (German)
9. sauerkraut (German)

The English language also grew from Indo-European. However, early English does not sound like the English we speak today. It almost sounds like a foreign language. Early English is also called *Old English.* It was made up of the languages used by groups of people called the Jutes, Angles, and Saxons who moved to England starting in 449 A.D. England was called Angle-land for a long time. In 1066 A.D. Old English started to change into *Middle English.* At that time a French duke named William conquered England. Many French people then moved to England. French words replaced some Old English words. The English language changed a great deal.

Talk About It

Say each Middle English word just the way it looks. Spell each word in modern English.

1. poyson **3.** botel **5.** citee **7.** melodye
2. nyght **4.** dayes **6.** ende **8.** thyng

Soon Middle English began to sound more like modern English. But English has not stopped changing. We still add many words to our language. Sometimes we still borrow words from other languages.

Talk About It

Here are some words borrowed from other languages. Use each word in a sentence. Tell your sentence.

1. skunk (Native American)
2. chipmunk (Native American)
3. raccoon (Native American)
4. boomerang (Native Australian)
5. almanac (Arabic)
6. shawl (Persian)
7. kimono (Japanese)
8. judo (Japanese)

Skills Review

Write the prepositional phrase in each sentence. Underline the preposition once. Underline its object twice.

1. A famous circus performed in our town last year.
2. My friends and I spent a day at the circus.
3. We saw horseback riders ride around the ring.
4. The clowns made everyone laugh with their funny tricks.
5. The band played a lively tune for the performers.
6. The trapeze artists flew through the air.
7. We watched them do their act high above our seats.
8. The end of the trapeze act was spectacular.
9. Some people left before the end.
10. I asked my friends not to leave without me.

Write each underlined word. Then write whether the word is a **noun, pronoun, adjective, verb,** or **adverb.**

11. Jumbo was one of the biggest elephants ever.
12. He lived peacefully at the zoo.
13. Children and adults visited Jumbo.
14. Everyone loved him dearly.
15. P. T. Barnum ran a circus in America.
16. He brought Jumbo to the United States.
17. Crowds of people watched him.
18. Some friends and I read a book about this elephant.

Write each sentence. Add commas where they are needed.

19. Lions tigers and monkeys performed in the circus.
20. Jumbo also performed and everyone loved him.
21. He walked danced and rode in the ring.
22. Yes everyone loved Jumbo the elephant.
23. "Norma do you know Jumbo's age?" asked Kim.

24. ''Elephants sometimes live to be 65'' Norma answered.
25. ''Jumbo did many wonderful tricks'' Carlos said.
26. People sat watched and cheered for Jumbo.
27. ''Jumbo loved to perform'' said Natalie.
28. We saw Jumbo in Philadelphia Pennsylvania at the circus.
29. Jumbo was very large but it moved quickly.
30. Children their parents and their friends watched it dance.
31. People rode on its back but Jumbo did not mind.
32. Did you ever see it Natalie?
33. No I never saw Jumbo perform.
34. ''People made a fuss over it'' said Kim ''and Jumbo loved it!''
35. An angry Jumbo bellowed stamped its foot and tossed its trunk.
36. Elephants are large but Jumbo grew to be the largest.
37. ''Jumbo was a credit to all pachyderms'' exclaimed Carlos.

Have you ever heard the expression "to let the cat out of the bag"? It means "to let a secret be found out." How did this expression get started? It began in old England where country fairs were held. Pigs were sold in the market there, and they were often wrapped in a sack.

Some sellers tried to trick the buyers. They would not wrap a pig in the bag, but instead they would put in a cat. Usually the buyer did not find out until opening the bag at home.

Careful buyers insisted that the bag be opened at the fair. If the seller was trying to cheat, it was discovered when the buyer "let the cat out of the bag."

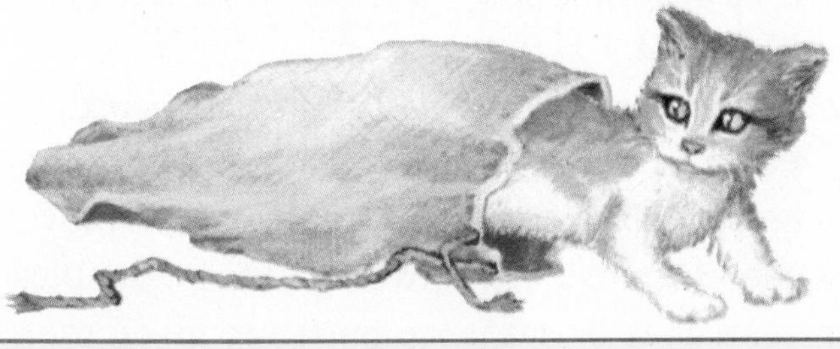

Exploring Language

Reviewing Dictionary Skills

You may be surprised at how much information you can find in a dictionary. Study this sample from a dictionary page.

bleak/boxing

bleak(blēk) *adj.* **1.** open and exposed to the wind; bare: *a bleak, barren, desert.* **2.** cold; chilling: *a bleak December day.* **3.** not cheerful or hopeful; gloomy: *Our team's prospects for winning were bleak.*—**bleak·ly,** *adv.*—**bleak·ness,** *n.*

bot·a·ny (bot'ən ē) *n.* the science or study of plants

bough(bou) *n.* a branch of a tree, especially a large or main branch.

bou·quet (bō kā,'bo͞o kā') *n* **1.** a bunch of flowers; especially one arranged and fastened together. **2.** fragrance or aroma.

Pronunciation Key

at; āpe; cär; end; mē; it; īce; hot; ōld; fôrk; wood; fo͞ol; oil; out; up; turn; sing; thin; this; hw in white; zh in treasure

The symbol ə stands for the sound of **a** in about; **e** in taken, **i** in pencil, **o** in lemon, and **u** in circus.

The *guide words* at the top of the page tell you that the entry words between **bleak** and **boxing** are listed alphabetically on this sample page. Each word on the page is an *entry word.* The entries above contain the following kinds of information.

1. An entry word of more than one syllable is divided into *syllables.* Notice the dots that separate the three syllables of **botany.**
2. The letters and symbols in parentheses show the *pronunciation* of the entry word. The symbols are explained by a *pronunciation key* on the page or by a complete *guide to pronunciation* elsewhere. This pronunciation key tells you to pronounce the vowels in **botany:** *o* as the *o* in *hot;* *ə* the *a* in *about;* and *ē* as the *ē* in *mē.*
3. Next, an abbreviation indicates the *part of speech,* or word group, of the entry word: *n.* means *noun; pron.* means *pronoun; v.* means *verb; adj.* means *adjective;* and *adv.* means *adverb.*
4. Then the entry lists the meanings of the word. Often examples of the word used in sentences or sentence parts are given too.

Many dictionaries have a Table of English Spellings that shows how sounds may be spelled in English. For each sound, the spellings are listed in the order they appear most often in words. Notice ā may be spelled eleven different ways.

Table of English Spellings

Sound	Spelling	Sound	Spelling
/a/	hand, have, laugh, plaid	/k/	cat, key, tack, chord, account, mosquito, Iraq, walk
/ā/	paper, rate, rain, pay, eight, steak, veil, obey, ballet, straight, gauge	/m/	mine, hammer, climb, salmon, hymn
/är/	car, heart, sergeant		

Talk About It

Use the dictionary samples to answer these questions.

1. Which entry words have two or more syllables?
2. What entry word has two pronunciations?
3. What sentence uses *bleak* meaning "gloomy"?
4. What parts of speech are *bough* and *botany*?
5. Look at the picture. Use the Table of English Spellings and your dictionary to find how you spell this word.
   lame, laum, lamb, lamm

Skills Practice

Use the dictionary samples to answer these questions.

1. Use the pronunciation key to help you say this sentence.
   (mī) (na bərz) (hav) (hyo͞oj) (rōz əz) (in) (ther) (yärd)
2. How many related meanings does the word *bouquet* have?
3. *Bleak* can be three parts of speech. What are they?
4. Write a sentence using the word *bough*.
5. Look at each picture. Use the Table of English Spellings and your dictionary to find how you spell these words.

sheark
shark

snaik
snake

snayl
snail

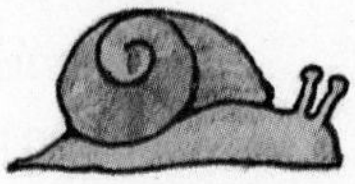

Sample Answer 1. My neighbors

A Story

Thinking About a Story

Almost everyone likes stories. Before you could read, maybe someone read stories to you. Do you remember your favorite ones? Stories can be about many different subjects. Some stories may be about an animal. Others might be about life in a family. Still others could be exciting adventure stories.

Stories may be about different ideas, but all stories share common parts. You can use these parts to talk about stories. You can also use them to write your own story.

1. The *plot* describes the action or events of the story. Usually the plot has a beginning, a middle, and an ending.
2. The *setting* tells where and when the story takes place. The setting in a story could change if the plot moves the action from one place to another.
3. The *characters* are people or animals in the story. You find what characters are like by what they say and do.

Every story has a beginning, a middle, and an ending. The *beginning* describes the characters and tells where and when the story takes place. The *middle* tells what happens to the characters. They usually have some problem that has to be solved. The *end* of the story tells how things turn out for the characters.

- Read this story and look for the setting, characters, and plot.

Maria's Slippers

It was the morning of Maria's tenth birthday. She wondered what her present would be. She looked in her house, but no one was inside. She looked around her yard, but no one was outside either. She sat on the back step feeling very sad.

She wondered if her family had forgotten her birthday. Then she felt something funny on her right bare foot. A little grey and white patch of fur was licking her toe. Before she could say anything, another little fur ball started licking her other toe. She looked as if she were wearing furry bedroom slippers.

Suddenly, she heard giggling behind her. She turned around to see her family in the doorway. She heard tiny little meows at her feet. She looked again. The little patches of fur were tiny kittens. Her family smiled and shouted, "Happy Birthday."

Talking About Stories

1. What was the main character's name?
2. What else did you know about the main character?
3. What was the setting of the story?
4. What happened in the beginning of the story?
5. What happened in the middle of the story?
6. How did the story end?

Practicing a Story

All authors face one problem when they write a story. First they must think of an idea. When they have decided on an idea, they must do some careful planning and take notes.

1. Think about the plot. You can use your own idea or you may use this map to help plan your plot. The main character of your story has an exciting adventure on the way home from school. Follow the dotted line. The dotted line *begins* at school and shows the path the character took home to the house marked END. What events might have happened to the character? Look at the two *X's* in the middle of the map. What two problems could your characters have faced at these places?
2. Think about the setting for your story. Write notes to describe the river, the forest, and the home.
3. Name the *main character.* Write notes to describe the main character. How will this person act in the story?

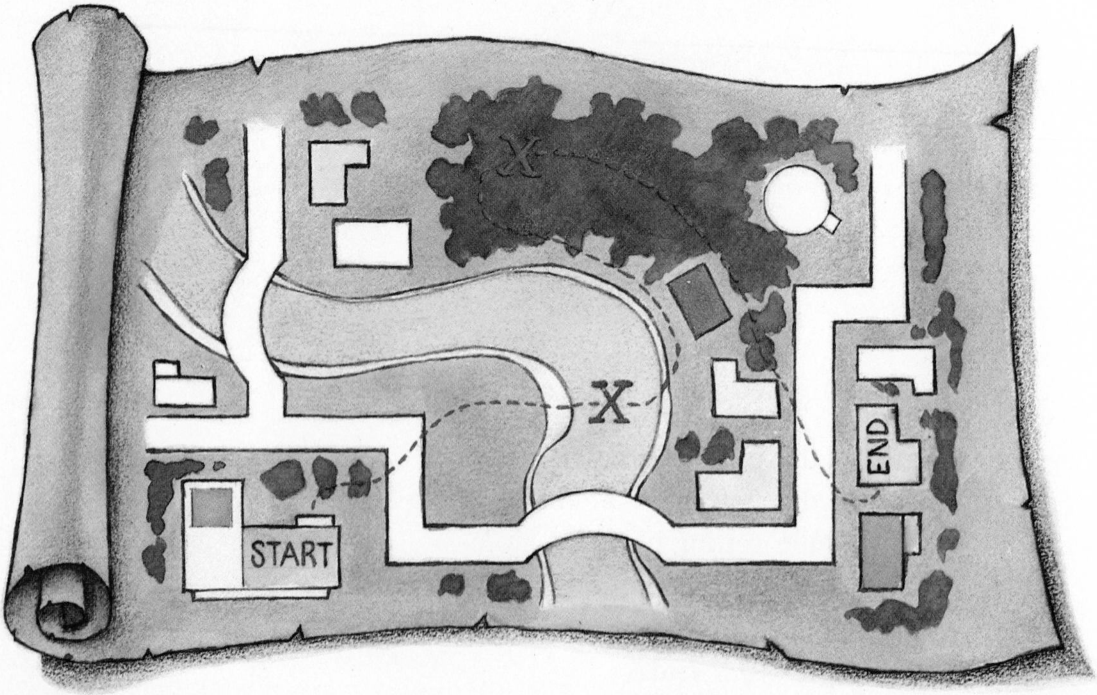

Writing Your Story

Write your story. Use your notes and the map to help you.

1. Write a paragraph about the main character and setting.
2. Write a paragraph about what happened to your main character. What problems did he or she face?
3. Write a paragraph that tells how things turned out.
4. Write a title for your story.

Edit Your Story

1. Did your story have a beginning, a middle, and an end?
2. Did you describe your main character clearly?
3. Did you describe the setting of the story?
4. Did you write a title for your story?
5. Did each sentence have a subject and a predicate?
6. Did you choose interesting adjectives and adverbs?
7. Did you indent the first word in each paragraph?
8. Did you use commas correctly?
9. Did you check your spelling?

Editing Symbols

- ≡ capitalize
- ¶ indent
- ℘ take out
- ∧ add

INDEPENDENT WRITING

A Story

Prewriting Science fiction writers use science facts and their imaginations to develop their plots. The settings of these stories may be in the present or far in the future. The action may take place on Earth or in outer space. The characters may be real, from outer space, or both. Think of a science fiction story. Plan the characters, plot, and setting. Make notes.

Writing Write a science fiction story using your notes. In the beginning describe the characters and the setting. In the middle explain the problem the characters face. In the ending tell how the problem was solved.

Editing Use the check questions and the editing symbols to edit your story.

Writing a Book Report

Thinking About Your Book Report

Stories are fun to read. They are fun to write. Stories are also fun to share with others. When you read a good book, you often want to tell your friends about its *plot, characters,* and *setting*. Those three parts helped you to read and write a story. You can also use them to *report* on a *book*. A book report helps you remember the book, lets you share it with others, and can help you learn how to express your thoughts in writing.

A *book report* tells about a story in two or three summary paragraphs. The summary tells enough about the story to interest the reader, but it doesn't give away the whole story. Follow these steps to write a book report.

1. Write the title and author of the book. Remember to underline the title.
2. In the first paragraph describe the main character and tell the setting where the character lives. The summary paragraph should tell what the main character says and does, and what the author says about the character.
3. Tell one or two important events that happened in the story. This second paragraph is also a summary paragraph.

● Read the following book report.

Little House on the Prairie

by Laura Ingalls Wilder

The Ingalls family leave their home in Wisconsin and travel to Kansas. They settle on the open prairie in Indian Territory. Pa and Ma and their three daughters, Mary, Laura, and Baby Carrie, live in a log house that Pa builds. Laura is a strong, brave young girl. She helps Pa build the house, helps Ma pick berries, and helps take care of her little sister.

The Ingalls family has many adventures. One time they fight a giant prairie fire. Another time they are trapped in their house, surrounded by wolves. They make an effort to get along with the Indians that live nearby. The family works hard to survive the dangers and the hardships of prairie life.

Thinking About Your Book Report

Read the book report again.

1. What are the title and author of the book?
2. Who is the main character?
3. Where does the main character live?
4. What kind of girl is Laura?
5. How does she help her family?

Writing Your Book Report

Choose a book that you have read and liked. Take notes on the parts of the book that you will use in your book report.

1. Write the title and author of the book.
2. Write a summary paragraph that describes the main character. Tell what the character says and does. Also tell the setting where the character lives.
3. Write a summary paragraph about the plot of the book. Tell about one or two important events that happened.

Edit Your Book Report

1. Did you write the title and author of the book?
2. Did you describe the main character and the setting?
3. Did you write a summary paragraph about the plot?
4. Did you indent the first sentence of each paragraph?
5. Did you begin your sentences with a capital letter?
6. Did you end your sentences with the correct punctuation?
7. Did you spell your words correctly?

Unit Review

Read each sentence. If the subject is compound, write **compound subject.** If the predicate is compound, write **compound predicate.** *pages 296–297*

1. The seals swam in the pool and delighted the boys.
2. The gorillas sat in the corner and ate their bananas.
3. Fifty boys and girls crowded around them.
4. Carl and his friend liked the elephants best.
5. The elephants stamped their feet and lifted their trunks.

If a sentence is compound, write **compound.** If a sentence is not compound, write **not compound.** *pages 298–299*

6. Our whole class went to the aquarium.
7. We got there early, but we waited in line.
8. A big codfish bumped the diver, and another nibbled his ear.
9. The diver brushed it away and went on with his job.

Write each pair of sentences as a compound sentence. *pages 300–301*

10. Thousands of pigeons live in our city. Some of them roost on our building.
11. I like the pigeons near my window. Sometimes they disturb me.
12. During the day many pigeons flock to the park. Some people feed them.

Write the prepositional phrase in each sentence. Underline the preposition once. Underline its object twice. *pages 304–305*

13. We saw many dogs in the dog show.
14. The people walked their dogs around the room.
15. All the dogs stood near their owners.
16. One dog left the show with first prize.

Unit Review

Write each underlined word. Write whether the word is a **noun, pronoun, verb, adjective,** or **adverb.** *pages 306–307*

17. The <u>soldiers</u> used a <u>large</u> eagle during the war.
18. <u>They</u> used <u>it</u> to scare the <u>enemy</u>.
19. The soldiers <u>tied</u> <u>colorful</u> ribbons around its <u>neck</u>.
20. The bird <u>spread</u> its <u>huge</u> wings and <u>flew</u> high above them.
21. The bird <u>screamed</u> <u>loudly</u> at the enemy <u>soldiers</u>.

Write each sentence. Add commas where they are needed. *pages 308–309*

22. Beavers are clever animals and they are useful.
23. They build repair and lengthen dams.
24. Beavers eat tree bark and they like some grasses.
25. "Beavers" said Ann "live near my home in Hillsdale."
26. They have broad heads powerful jaws and round ears.
27. In Yellowstone Park Wyoming beavers are protected.
28. "Have you ever seen a beaver work Emily?" asked Ann.
29. "The beavers finished the dam on Saturday" said Sam.
30. Beavers build dams with branches stones and mud.
31. I saw beavers on Tuesday June 12 1982 at the zoo.

A story has characters, setting, and a plot. The plot has a beginning, a middle, and an ending. Write a story using your own idea, or you can use one of these topics:

a story about a baby animal and its adventure
a story about a character's trip to a strange place
a story about something that happened on your vacation *pages 316–319*

a. Write a paragraph describing the main characters.
b. Write a paragraph about what happened to your character. Tell about the setting.
c. Write a title for your story.

A Story

A *story* has three main parts. The *plot* is the action of the story. The *setting* is the place and time of the action. The *characters* are the people or animals in the story.

In the following story, the characters are a ten-year-old Polynesian boy named Mafatu and his dog Uri. The setting is the ocean near a desert island on which Mafatu and Uri have been stranded. A shark has been breaking into a bamboo trap that Mafatu has built to catch fish. Mafatu fears the sea but knows he must stop the thief in order to survive.

This story is from a book entitled Call It Courage. The book was awarded the Newbery Medal for being a distinguished contribution to children's literature.

Call It Courage

by ARMSTRONG SPERRY

Fishing with a line took too long when you were working against time. Mafatu could not afford to have his trap robbed. Twice it had been broken into, the stout bamboos crushed and the contents eaten. It was the work either of a shark or of an octopus. That was certain. No other fish was strong enough to snap the tough bamboo.

Mafatu's mouth was set in a grim line as he worked away on his knife. That old hammerhead—undoubtedly he was the thief! Mafatu had come to recognize him; for every day when the boy went out with his trap, that shark, larger than all the others, was circling around, wary and watchful. The other sharks seemed to treat the hammerhead with deference.

Hunger alone drove Mafatu out to the reef to set his trap. He knew that if he was to maintain strength to accomplish all that lay ahead he must have fish to add to his diet of fruit. But often as he set his trap out by the barrier-reef, the hammerhead would approach, roll over slightly in passing, and the cold gleam of its eye filled Mafatu with dread and anger.

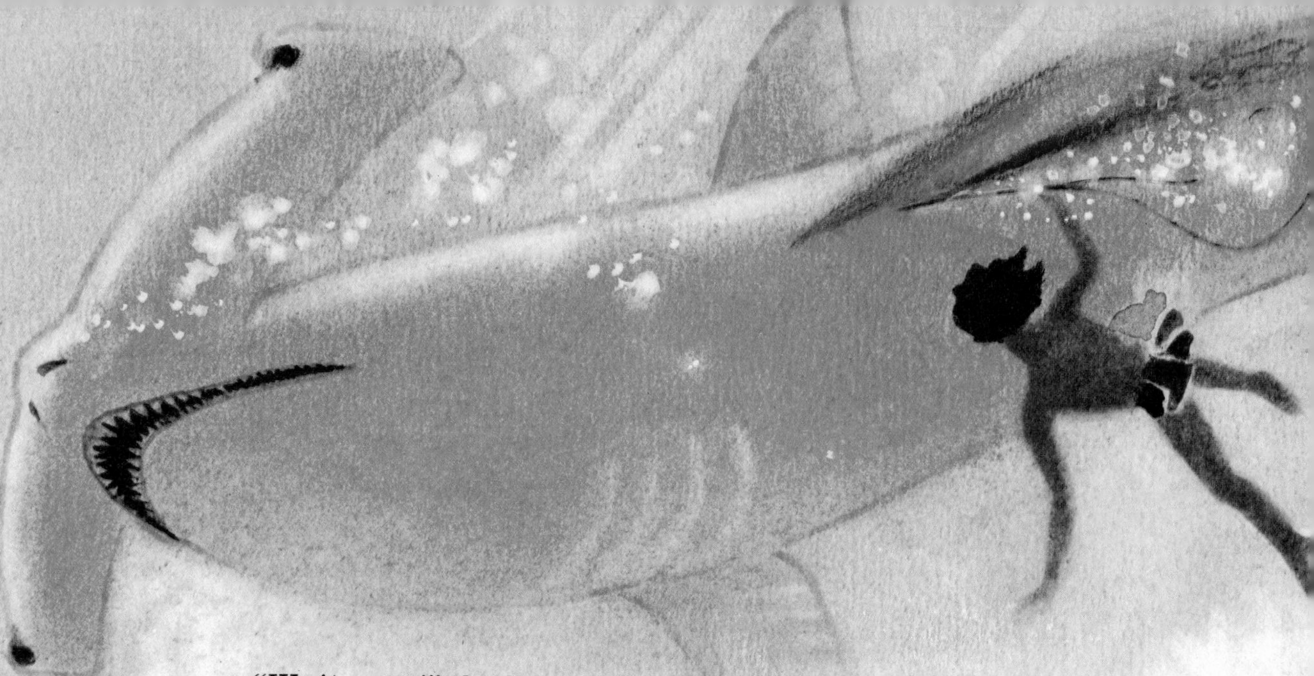

"Wait, you!" the boy threatened darkly, shaking his fist at the ma'o. "Wait until I have my knife! You will not be so brave then, Ma'o. You will run away when you see it flash."

But the morning that the knife was finished, Mafatu did not feel so brave as he would have liked. He hoped he would never see the hammerhead again. Paddling out to the distant reef, he glanced down from time to time at the longbladed knife where it hung about his neck by a cord of sennit. It wasn't, after all, such a formidable weapon. It was only a knife made by a boy from a whale's rib.

Uri sat on the edge of the raft, sniffing at the wind. Mafatu always took his dog along, for Uri howled unmercifully if he were left behind. And Mafatu had come to rely upon the companionship of the little yellow dog. The boy talked with the animal as if he were another person, consulting with him, arguing, playing when there was time for play. They were very close, these two.

This morning as they approached the spot where the fish trap was anchored, Mafatu saw the polished dorsal of the hated hammerhead circling slowly in

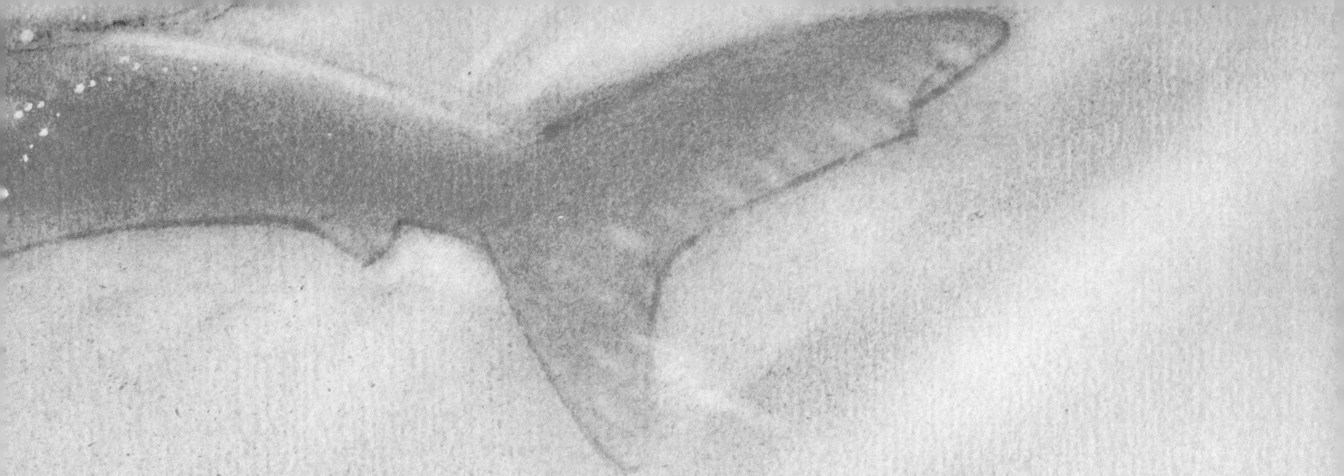

the water. It was like a triangle of black basalt, making a little furrow in the water as it passed.

"Aiá, Ma'o!" the boy shouted roughly, trying to bolster up his courage. "I have my knife today, see! Coward who robs traps—catch your own fish!"

The hammerhead approached the raft in leisurely fashion; it rolled over slightly, and its gaping jaws seemed to curve in a yawning grin. Uri ran to the edge of the raft, barking furiously; the hair on the dog's neck stood up in a bristling ridge. The shark, unconcerned, moved away. Then with a whip of its powerful tail it rushed at the bamboo fish trap and seized it in its jaws. Mafatu was struck dumb. The hammerhead shook the trap as a terrier might shake a rat. The boy watched, fascinated, unable to make a move. He saw the muscles work in the fish's neck as the great tail thrashed the water to fury. The trap splintered into bits, while the fish within escaped only to vanish into the shark's mouth. Mafatu was filled with impotent rage. The hours he had spent making that trap—but all he could do was shout threats at his enemy.

Uri was running from one side of the raft to the other, furious with excitement. A large wave sheeted across the reef. At that second the dog's shift in weight tipped the raft at a perilous angle. With a helpless yelp, Uri slid off into the water. Mafatu sprang to catch him but he was too late.

Instantly the hammerhead whipped about. The wave slewed the raft away. Uri, swimming frantically, tried to regain it. There was desperation in the brown eyes—the puzzled eyes so faithful and true. Mafatu strained forward. His dog. His companion . . . The hammerhead was moving in slowly. A mighty rage stormed through the boy. He gripped his knife. Then he was over the side in a clean-curving dive.

Mafatu came up under his enemy. The shark spun about. Its rough hide scraped the flesh from the boy's shoulder. In that instant Mafatu stabbed. Deep, deep into the white belly. There was a terrific impact. Water lashed to foam. Stunned, gasping, the boy fought for life and air.

It seemed that he would never reach the surface. Aué, his lungs would burst! . . . At last his head broke water. Putting his face to the surface, he saw the great shark turn over, fathoms deep. Blood flowed from the wound in its belly. Instantly gray shapes rushed in—other sharks, tearing the wounded hammerhead to pieces.

Uri—where was he? Mafatu saw his dog then. Uri was trying to pull himself up on the raft. Mafatu seized him by the scruff and dragged him up to safety. Then he caught his dog to him and hugged him close, talking to him foolishly. Uri yelped for joy and licked his master's cheek.

It wasn't until Mafatu reached shore that he realized what he had done. He had killed the ma'o with his own hand, with naught but a bone knife. He could never have done it for himself. Fear would have robbed his arm of all strength. He had done it for Uri, his dog. And he felt suddenly humble, with gratitude.

Creative Activities

1. **Creative Writing** Imagine another problem of survival that Mafatu and Uri could face on the island. For example, they might have to protect themselves during a storm or start a fire in wet weather. Write a story about the problem. In the beginning describe the characters and setting. In the middle explain the problem that the characters face. In the ending tell how the problem is solved.
2. Finish reading the book Call It Courage. Choose another incident that tells about a problem Mafatu faced. Share the incident with the class by reading it aloud or telling it in your own words.

End-of-Year Review

Some of the groups of words below are sentences. Other groups are not. Write each group of words that is a sentence. If a group of words is not a sentence, write **not a sentence.** *pages 2–3*

1. A bus.
2. The driver honks his horn.
3. Stopped the bus.
4. Fell all night.
5. Rain washes the bus.
6. A bad storm.

Write each of the following sentences. Begin each sentence with a capital letter. End each sentence with the correct punctuation mark. Decide whether each sentence is **declarative, interrogative, imperative,** or **exclamatory.** *pages 4–7*

7. what a storm that was
8. did you see the tree fall
9. look out the window
10. the tree fell in the road
11. what a noise it made
12. we heard claps of thunder
13. the storm ended early
14. did people move the tree

Write each sentence below. Draw a line between the subject part and the predicate part. Draw one line under the subject part. Draw two lines under the predicate part. *pages 10–11*

15. Four yellow hens ran away.
16. A farmer chased the hens.
17. The animals headed for town.
18. Two ducks ran after the hens.
19. Children found the ducks.
20. The sheriff saw the hens.

Write each noun in each sentence. After each noun, write whether it names a **person, place, thing,** or **idea.** Write whether it is **common** or **proper.** *pages 36–38, 46–47*

21. Laurie saw a footprint on the ground.
22. A friend followed the girl to a cave.
23. Bill admired the beauty of Overlook Mountain.

End-of-Year Review

Write the plural form of each noun. *pages 38–41*

24. beach
25. fox
26. child
27. man
28. fly
29. goose
30. kiss
31. foot

Change the word at the end of the sentence to make a possessive noun. Write the possessive noun. *pages 50–51*

32. Irene saw the ___ car. (teacher)
33. The ___ faces showed smiles. (children)
34. The ___ drivers waved. (cars)

Write the action verb. Then write the object of the verb. *pages 72–75*

35. Ronnie saw a cat.
36. The cat licked its paw.
37. Ronnie brought a bowl.
38. The cat drank milk.

Write the verb in each sentence. Write whether the verb is in the **present, past,** or **future** tense. *pages 76–77*

39. Rita will eat her lunch.
40. Children run in the park.
41. Miyo hurried to the field.
42. A cat climbs a tree.
43. Clouds filled the sky.
44. The park will close soon.

Write the correct form of the verb in the present tense. *pages 78–79*

45. Sue ___ a flower. (pick)
46. A boy ___ a ball. (toss)
47. My friend ___ us. (watch)
48. A dog ___ a bone. (bury)
49. Roy ___ bones to him. (carry)
50. The dog ___ Roy. (obey)

Read each sentence. Write the verb in the past tense. *pages 80–81, 88–91*

51. Roy asks for a flower.
52. A flower grows here.
53. I give it to a friend.
54. My friend plants a seed.
56. Amy begins a story.
56. Bill drinks some milk.
57. You study hard.
58. We stay at home.

Read each sentence. Write the correct form of the verb *have*. *pages 84–85*

59. We ___ a problem. (present)
60. Sue ___ several colds. (past)
61. She ___ a sore throat. (past)
62. You ___ the message. (present)
63. Dave ___ the report. (present)
64. He ___ the typewriter. (past)

Write the correct past tense form of each verb in parentheses. *pages 86–87*

65. Pete has ___ Sue often. (phone)
66. They have ___ for hours. (talk)
67. Sue has ___ her report. (begin)
68. Pete has ___ his facts. (share)
69. Pete has ___ his report. (type)
70. Pete and Sue have ___. (finish)

Read each pair of sentences. In the second sentences replace the underlined words with pronouns. Write whether each pronoun is a **subject** or an **object** pronoun. *pages 112–119*

71. Cheryl met friends at the bus.
Cheryl recognized the friends.
72. Bob wore a new jacket.
The jacket fits Bob perfectly.
73. Meg hurried to the bus.
Meg got on the bus first.
74. Bob and I saw Cheryl.
Bob and I waved to Cheryl.

Write the correct possessive pronoun for each blank. *pages 122–123*

75. The twins row the boat.
The boat is ___. (hers, theirs)
76. Bob has new sneakers.
He jogs in ___ sneakers. (her, his)
77. Alison has blue shoes.
___ shoes are shiny. (Her, Hers)
78. Do you have a tennis racket?
Is this racket ___? (yours, our)

Draw a line between the subject part and the predicate part. Draw one line under the simple subject. Draw two lines under the simple predicate. *pages 152–157*

79. A group of children invented a new game.
80. The new game has a secret name.
81. Three children in the class wrote a story about the game.

Write whether each sentence has a compound subject or a compound predicate. *pages 158–161*

82. Polly and Tim had a party.
83. Roy came to the party and played the piano.
84. Jan and her brothers played a magic trick.
85. The children played games and sang songs.

Write each adjective in these sentences. After each adjective, write the noun it describes. *pages 192–193*

86. A young musician plays a shiny flute in the bright sun.
87. A brown dog with sad eyes listens carefully.
88. A large crowd of happy people gathers around.

Write the correct form of the adjective. Remember some adjectives use **more** or **most.** *pages 194–195, 200–201*

89. Norman has a ___ voice than Dick. (soft)
90. The trumpet made a ___ sound than the flute. (loud)
91. The oboe makes the ___ sound of all. (beautiful)
92. Jim is a ___ player than Bob. (careful)

Write each of these adjectives with **-er** and **-est** endings. *page 200*

93. noisy
94. fast
95. flat
96. dim
97. sad
98. happy
99. hot
100. roomy

Write each sentence, capitalizing the proper adjective. *page 201*

101. I enjoy mexican food.
102. He wore an irish scarf.
103. We visited an african desert.
104. She saw the italian flag.

Write each verb. Write whether the verb is an **action verb** or a **linking verb.** *pages 226–227*

105. Nadia is a dancer.
106. She dances on her toes.
107. Antonio was an acrobat.
108. He hung from his toes.

Write the word that follows the linking verb. (Do not count *a* or *an*.) Write whether the word is a **noun** or **adjective**. Then write the word to which the noun or adjective is connected. *pages 228–229*

109. Ruth is a doctor.
110. She is happy.
111. Some patients are children.
112. Ruth is alert.
113. Her patients are grateful.
114. She is careful.

Decide if each verb should be in the present or past tense. Write the correct form of the verb to complete each sentence. *pages 230–231*

115. Luis ___ baking bread yesterday. (was, were)
116. The children ___ helping him that day. (was, were)
117. He ___ baking cakes now. (am, is, are)
118. The children ___ watching him today. (am, is, are)

Write each underlined word. Add an apostrophe. *pages 238–239*

119. <u>Toms</u> the captain of our team.
120. <u>Hes</u> the youngest boy.
121. Our <u>teams</u> ahead!
122. <u>Theyre</u> cheering our team.
123. All the <u>students</u> cheers help.
124. <u>Im</u> so excited.
125. Many <u>boys</u> spirits are high.
126. <u>Were</u> very glad.

Write each adverb. Then write the word it describes. *pages 260–262*

127. The creature grinned strangely.
128. It jumped wildly.
129. We stared around.
130. The creature moved quietly.

Add **-er, -est, more,** or **most** to the words in parentheses. *pages 262–263*

131. Jerry ran ___ than Earl did. (long)
132. Jerry practiced ___ than Earl. (frequently)
133. Claire practiced the ___ of all. (happily)
134. She came the ___ of all to breaking the record. (close)
135. Jerry came ___ to the record than Earl. (near)
136. Sally talked ___ than Ellen. (freely)
137. Who would be the ___ racer in the class? (fast)
138. Mike raced the ___ of the group. (rapidly)
139. Alice remained the ___ of all. (cool)

Change each adjective to an adverb. Write the adverb. *pages 264–265*

140. swift **141.** crazy **142.** complete **143.** soft

Write each sentence. Use capital letters where necessary. *pages 268–269*

144. dr. boulez opened the boulez laboratory in july.
145. ms. smith and mr. j.r. fox arrived from england on monday.

Write whether each sentence has a **compound subject** or **compound predicate,** or whether it is a **compound sentence.** *pages 296–299*

146. Harry and Ann went to the aquarium.
147. The dolphins entertain, and their trainer rewards them.
148. They jump and catch fish high in the air.

Write each underlined word. Then write whether the word is a **noun, pronoun, adjective, verb,** or **adverb.** *pages 306–307*

149. <u>Harry</u> and Ann <u>feed</u> their <u>dog</u> <u>daily</u>.
150. <u>They</u> play with <u>him</u> and take him for <u>long</u> <u>walks</u>.
151. They <u>brush</u> his <u>soft</u> fur <u>frequently</u>.
152. His <u>fur</u> is <u>wet</u> from the <u>rain</u>.

Write each sentence. Add commas where they are needed. *pages 308–309*

153. "What will you do for the summer Ann?" asked Jane.
154. "I don't know" said Ann "if I'll go anywhere."
155. I guess I'll stay here read books and go swimming.
156. We're leaving on Tuesday June 30 1984 for a trip.
157. We'll be visiting Denver Colorado then.
158. I hope to see bears mountains and a waterfall.
159. Well I expect to get a post card.
160. Of course I'll send you one from Denver and I'll also write you from Yellowstone Park.
161. Tom George and Tim want post cards of Indians.
162. "It sounds like a nice trip" said Ann.

Handbook Contents

I. GRAMMAR AND USAGE 337-345
Sentences 337-338
Definition 337
Parts of Sentences 337
Kinds of Sentences 338
Parts of Speech 338-345
Noun 338
Verb 339
Pronoun 343
Adjective 344
Adverb 344
Interjection 345
Preposition 345
Conjunction 345
II. MECHANICS 345-348
Capitalization 345
Punctuation 346
Capitalization and Punctuation in Conversation. 348
III. SPELLING 349-350
Spelling Nouns 349
Spelling Verbs 349
Spelling Adjectives 350
Spelling Adverbs 350
IV. VOCABULARY 351-353
V. SPECIAL FORMS 354-356
Friendly Letter 354
Business Letter 355
Book Report 355
Outline 356
VI. DIAGRAMING 357

Handbook

I. Grammar and Usage

Sentences

DEFINITION

A **sentence** is a group of words that state a complete idea. page 2 MORE PRACTICE, page 358

Virginia painted a lovely picture. James lost his shoes.

PARTS OF SENTENCES

The **subject part** of a sentence names whom or what the sentence is about. The subject part may have one word or more than one word. pages 10, 152 MORE PRACTICE, pages 359, 366

A large circus arrives in town every spring.

The tall girl on the high wire performs many tricks.

The **predicate part** of a sentence tells what action the subject part does. The predicate part may have one word or more than one word. pages 10, 152, 156 MORE PRACTICE, pages 359, 366

The family planted a garden. Many flowers bloomed.

The **object of a verb** receives the action of the verb. It answers the question *whom?* or *what?* after an action verb. page 74 MORE PRACTICE, page 362

Anthony broke his glasses. The visitor opened the door.

The **simple subject** of a sentence is the main word in the subject part. page 154 MORE PRACTICE, page 366

The little girl played outside. The boy walked with crutches.

The **simple predicate** is the main word or group of words in the predicate part. page 156 MORE PRACTICE, page 366

The horse jumped over the bush. The parents clapped at the end.

A **compound subject** has two or more simple subjects that have the same predicate. The subjects are joined by **and.** pages 158, 296 MORE PRACTICE, pages 366, 367

Snow and sleet fell all night. Mary and her friends skated.

A **compound predicate** is a predicate that has two or more verbs that have the same subject. The verbs are joined by **and.** pages 160, 297 MORE PRACTICE, page 367

Betty fed the pig and hugged it. The pig squealed and squirmed.

KINDS OF SENTENCES

A **declarative sentence** is a sentence that makes a statement or tells something. page 4 MORE PRACTICE, page 358

The teacher read a story to the class.

The children looked at the pictures.

An **interrogative sentence** is a sentence that asks something. page 4 MORE PRACTICE, page 358

What did you do in school today?

Do you know which country grows the most rice?

An **imperative sentence** is a sentence that tells or asks someone to do something. page 4 MORE PRACTICE, page 358

Honk your bicycle horn. Wait for me at the desk.

An **exclamatory sentence** is a sentence that shows excitement or strong feeling. page 5 MORE PRACTICE, page 358

How the trees bend in the wind!

What an awful sound the wind makes!

A **simple sentence** is a sentence that has one subject part and one predicate part. page 298 MORE PRACTICE, page 375

The children played games.

Miranda watched the game.

A **compound sentence** is a sentence that contains two simple sentences joined by *and* or *but*. page 298 MORE PRACTICE, page 375

Paul read a book, and Joan watched TV.

Mr. Frantz cleaned the garage, but Natalie mowed the lawn.

Parts of Speech

NOUN

A **noun** is a word that names a person, place, thing, or idea. pages 37, 228, 306 MORE PRACTICE, pages 360, 376

The ships sailed from the harbor.

The friendship of the children delighted the teacher.

A **singular noun** is a noun that names one person, place, thing, or idea. page 38 MORE PRACTICE, page 360

The horse raced in the field. A turtle lives in our pond.

A **plural noun** is a noun that names more than one person, place, thing, or idea. page 38 MORE PRACTICE, page 360

The children have two dogs. The dogs live in small houses.

A **compound noun** is a noun made up of two or more other words. You can usually figure out the meaning of a compound noun if you know the meanings of the smaller words that form it. page 40 MORE PRACTICE, page 360

Did the motorcycle have a sidecar?

A **common noun** is a noun that names any person, place, thing, or idea. page 46 MORE PRACTICE, page 361

A shepherd watched his sheep. The dog followed the canary.

A **proper noun** is a noun that names a special person, place, thing, or idea. A proper noun can be one word or more than one word. page 46 MORE PRACTICE, page 361

John Campos lives on Park Way. Claudia attends South School.

A **possessive noun** is a noun that names who or what has something. page 50 MORE PRACTICE, page 361

The woman's hand touched my cheek. Who hid Andre's hat?

VERB

An **action verb** is a word that names an action. It may contain more than one word. It may have a main verb and a helping verb. pages 72, 226 MORE PRACTICE, pages 362, 376

The girl finds the boy. The boy hides behind the chair.

The **object of a verb** receives the action of the verb. It answers the question *whom*? or *what*? after an action verb. page 74 MORE PRACTICE, page 362

The coach lectures the players.

The **present tense** of a verb names an action that happens now. page 76 MORE PRACTICE, page 362

The plant needs water and plant food.

Chickens eat corn and grains.

The **past tense** of a verb names an action that already happened. page 76 MORE PRACTICE, page 362

The Pilgrims celebrated the first Thanksgiving.

The team played well yesterday.

The **future tense** of a verb names an action that will take place in the future. page 77 MORE PRACTICE, page 362

Snow will fall soon. We will need heavy coats.

A **helping verb** helps the main verb to name an action or make a statement. pages 86, 88, 90 MORE PRACTICE, page 363

Astronauts have landed.

Marsha has picked the beans.

The **past tense** of a verb with **have** names an action that began in the past and may still be going on. The **past tense** with **have** uses the helping verb **have** or **has** and the main verb in the past tense. page 86 MORE PRACTICE, page 363

The children have dug a hole.

The pony has jumped the fence.

The **present tense** of the helping verb **be** *(am, is, are)* and a main verb ending with **-ing** name an action that continues in the present. page 236 MORE PRACTICE, page 371

I am selling buckets of fish. You are helping the clerk.

The **past tense** of the helping verb **be** *(was, were)* and a main verb ending with **-ing** name an action that began in the past and continued for a time. page 236 MORE PRACTICE, page 371

The sun was shining.

Many people were playing.

A **linking verb** is a verb that connects the subject part with a noun or adjective in the predicate part. It tells what the subject is or is like. page 226 MORE PRACTICE, pages 370, 371

Today is Halloween.

Our costumes are scary.

Use an **-s** or **-es** to form the present tense of a verb when the subject is a singular noun or *it, he,* or *she.* page 78 MORE PRACTICE, pages 362, 365

The cat races around the room.

It leaps onto the sofa.

Do not use an **-s** or **-es** to form the present tense of a verb when the subject is a plural noun or *I, you, we,* or *they.* page 78 MORE PRACTICE, pages 362, 365

The rabbits eat lettuce in our garden.

They hop away.

Add an **-s** to the main verb in the predicate to form the present tense when the subject is a singular noun and the predicate is compound. page 164 MORE PRACTICE, page 367

Xi buys and sells antiques.
Mabel also repairs and paints furniture.

Use the plural form of the verb in the present tense when the parts of a compound subject are connected by **and.** page 164 MORE PRACTICE, page 367

The ducks and geese swim in the pond.
Otto and Miguel watch from the bank.

Use **has** for the present tense of the verb **have** when the subject is a singular noun or *it, he,* or *she.* page 84 MORE PRACTICE, page 363

The dog has a bone.
He has a ball.

Use **have** for the present tense of the verb **have** when the subject is a plural noun or *I, you, we,* or *they.* page 84 MORE PRACTICE, page 363

The children have toys.
I have a cold.

Use the forms of **be** in the present and past tense as shown in this chart. page 226 MORE PRACTICE, page 360

Present		Past		Present		Past	
I	**am**	I		You		You	
She		She	**was**	We	**are**	We	**were**
He	**is**	He		They		They	
It		It					

The past tense of some verbs is not formed in the regular way. These verbs do not change to the past tense by adding **-ed.** They have special forms that do not follow any rules. You must learn these special forms. page 90 MORE PRACTICE, page 363

Plants grow best in sunlight.
The violets grew new blooms last week.
The ivy has grown very fast.

Use special forms of the **past** tense for these verbs. pages 88-91
MORE PRACTICE, page 363

Present	Past	Past Tense with Have
begin	began	have, has begun
blow	blew	have, has blown
break	broke	have, has broken
bring	brought	have, has brought
choose	chose	have, has chosen
come	came	have, has come
do	did	have, has done
draw	drew	have, has drawn
drink	drank	have, has drunk
drive	drove	have, has driven
eat	ate	have, has eaten
fall	fell	have, has fallen
feel	felt	have, has felt
fly	flew	have, has flown
freeze	froze	have, has frozen
give	gave	have, has given
go	went	have, has gone
grow	grew	have, has grown
have	had	have, has had
know	knew	have, has known
lay	laid	have, has laid
leave	left	have, has left
let	let	have, has let
lie	lay	have, has lain
lose	lost	have, has lost
ride	rode	have, has ridden
ring	rang	have, has rung
rise	rose	have, has risen
run	ran	have, has run
say	said	have, has said
see	saw	have, has seen

Present	Past	Past Tense with Have
sing	sang	have, has sung
sit	sat	have, has sat
speak	spoke	have, has spoken
steal	stolen	have, has stolen
swim	swam	have, has swum
take	took	have, has taken
teach	taught	have, has taught
think	thought	have, has thought

PRONOUN

A **pronoun** is a word that takes the place of one or more nouns. pages 112, 307 MORE PRACTICE, pages 364, 376

Denise played on the sidewalk. She fell and scratched her hand.

Two strangers spoke to Frank. They asked him for the time.

A **subject pronoun** is a pronoun that is used as the subject of a sentence. page 114 MORE PRACTICE, page 364

Elsie and Helen went to school. They borrowed two books.

The canary lived in a cage. It sang all day long.

An **object pronoun** is a pronoun that is used as the object of a verb. page 116 MORE PRACTICE, page 364

The boy kicked the ball. Sanya caught it.

Jason delivered the boxes. The dealer stacked them.

This chart shows the use of subject pronouns and object pronouns. page 118 MORE PRACTICE, page 365

Subject	Pronouns	Object	Pronouns
I	we	me	us
you	you	you	you
she, he, it	they	her, him, it	them

A **possessive pronoun** is a pronoun that names who or what has something. page 122 MORE PRACTICE, page 365

Mary washed her new bicycle.

The children found their ball.

Handbook

ADJECTIVE

An **adjective** is a word that describes a noun or pronoun. pages 192, 228, 306 MORE PRACTICE, pages 368, 376

Little Adam tipped his red hat.

The silly clown jumped over a tiny stick.

An adjective ending in **-er** compares two nouns. An adjective ending in **-est** compares more than two nouns. page 194 MORE PRACTICE, page 369

The flute makes a softer sound then the trombone.

The drums play the loudest music in the band.

A **proper adjective** is an adjective formed from a proper noun. Begin a proper adjective with a capital letter. page 201 MORE PRACTICE, page 369

The class learned a Spanish dance.

Use **more** before most adjectives with two or more syllables when comparing two nouns. page 196 MORE PRACTICE, page 369

Swimming was more popular at camp than canoeing.

Sailing was more difficult than canoeing.

Use **most** before most adjectives with two or more syllables when comparing more than two nouns. page 196 MORE PRACTICE, page 369

The President has the most difficult job of all the jobs in the country.

The President lives in the most beautiful home in America.

ADVERB

An **adverb** is a word that describes an action. pages 260, 306 MORE PRACTICE, pages 372, 376

The monkeys chattered noisily.

The elephant walked slowly.

Add **-er** to one-syllable adverbs when comparing two actions. Add **-est** to one-syllable adverbs when comparing more than two actions. page 262 MORE PRACTICE, page 373

Laurel can swim faster than her pet dog.

Audry tried hardest of all the children.

Use **more** before most adverbs ending in **-ly** when comparing two actions. page 262 MORE PRACTICE, page 373

The sun shines more brightly today than yesterday.

It shone most brightly of all on Tuesday.

INTERJECTION

An **interjection** is a word or group of words that expresses strong feeling. It is followed by an exclamation mark. page 5

Oh! How lovely! MORE PRACTICE, page 358

PREPOSITION

A **preposition** is a word that relates a noun or pronoun to another word. page 304 MORE PRACTICE, page 376

Rain fell from the sky. The twins went to the store.

A **prepositional phrase** is a group of words that begins with a preposition and ends with a noun or pronoun. page 304

The cat sleeps under the table. MORE PRACTICE, page 376

The books are on the desk.

CONJUNCTION

A **conjunction** is a word that joins words or groups of words. page 298 MORE PRACTICE, page 376

Some crocodiles live in Florida, but others live in Africa.

II. Mechanics

Capitalization

Use a **capital letter** to begin the first word of every sentence. pages 6, 268 MORE PRACTICE, pages 358, 373

The rocket landed. Where did it land?

Use a **capital letter** to begin each important word of a proper noun. A proper noun is a noun that names a special person, place, thing, or idea. page 268 MORE PRACTICE, page 373

Art Jones is from Dallas. Tom lives on Tyler Drive.

Use a **capital letter** to begin the names of the months and days of the week. page 268 MORE PRACTICE, page 373

We leave on Monday, June 26. The show will be this Friday.

Use a **capital letter** for each initial in a person's name. Use a period after an initial. page 268 MORE PRACTICE, page 373

Edwin C. Jones is our grocer. T. A. Edison was an inventor.

Use a **capital letter** to begin each important word in a book title. Always begin the first word of a title with a capital letter. page 268 MORE PRACTICE, page 373

Have you read *Moby Dick?* *The Great Brain* is a good book.

Punctuation

Use a **period** (.) at the end of a declarative or an imperative sentence. page 6 MORE PRACTICE, page 358

Use a **question mark** (?) at the end of an interrogative sentence. page 6 MORE PRACTICE, page 358

Where is the library?

Do you have a book?

Use an **exclamation mark** (!) at the end of an exclamatory sentence or an interjection. page 6 MORE PRACTICE, page 358

What a silly costume you have! Ouch!

Use a **comma** (,) to set off words such as yes, no, and well when they begin a sentence. pages 14, 168, 308 MORE PRACTICE, pages 368, 376

No, I do not have your pencil.

Use a **comma** (,) to set off the name of a person who is spoken to directly in a sentence. pages 14, 168, 308 MORE PRACTICE, pages 368, 376

Please pass the vegetables, Tom.

Use a **comma** (,) to separate the name of the day from the date, and the date from the year. Use a **comma** (,) after the year when it appears with the date in the middle of a sentence. pages 14, 168, 308 MORE PRACTICE, pages 368, 376

We will arrive on Thursday, May 6, 1982, in Denver.

Use a **comma** (,) to separate the name of a city and state. Use a **comma** (,) after the name of a state when it appears with a city name in the middle of a sentence. pages 14, 168, 308 MORE PRACTICE, pages 368, 376

She was born in Toledo, Ohio, many years ago.

Use a **comma** (,) to separate each noun in a series of three or more nouns. pages 168, 308 MORE PRACTICE, pages 368, 376

Tom, Ed, and Sue worked.

Ted read stories, poems, and plays.

Use a **comma** (,) to separate each verb in a series of three or more verbs. pages 168, 308 MORE PRACTICE, pages 368, 376

The girls hop, skip, and jump.

Tom cuts, sews, and fits suits.

Use a **comma** (,) before the conjunctions and or but in a compound sentence. page 308 MORE PRACTICE, page 376

The band played, and the children danced.

When writing conversation, use a **comma** (,) to separate the spoken words from the person who is saying them. Place the **comma** before the quotation marks. page 308 MORE PRACTICE, pages 368, 376

"Let's sit out this dance," suggested June.

If a speaker asks a question, use a **question mark** (?) instead of a comma before the end quotation marks. page 308 MORE PRACTICE, pages 368, 376

"Do you know how to waltz?" asked Ted.

If a speaker's name comes in the middle of the spoken words, use **commas** (,) to separate the spoken words from the speaker's name. page 308 MORE PRACTICE, pages 368, 376

"I'll ask Dad to teach me," said June, "and then I'll teach you."

Add an **apostrophe** and **s** ('s) to form the possessive of most singular nouns. pages 50, 238 MORE PRACTICE, page 372

The bird's nest was full of eggs.

Add an **apostrophe** (') to form the possessive of plural nouns that end with **s.** pages 50, 238 MORE PRACTICE, page 372

Some animals wandered through the scouts' camp.

Add an **apostrophe** and **s** ('s) to form the possessive of plural nouns that do not end with **s.** pages 51, 238

This store sells women's clothes on the third floor.

Use an **apostrophe** (') to form a **contraction.** A **contraction** is a word made up of two words. The words are joined together to make one word. page 238 MORE PRACTICE, page 372

Aren't you going on a picnic?

Capitalization and Punctuation in Conversation

Use **quotation marks** (“ ”) to show the exact words that a person speaks. They show where the conversation starts and where it stops. When a conversation begins with a new speaker, indent the first word. page 170 MORE PRACTICE, page 368

“Your automobile should run perfectly now,” the smiling mechanic said to Father.

“I certainly hope so,” Father replied.

Use conversation words such as *asked, shouted,* and *cried* to show how a person is speaking. Use a **comma** (,) to divide the spoken words from the person who is saying them. The comma always comes before the quotation marks. page 170 MORE PRACTICE, page 368

“The weather report was good,” explained Mother, “and we should have a wonderful trip.”

If the speaker asks a question, use a **question mark** (?) instead of a comma before the end quotation marks. page 171 MORE PRACTICE, page 368

“Joan, have you packed all your things?” asked Mother.

Capitalize the first word of the **quotation** as you do in any sentence. page 171 MORE PRACTICE, page 368

“Joan answered, “To be sure, I'll check my list again.”

When the conversation words and the speaker's name follow the **quotation**, do not capitalize the first word after the quotation. Always capitalize proper nouns. page 171 MORE PRACTICE, page 368

“The dog is acting strange,” a worried Andy remarked.

When the speaker's name and conversation words come in the middle of the **quotation**, use **commas** (,) to divide the spoken words from the speaker's name. page 171 MORE PRACTICE, page 368

“Perhaps the dog senses our leaving,” said Mother, “and he is nervous.”

Use a **period** (.) at the end of the complete quotation or sentence. page 171 MORE PRACTICE, page 368

“It's too bad we can't take Ruff with us,” sighed Andy.

III. Spelling

Spelling Nouns

To make most singular nouns plural, add **-s.** page 38 MORE PRACTICE, page 360

cow/cows horse/horses bed/beds

If a singular noun ends with **s, ss, x, ch, sh,** or **z,** add **-es** to form the plural. page 38 MORE PRACTICE, page 360

box/boxes bus/buses bench/benches dish/dishes

If a singular noun ends with a consonant and **y,** change the **y** to **i** and add **-es** to form the plural. page 40 MORE PRACTICE, page 360

butterfly/butterflies country/countries sky/skies

If a singular noun ends with a vowel and **y**, add **-s** to form the plural. page 40 MORE PRACTICE, page 360

key/keys boy/boys day/days

Many singular nouns ending in **f** or **fe** add **-s** to form the plural in the usual way. page 41 MORE PRACTICE, page 360

roof/roofs safe/safes cliff/cliffs

For some singular nouns that end in **f** or **fe,** change the **f** to **v** and add **-s** or **-es** to form the plural. page 41 MORE PRACTICE, page 360

life/lives shelf/shelves loaf/loaves wife/wives

Spelling Verbs

If a verb ends in a consonant and **y**, change the **y** to **i** and add **-es** to make the correct form of the present tense. page 78 MORE PRACTICE, page 362

try/tries worry/worries study/studies

If a verb ends in a vowel and **y**, add **-s** to make the correct form of the present tense. page 79 MORE PRACTICE, page 362

play/plays say/says obey/obeys

If a verb ends in a consonant and **y**, change the **y** to **i** and add **-ed** to form the past tense. page 80 MORE PRACTICE, page 362

study/studied hurry/hurried try/tried

If a verb ends in a vowel and **y**, add **-ed** to form the past tense. page 80 MORE PRACTICE, page 362

play/played obey/obeyed stay/stayed

If a verb ends in a consonant, vowel, consonant, double the last consonant and add **-ed** to form the past tense. page 81 MORE PRACTICE, page 362

shop/shopped beg/begged knit/knitted

Spelling Adjectives

If an adjective ends in **e**, drop the **e** and add **-er** or **-est** to make the correct form of the adjective. page 195 MORE PRACTICE, page 369

sane	late	nice
saner	later	nicer
sanest	latest	nicest

If an adjective ends with a consonant and **y**, change the **y** to **i** and add **-er** or **-est** to make the correct form of the adjective. page 200 MORE PRACTICE, page 369

happy	funny	pretty
happier	funnier	prettier
happiest	funniest	prettiest

If a one-syllable adjective ends with a consonant, vowel, consonant, double the last consonant and add **-er** or **-est** to make the correct form of the adjective. Adjectives that end in **w, x**, or **y** are exceptions to this rule. page 200 MORE PRACTICE, page 369

dim	hot	big
dimmer	hotter	bigger
dimmest	hottest	biggest

Spelling Adverbs

Add **-ly** to some adjectives to form an adverb. page 264 MORE PRACTICE, page 373

quiet/quietly sudden/suddenly final/finally

Change **y** to **i** and add **-ly** to form an adverb from an adjective that ends in **y**. page 264 MORE PRACTICE, page 373

happy/happily busy/busily easy/easily

IV. Vocabulary

A **compound noun** is a noun made up of two or more other words. page 42 MORE PRACTICE, page 360

The campers went on a hayride.

Peter explored the lakeside.

An **abbreviation** is the shortened form of a word. page 48 MORE PRACTICE, page 361

Common Abbreviations Used in Writing	Title Stands for	Abbreviations Used in Addresses, Lists	Stands for
Mr.	a man	Ave.	Avenue
Dr.	Doctor	Blvd.	Boulevard
Rev.	Reverend	Dr.	Drive
Sr.	Senior	Rd.	Road
Jr.	Junior	Rte.	Route
Mrs.	a married woman	St.	Street
		Co.	Company
		Inc.	Incorporated

A **prefix** is a letter or group of letters added to the beginning of a word. page 202 MORE PRACTICE, pages 363, 370

Prefix	Example	Meaning
mis-	badly, in the wrong way	Did you know you misspelled my name?
re-	again	Please rewrite my name.
un-	opposite of	Jack untied his shoelaces.
pre-	before	Sally premixed the cake batter.

Handbook

A **suffix** is one or more letters added to the end of a word. page 202 MORE PRACTICE, pages 361, 370

Suffix	Meaning	Example
-er	one who	printer (one who prints)
-or	one who	sailor (one who sails)
-ness	the state of being	happiness (state of being happy)
-less	without	senseless (without sense)
-y	having	thirsty (having thirst)
-ful	full of	careful (full of care)

A **synonym** is a word that has nearly the same meaning as another word. page 204 MORE PRACTICE, pages 370, 372

The large hall filled with people.
The big hall filled with people.
The silent audience broke into applause.
The quiet audience broke into applause.

An **antonym** is a word that means the opposite of another word. page 232 MORE PRACTICE, page 371

Susan began reading the book on Monday.
She finished reading it on Friday.
The train arrives in the station at ten.
The train leaves at eleven.

Homonyms are words that sound alike but have different spellings and different meanings. page 126 MORE PRACTICE, page 365

They're playing with their gifts.
The two waiters wanted to go home, too.

A **homograph** is a word that is spelled the same way as another word but has a different meaning. page 270 MORE PRACTICE, page 374

Lena lowered her head in the wind.
Be sure to wind your watch.
Helen left her umbrella behind.
Make a left turn at the crossroads.

A **simile** is a comparison of two different things with the use of **like** or **as.** page 58

The mountain water was as cold as an ice cube.

A **metaphor** is a comparison of two different things without the use of **like** or **as.** page 58

To the thirsty hikers, the water was ambrosia!

Personification is the use of words to give things and animals human qualities. page 59

The stream played hide and seek among the rocks.

A **contraction** is a word made up of two words. The words are joined together to make one word. page 238 MORE PRACTICE, page 371

These charts show contractions of pronouns with the present tense of the verb **be**, pronouns with **have** and **has**, and pronouns with **had**.

Contraction	Short For
I'm	I am
you're	you are
he's	he is
she's	she is
it's	it is
we're	we are
they're	they are

Contraction	Short For
I've	I have
you've	you have
he's	he has
she's	she has
it's	it has
we've	we have
they've	they have

Contraction	Short For
I'd	I had
you'd	you had
he'd	he had
she'd	she had
it'd	it had
we'd	we had
they'd	they had

Handbook

V. Special Forms

Friendly Letter

Use this this form to write a friendly letter. page 62

Heading →	63 Barrow Street Boston, Massachusetts 68102 January 14, 19__
Greeting →	Dear Kenny,
Body →	We had a lot of fun in the snow last week. A howling blizzard swept through our town on Monday. Jo Ann, Tommy, Amy, and I built a huge snow fort with a wall that was five feet high. It had a long, dark tunnel, too. Mom gave us delicious sandwiches and a thermos of hot, creamy chocolate for a picnic. Later we had an exciting snowball fight, but the dog kept catching the snowballs! I wish you could have been with us.
Closing →	Your friend,
Signature →	Charles

Use this form to address an envelope.

Return Address →	Charles Kinney 63 Barrow Street Boston, Massachusetts 68102
Address →	Kenny Brody 8657 Gulf Road El Paso, Texas 68705

Business Letter

Use this form to write a business letter. page 102

Heading →	130 Hugh Street Omaha, Nebraska 58412 May 17, 19__
Inside Address →	Brown's Sporting Goods 473 Ocean Avenue Johnson, New York 11005
Greeting →	Dear Brown's Sporting Goods:
	I want to order a warm-up suit. I read your ad about the sale in this morning's newspaper. I want a suit that is red with blue stripes. My size is small. I am sending a check for the sale price of $20.00.
Closing →	Yours truly,
Signature →	Jan L. Hanson Jan L. Hanson

Book Report

Follow these steps to write a book report. A book report tells about a story in two or three summary paragraphs. page 312

1. Write the title and author of the book.
2. In the first summary paragraph, describe the main character and tell the setting where the character lives.
3. In the second summary paragraph, tell one or two important events that happened in the story.

Little House on the Prairie
by Laura Ingalls Wilder

The Ingalls family leave their home in Wisconsin and travel to Kansas. They settle on the open prairie in Indian Territory. Pa and Ma and their three daughters, Mary, Laura, and Baby Carrie, live in a log house that Pa builds. Laura is a strong, brave little girl. She helps Pa build the house, helps Ma pick berries, and helps take care of her little sister.

The Ingalls family has many adventures. One time they fight a giant prairie fire. Another time they are trapped in their house, surrounded by wolves. They make an effort to get along with the Indians that live nearby. The family works hard to survive the dangers and hardships of prairie life.

Outlines

Use this form to arrange ideas into an outline. page 278

Main subject	→	**Fur Traders in the West**
Main heading	→	**I.** Fur traders in the West
Subheadings	→	A. Found new lands
		B. Found new routes for pioneers
Main heading	→	**II.** Fur traders in the mountains
Subheadings	→	A. Called mountaineers
		B. Learned many Indian skills

The main headings should be developed into topic sentences for the report. The subheadings should be developed as detail sentences for the paragraphs in the report.

VI. Diagraming

You can examine parts of speech and how words work in a sentence by using diagrams. The sentence patterns below show how different sentences can be diagramed.

Simple Sentence with Action Verb

PATTERN 1

Horses run.

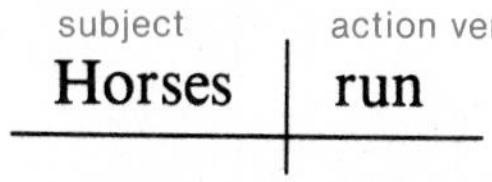

PATTERN 2

Cows eat grass.

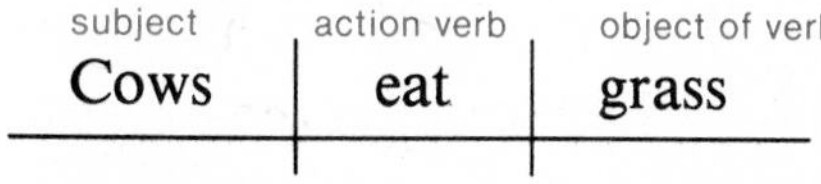

Simple Sentence with Adjective and Adverb

PATTERN 3

Young horses walk slowly.

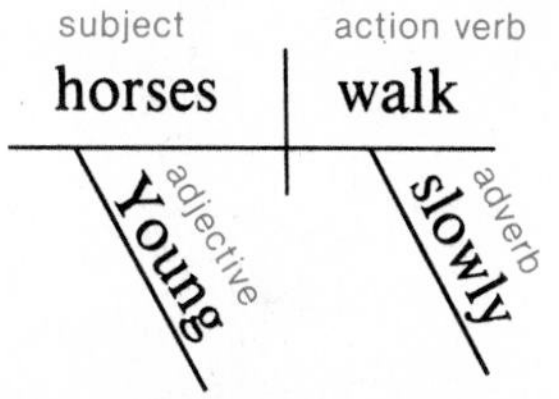

Simple Sentence with Linking Verb

PATTERN 4

Elephants are huge.

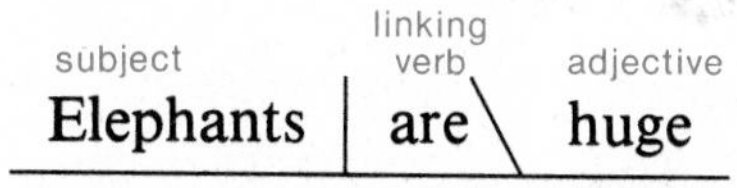

PATTERN 5

Ants are insects.

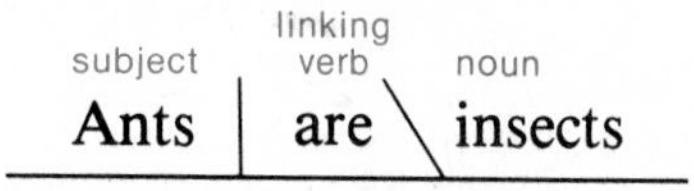

Compound Sentence

PATTERN 6

Dogs run, but birds fly.

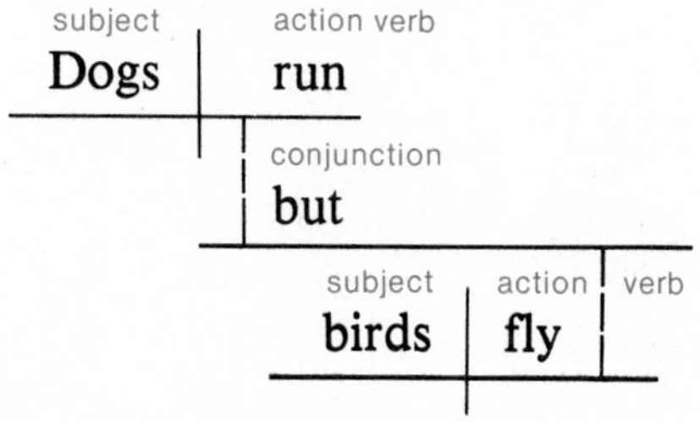

More Practice

Reviewing Sentences, pages 2–3

Some of the groups of words below are sentences. Other groups are not. Write **sentence** if the group of words is a sentence. If a group of words is not a sentence, write **not a sentence.**

1. The Mendez family drives away.
2. The dog runs away.
3. The police.
4. José Mendez looks around.
5. The neighbors search their yard.
6. Nilda Mendez writes a sign.
7. Hangs the sign in town.
8. Knocks on doors.
9. The sad family.
10. They look everywhere.

Four Kinds of Sentences, pages 4–5

Read each sentence. Decide what kind it is. Write whether each sentence is **declarative, interrogative, imperative,** or **exclamatory.**

1. Will the family find the dog?
2. How unhappy they are!
3. They hear a noise.
4. What is that sound?
5. Open the door.
6. What a surprise!
7. The dog is at the door.
8. How did it get home?
9. Give the dog some food.
10. The family is relieved.

Capitalizing and Punctuating Sentences, pages 6–7

Write each of the following sentences. Begin each sentence with a capital letter. End each sentence with the correct punctuation mark.

1. a new boy joins our class
2. his name is Kevin
3. where did he come from
4. he came from another city
5. make him feel welcome
6. how unfriendly he is
7. come back
8. why does he walk away
9. the boy solves the mystery
10. the real Kevin appears

Subject Parts and Predicate Parts, pages 10–11

Write each sentence. Underline each subject part.

1. Mrs. Kornfeld loses her ring.
2. The detective finds a feather.
3. A friend sees a tree.
4. Mr. Kornfeld sees a nest.
5. The detective smiles.
6. The yellow bird sings.

Write each sentence. Underline each predicate part.

7. Birds sit on eggs in the nest.
8. One bird brings food.
9. The detective puts a shiny penny near a window.
10. Another bird takes the penny.
11. The detective finds the ring in the nest.

Building Sentences, pages 12–13

Add words to the subject or predicate part of each sentence. Write the sentences.

1. Bells rang.
2. People rushed.
3. The crowd waited.
4. The owner phoned.
5. A man climbed.
6. A woman shouted.
7. The child laughed.
8. A person escaped.

Using Commas, pages 14–15

Write each sentence, using commas where necessary.

1. What are you reading now Joan?
2. Well it seems to be a true detective story.
3. It tells about something that happened on March 15 1975.
4. Wasn't the story reported in a Rome New York newspaper then?
5. In 1975 I was living in Lancaster Pennsylvania.
6. The story remains a mystery Betty until I've read all about it.

More Practice

Reviewing Nouns, pages 36–39

Write each noun. After each, write **person, place, thing,** or **idea.** Then write **singular** if the noun is singular and **plural** if it is plural.

1. The children visited the museum.
2. Maria looked at the Egyptian mummies.
3. Judy admired the precious stones.
4. The museum gave pleasure to the children.

Forming Plural Nouns, pages 40–43

Write the plural form of each noun.

1. zoo	4. ray	7. box	10. life	13. cross
2. roof	5. child	8. crate	11. leaf	14. goose
3. lunch	6. fig	9. woman	12. family	15. daisy

Compound Nouns, pages 42–43

Write each compound noun. Draw a line between the two words. Then write what each compound noun means.

1. A heavy rainstorm hit the area.
2. The downpour caused a lot of damage.
3. Many backyards filled with water.
4. People drove on the sidewalk.

Write a compound noun to replace the underlined words.

5. The tourists boarded a <u>boat that sails</u>.
6. The <u>light of the moon</u> gave a soft glow.
7. At <u>the time of night</u> the group could see the city's lights.
8. They watched the blinking <u>house with a light</u>.
9. It guided the ships away from the <u>line of the shore</u>.
10. The boat sailed until the <u>rise of the sun</u>.

Common and Proper Nouns, pages 46–47

Write each noun. Write whether it is **common** or **proper.**

1. The ship traveled into the port.
2. The tourists saw the Panama Canal.
3. Mrs. Potts pointed to the Andes Mountains.
4. The Hawaiian Islands appeared on the horizon.

Abbreviations, pages 48–49

Change each underlined word to an abbreviation. Write the new phrase.

1. The Good Idea <u>Company</u>
2. 3:00 <u>post meridiem</u>
3. <u>Friday, February</u> 2
4. 8:36 <u>ante meridiem</u>
5. <u>Mister</u> Adam Jones
6. Mill <u>Road</u>

Possessive Nouns, pages 50–51

Change the word at the end of the sentence to make a possessive noun. Write each sentence.

1. The passengers board Captain ___ airplane. (River)
2. The ___ baggage arrived. (attendants)
3. The ___ dinners were prepared. (travelers)
4. The ___ engine started. (plane)

Suffixes, pages 52–53

In each sentence find each word that has the suffix **er, or, ness,** or **less.** Write each word and then write what it means.

1. The concert began with a banjo player.
2. A singer sang a folk song.
3. One song told of a friendless child.
4. The performers spread gladness.

More Practice

Action Verbs, pages 72–73

Write each sentence. Underline the action verb.

1. The air hummed with excitement.
2. Runners raced around the track.
3. Our team broke the old record.
4. Jenny set a new record.

Objects of Verbs, pages 74–75

Read each sentence. Write the verb and the object of the verb.

1. The coach blows her whistle.
2. The runners take their places.
3. The starter raises the gun.
4. The starter pulls the trigger.
5. The runners start the race.
6. The winner crosses the line.

Verb Tenses, pages 76–77

Read each sentence. Write the verb. Then write whether each verb is in the **present, past,** or **future** tense.

1. Ralph will chase the ball.
2. It lands in his glove.
3. The players worked hard.
4. The rain will fall all day.

Using the Present Tense, pages 78–79

Write each sentence. Use the verb in the present tense.

1. The fan ___ to the game. (run)
2. Sandy ___ for the basket. (shoot)
3. He ___ two points. (score)
4. He ___ the rules. (study)
5. Carmen ___ in the air. (leap)
6. She ___ the ball. (catch)
7. The fans ___. (clap)
8. One player ___ home. (stay)

Using the Past Tense, pages 80–81

Write each sentence. Use the verb in the past tense.

1. The captain worries about rain.
2. The players share their lunches.
3. They obey the coach.
4. He drags out the plastic cover.
5. They cover the wet field.
6. The boys enjoy the rain.

Present and Past of *Have,* pages 84–85

Write each sentence. Use the correct form of the verb **have.**

1. Jorge ___ a pencil. (present)
2. They ___ the puzzle. (past)
3. You ___ an eraser. (present)
4. Kay ___ the right word. (past)

Past Tense with *Have,* pages 86–87

Write each sentence. Use each verb in the past tense.

1. Tom has ___ the house this summer. (paint)
2. His sisters have ___ him. (help)
3. They have ___ the old paint. (scrape)
4. Their friends have ___ them. (watch)
5. Carpenters have ___ the windows. (fix)
6. The mason has ___ the walk. (cement)

Irregular Verbs, pages 88–91

Write each sentence. Use each verb in the past tense.

1. The players have ___ badly. (do)
2. Perry has ___ the water. (drink)
3. The audience has ___ quietly. (sit)
4. Has the team ___ the game? (lose)
5. The coach ___ angry. (grow)
6. People have ___ asleep. (fall)

Prefixes, pages 92–93

Change the underlined words to one word that has a prefix.
Write the new word.

1. Leona <u>placed in the wrong way</u> her keys.
2. Her daughter <u>did the opposite of lock</u> the door for her.
3. The keys <u>appeared again</u> the next day.
4. She <u>did the opposite of cover</u> them in her drawer.

More Practice

Pronouns, pages 112–113

Read each pair of sentences. The second sentence in each pair has one or more pronouns. Write each pronoun. Then write the noun or nouns each pronoun replaces.

1. Nan wrote a report about ants. She wrote it in the library.
2. Nan read articles about ants. She found them in books.
3. Two boys made an ant farm. They watched the ants work.
4. Our class liked the report. We listened to it quietly.

Pronouns as Subjects, pages 114–115

Read each pair of sentences. Write the second sentence. Use the correct subject pronoun in place of the underlined words.

1. Jason drives a truck. <u>The truck</u> has a CB radio.
2. Jason drives cross-country. <u>Jason</u> drives long distances.
3. Other drivers call Jason. <u>The drivers</u> ask about the weather.
4. Beth and I met Jason. <u>Beth and I</u> asked many questions.

Pronouns as Objects, pages 116–117

Read each pair of sentences. In the second sentence some words are underlined. Write the object pronoun that can be used in place of the underlined words.

1. One driver called Jason on the CB radio. The driver asked <u>Jason</u> for help.
2. Jason answered the driver's call. Jason answered <u>the call</u> in less than a minute.
3. The driver told Jason about two flat tires. Glass on the road caused <u>the tires</u> to go flat.
4. Jason visited our class. Jason showed <u>our class</u> some pictures.

Using Subject and Object Pronouns, pages 118–119

Write each sentence. Use the correct pronoun.

1. Sue said to Mr. Ray, "___ need help." (I, me)
2. "Tell ___ about the problems," answered Mr. Ray. (I, me)
3. Sue told ___ about the worst problems. (he, him)
4. Mr. Ray helped ___ quickly. (she, her)

Possessive Pronouns, pages 122–123

Write each sentence. Use the correct possessive pronoun.

1. The students read ___ reports. (their, theirs)
2. Carl read ___ first. (his, theirs)
3. Then Andrea read ___ . (her, hers)
4. It told about ___ trip to Mexico. (her, hers)

Subject-Verb Agreement, pages 124–125

Write each sentence. Use the present tense of the verb.

1. Nancy enjoys television.
   She ___ television every evening. (watch)
2. Nancy looks for programs about nature.
   They ___ Nancy many new facts. (teach)
3. Nancy tells the club members about the nature programs.
   They ___ very carefully. (listen)
4. Nancy's uncle brings her books about nature.
   He ___ the books from the library. (borrow)

Words Often Confused, pages 126–127

Read each sentence. Write the correct word for each blank space.

1. "Do ___ friends visit you often?" (you're, your)
2. "Yes, ___ good to see them." (its, it's)
3. They bring ___ books. (their, there, they're)
4. ___ fun to read. (Their, There, They're)

More Practice

Reviewing Sentences, pages 152–153

Write each sentence. Underline each subject part.

1. Many people invent new things.
2. These inventions help us.
3. Some discoveries keep us warm.
4. Other inventions keep us cool.

Write each sentence. Underline each predicate part.

5. The Chinese invented many things.
6. A Greek man made a press for fruit.
7. Johannes Gutenberg worked on a printing press.
8. Gutenberg invented movable type.

Simple Subjects, pages 154–155

Write the subject part. Draw one line under the simple subject.

1. My brother has a workshop.
2. He invents new toys.
3. One toy has a battery.
4. A green robot walks in circles.

Simple Predicates, pages 156–157

Write each predicate part. Underline the simple predicate.

1. Lu read about inventors.
2. He wrote a good report.
3. Peg read about George Eastman.
4. He invented a camera.

Compound Subjects, pages 158–159

Write the subject part of each sentence. If the subject is compound, write **compound.**

1. Alexander Graham Bell and Thomas Edison worked hard.
2. The telephone first rang in 1876.
3. Homes and offices needed telephones.
4. People enjoyed the new invention.

Compound Predicates, pages 160–161

Write the predicate part of each sentence. If the predicate is compound, write **compound.**

1. People called and talked on the telephone.
2. They made meals and cleaned rooms by lamplight.
3. People sat by their telephones.
4. They read books and played games by the flickering lights.
5. Everybody laughed and joked about the blackout.

Agreement of Verbs with Compound Subjects, pages 164–165

Write each sentence. Use each verb in the present tense.

1. Lucy ___ a list of inventions. (read)
2. Lucy and her parents ___ the museum. (visit)
3. The guard ___ them many things. (show)
4. Lucy and the guard ___ about inventors. (talk)
5. Lucy and the visitors ___ to the guard. (listen)

Building Sentences with Compound Subjects and Compound Predicates, pages 166–167

Combine each group of sentences to make one sentence.

1. The Chinese invented paper. The Chinese invented porcelain. They also invented gunpowder.
2. The plow was invented long before B.C. dating. The wheel was invented even earlier.
3. What invention was Edwin Land identified with? What invention was George Eastman identified with?
4. The fluorescent light was invented about 1935. Radar was invented about the same time.

Using Commas in Writing, pages 168–169

Write each sentence. Add commas where they are needed.

1. A. G. Bell worked as a scientist teacher and inventor.
2. He was born on March 3 1847 in Edinburgh Scotland.
3. Bell lived in Canada England and America.
4. He studied invented and helped others during his life.
5. Well he certainly was a brilliant man.
6. Miss Adams I'd like to read a biography of Bell.

Punctuating a Conversation, pages 170–171

Write each sentence, adding the correct punctuation.

1. Can you help me clean the car? asked Father.
2. Let me finish mowing the lawn replied Timmy.
3. Hurry up, urged Father. I need you here.
4. Ten more minutes said Timmy and I'll be through.
5. Father called, Bring the dustpan with you.

Adjectives, pages 192–193

Write each adjective that appears in each sentence. After each adjective, write the noun it describes.

1. The new group performs during assembly.
2. The talented students practice after school.
3. The teacher is a famous singer.
4. The group sings favorite songs.
5. Four girls sing in a quartet.
6. The boys practice pretty songs.
7. The music echoes in the huge auditorium.
8. The teacher looks out at the empty seats.
9. The teacher pulls the heavy curtain.
10. A curious visitor stops and listens.

Adjectives That Compare, pages 194–195

Write each sentence with the correct form of the adjective.

1. The visitor listened for a ___ time than I did. (long)
2. The songs were the ___ songs on the radio. (late)
3. The group seemed ___ than the other singing group. (loud)
4. This was a much ___ group than the other. (large)

Using *More* and *Most* to Compare, pages 196–197

Write the correct form of the adjective for each sentence.

1. Eva has the ___ voice in the whole group. (more pleasant, most pleasant)
2. The tenors have ___ voices than the baritones. (more joyous, most joyous)
3. The soprano singer has the ___ voice of all. (more delicate, most delicate)
4. Dan has ___ songs than the other bass singer. (more difficult, most difficult)

Spelling Adjectives, page 200

Write each adjective with an **-er**. Then write each with **-est**.

1. happy	3. noisy	5. heavy	7. roomy	9. sunny
2. mushy	4. lazy	6. juicy	8. busy	10. sandy

Capitalizing Proper Adjectives, page 201

Write each sentence. Capitalize the proper adjective.

1. The french artist plays the accordian well.
2. We can enjoy the canadian Ballet on television.
3. People in Canada can enjoy the detroit Symphony.
4. Do jamaican drums sound strange to you?

More Practice

Prefixes and Suffixes, pages 202–203

Write each underlined word. Then write the word's meaning.

1. Chip doesn't have a squeaky voice.
2. The audience listened to the delightful song.
3. They were unaware of his nervousness.
4. He was not careless with the notes.
5. The audience was in a cheerful mood.
6. They listened to an unplanned encore.

Adjective Synonyms, pages 204–205

Read the word after each sentence. Write the word that is the synonym for the underlined word.

1. The group gave a brilliant performance. (splendid, dull, boring)
2. The boys and girls applauded in the crowded auditorium. (empty, full, small)
3. The happy faces pleaded for another song. (hopeless, unhappy, joyful)
4. A slender girl in the front row jumped up and down. (thin, wealthy, tired)

Linking Verbs, pages 226–227

Write the verb in each sentence. If the verb names an action, write **action verb** after the verb. If the verb is a linking verb, write **linking verb** after the verb.

1. Jan works very hard.
2. She is a musician.
3. She plays the violin.
4. Jan practices every day.
5. Her days are pleasant.
6. She practiced last week.
7. Mark was a pianist.
8. He is Jan's friend.
9. Mark visits often.
10. The teacher praised them.
11. They were very good.
12. The musicians were happy.

Nouns and Adjectives After Linking Verbs, pages 228–229

Write the word that follows the linking verb. (Do not count words such as *a, an,* or *the*). If the word is a noun, write **noun.** If the word is an adjective, write **adjective.** Then write the word to which the noun or adjective is linked.

1. George is a racer.
2. Sometimes the job is dangerous.
3. George is fearless.
4. His parents were spectators.
5. His mother was quiet.
6. George was calm.

Using Linking Verbs in the Present and Past Tenses, pages 230–231

Write each sentence. Use the correct form of the linking verb.

1. Tina and Chuck ___ comedians. (is, are)
2. Tina ___ funnier than Chuck. (is, are)
3. I ___ a fan of theirs. (is, am)
4. Tina and Chuck ___ good last night. (was, were)
5. Chuck ___ funnier than Tina this time. (was, were)

Verb Antonyms, pages 232–233

Write each sentence. Use an antonym for the underlined word.

1. Jon <u>finished</u> college this year. (started, quit, completed)
2. His family was <u>proud</u>. (happy, amazed, ashamed)
3. His parents <u>arrived at</u> his graduation. (watched, left, awaited)
4. They <u>smiled</u> at their son. (grinned, laughed, frowned)

Verbs Ending in *-ing*, pages 236–237

Write each sentence with the correct form of the verb **be.**

1. My job ___ starting today. (is, are)
2. I ___ working now for a florist. (am, was)
3. Today these flowers ___ beautiful. (are, were)
4. I ___ watering a plant last night. (am, was)
5. Yesterday it ___ wilting. (was, were)

More Practice

Using Apostrophes in Possessives and Contractions, pages 238–239

Write each sentence, adding the apostrophe in the correct place. Write what each possessive or contraction means.

1. Tami is a printers helper.
2. She uses the artists ink.
3. The workers jobs are hard.
4. Theyre very good at their work.
5. Im a keen observer.
6. Tami reads the books pages.
7. Tamis father is pleased.
8. Its fun to watch workers.
9. Weve looked at the presses.
10. Her fathers friend is pleasant.

Verb Synonyms, pages 240–241

Write each sentence. Use the verb in parentheses that most closely names the action.

1. The fans ___ with excitement. (scream, speak)
2. Many eager fans ___ onto the field. (walk, dash)
3. A funny clown ___ during halftime. (works, performs)
4. Attendants ___ from the stands. (rush, step)
5. The announcer ___ above the noise. (calls, shouts)
6. Then the clown ___ back into the stands. (goes, scurries)

Adverbs, pages 260–261

Write the adverb in each sentence and the word it describes.

1. I visited once.
2. Mr. Atkins eagerly greeted me.
3. He laughed sometimes.
4. He often talked.
5. His dog barked wildly.
6. He ran everywhere.
7. Mr. Atkins spoke angrily.
8. The dog cried softly.
9. Mr. Atkins patted him gently.
10. The dog's tail wagged happily.
11. Then he ate.
12. He chewed noisily.
13. Later he finished.
14. His eyes closed slowly.
15. He slept deeply.
16. I looked around.
17. Suddenly I jumped.
18. I laughed loudly.

Using Adverbs to Compare, pages 262–263

Write each sentence. Use **-er, -est, more,** or **most** to make the correct form of the adverb.

1. Mr. Atkins ran ___ than a flash. (quick)
2. He raced ___ than his son. (fast)
3. Mr. Atkins ran the ___ of all. (smoothly)
4. He also ran the ___ in the family. (fast)
5. Mrs. Atkins improved the ___ in the family. (rapidly)
6. Mrs. Atkins tried the ___. (hard)
7. She practiced ___ than Mr. Atkins. (regularly)

Forming Adverbs from Adjectives, pages 264–265

Change each adjective to an adverb. Write the adverb.

1. A doll swung ___. (merry)
2. Its eyes shone ___. (bright)
3. I walked to it ___. (slow)
4. I touched it ___. (curious)
5. It moved ___. (light)
6. I heard ___. (clear)
7. Mr. Atkins worked ___. (busy)
8. He painted ___. (swift)
9. The toys sat ___. (silently)
10. The dog watched ___. (sleepy)
11. Mr. Atkins whistled ___. (soft)
12. He hammered ___. (quick)

Reviewing Capitalization, pages 268–269

Write each sentence. Use capital letters correctly.

1. mr. edwin t. atkins has an interesting job.
2. my visit to his shop on tuesday was quite an adventure.
3. they are all in dameron, maryland.
4. mr. e. atkins makes things for television and movies.
5. my friend, j. d. copeland, read about this work.
6. it was in a book called *monster makers*.
7. j. d. and I are going to write a book called *giggly ghost*.
8. we will take it to mr. atkins in june.

More Practice

Homographs, pages 270–271

Two sentences with underlined words are followed by two meanings. Write the letter of the correct meaning next to each sentence.

1. Who invented the bat and ball? Do you mean a bat that flies?
   (a) baseball **(b)** animal
2. He rode a camel in the desert. They desert the sinking ship.
   (a) abandon **(b)** hot, sandy area
3. The cow grazed quietly. Nobody could cow that umpire!
   (a) a farm animal **(b)** to overawe
4. The wolf watched the sheep. Do you ever wolf your breakfast?
   (a) a wild animal **(b)** to eat greedily
5. Light that match carefully. Were your slippers a match?
   (a) one of a pair **(b)** a splinter that catches fire

Understanding Words from Context, pages 272–273

Read each sentence. Write the underlined word in each sentence. Then write what you think each underlined word means.

1. Miko was out sick yesterday. Her absence from school was noted by her teacher.
2. Joel Jackson is an apprentice to a printer. He is learning the printing business. He will be able to get a job as a printer.
3. Sandford is very timid. He is even too shy to ask people the time.
4. The boat was submerged in the lake. It went under the water. It took twelve workers to get it out.
5. This tea was voted superior. The quality of the tea was better than all the others. Five out of six judges liked it best.

Reviewing Compound Subjects and Predicates, pages 296–297

Write each sentence. If the subject is compound, write **compound subject.** If the predicate is compound, write **compound predicate.**

1. Cindy and Karen stayed home with their mother.
2. Mr. Schultz and Otto went fishing on a big boat.
3. Otto fished and drank water all day.
4. The sky and the water were very blue.

Compound Sentences, pages 298–299

Write each compound sentence. If a sentence is not compound, write **not compound.**

1. The girls got up early, and their father loaded the car.
2. The girls made a nice lunch.
3. Kay caught the first fish, but Meg caught the biggest one.
4. The girls held the fish up, and the captain took a picture.

Read each pair of simple sentences. Make them into one compound sentence, using the conjunction in parentheses. Write the new sentence. Place a comma where it belongs.

5. Bees buzzed among the flowers. Black wasps covered the grapes on the terrace. (and)
6. Edda stretched out upon a lounge chair. Her cat curled up at her feet. (and)
7. A wasp landed on the arm of Edda's chair. Edda shooed it away with her book. (but)
8. Later, the wasp landed near the cat. The cat swatted it with her paw. (but)
9. The wasp buzzed angrily. Edda abandoned her place on the terrace. (and)

Building Compound Sentences, pages 300–301

Write each pair of sentences as a compound sentence.

1. Tigers can run very fast. They tire quickly.
2. A tiger makes many sounds. The roar is its loudest sound.
3. People admire a tiger's beauty. They also admire its strength.
4. Tigers have sharp eyesight. They also have a good sense of smell.

Prepositions and Prepositional Phrases, pages 304–305

Write the prepositional phrase in each sentence. Underline the preposition once. Underline its object twice.

1. Seals spend much time in the water.
2. Fur seals have thick coats of fine hair.
3. Sea lions walk with all four flippers.
4. Some seals are slow and clumsy on the ice.

Parts of Speech in Sentences, pages 306–307

Write each underlined word. Write whether the word is a **noun, pronoun, verb, adjective,** or **adverb.**

1. The <u>MacLeans</u> <u>owned</u> some rich farm <u>land</u>.
2. <u>They</u> raised <u>cows</u>, <u>horses</u>, and some <u>noisy</u> <u>ducks</u>.
3. <u>Sometimes</u> the <u>ducks</u> got loose and <u>quacked</u> <u>wildly</u>.
4. The <u>whole</u> <u>family</u> <u>ran</u> after the <u>frightened</u> <u>ducks</u>.

Reviewing Commas, pages 308–309

Write each sentence. Add the commas where they are needed.

1. "Chimpanzees gibbons and gorillas are all apes" explained Dad.
2. Chimps can be tamed easily and they are good performers.
3. Scientists study chimpanzees in Atlanta Georgia.
4. "They eat fruit and leaves" Donna said.
5. "Does the chimpanzee" asked Jack "have a tail?"

SERIES E Macmillan English

Workbook

Unit 1
Reviewing Sentences 379
Four Kinds of Sentences 380
Capitalizing and Punctuating Sentences 381
Subject Parts and Predicate Parts 382
Building Sentences 382
Using Commas 383
Parts of a Book 384
Putting Ideas in Order 385
Independent Writing: Writing a Time-Order Paragraph 385
How to Edit Your Work 386

Unit 2
Reviewing Nouns 386
Plural Nouns 387
Compound Nouns 388
Common and Proper Nouns 389
Abbreviations 389
Possessive Nouns 390
Suffixes 390
Using the Dictionary 391
Words that Describe Senses 392
Independent Writing: Writing a Descriptive Paragraph in a Friendly Letter 392

Unit 3
Action Verbs 393
Objects of Verbs 394
Verb Tenses 395
Using the Present Tense 396
Using the Past Tense 396
Present and Past of *Have* 397
Past Tense with *Have* 397
Irregular Verbs 398
More Irregular Verbs 398
Verb Prefixes 399
Using the Library 399
Reading Graphs and Tables 400
Facts in Paragraphs 401
A Factual Paragraph in a Business Letter 402
Independent Writing: Writing a Business Letter 402

Unit 4
Pronouns 403
Pronouns as Subjects 404
Pronouns as Objects 405
Using Subject and Object Pronouns 406
Possessive Pronouns 407
Subject-Verb Agreement 407
Words Often Confused 408
Fact and Opinion 408
Reasons in a Persuasive Paragraph 409
Independent Writing: Writing an Editorial 409

Unit 5
Reviewing Sentences 410
Simple Subjects 411
Simple Predicates 412
Compound Subjects 413
Compound Predicates 413
Agreement of Verbs with Compound Subjects 414
Building Sentences with Compound Subjects and Compound Predicates 415
Using Commas in Writing 416
Punctuating a Conversation 417
Independent Writing: Writing a Conversation 417

Workbook

Unit 6
Reviewing Adjectives 418
Adjectives That Compare 418
Using *More* and *Most* to Compare 419
Spelling Adjectives 420
Capitalizing Proper Adjectives 420
Prefixes and Suffixes 421
Adjective Synonyms 421
Using Reference Works 422
Reviewing Paragraphs 423
Independent Writing: Writing a Summary Report 424

Unit 7
Linking Verbs 425
Nouns and Adjectives After Linking Verbs 426
Using Linking Verbs in the Present Tense 427
Using Linking Verbs in the Past Tense 427
Verb Antonyms 428
Verbs Ending in *ing* 428
Using Apostrophes in Possessive and Contractions 429
Using Note-Taking Skills 430
Independent Writing: Writing a Two-Paragraph Report 430

Unit 8
Reviewing Adverbs 431
Using Adverbs to Compare 432
Forming Adverbs from Adjectives 433
Reviewing Capital Letters 434
Homographs 435
Understanding Words from Context 436
Developing a Two-Part Outline 437
Outlining a Two-Paragraph Report 438
Independent Writing: Writing a Two-Paragraph Historical Report 438

Unit 9
Reviewing Compound Subjects and Predicates 439
Compound Sentences 440
Building Compound Sentences 441
Prepositions and Prepositional Phrases 442
Parts of Speech in Sentences 443
Reviewing Commas 444
Review: Using the Dictionary 445
Independent Writing: Writing a Story 446

Workbook

Reviewing Sentences pages 2-3

A **sentence** is a group of words that state a complete idea.
Sentence: Tourists usually visit the pyramids in Egypt.
Not a Sentence: visit the pyramids in Egypt.

A. Read each group of words. Write each sentence. If a group of words is not a sentence, **write not a sentence.**

1. Egyptians built the pyramids out of stone blocks.
2. Used limestone for making the blocks.
3. Pyramids have square bases.
4. Each side of an Egyptian pyramid.
5. Faces a compass point.
6. The ruins of 35 pyramids still stand in Egypt.
7. Many people from all over the world.
8. Long ago people buried rulers in pyramids.
9. The Egyptians believed a man's body must be preserved.
10. The Great Pyramid of Cheops at Gizeh.
11. The largest pyramid ever built.
12. The base covers thirteen acres.
13. Some museums have an entire pyramid.

B. Make a complete sentence out of each group of words from the exercise above that is not a sentence. Write the new sentence.

C. Read this paragraph about a trip to Egypt. Then rewrite the paragraph. Be sure each group of words is a complete sentence.

Mei went to Gizeh by car. An old lady rode a camel. Beside the road. Loaded down with red onions. Many small farms along the Nile River. The farmland ended suddenly. Miles of yellow-brown desert sand. Near the pyramids people sold cold drinks. Rode a camel. Mei followed the guide into the Great Pyramid. Crawled through dark tunnels. Now museums all over the world keep the treasures.

Four Kinds of Sentences pages 4-5

A **declarative sentence** makes a statement or tells something.
Giant redwood trees grow in California.

An **interrogative sentence** asks something.
Have you seen a picture of a redwood tree?

An **imperative sentence** tells or asks someone to do something.
Please show the slides of the redwood trees again.

An **exclamatory sentence** shows excitement or strong feeling.
How beautiful those trees look!

Divide your paper into four sections. Head each section **declarative sentence, interrogative sentence, imperative sentence,** and **exclamatory sentence.** Then write each of these sentences under the correct heading.

1. How tall does the sequoia grow?
2. What an enormous piece of wood I saw!
3. Is it part of a sequoia?
4. Who spotted that tree first?
5. It stood for over 1,300 years.
6. What a beautiful scene that is!
7. Tourists visited the forest.
8. Tell us how this wood came here.
9. The Painted Desert is in Arizona.
10. Spanish explorers named it.
11. Have you ever seen it?
12. How colorful it is!
13. Does the desert really change colors?
14. Heat causes the changes in colors.
15. The Painted Desert is a spectacular sight at sunset.
16. How many colors do you see?
17. I see red, yellow, blue, and lilac.
18. Take a picture of the hills in the Painted Desert.

Capitalizing and Punctuating Sentences pages 6-7

Use a **capital letter** to begin the first word of every sentence.

Use a **period (.)** at the end of a declarative or an imperative sentence.

A fawn hides behind a big tree.   Walk quietly.

Use a **question mark (?)** at the end of an interrogative sentence.

Did you see a raccoon?

Use an **exclamation mark (!)** at the end of an exclamatory sentence.

How fast the rabbit moved!

Write each of the following sentences. Begin each sentence with a capital letter. End each sentence with the correct punctuation.

1. imagine a woman in a forest of giant sequoias
2. how tiny she felt
3. why did she choose this tree
4. it was healthy and green
5. what a crash it made
6. how did the workers move this piece
7. the workers cut it into twelve sections
8. how heavy they were
9. tell the group one more thing
10. where is this slice of sequoia displayed
11. it is in The American Museum of Natural History in New York City
12. joyce saw it there
13. what other interesting things are at that museum
14. we saw an exhibit with animals from Africa
15. a lady made origami figures
16. what is origami
17. origami is the art of folding paper
18. it started in Japan
19. a special room exhibits precious gems

Workbook

Subject Parts and Predicate Parts pages 10-11

The **subject part** of a sentence names whom or what the sentence is about. The subject part may have one or more than one word.

Heavy rain fell on the city.

The **predicate part** of a sentence tells what action the subject part does. The predicate part may have one or more than one word.

Heavy rain fell on the city.

Write the sentences below. Draw a line between the subject part and the predicate part of each sentence. Draw one line under the subject part. Draw two lines under the predicate part.

(1) An angry wind rattles the windows. **(2)** The whole house creaks. **(3)** The rain stops. **(4)** My parents stand in the messy yard. **(5)** Someone has torn the leaves from the trees. **(6)** The wind tossed twigs all around.

Building Sentences pages 12-13

Every sentence has a subject part and a predicate part. Some telling sentences are very shot. You can make these sentences tell more by adding words to describe the subject part or the predicate part.

The sky darkened.	The bright sky darkened.
The sky darkened.	The sky darkened suddenly.

Write the following sentences. Underline the subject part in each sentence one. Circle the predicate part in each sentence. Then write new sentences by adding words to the part of the sentence indicated in parentheses.

1. A storm started . (predicate part)
2. The wind blew . (subject part)
3. Trees fell . (predicate part)
4. Streets flooded . (subject part)
5. Electric lines snapped . (predicate part)
6. The rain stopped . (subject part)

Using Commas pages 14-15

Use a **comma (,)** to set off words such as *yes, no,* and *well* when they begin a sentence.

Yes, I enjoy books about magic.

Use a **comma (,)** to set off the name of a person who is spoken to directly in a sentence.

Alice, have you read about Harry Houdini? I read one book, Kim.

Use a **comma (,)** to separate the day from the date and the date from the year. Use a **comma (,)** after the year when it appears with the date in the middle of a sentence.

Our teacher invited a magician to speak to our class on Monday, November 9, 1984, about famous magicians.

Use a **comma (,)** to separate the name of a city and state. Use a **comma (,)** after the name of a state when it appears with a city name in the middle of a sentence.

The magic show in Sioux City, Iowa, featured amateur performers.

Write each sentence. Add commas where they are needed. After each sentence write the number of commas you added.

1. No I never read a book about Harry Houdini.
2. Erich Weiss was born in Appleton Wisconsin in 1874.
3. Yes Houdini wrote articles about some daring tricks.
4. Erich Weiss used Houdini as his stage name Tina.
5. Houdini often performed his incredible tricks in cities such as New York City New York and Los Angeles California.
6. The magician first escaped from inside a water tank at the Circus Busch in Berlin Germany.
7. I saw the movie about his life on Friday June 8 of this year.
8. People of other cities such as Paris France and London England followed his adventures closely Kathleen.
9. Tina can you imagine doing that trick?
10. On Halloween October 31 1926 Houdini became sick and died.

Parts of a Book pages 18-19

The **title page** shows the name, author, publisher, and place of publication of a book.

The **copyright date** tells when a book was published.

The **table of contents** lists the names of the chapters or units.

The **index** is an alphabetical list that tell on what pages information appears.

Use the sample pages on the right to answer these questions. Number your paper from **1** to **12**. Write both the answer to each question and **title page, copyright page, table of contents,** or **index** to show where you found each answer.

1. When was the book published?
2. What is the name of the author?
3. Which chapter tells about famous magicians?
4. What is the title of the book?
5. On which page are there two magic tricks?
6. Which chapter tells about practicing magic tricks?
7. On which page is the Disappearing Dime trick?
8. What chapter tells what a magician needs?
9. What company published this book?
10. On which page is there a trick using an envelope?
11. How many pages of magic tricks are there in this book?

Title Page

MAKING MAGIC

Harve U. A. Chance

Top Hat Publishing Co.
Quicksburg, Virginia

Copyright Page

Copyright © 1984
Top Hat Publishing Co.
All rights reserved.

Table of Contents

Contents

1. What You Need	3
2. How to Practice	15
3. Amazing Tricks	21
4. Great Magicians	37

Index

Magic Tricks	21-36
Disappearing Dime	21
Empty Envelope	21
Fancy Finger Work	22
Hollow Hat	23

Workbook

Putting Ideas in Order pages 20-21

The **topic sentence** states the main idea of a paragraph. The **detail sentences** tell more information about the topic sentence. **Time-order words** help the reader follow the order of the paragraph. Some time-order words are *first, next, then, finally,* and *at last.*

Read the group of sentences below. Write the topic sentence. Write the detail sentences in the correct order after the topic sentence. Use the time-order words to help you.

Finally the bird ties the strands into a hanging nest. Then the bird weaves in other strands. First the bird twists strips of leaves around a twig. Some birds weave their nests.

Independent Writing: Writing a Time-Order Paragraph pages 22-25

Some paragraphs tell about events in time order. The **topic sentence** states the main idea of the paragraph. The **detail sentences** tell the order that the events happen and may use time-order words to help show the order of events.

Prewriting A paragraph that gives directions is written in time-order. Suppose that you are writing directions on how to do something for the class bulletin board. You might explain how to give a party or how to make a silly invention. If you prefer, you may choose your own topic. Imagine a series of events you could use in your paragraph. Make up lively details as you think of each one. Jot down some notes to help you remember.

Writing Write a paragraph explaining how to make something. Start your paragraph with a topic sentence. Then write a sentence about each step in the directions. Use time-order words to show the order of the steps in your paragraph.

Editing Use the check questions on page 26 and the editing symbols to edit your paragraph.

How to Edit Your Work page 27

Editing symbols are used to show mistakes in writing.

¶ This symbol means to indent the first word in a paragraph.

≡ These lines mean to make a capital letter.

∧ A caret means something has been left out or is being corrected. You add missing letters or words above the correction.

ℓ This symbol means delete, or take something out.

Look at the time-order paragraph below. Rewrite the paragraph. Use the editing marks. Make the necessary corrections.

maria wanted a part in the school play first maria studied Then Maria auditioned for the part. At last list of students came out. Maria had a part in the play

Reviewing Nouns pages 36-37

A **noun** is a word that names a person, place, thing, or idea.

person — thing
Karla wound the new clock.

person — idea — place
Bob enjoys the excitement on the *field*.

A. Make five columns on your paper. Then write **person, place, thing,** or **idea** at the top of each column. Write each word in the box under the correct heading.

bicycle	freedom	joy	sister	glass
janitor	playground	pajamas	country	friend
darkness	store	bakery	honor	planet
stone	peace	mother	book	teacher

B. Write five sentences of your own. Use two nouns from the box in each one. Circle the nouns.

Plural Nouns pages 38-41

To make most singular nouns plural, add **-s**.
If a singular noun ends with **s, ss, x, ch, sh,** or **z**, add **-es** to form the plural. Some singular nouns form the plural in a different way. If a singular noun ends with a consonant and **y**, change the **y** to **i** and add **-es** to form the plural. If a singular noun ends in a vowel and y, add **-s** to form the plural. Many singular nouns ending in **f** or **fe** add **-s** to form the plural. For some singular nouns ending in **f** or **fe**, change the **f** to **v** and add **-s** or **-es** to form the plural.

A. Study the word-search puzzle. Ten nouns are written in it. They go **down** and **across**. They are not written on the diagonal. On your paper write the ten nouns hidden in the puzzle.

F	O	O	T	I	S	D
W	M	A	N	V	K	G
B	O	X	A	R	M	Y
U	U	M	S	A	Z	T
L	S	R	P	S	U	I
B	E	A	C	H	Q	X

B. Now write the plural form of each noun you found.

C. Write the plural form of each of these nouns.

1. fox
2. child
3. roof
4. canary
5. woman
6. birch
7. Monday
8. dress
9. ox
10. wish
11. life
12. bus

D. Write each sentence. Draw a line under each plural noun.

13. The students held a dance contest.
14. Two children made signs about the contest.
15. Rita posted the rules.
16. Partners signed up after school on Wednesday.

Workbook

Compound Nouns pages 42-43

A **compound noun** is a noun made up of two or more other words.

A *mailbox* is a *box* used for the *mail*.

A *goldfish* is a *fish* that is *gold*.

A. Read the paragraph. In each sentence you will find a compound noun. Write each compound noun and its meaning on your paper.

(1) People once mined coal in the Pennsylvania countryside. **(2)** These days many people enjoy the outdoors there. **(3)** During the wintertime many people ski. **(4)** From March to November people go rafting on whitewater. **(5)** The woodland along the Lehigh River is beautiful. **(6)** Several rafting companies are located near the riverbanks. **(7)** They rent everything but courage. **(8)** In cool weather most people wear the tops of wetsuits. **(9)** The rapids can feel like a rollercoaster. **(10)** The Lehigh River has no waterfalls.

B. Make ten compound nouns by combining some of the words below. The nouns you make are things you might see on a rafting trip.

flowers	prints	foot	berries	butter	rattle
life	shine	wild	flies	snakes	fish
rooms	sun	blue	mush	hooks	dragon

C. Look carefully at the puzzle below. There are eight compound words hidden in this puzzle. All words read from left to right. Write each compound word.

```
Q S P E L L B O U N D
C R O S S W O R D B A
A T Y P E W R I T E R
N I G H T M A R E X F
D S H I P S H A P E R
L O O S E L E A F D U
E D A Y L I G H T C I
L P I N E A P P L E T
```

Workbook

Workbook

Common and Proper Nouns pages 46-47

A **common noun** is a noun that names any person, place, thing, or idea.

boy city machine freedom

A **proper noun** is a noun that names a specific person, place, thing, or idea.

Tom Denver Golden Gate Bridge

Write the items in this list. Use capital letters where they are needed in proper nouns. Leave the common nouns as they are.

1. great lakes
2. a great book
3. texas
4. a doctor's office
5. dr. jonas salk
6. friday
7. martha washington
8. a fine lady
9. empire state building

Abbreviations pages 48-49

An **abbreviation** is a short form of a word. You may use an abbreviation to shorten a person's title, such as *Dr.* for Doctor or *Jr.* for Junior. Abbreviations can be used in addresses, such as *Rd.* for Road or *St.* for Street. You may also abbreviate days, months, and times of a day. An abbreviation is often followed by a period.

Rewrite these groups of words using abbreviations where you can.

1. Mister Duncan Marks, Senior
2. Perfect Cat Foods, Incorporated
3. 20-01 Littlepaws Boulevard
4. Queens, New York
5. Doctor Jane Sun Medical Doctor
6. The Clearwater Company
7. 15 Community Avenue
8. Goodland, Indiana

In the paragraph below abbreviations have been used incorrectly. Rewrite the paragraph using the long form of each abbreviation.

(1) Holly goes to Garden Rd. Schl. **(2)** Jr. sits next to Holly in the class. **(3)** The boy lives on Sutter St. **(4)** Holly visits Jr. on Sat. **(5)** Holly sees Dr. Smith at Junior's house. **(6)** Jr. visits Dr. Smith on Mon. **(7)** Jr. passes the Marvel Sports Co. on the way.

Possessive Nouns pages 50-51

A **possessive noun** is a noun that names who or what has something.
Add an **apostrophe** and **s ('s)** to form the possessive of most singular nouns. Add an **apostrophe (')** to form the possessive of plural nouns that end with s. Add an **apostrophe** and **s ('s)** to form the possessive of plural nouns that do not end with *s*.

Write each sentence. Use the possessive form of the noun in parentheses.

(1) Our class visited Dr. (Brown) laboratory. **(2)** Mrs. Wood drove the (school) van. **(3)** Many (scientists) workrooms were interesting. **(4)** I liked the modern tools in the (groundkeeper) garage. **(5)** The mechanics measured some (automobiles) exhaust. **(6)** The mechanics design (tomorrow) clean-air engines. **(7)** Maybe the air the (mechanics) children breathe will be cleaner.

Suffixes pages 52-53

A **suffix** is one or more letters added to the end of a word.

Suffix	Meaning	Example
-er	one who	maker (one who makes)
-or	one who	actor (one who acts)
-ness	the state of being	kindness (state of being kind)
-less	without	breathless (without breath)

1. Write the name for a person who does these things. Add **-er** or **-or** to each of these words.

spell	invent	explore	build	teach	act
sail	govern	collect	visit	farm	drive

2. Write each word. Then write what it means.

foolishness	sleepless
thankless	cleverness
graceless	endless

Workbook

Using the Dictionary pages 56-57

A **dictionary** is an alphabetical list of *entry words. Guide words* at the top of each page show the first and last entry words on that page. An *entry word* is divided into *syllables*. If a word has more than one *meaning*, the meanings are numbered. Sometimes a sample sentence or phrase shows how the word is used.

1. Below are guide words on two pages of a dictionary.

buckle/bugle	**53**	**compass/complex**	**67**

On which page would you find each of these entry words?

bug	complain	competent
compel	buggy	company
buffalo	complete	budge

2. Study the sample dictionary page. Then answer the questions.

a. What are the guide words?

b. What is a looking glass?

c. Which word has the most related meanings? How many meanings does it have?

d. What does *looby* mean?

e. Which words have two related meanings?

f. What is the first meaning of *lookout*?

g. Which words have only one meaning?

looby/lookout

loo•by (loo bē) *n.* a clumsy person

look[1] (look) *v.* **1.** to make sure (that something is done) **2.** to find by using the eyes **3.** to stare in wonder or surprise.

look[2] (look) *n.* **1.** the action of looking; glance **2.** the way one appears

looking glass *n.* mirror

look•out (lookout) *n.* **1.** one who watches **2.** a high place from which a large area may be observed.

Workbook

Words That Describe Senses pages 58-59

Using words that describe how things look, sound, smell, taste, or feel can make your writing more vivid. You can also create vivid mental pictures by comparing one thing to something else.
A **simile** is a comparison of two different things with the use of *like* or *as:* Her cheeks are as red as roses.
A **metaphor** is a comparison of two different things without the use of *like* or *as*: Her cheeks are roses.
Personification is the use of words to give things and animals human qualities: The thorny roses guarded the yard.

Match the words in both columns to complete the comparisons. Write each sentence. Then write whether each sentence is a **simile, metaphor,** or **personification.**

1. The highway	that holds us together.
2. Friendship is a thread	steals my voice.
3. Fear	unrolls like a pale ribbon.

Independent Writing: Writing a Descriptive Paragraph in a Friendly Letter pages 60-65

You write a **friendly letter** to share your feelings and ideas. A friendly letter has a special form with five parts. Use your address and today's date in the *heading*. Write the first name of the person you are writing to in the *greeting*. In the *body* write your message. After the *closing* write your *signature*.

Prewriting Plan a letter to a friend. Think of a place you visit often. Make notes about sights, sounds, and feelings. Practice using similes, metaphors, and personifications in your descriptions.

Writing Write a letter to a friend. Describe the place you visit in the body paragraph. Use vivid words for sights, sounds, and feelings.

Editing Use the check questions on page 65 and the editing symbols to edit your letter.

Action Verbs pages 72-73

> An **action verb** is a word that names an action.
>
> The dog chases the frisbee.
>
> The surfboard glided over the waves.

Write each sentence. Underline the action verb.

1. Lisa enters a contest for skateboard beginners.
2. Some friends make a skateboard at the recreation center.
3. Conni selects wood for the board.
4. Maria paints a design.
5. Juan finds the wheels on an old skateboard.
6. The friends went to a skateboard park near the center.
7. Lisa rented a helmet.
8. Lee wore elbow pads.
9. One instructor demonstrated a special trick.
10. Tina tightened the wheels before the contest.
11. Another instructor performed another trick.
12. Carlos turned the board in a full circle.
13. Lisa practiced these tricks.
14. Lisa polished the new skateboard.
15. The spectators applauded the tricks.

Write these sentences. Circle the action verb in each one.

(1) Some people jump waves on their boards. **(2)** Beth aims her board toward the crest of a wave. **(3)** Beth sails over it. **(4)** Beth soars into the air for a few seconds. **(5)** Beth lands in the calm water ahead of the wave. **(6)** Jennifer stands on her board. **(7)** Jennifer grabs the boom at the bottom of the sail. **(8)** Jennifer tilts the sail. **(9)** Wind fills the sail. **(10)** Jennifer leans backward over the water. **(11)** The wind carries Jennifer along. **(12)** Jennifer wonders about the beginning of surfboards. **(13)** In 1967 two friends invented a new sport. **(14)** The two friends built the first wind-surfboard in a garage. **(15)** Hoyle Schweitzer sold a few boards to friends. **(16)** Schweitzer started Windsurfing International Inc. **(17)** This company manufactures sailboards.

Objects of Verbs pages 74-75

The **object of a verb** receives the action of the verb. It answers the question *whom?* or *what?* after an action verb.

V O V O

Lisa cuts the paper. Ali creates the design.

Write each sentence. Circle the action verb in each one. Then draw one line under the object of the verb.

(1) Kim Rose started a new hobby. **(2)** Kim drew illustrations for science. **(3)** Kim now designs books with model buildings. **(4)** People make these buildings. **(5)** Kim Rose built a model Empire State Building. **(6)** Kim studied photographs. **(7)** Kim visited the building. **(8)** Kim drew each side. **(9)** Kim added many details. **(10)** Kim designed the model.

(11) José Rodriguez built a model Brooklyn Bridge. **(13)** José cut the pages. **(14)** José used sharp scissors. **(15)** José Rodriguez colored the details. **(16)** The boy folded each part. **(17)** José glued the pieces together. **(18)** People liked the model. **(18)** José's sister wants a model. **(19)** José's sister prefers a tall model building.

Read each sentence. Write the verbs. Then write the object of the verb.

1. Molly likes puppets.
2. Molly makes hand puppets.
3. The girl uses various materials.
4. Molly uses cloth.
5. Molly creates a mouth.
6. Molly draws the eyes.
7. The girl finds a white sock.
8. Molly glues these features.
9. Molly's puppet performs an entire show.
10. People like the performance.
11. Molly wants more puppets.

Verb Tenses pages 76-77

The **tense** of a verb shows when the action takes place. The **present tense** of a verb names an action that happens now. The **past tense** names an action that happened already. Most verbs end in *-ed* in the past. The **future tense** of a verb names an action that will take place in the future.

The referee blows the whistle. **Present**
The race started. **Past**
The race will last for two hours. **Future**

A. Write these sentences. Underline the verb in each one. Then write **past, present,** or **future** to show the tense of the verb.

1. Judge William Cooper founded Cooperstown in 1786.
2. Meg will visit the Baseball Hall of Fame next summer.
3. The young girl returned from Cooperstown yesterday.
4. In the morning Ann visited the National Baseball Library.
5. The library shows films every day.
6. The old people enjoyed the old films most.
7. Fran learned about early professional players.
8. Anita will enjoy the pictures of Jackie Robinson.
9. Cooperstown boasts other museums.
10. The Farmers' Museum celebrates frontier life.

B. Make a chart like this one on your paper. Write the present, past, and future tenses of each verb. Fill in the missing verb forms.

Present	Past	Future
	helped	
shows		
		will explain
travels		
	displayed	

Using the Present Tense pages 78-79

> The **present tense** of a verb names an action that happens now. For most verbs in the present tense, add *-s* or *-es* to agree with a singular noun or *it, she,* or *he.*
> When a verb ends with a **consonant** and **y,** change the *y* to *i* and add *-es.*
>
> When a verb ends in a **vowel** and **y,** add *-s* to make the correct form of the present tense.
>
> fold/folds match/matches deny/denies obey/obeys

Write each sentence using the verb in parentheses in the present.

1. Sailors *(climb)* on the old boat.
2. The ferry *(pull)* out.
3. Some fish *(skim)* the water.
4. Ben *(grab)* the camera.

Using the Past Tense pages 80-81

> The **past tense** of a verb names an action that already happened. Most verbs end in *-ed* in the past tense. Verbs that already end in *-e* drop the *e* and add *-ed.*
> When a verb ends in a **consonant** and **y,** change the *y* to *i* and add *-ed.*
> When a verb ends in a **vowel and y,** just add *-ed.*
> When a verb ends in **consonant, vowel, consonant,** double the last consonant and add *-ed.*
>
> tow/towed scare/scared try/tried enjoy/enjoyed flop/flopped

Write each sentence using the verb in parentheses in the past tense.

(1) Last year Barry and Jay (visit) Yellowstone National Park. **(2)** The boys (stay) away from the tourist attractions. **(3)** Instead these tourists (live) in the park for a week. **(4)** The boys (camp) under the stars. **(5)** The campers (hike) through the forests. **(6)** The boys (fish) in the park's streams. **(7)** The boys (scrub) the fish in icy waters. **(8)** The boys (nap) in the long afternoons. **(9)** Barry (fry) the fish. **(10)** Barry (spot) elk, moose, and buffalo. **(11)** The boys (stop) feeling out of place in the wilderness.

Present and Past Have pages 84-85

The **present and past tense** of the verb *have* are formed in a different way from most other verbs. Look at this chart:

Subject	Present Tense	Past Tense
singular noun or *it, she,* or *he*	has	had
plural noun or *I, you, we,* or *they*	have	had

Write each sentence using the correct form of the verb *have*.

1. Sara ____ a good story about her pet yesterday. (past)
2. Joan ____ more ideas now for the hamster cage. (present)
3. The cats ____ fun every morning in the garden. (present)
4. Lee ____ his dog on a leash each day in the park. (past)
5. Our parrots ____ many words for you last week. (past)
6. Those parrots ____ even more words for you. (present)
7. Tony ____ a raccoon at the last science show. (past)
8. Carlo always ____ a picture of his pet with him. (present)

Past Tense with Have pages 86-87

The **past tense with have** may be used to tell about an action that began in the past and is still going on. It may also tell about an action that did not happen at a definite time in the past.

The play has started. (still going on)
The actors have performed many roles. (not at a definite time)

Write these sentences. Write **has** or **have** for each blank.

1. John Clark Donahue ____ improved the Children's Theatre Company.
2. John ____ headed the actors.
3. John ____ worked with adults as well.
4. John Donahue ____ produced many original plays.
5. The actors ____ rehearsed.
6. The painter ____ finished the sets.
7. Sid ____ raised the curtain.

Workbook

Workbook

Irregular Verbs pages 88-89

Some verbs do not change to the past tense by adding **-ed.** These verbs have special forms. To review some of these verbs you may want to look at the chart on page **88** again.

Write each sentence using each verb in parentheses in the past tense with *have.*

(1) Helen (write) to Barbara about the trip. **(2)** Helen (go) to Chicago last summer. **(3)** Some friends (grow) up in Chicago. **(4)** The family (go) there many times. **(5)** The girls (swim) in Lake Michigan. **(6)** Helen and Joan (do) many pleasant things in Chicago. **(7)** The girls (run) along Lake Shore Drive together. **(8)** The girls (sit) on the beach. **(9)** The girls (drink) lemonade at a sidewalk restaurant. **(10)** The girls (begin) to explore the Field Museum of Natural History. **(11)** The girls (lose) a package in the Museum of Science and Industry. **(12)** The girls (see) some paintings in the Art Institute.

More Irregular Verbs pages 90-91

You may want to review some of these verbs. Look at the chart on page 90 for help.

Write each sentence. Use the correct form of the verb in parentheses in the past tense.

(1) The alarm clock (ring). **(2)** Lenny (lie) in bed for a minute. **(3)** Lenny (think) about the bike race. **(4)** Lenny (eat) a good breakfast. **(5)** Then Lenny (take) the bike out of the garage. **(6)** His mother (speak) with him. **(7)** Lenny has (ride) in races before. **(8)** "I have (think) about the race almost all night," Lenny (say). **(9)** "That last race has (teach) me a lesson. **(10)** I (feel) too sure of winning," Lenny said. **(11)** "I have (set) out some lunch for you," his mother said. **(12)** "I have (freeze) a can of juice. I have (leave) a sandwich on the counter." **(13)** His heart (rise) and (fall) in his chest. **(14)** After the signal sounded, Lenny (ride) as hard as he could.

Verb Prefixes pages 92-93

A **prefix** is a letter or group of letters added to the beginning of a word. A prefix changes the meaning of a word.

Prefix	**Meaning**	**Prefix**	**Meaning**
mis-	badly, in the wrong way	*un-*	opposite of
re-	again	*pre-*	before

Write each word and its meanings.

repaint	reweave	unclose
unload	unmade	misunderstand
prepack	remove	rejoin
prejudge	undress	unveil

Using the Library pages 96-97

The library has many *reference works* that you may use to write a report. An *encyclopedia* is a book or set of books that gives information about many subjects. An *almanac* is a single book that is printed every year. It lists the latest facts and figures about records, events, and people.

To find a book in the library, you use the *card catalog.* The three types of cards in the card catalog are the *author card,* the *title card,* and the *subject card.*

Write **almanac, encyclopedia, author card, subject card,** or **title card** to tell where you could find the answers to the following questions.

1. What is the name of a book by Betty Miles?
2. Who won the World Series in 1980?
3. Who wrote *My Backyard History Book?*
4. What are some facts about fire ants?
5. How many books about bicycling does the library have?

Reading Graphs and Tables pages 98-99

A **graph** shows information in picture form.

Jenny managed the book club orders for her class. At the end of the year she made this graph. Use the graph to answer the questions

1. How many science books were ordered last year?
2. Which kind of book was ordered least often? How many were ordered?
3. How many animal stories were bought?
4. Which two kinds of books were equally popular? How many of each kind were ordered?

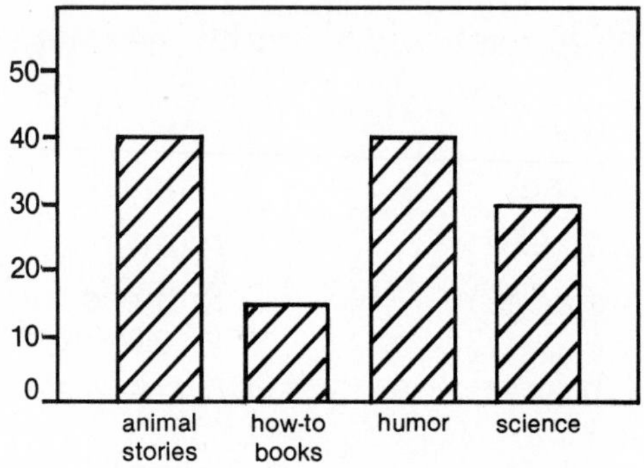

A **table** is another way of presenting information. A table is made up of columns and rows.

Use this table to answer the questions.

CLASS	MANAGER	BOOK CLUB ORDERS
Ms. Green	Renee	17
Mr. Fisher	Carl	32
Mr. Peters	Kim	12
Mrs. Holland	Lisa	25

1. Who managed the book club in Mrs. Holland's class?
2. How many orders did Lisa get?
3. Whose class gave the most orders?
4. Which manager got the fewest orders?

Facts in Paragraphs pages 100-101

A paragraph of facts gives information about a subject. The topic sentence states the main idea. Each detail sentence gives facts that support the main idea. You can arrange the facts by using answers to the questions *who, what, where, when,* and *how.*

Read the paragraphs below. Look for facts about the main ideas. Then answer the questions.

Racquetball is an exciting indoor sport for two to four players. The game is played against all four walls in a small room called a court. The players use a racquet to hit a rubber ball against the four walls of the racquetball court. The game begins with a serve. The first player bounces the ball and hits it against the front wall. The other player or team returns the ball. The winner is the first to score 21 points.

1. Which sentence is the topic sentence?
2. Where is racquetball played?
3. What is used to hit the ball?
4. What kind of ball is used?
5. Who serves the ball?
6. When does the game end?

Basketball achieved wide popularity soon after it was invented. Basketball was first played in a YMCA in Massachusetts in 1891. A young athlete desired a new indoor game for the cold weather. His new game was played with a soccer ball and fruit baskets that were nailed to the gymnasium walls. Many groups began playing their own versions of the game.

1. Which sentence is the topic sentence of the paragraph?
2. Where and when was basketball first played?
3. Who invented the new game?
4. Why did he create this new game?
5. What equipment was used to play the first game of basketball?

A Factual Paragraph in a Business Letter pages 102-103

If you write to a business to ask for information, place an order, or complain about something, you write a *business letter.* The letter contains a *heading,* an *inside address,* a *greeting,* a *body,* a *closing,* and a *signature.* In the body you should use facts to explain the purpose of the letter. Use a colon (:) after your greeting.

Use the business letter below that Erica wrote to answer the questions.

417 Oak Road
Newark, New Jersey 07102
April 9, 1982

Marvel Sports Company
36 Raymond Highway
Newark, New Jersey 07102

Dear Marvel Sports Company:
I want to participate in your fishing contest. I saw your poster. Please send me the entry forms.

Yours truly,
Erica Turner
Erica Turner

1. What information is given in the inside address?
2. What is the greeting?
3. What other greeting could you use?
4. What are the last two parts of a business letter?

Independent Writing: Writing a Business Letter pages 104-105

Prewriting Imagine you have decided to write a letter to the Bestever Book Club. Study the graph on page 399. Make notes of facts to include that will help the book club choose new books.

Writing Write a letter to the Bestever Book Club. Use your own address for the heading. The Club's address is: 815 Hammock Road, Holiday, Florida 33590. Begin the body with a good topic sentence. Use facts. Explain which three kinds of books were most popular in your class. Give facts in the detail sentences. Sign your name.

Editing Use the check questions on page 105 and the editing symbols to help you edit your business letter.

Pronouns pages 112-113

A **pronoun** is a word that takes the place of one or more nouns.

The students decided on a play. Then they performed it.

Some pronouns are *I, you, it, he, she, we, they, me, him, her, us, them.*

Read each pair of sentences. The second sentence in each pair has one or more pronouns. Write the second sentence. Then draw a line under each pronoun. Write the noun or nouns each pronoun replaces.

1. Judith Hoffman visited Tony Auditore in Brooklyn.
   She interviewed him for a newspaper story.
2. Mr. Auditore has several thousand bees.
   He keeps them in his backyard.
3. Mr. Auditore ordered the first beehive in the mail.
   It came in a package of 12,000 bees.
4. The bees were in a three-pound package.
   They buzzed loudly.
5. Every day the bees gather pollen from nearby parks.
   They return home in the evening.
6. Sometimes Mr. Auditore watches the bees.
   He stands in the yard.
7. Some bees rest on Mr. Auditore.
   Then they return to the hive.
8. The photographer took pictures.
   They accompanied the story about Mr. Auditore.
9. Judith wrote an interesting story.
   It told the facts from the interview.
10. The science class read the story in class.
    They enjoyed it.
11. The teacher showed some slides on bees.
    She carried them in a special case.
12. The students will study plants next week.
    They will bring in plants from home.

Pronouns as Subjects pages 114-115

The **subject part** of a sentence names whom or what the sentence is about. A **subject pronoun** is a pronoun that is used as the subject part of a sentence. The subject pronouns are *I, you, it, she, he, we,* and *they.*

Barbara goes to plays. <u>She</u> likes musicals.

Read each pair of sentences. Write the second sentence. Use the correct pronoun in place of the words in parentheses.

1. Luke and Arleen live in Paris.
   (Luke and Arleen) ride the subway to school.
2. The subway is called the Métro.
   (The subway) is quiet, inexpensive, and fast.
3. Builders started the Paris subway in 1898.
   (Builders) still work on the subway.
4. The wheels on the train are made of rubber.
   (The wheels) are very quiet.
5. Arleen likes the shows in the stations.
   (Arleen) browses through the paintings on the way home.
6. Luke likes the performers.
   (Luke) prefers the jugglers.
7. You and I like the Métro.
   (You and I) visited Luke and Arleen.
8. London had the first subway system.
   (London) now has seven systems.
9. Londoners call the subway "the tubes."
   (Riders) use elevators in some stations.
10. Boston had the first subway system in America.
    (The subway system) had one and a half miles of tracks.
11. New York has the largest subway system in the world.
    (Lucy) traveled from one end of the subway to the other.
12. San Francisco has a new system.
    (San Francisco) shares the system with Oakland.

Pronouns as Objects pages 116-117

The **object of the verb** receives the action of the verb. An **object pronoun** is a pronoun that is used as the object of the verb. The object pronouns are *me, you, it, her, him, us,* and *them.*

Tina brought a plant. Tina brought it.

Read each pair of sentences. Write the second sentence. Use the correct pronoun in place of the words in parentheses.

1. Arthur Sheppard planned a garden for blind people.
Arthur planted (the garden) on a rooftop.

2. Arthur asked Allison Johnston for help.
Mr. Sheppard asked (Ms. Johnston) about scented plants.

3. Ms. Johnston owns a plant nursery.
Allison has managed (the nursery) for years.

4. Allison suggested certain bushes.
Ms. Johnston purchased (the bushes) on sale.

5. Arthur hired Sharon and David.
Mr. Sheppard hired (Sharon and David) last week.

6. Allison invited Harry and me to the garden.
Ms. Johnston called (Harry and me).

7. Ms. Johnston took Harry inside.
Allison showed (Harry) around.

8. Harry planted a garden.
Harry enjoyed (the garden) very much.

9. Jeff and Lupe played outside.
Lupe saw (the tree) across the street.

10. Jeff saw acorns under the tree.
Lupe gathered (the acorns) for her mother.

11. Jeff heard a cardinal sing high in the tree.
Jeff showed (the bird) to Lupe.

12. Jeff reached for the first branch.
Lupe helped (Jeff) up.

Using Subject and Object Pronouns pages 118-119

A **subject pronoun** is a pronoun that is used as a subject of a sentence. It tells *who* or *what* does the action. The subject pronouns are *I, you, it, she, he, we,* and *they.*

Jay answered the telephone. He took a message.

An **object pronoun** is a pronoun that is used as the object of a verb. It receives the action of the verb. The object pronouns are *me, you, it, her, him, us,* and *them.*

Mary left a message. Mary left it.

Write each sentence. Replace the words in parentheses with the correct pronouns.

1. Carlos and Lita planned (a trip).
2. (Carlos and Lita) had read a book about old railroads.
3. (The book) inspired (Carlos and Lita).
4. (Lita) bought two tickets for a day trip.
5. (The tickets) were a birthday present for Carlos.
6. Lita knew (Carlos) well.
7. (Carlos) likes (the present).
8. (Carlos) took pictures.
9. (Carlos) developed (the pictures).
10. Then (Carlos) told (John and me) about the trip.
11. (Mark) received a guitar for his birthday.
12. (The guitar) was a folk guitar.
13. (Mark) played guitar with Maria.
14. (Maria) plays the mandolin.
15. (The mandolin) has eight strings.
16. Maria taught (Mark).
17. (Mark and Maria) liked bluegrass music.
18. Mark and Maria received (bluegrass records).
19. They practiced (new songs) every day.
20. Mark and Maria played (some new songs) for us.

Workbook

Possessive Pronouns pages 122-123

A **possessive pronoun** is a pronoun that names *who* or *what* has something. Possessive pronouns that appear **before a noun** are *my, your, its, her, his, our,* and *their.* Possessive pronouns that **stand alone** are *mine, yours, hers, his, ours,* and *theirs.*

Mei recited her poem. The poem is hers.

Write each sentence. Replace the words in parentheses with the correct possessive pronoun.

(1) Juanita visits (her, hers) grandmother at work. **(2)** Mrs. Ortiz works at (her, hers) gas station. **(3)** The big garage on the corner is (her, hers). **(4)** Sally and Victor ask Mrs. Ortiz to fix (their, theirs) car. **(5)** Sometimes (its, it's) engine needs fixing. **(6)** The old green car is (their, theirs). **(7)** (My, Mine) brothers and I run a towing company. **(8)** All the trucks on the lot are (our, ours). **(9)** Do you like any of (mine, my) trucks?

Subject-Verb Agreement pages 124-125

Verbs agree with the subject pronouns in a sentence. When the subject is *it, she,* or *he,* add *-s* or *-es* to most verbs in the present tense. When the subject is *I, you, we,* or *they,* do not add anything to the verb in the present tense.

I write. He writes.

Write each numbered sentence. Use the correct form of the verb in parentheses in the present tense.

(1) We (enjoy) boat trips. **(2)** We (charter) a fishing boat. **(3)** It (leave) after midnight from Montauk, Long Island. **(4)** We (pack) field glasses, food, and warm clothing. **(5)** Gil Davis (stand) on deck. **(6)** I (stay) with him. **(7)** We (peer) into the dark sky. **(8)** Gil (talk) about birdwatchers. **(9)** I (listen) quietly.

Workbook

Words Often Confused pages 126-127

Homonyms are words that sound alike but have different spellings and different meanings. Look at the chart below.

Word	Meaning	Word	Meaning
their	belonging to them	its	belonging to it
there	in that place	it's	it is
they're	they are	your	belonging to you
		you're	you are

Choose the correct homonym in parentheses. Then write each sentence.

(1) ("Their, There, They're) is the turnoff for the country fair," Scott said. **(2)** ("You're, Your) going to have a good time, Dan," he added.

(3) ("Its, It's) the biggest country fair in our state," Lilly bragged. **(4)** "The Cutlers will be showing (there, their, they're) prize hogs." **(5)** ("There, They're, Their) enormous!" she said. "I stood next to a big black one once. (Its, It's) side was as big as a blackboard!"

Fact and Opinion pages 132-133

A **fact** is a statement that can be checked to find out if it is true.

Fact: Water boils at a temperature of 212°F.

An **opinion** is what a person believes or thinks is true.

Opinion: Spring is the nicest season of the year.

Write these sentences. Then write **Fact** or **Opinion** beside each one.

1. The local 4-H Club offers lessons on the care of farm animals.
2. Club members have the best training for careers in farming.
3. 4-H Club programs include the animal sciences and agriculture.
4. Children in cities and on farms may join the 4-H Club.
5. Every 4-H activity is both interesting and useful.
6. A 4-H Club fair offers an endless variety of shows and contests.

Reasons in a Persuasive Paragraph pages 134-135

Sometimes you write a paragraph to persuade people to agree with your opinion. The *topic sentence* states the opinion. Then several *detail sentences* give facts or reasons to support the opinion in the topic sentence.

The headings below state opinions. Write each opinion. Then find the detail sentences below that support them. List each detail under the correct opinion.

Summer is my favorite season.
The trees are bare.
We can grow vegetables.
Heating is expensive.

Winter is the worst time of year.
People spend more time outdoors.
Overcoats are a nuisance.
Summer vacation is relaxing.

Now write your own persuasive paragraph about a season. First choose a season and think of an opinion. Then think of three or four facts or reasons to support your opinion. Put the detail sentences in an order that makes sense.

Independent Writing: Writing an Editorial page 138

An **editorial** is a report that expresses the opinion of the editorial board of a newspaper. The topic sentence states the opinion. The detail sentences state facts or reasons to support the opinion.

Prewriting Imagine that you are the editor of a school newspaper. Use the following topic for an editorial or choose a topic of your own: *It is not easy to be a leader.* Think of as many reasons as you can to support the statement you choose. Write some notes to help you remember your ideas.

Writing Write an editorial to persuade your schoolmates to agree with your opinion. Write your topic sentence. Then choose the best reasons to support it. Put them in an order that makes sense.

Editing Use the check questions on page 139 and the editing symbols to edit.

Reviewing Sentences pages 152-153

The **subject part** of a sentence names whom or what the sentence is about. The subject part may have more than one word. The **predicate part** of a sentence tells what action the subject part does. The predicate part may have one word or more than one word.

The eager students / participated in a new project.

A. Write each sentence. Draw a line between the subject part and the predicate part.

(1) Two fifth grade teachers started a job program in their school. **(2)** Their students selected a group of four classmates. **(3)** This group matched jobs and students. **(4)** The teachers posted a list of the available jobs. **(5)** Students applied for certain positions. **(6)** The four classmates gave the best jobs to the most suitable workers. **(7)** Students earn chips for their work. **(8)** Most workers make four or five chips a week. **(9)** Some fifth-graders save their chips. **(10)** The bank pays interest every week. **(11)** Some children spend their chips in a special lunchroom. **(12)** Other students buy things at special sales.

B. The subject and predicate parts of five sentences are mixed up in the two columns below. Join each subject to a predicate to write a complete sentence. Then draw one line under each subject part. Draw two lines under each predicate part.

1. A blue and yellow truck	A street theater play
2. begins.	pulls up to a street corner.
3. gathers around the truck.	The sides of the truck
4. open into a platform.	Neighborhood children
5. The play	has three short acts.

Workbook

Simple Subjects pages 154-155

The **subject part** of a sentence names whom or what the sentence is about. The **simple subject** of a sentence is the main word in the subject part.

Pastel colors signal spring.

Write each sentence. Draw a line under the subject part of each sentence. Circle each simple subject.

1. Color surrounds us.
2. Signs in yellow and black warn us of danger.
3. We use the names of many colors in our language.
4. Paco feels sad once in a blue moon.
5. Ron was green with envy.
6. Juan turned purple with rage.
7. Most people see colors.
8. Only some animals cannot see colors.
9. People respond to colors.
10. Colors change our moods.
11. Bright pink calms many people.
12. Some scientists study colors.
13. Scientists report the findings.
14. One scientist studied the effect of color on children.
15. The scientist visited a school in Canada.
16. The scientist changed the color in a classroom.
17. Blue relaxed the children in the room.
18. The cool color lowered blood pressures.
19. Bright orange affected the children.
20. Color affected all of the children.
21. Artists use a wide range of colors.
22. The art students mix different colors together.
23. Some artists place these paints on a palette.
24. The artists start with the primary colors.

Simple Predicates pages 156-157

The **predicate part** of a sentence tells what action the subject part does. The **simple predicate** is the main word or group of words in the predicate part of a sentence.

predicate part

Color protects many animals.

Write each sentence. Draw a line under the predicate part of each sentence. Circle the simple predicate.

(1) Certain animals change colors. **(2)** Some lizards live in trees. **(3)** These animals match the leaves or bark around them. **(4)** Certain lizards change color within seconds. **(5)** These lizards develop black spots or dark streaks. **(6)** Snowshoe rabbits change color in different seasons. **(7)** These animals turn white in winter. **(8)** The rabbits imitate the color of snow. **(9)** A white polar bear almost disappears on the white snow. **(10)** A flatfish's body has the same color as the ocean floor. **(11)** Pheasants show brown feathers. **(12)** These colors match the same shade as their surroundings. **(13)** Some moths match the exact colors of certain trees. **(14)** They disappear on the trees. **(15)** Many shrimp change to the color of seaweed. **(16)** Some birds use their color for protection. **(17)** Color protects many animals from their enemies.

(18) Color helps creatures in other ways. **(19)** Certain colors lead insects to their food. **(20)** Bright flowers attract insects during the day. **(21)** Pale flowers attract moths at night. **(22)** Some blossoms have colored guidelines. **(23)** These bright marks lead insects into the flowers. **(24)** These animals remain motionless. **(25)** An enemy rarely detects their presence. **(26)** Enemies need sharp vision. **(27)** They also must move very quickly. **(28)** Leafhopper insects look like thorns. **(29)** They land on the stem of the plant. **(30)** A praying mantis resembles a torn leaf. **(31)** A frogfish displays ragged fins. **(32)** These fins look like floating seaweed. **(33)** Animals adapt for survival in nature.

Compound Subjects pages 158-159

A **compound subject** has two or more simple subjects that have the same predicate. The subjects are joined by *and.*

Write each sentence. Underline the subject part. Then if the subject is compound, write **compound** above it. Circle the word *and* that joins the simple subjects.

1. Meriwether Lewis and William Clark lived near Thomas Jefferson.
2. President Jefferson spoke with the two old men.
3. Jefferson and the U.S. government hired them.
4. Lewis and Clark organized an expedition.
5. The two men gathered others for the trip.
6. Soldiers and scouts left St. Louis in 1803.
7. Ice and snow slowed their journey.
8. A French guide and his Indian wife helped the explorers.
9. Lewis and Clark separated for part of the trip home.

Compound Predicates pages 160-161

A **compound predicate** is a predicate that has two or more verbs that have the same subject. The verbs are joined by *and.*

Write each sentence. Underline the predicate part of each sentence. If the predicate is compound, write **compound** above it.

1. Jefferson liked and trusted Meriwether Lewis.
2. The explorers looked for a land route to the Pacific and collected information about the West.
3. The group met and trained in Illinois.
4. The two men started the journey and spent the winter in North Dakota.
5. The adventurers saw the Missouri River and followed it.
6. The Indian woman interpreted languages and explained Indian customs.

Agreement of Verbs with Compound Subjects pages 164-165

When the subject of a sentence is a singular noun, *-s* or *-es* is added to the verb to form the present tense. When the subject is a plural noun, the verb does not change. A compound subject is like a plural subject. When a sentence has a compound subject, nothing is added to the verb in the present tense.

Singular Subject: Anne likes acrobats.
Plural Subject: Her friends like acrobats.
Compound Subject: Anne and her friends like acrobats.

A. Write these sentences. Use the correct form of the verb in the present tense.

1. Richard and I (like, likes) the Flying Karamozov Brothers.
2. The four performers (come, comes) from the West Coast.
3. Howard and Timothy (juggle, juggles) together.
4. Samuel (tell, tells) funny jokes.
5. The jugglers (play, plays) drums with tenpins.
6. Paul (laugh, laughs) about the silly story.
7. Torches and balls (fly, flies) across the stage.
8. An audience volunteer (stand, stands) still.
9. Heavy objects (whizz, whizzes) by Mei from all directions.
10. Howard and Timothy (perform, performs) in a play.
11. Their two cats (do, does) tricks.
12. The Karamazovs (toss, tosses) the cats into the air.
13. The grey cat and the black cat (remain, remains) calm.
14. One cat (wear, wears) a little red cape.
15. The final act (thrill, thrills) the audience.
16. Plates and glasses (fall, falls) onto a table.
17. The performers (set, sets) a table with amazing speed.
18. The curtain (close, closes).
19. Ines and a friend (clap, claps).

B. Look at the sentences again. Write **compound** above each compound subject. Write **plural** above each plural subject. Write **singular** above each singular subject.

Building Sentences with Compound Subjects and Compound Predicates pages 166-167

Sometimes you write short sentences. You can make your sentences more interesting by combining the subject part or the predicate part of different sentences.

Simple Subjects:	The owners wait for the circus. The trainers wait for the circus.
Compound Subject:	The owners and the trainers wait for the circus.
Simple Predicates:	The acrobats twist in the air. The acrobats turn in the air.
Compound Predicate:	The acrobats twist and turn in the air.

Combine each pair of sentences to make one longer sentence. Write your new sentence.

1. Mickey goes to the show. Jane goes to the show.
2. The gray cat sits in the box. The black cat sits in the box.
3. The big cats enter a cage. The big cats jump onto the platforms.
4. Rubber balls bounce. Rubber balls fly through the air.
5. Howard dances. Howard sings silly songs.
6. Trapeze artists perform amazing tricks. Tightrope walkers perform amazing tricks.
7. The costumes sparkle. The costumes glitter.
8. The lions growl. The lions roar.
9. Dogs run around the ring. Horses run around the ring.
10. Elephants stand on their back legs. Elephants sit.
11. Monkeys jump around the cages. Monkeys climb around the cages.
12. Some clowns trick each other. Some clowns help each other.
13. The Master of Ceremonies directs attention to the center. The Master of Ceremonies announces the performers.
14. The snake charmer blows a horn. The snake charmer controls the snake.
15. The conductor reads the music. The band reads the music.

Using Commas in Writing pages 168-169

Use a **comma (,)** to separate each noun or verb in a series of three or more nouns or verbs.

Winter sports include skiing, ice hockey, and ice skating.

Use a **comma (,)** to set off such words as *yes, no,* and *well* when they begin a sentence.

Yes, I like winter sports.

Use a **comma (,)** to set off the name of a person who is spoken to directly in a sentence.

Jason, please bring your sled.

Use a **comma (,)** to separate the name of the day from the date, and the date from the year.

Jan skated on Thursday, November 18, 1982.

Use a **comma (,)** after the year when it appears with the date in the middle of a sentence.

A new skating rink opened Monday, February 15, 1980, in our town.

Use a **comma (,)** to separate the names of a city and state.

One popular winter resort is in Stowe, Vermont.

Use a **comma (,)** to separate the name of a state when it appears with a city name in the middle of a sentence.

The scenery of Providence, Rhode Island, is beautiful.

Write each sentence. Add commas where they are needed.

1. Richard have you been on an iceboat?
2. Yes I enjoy the sport.
3. In New York State iceboats speed across Lake Champlain Lake George Lake Onodagna and Lake Greenwood.
4. In 1790 Oliver Booth of Poughkeepsie New York made the first iceboat in the United States.
5. On Saturday January 15 1983 Richard won a race.
6. Iceboating is popular in Madison Wisconsin.
7. Iceboats race pound and skim over the ice.

Workbook

Punctuating a Conversation pages 170-171

Conversation tells the exact words spoken by people to one another. Each time a new speaker begins, the first word is indented. Quotation marks go before and after the exact words a person speaks. The first word of a quotation is always capitalized. A comma usually separates the spoken words from the rest of the sentence. A period goes at the end of the complete quotation or sentence. If the speaker asks a question, the quotation ends with a quotation mark.

Read this conversation. Then write it correctly. Be sure to follow all of the guidelines for writing conversation.

How will you use those legs Joe asked. I am building a walking machine Mary replied these mechanical legs will carry a robot. Why does your robot need legs Joe wondered. Wheels cannot move in sand or mud or climb steep hillsides Mary explained. This robot will be complex. The bottom of each leg will be sensitive. It will send information to a computer Mary continued. Then the computer will send instructions to the leg Mary finished. Walking is easier for me Joe laughed.

Independent Writing: Writing a Conversation pages 180-181

Prewriting Imagine that you are selling a robot to someone named Mr. Danielli. The robot does household chores. Think of the things the robot can do. Think of the questions a customer might ask as well. Jot down notes about your ideas to help you remember.

Writing Write the conversation between you and Mr. Danielli.

Editing Use the check questions on page 181 and editing symbols to edit your conversation.

Reviewing Adjectives pages 192-193

An **adjective** is a word that describes a noun or a pronoun.
An **adjective** tells *how many* or *what kind.*

Skiers wear bright clothes on ski slopes.

Write each sentence. Circle each adjective. Draw a line under the noun it describes.

(1) Bonita likes fresh air and pretty views. **(2)** Bonita and two friends take long hikes. **(3)** They climb the famous Mount Whitney in California.

(4) Narrow roads enter the thick forest. **(5)** The children followed a narrow path through the tall trees. **(6)** Low branches scraped off the knitted caps. **(7)** Feathery moss formed a soft carpet.

Adjectives That Compare pages 194-195

An **adjective** ending in **-er** compares two nouns. An **adjective** ending in **-est** compares more than two nouns.

Ming swims a farther distance than Pete.
Mary swims the farthest distance of all.

If an adjective ends in *e*, drop the *e* and add **-er** or **-est** to make the correct form of the adjective.

Some streets are wider than others.
Bush Street is the widest of all.

Write each sentence with the correct form of the adjective.

(1) South America has the ____ mountain chain on earth. (long) **(2)** The Andes Mountains are ____ than the Rocky Mountains. (tall) **(3)** Mt. Aconcagua is the ____ point on the continent. (high) **(4)** The ____ point on the continent is the southern tip of South America. (cold) **(5)** The ____ tropical forest in the world is also in South America. (large)

Workbook

Using More and Most to Compare pages 196-197

Use **more** before some adjectives when comparing two nouns.
Dan's stories are more amusing than mine.

Use **most** before adjectives with two or more syllables when comparing more than two nouns.
Yesterday I enjoyed the most interesting talk with Jill I have ever had.

A. Write six sentences comparing two nouns. Use pair of words below.

1. colorful leaves
2. cautious child
3. modern building
4. unusual sight
5. important idea
6. enjoyable trip

B. Write six sentences comparing two or more nouns. Use each pair of words below.

1. comfortable chair
2. cheerful morning
3. friendly waiter
4. careful decision
5. important idea
6. beautiful scene

C. Write the following letter. In each sentence use **more** or **most** to complete the comparison.

Dear Candy,

(1) Your Aunt Kate and I just returned from the ____ delightful vacation we have ever had. **(2)** Aunt Kate was ____ eager for the trip than I was. **(3)** Her work is ____ demanding than mine.

We visited Rocking Horse Farm. **(4)** Rocking Horse Farm had the ____ appealing picture of all in the *Farm and Inn Guide.* **(5)** Rooms at the farm were ____ comfortable than other hotel rooms. **(6)** The farm was the ____ charming place we ever visited. **(7)** The meals were the ____ delicious food in the world. **(8)** Mr. Fratatoni was even ____ gracious than your Aunt Kate. **(9)** To top all that, the farm is located in some of the ____ beautiful country in the Northeast.

Affectionately,

Workbook

Spelling Adjectives page 200

If an adjective ends with a **consonant** and **y**, change the **y** to **i** and add **-er** or **-est** to make the correct form of the adjective.

silly ⟶ sillier ⟶ silliest

If a one-syllable adjective ends with **consonant, vowel, consonant,** double the last consonant and add **-er** or **-est** to make the correct form of the verb.

slim ⟶ slimmer ⟶ slimmest

A. Write each of these words with an **-er** and an **-est** ending.

stormy	cloudy	happy	hot	pretty	mad
busy	rocky	mushy	skinny	risky	sag
catchy	big	rainy	sticky	moody	dry

B. Write each sentence. Use the correct form of the adjective in parentheses.

1. Your cat is (thin) than mine.
2. My cat is the (thin) one in the show.
3. A dog in a bathtub is the (wet) thing in the world.
4. My dog's fur is (wet) than a waterfall.

Capitalizing Proper Adjectives page 201

A **proper noun** names a special person, place, thing, or idea. A **proper adjective** is an adjective formed from a proper noun.

a. Korean dress c. Irish sweater
b. French accent d. Idaho potato

Write each sentence, capitalizing the proper adjective.

1. Virginia likes hawaiian folk music.
2. Our museum collects unusual asian dolls.
3. Devora studies the history of the israeli people.
4. Julie practices on a spanish guitar.
5. Carol's father works on the alaskan pipeline.

Prefixes and Suffixes pages 202-203

A **prefix** is one or more letters added to the beginning of a word. A **suffix** is one or more letters added to the end of a word. Look at the chart.

		Meaning	Example
Prefix	*un-*	not	unusual (not usual)
Suffix	*-y*	having	thirsty (having thirst)
	-ful	full of	careful (full of care)
	-less	without	harmless (without harm)

Write these sentences. Circle the words that end with *-y, -ful,* or *-less*. Then write the meaning of each word you circled.

(1) Iris and Liz were restless. **(2)** They agreed on a useful activity. **(3)** They made those wonderful sugarless cookies. **(4)** The cookies were the crunchy type.

(5) The girls were careful with the recipe. **(6)** At first the batter was lumpy. **(7)** The lumps were harmless. **(8)** The cookies were tasty.

Adjective Synonyms pages 204-205

A **synonym** is a word that has nearly the same meaning as another word. For example, *tasty* and *delicious* are synonyms.

Write each sentence. Replace each underlined word with a synonym from the box.

numerous
unusual
fat
dangerous
expensive
enormous
foolish

(1) Betsy tests toys for <u>many</u> manufacturers. **(2)** She finds out if their toys are <u>unsafe</u>. **(3)** She handles <u>rare</u> and <u>costly</u> toys. **(4)** Sometimes Betsy feels <u>silly</u>. **(5)** Her office is full of <u>plump</u> bears, <u>huge</u> trucks and other funny things.

Workbook

Using Reference Works pages 208-209

An **encyclopedia** gives information about many subjects. An **almanac** gives the latest facts and figures. An **atlas** is a book of maps. **Periodicals** are newspapers and magazines that are published at certain periods of time.

Divide your paper into four sections. Write **encyclopedia, almanac, atlas,** and **periodicals** at the top of each section. Then write each of the following topics under the heading that tells where you would find information about it.

1. News of a recent discovery in medicine
2. A list of winners of the Nobel Peace Prize
3. The number of cities named Adams in the U.S.
4. A relief map of South America
5. A short biography of Sojourner Truth
6. Photographs of today's world leaders
7. A graph of the number of cars sold last year
8. A review of a new book
9. The number of square miles in Texas
10. The shapes of cut diamonds
11. A road map of Michigan
12. The number of students in college last year
13. A table of movie show times in your town
14. A map of the major rivers in the United States
15. Pictures of many different breeds of dogs
16. A diagram of the parts of the brain
17. A chart of recent population figures for ten countries
18. A map of downtown Seattle, Washington
19. The times of the ten fastest runners in the world
20. An article about the star of a new movie
21. Information about trees
22. A map showing the weather for next weekend
23. A map of the islands in the Pacific Ocean
24. A chart showing how oil was used in the U.S. last year

Reviewing Paragraphs pages 210-211

You can use four different kinds of detail sentences in writing paragraphs. **Time-order details** describe events in the order they happened. **Descriptions** tell how things look, sound, smell, feel, or taste. **Facts** provide information about a subject. **Reasons** explain an opinion or a point of view.

Write each topic sentence. Beside each one, write **time order, descriptions, facts,** or **reasons** to tell what kind of detail sentence that paragraph requires.

1. It is easy to bake a cake.
2. Dogs make good pets.
3. Daniel Boone was a famous pioneer.
4. I see the zoo from my window.

Read each detail sentence below. Match each sentence to the topic sentence above by writing **time order, descriptions, facts,** or **reasons.**

5. First add water, flour, and eggs.
6. Add yeast to the batter.
7. They make good companions.
8. One lion has a large mane and looks ferocious.
9. Puppies keep your feet warm.
10. The black seal swims in a large pool.
11. Daniel Boone learned much from friendly Indians near his childhood home in Pennsylvania.
12. Boone explores the unknown forests of Kentucky.
13. He opened the Wilderness Trail in the West.
14. The elephants live in a large round house.
15. There are several tigers.
16. His wife Rebecca guarded the children and the cabin.
17. Bake the cake for twenty minutes.
18. Dogs are very loyal.
19. Spread the icing on the cake.
20. Prepare a platter for the cake.

Independent Writing: Writing a Summary Report pages 214-215

A *summary paragraph* briefly states only the most important facts about a subject. The paragraph has a topic sentence and detail sentences.

Prewriting Imagine that you are a reporter for the local newspaper. You will write a summary paragraph about a new protective suit for firefighters. Read the selection and the interview with a fire chief below. Then make notes on the important ideas.

Fire departments use special clothes in all situations. Fire-fighters' helmets, long coats, and boots protect them. Some fires burn more hotly than others. Then a firefighter needs better protection.

Science has developed a suit which reflects heat. This new suit covers every part of the body. It is made of a special heavy cloth which resists fire. The cloth is coated with aluminum to reflect heat. The person sees through a glass visor in the hooded helmet. The suits are somewhat costly.

City firefighters often use the new suits. They can now walk through fire to save lives.

Q: Will our fire department receive the suits?

A: I spoke in favor of the suits. I said that we needed them. The town finally voted to buy three suits.

Q: What reasons did you state?

A: I said that some fires are too hot for the usual equipment. I said that only these suits can help firefighters save trapped people at such times. We must be ready.

Q: Are our firefighters familiar with the suits?

A: They like the new suits. However, they need some special training. I am certain that expense is worthwhile.

Writing Write a summary paragraph about the firefighters' new protective suit. Use a clear topic sentence. Then write detail sentences using your notes on the important ideas. Follow the steps for writing a summary on page 215.

Editing Use the check questions on page 215 and the editing symbols to edit your summary paragraph.

Linking Verbs pages 226-227

An **action verb** is a word that names an action.

The orchestra practiced yesterday.

A **linking verb** is a verb that connects the subject part with a noun or adjective in the predicate part. It tells what the subject is or is like. The most common linking verb is *be.* The forms of be are *am, is,* and *are* in the present tense and *was* and *were* in the past tense.

Miss Magee is the dramatics teacher.

Write each sentence. Draw a line under the verb. Write **action verb** for each action verb. Write **linking verb** for each linking verb.

1. Phillip T. Young teaches music.
2. He is an expert.
3. He arranged a show.
4. Mr. Young displayed 305 old instruments in a museum.
5. The glass cases were full.
6. Visitors saw many musical instruments.
7. Some instruments were strange.
8. One horn was long.
9. An old violin was small.
10. Many stringed instruments are fragile.
11. Many items were rare.
12. Keyboards are delicate.
13. All the instruments were silent.
14. Many collectors came to the show.
15. Some people were musicians.
16. Pilar Diaz is a fine violinist.
17. Mrs. Diaz collects music.
18. One collector bought an old piano.
19. The piano was 150 years old.
20. The people danced at the show.
21. Ms. Diaz was happy.

Nouns and Adjectives After Linking Verbs pages 228-229

A **noun** is a word that names a person, place, thing, or idea.
An **adjective** is a word that describes a noun or a pronoun.
A linking verb connects, or links the subject with a noun or adjective that follows it.

Chorus members are students. The uniforms are new.

Write each sentence. Draw a line under each linking verb. Write **noun** above each noun that the linking verb connects to a word in the subject part of the sentence. Write **adjective** above each adjective that is connected to a word in the subject part.

1. I am a musician.
2. My instrument is the flute.
3. My flute is silver.
4. Our band is excellent.
5. Our music is exciting.
6. Our marches are famous.
7. John Philip Sousa is the composer.
8. The band members are children.
9. Our concerts are fun.
10. Mrs. Trainor is our leader.
11. She is a teacher.
12. Our schedule was crowded.
13. The audiences were pleased.
14. The street was our stage.
15. We were the best.
16. The Star Spangled Banner was triumphant.
17. It is a classic.
18. The weather was nice.
19. Tina Ortiz is a good musician.
20. She is a soloist.
21. She is a drummer.
22. Her solo was perfect.

Using Linking Verbs in the Present Tense page 230

The following rules tell how to use the **linking verb** *be* in the present tense. Use *am* in the present tense when the subject is *I*.

I am cheerful. I am first.

Use *is* in the present tense when the subject is *it, she, he,* or a singular noun.

Mike is a carpenter. He is skillful.

Use *are* in the present tense when the subject is *we, you, they,* a plural noun or a compound subject.

These students are helpful. They are careful.

Write each sentence. Use the correct form of *be* in the present.

1. Greenland ____ a country.
2. It ____ an island.
3. Life ____ quiet in Greenland.
4. Summers ____ pleasant.
5. They ____ poor.
6. I ____ surprised.
7. Helicopter flights ____ expensive.
8. Marcia ____ a pilot.

Using Linking Verbs in the Past Tense page 231

The following rules tell how to use the linking verb *be* in the past tense. Use *was* in the past tense when the subject is *I, it, she, he,* or a singular noun.

Jan was a runner. She was quick.

Use were in the past tense when the subject is *we, you, they,* a plural noun, or a compound subject.

Kim and Lee were dancers. They were partners.

Write each sentence. Use the correct form of *be* in the past tense.

1. The winter ____ long.
2. The wind ____ fierce.
3. We ____ tired.
4. Our equipment ____ poor.
5. It ____ old.
6. Our clothes ____ heavy.
7. The dogs ____ exhausted.
8. Sandra ____ determined.
9. She ____ a leader.
10 I ____ encouraged.

Verb Antonyms pages 232-233

An **antonym** is a word that means the opposite of another word. For example, an antonym for *hot* is *cold.*

Read each sentence. Write each sentence with the word that is an antonym for the underlined word.

1. Some chemicals weaken cloth. (buy, strengthen)
2. One new chemical pollutes the water. (heighten, purifies)
3. The news saddened the anxious family. (cheered, woke)
4. Mei and Iris begin their long trip. (enjoy, complete)
5. The train departs at 11:15 A.M. (arrives, howls)
6. The conductor grabs the brake handle. (releases, stirs)
7. He shouts to his assistant. (hums, whispers)
8. The new music pleases my parents. (upsets, interests)

Verbs Ending in ing pages 236-237

Am, is, or *are* and a main verb ending with *-ing* name an action that continues in the present. *Was* or *were* and a main verb ending with *-ing* name an action that began in the past and continued for a time.

Present: I am, it, he, she *is* you, we, they *are*
Past: I, it, he, she *was* *you, we, they were*

Write each sentence. Use the correct form of the verb *be* in each blank.

(1) Right now we ____ visiting the Boston Children's Museum. **(2)** Yesterday my friends ____ exploring an Indian wigwam. **(3)** Kristi ____ tasting Indian foods now. **(4)** Today Dan and Andrea ____ running a supermarket. **(5)** Andrea ____ managing the checkout counter a minute ago. **(6)** Some children ____ learning about blindness right now. **(7)** John and Sue ____ using a Braille typewriter now. **(8)** Yesterday Miguel ____ filming a TV show. **(9)** Tina ____ reading the news.

Using Apostrophes in Possessives and Contractions pages 238-239

A **possessive noun** is a noun that shows who or what has something. Add an **apostrophe** and **s ('s)** to form the possessive of most singular nouns. For example, The tower's walls are straight.
Add an **apostrophe (')** to form the possessive of a plural noun that ends with *s.* For example, The girls' plans are interesting.
Add an **apostrophe** and **s ('s)** to form the possessive of a plural noun that does not end with *s.* For example, The men's designs are excellent.

A **contraction** is a word made up of two words. The words are joined together to make one word. An **apostrophe (')** replaces the letter or letters dropped from the second word.

I have *I've* *He had* *He'd*

Write each sentence. Add the apostrophe in the correct place. Then write what each possessive means.

1. The programs name is "Architects in the Schools."
2. The projects leaders are Barbara and Allan Anderson.
3. You should see the young architects designs.
4. One students blueprints won an award.

Write each sentence. Change the underlined words into contraction. If you need help, look at the chart on page 239.

5. I am going out now.
6. I have errands.
7. It is late.
8. I am leaving
9. It is time to go.
10. We had better run.
11. They are waiting.
12. We are in a hurry.
13. She is tired.
14. You are ready now.
15. You had planned this.
16. I hope you have had lunch.
17. They are hungry.
18. They had had soup.
19. It is finished.
20. He has eaten dessert.
21. We have no time.
22. I have enjoyed my visit.
23. You have been nice.
24. They are expecting us.
25. We have visited before.
26. You had better rush.

Using Note-Taking Skills pages 244-245

As you gather information for a report, take notes on the most important facts. Your notes can be in *complete sentences* or in groups of words called *phrases.*

Take notes on the interview with an American historian. Then take notes on the selection on the right. Use them in the next lesson on reports.

Q: What kinds of roads did the first pioneers find in North America?
A: The first roads were trails used by American Indians. At first the Indians burned away thick brush in the summer. Later the Indians cut trails. Many walkers and large animals improved these dirt trails.

Pioneers built wider roads along the Indian trails. Planks and logs helped people across muddy areas. However the roads often needed repairs. Wagons and coaches of the 1800s required better roads. People built toll roads and covered them with tons of crushed stones.

Independent Writing: Writing a Two-Paragraph Report pages 250-251

A *two-paragraph report* has one main subject. Each paragraph tells about a different part of the subject. Each has a topic sentence and detail sentences.

Prewriting Reread the interview and article above. Study your notes and organize them. You will write a two-paragraph report about the early roads of North America. The report will tell how roads began and changed.

Writing Write a two-paragraph report about the early roads of North America. In the first paragraph describe the first roads and how they improved. In the second paragraph tell how the pioneers changed the early roads.

Editing Use the checklist on page 251 and the editing symbols to edit your two-paragraph report.

Reviewing Adverbs pages 260-261

An **adverb** is a word that describes an action. An adverb may tell *how, when, where,* or *how often* an action is done.

A. Write each sentence. Circle the adverbs. Draw an arrow from each adverb to the action it describes.

(1) Tangoonarak arrives early. **(2)** The old man sits down. **(3)** He chooses a stone carefully. **(4)** He handles each one gently. **(5)** Then he studies the stone. **(6)** Next he picks up a tool. **(7)** He carves slowly. **(8)** Tangoonarak works thoughtfully. **(9)** He sands the stone briskly. **(10)** He polishes it well. **(11)** Finally he finishes the statue of a young seal.

B. Write **how, when, where,** or **how often** above each adverb in the sentences you wrote.

C. Divide your paper into four sections. Head each one **how, when, where,** or **how often.** Then write each of these adverbs under the correct heading.

silently	nearby	freely	gracefully	now	hourly
yesterday	later	weekly	repeatedly	below	downtown

D. Read each sentence. Then complete each one with an adverb of your own. Use the words in parentheses to guide your choice.

1. Litchia (*how often*) works in the shop with Tangoonarak.
2. She sits (*where*) and carves small works of art.
3. Litchia handles each tool (*how*) during the work.
4. She finishes a statue (*when*) for other people of the village.
5. The walrus of sandstone shines (*how*) on the windowsill.
6. People (*how often*) want more of Litchia's fine work.
7. They wait (*where*) the shop.

Workbook

Using Adverbs to Compare pages 262-263

Add **-er** to some adverbs when comparing two actions.
Agapow carves faster than Tangoonarak does.

Add **-est** to some adverbs when comparing more than two actions.
Tangoonarak's dog team is the fastest team in Alaska.

Use **more** before most adverbs that end in **ly** when comparing two actions.
One carver worked more carefully than the other.

Use **most** before most adverbs ending in **ly** when comparing more than two actions.
Of all the old people, my grandfather spoke most wisely.

A. Draw this chart. Fill in the missing forms of each adverb.

Adverb	When 2 actions are compared	When more than 2 actions are compared
fast		
	more happily	
		most quietly
		latest

B. Write each sentence. Add **more** or **most** to complete each comparison.

1. The big dog waited ____ patiently than the little one.
2. Their sled ran ____ quickly than mine.
3. Of all the trainers Alivukuk handles the dogs ____ gently.
4. My sister packs the sled ____ slowly than I do.
5. My brother packs the ____ neatly of all.
6. Snow falls ____ silently here than anywhere else.
7. Alivukuk knows the weather ____ surely than anyone.
8. We must travel ____ swiftly than we traveled yesterday.
9. The snow gathers ____ deeply during the night than during the day.
10. The sled dogs pull ____ eagerly of all during a storm.
11. Birds stand ____ quietly than before on the snowy limbs.
12. Our sleds slide ____ smoothly of all on the level ground.
13. Alivukuk sings ____ joyfully at the top of a high hill.

Forming Adverbs from Adjectives pages 264-265

Add **-ly** to some adjectives to form an adverb. **bold** + **ly** = **boldly**
Change **y** to **i** and add **-ly** to form an adverb from an adjective that ends in **y**. **steady** + **ly** = **steadily**

A. Change each adjective in parentheses to an adverb. Write the new sentence.

1. The fifth-grade class waited ____ for the results (anxious)
2. Everyone completed the program ____ this year. (satisfactory)
3. The audience cheered ____. (wild)
4. The team marched ____ across the field. (proud)
5. The stock price dropped ____. (rapid)
6. The children ____ went to a stockholder's meeting. (quick)
7. The meeting started ____. (slow)
8. The students asked ____ about the stock. (polite)
9. The company officers answered ____. (nervous)
10. The other stockholders talked ____. (endless)
11. The students ____ left. (final)
12. They fared ____ on the stockmarket. (successful)
13. In 1929 the stock market fell ____. (dangerous)
14. President Roosevelt ____ created jobs. (generous)
15. Citizens ____ accepted them. (grateful)
16. The country recovered ____. (gradual)
17. Business people buy stock ____. (careful)
18. Stock value increased ____ during World War II. (great)
19. Stock buyers ____ lose all their money. (rare)
20. The stock market ____ goes up and down. (constant)

B. Write each of the following adjectives. Beside each one write its adverb form.

earnest	playful	ready
final	nice	greedy
strange	thoughtful	thankful
dreadful	happy	bushy

Reviewing Capitalization pages 268-269

Use a **capital letter** to begin the first word of every sentence.
Use a **capital letter** to begin each important word of a proper noun.
Use a **capital letter** to begin the names of the months and days of the week.
Use a **capital letter** for each initial in a person's name. Use a **period (.)** after an initial.
Use a **capital letter** to begin each important word in a book title. Always begin the first word of a title with a **capital letter**.

A. Write each sentence. Add capital letters where they are needed.

(1) sir arthur conan doyle was a famous english author. **(2)** his most famous book was *the adventures of sherlock holmes.* **(3)** the book first appeared in october 1891 in the strand magazine. **(4)** the character sherlock holmes was a very clever detective. **(5)** his faithful assistant's name was dr watson. **(6)** holmes and watson solved many cases together. **(7)** watson was also a shrewd detective. **(8)** *the adventures of sherlock holmes* earned conan doyle great popularity.

B. Write each sentence. Add capital letters where they are needed.

1. last august, mrs. collins went to the dentist.
2. dr. ortiz examined her.
3. the dr. became a dentist in mexico.
4. he found two bad teeth.
5. he gave mrs. collins another appointment.
6. the dr. scheduled her for monday, august 27.
7. mrs. collins went to dr. ortiz's office on park avenue.
8. she read a book called *the grapes of wrath* in the waiting room.
9. the dr. fixed her teeth in two hours.
10. mrs. collins gladly left park avenue.

Homographs pages 270-271

Homographs are words that are spelled the same way, but have different meanings. Sometimes homographs even have different pronunciations.

Beth will record the lecture.	*record* rhymes with *board*
Beth played a record for me.	*record* rhymes with *herd*

Write each pair of sentences. Circle the homographs. Write the meaning of each homograph beside its sentence.

1. A white dove flew into the tree next door.
   The boy dove into the icy water of the pond.
2. Jean sails her boat every summer in the bay.
   Two dogs bay at the moon from a hilltop.
3. Stan took the lead at the end of the race.
   The coach wrote all the names with a lead pencil.
4. Please do not lean on that old chest of drawers.
   Our lean and bony dog sleeps beside the chest.
5. Take charge of the store for a minute, please.
   The parts for the model ship are minute.
6. Clouds hide the sun before a thunderstorm.
   The hide of a whale is tough and very thick.
7. A green vine winds up the side of the house.
   Winds wear down mountains over long centuries.
8. Everyone at the party wore a bow on their shirts.
   The bow of the ship moved up and down on the waves.
9. Jimmy stood close by his sister in the picture.
   Donna and Erin close their eyes before the flash.
10. There is a tear in the curtain on the stage.
    A tear ran slowly from the corner of my eye.
11. Tina will watch the new group on Thursday night.
    Small letters formed a message on the old watch.
12. The colors on that tie are very bright.
    Did you tie the dog on its leash in the backyard?

Understanding Words from Context pages 272-273

> You can figure out the meaning of a word by thinking about the other words in a sentence.

A. Write each sentence. Then write what you think each underlined word means.

1. The intention of this family meeting is to divide the housework.
2. Sue appointed Barry to make a work chart.
3. The plan will work smoothly if you heed your name on the chart and do your own job.
4. Dan is a good worker. When confronted by a messy room, he works until the room is spotless.
5. Perishable fruit will spoil if it is not kept cool.
6. The family consumed the fine dinner quickly.
7. There was no plain food. Everything was elaborate.
8. When I want to be alone, I visit an isolated cabin the woods.
9. Over the years, the river carved a gully in the valley.
10. The baby was afflicted with a red rash.
11. Teri's dog gamboled playfully with a ball in the yard.
12. A huge whale breached the surface of the sea, and it fell back again with a splash.
13. Helicopters hover like bees above the busy airport.
14. The scientist felt awe before the endless millions of stars.
15. Carol told me her convictions about the matter in question.
16. A silent instinct guides animals over their long journeys.
17. Fred's early ancestors came to America from England in 1899.
18. The high crest of each wave tossed foam across the small deck.
19. An army of homeless ants arrived to colonize the empty house.

B. Look up the underlined words to check their meanings. Then write your own sentence using each word. The other words in the sentence should give clues to the meaning of the word.

Workbook

Developing a Two-Part Outline pages 278-279

An *outline* is a plan for arranging ideas in a report. The main subject is shown in the title of the outline. In a two-part outline, Roman numerals **I** and **II** identify the main headings. The main headings give the main idea in each paragraph. Capital letters **A, B, C,** and so on, identify the subheadings. The subheadings give the supporting details in each paragraph.

A. Read this report. Then follow the directions.

Stagecoaches

American stagecoaches of the 1800s were built well. The bodies of the coaches were carefully made of the strongest white oak. They were often beautifully painted. Passengers inside sat on soft cushions, and springs were added under the seats in later years. These comfortable, sturdy coaches could carry about seven people and many packages.

The stagecoach was an important means of travel before railroads were built. Large cities of the day, such as Boston, New York, Philadelphia, and Washington were connected mainly by stagecoaches. A large coach drawn by a team of horses could travel along at about 10 miles per hour.

Use the following steps to write an outline for the two-paragraph report.

1. Write the title of the outline.

2. Write the first heading and subheading.

I.

A.

3. Write two more subheadings, B and C.

4. Write the main heading of the second paragraph.

II.

5. Write two subheadings beneath the second heading.

Workbook

Outlining a Two-Paragraph Report pages 280-281

An outline for a two-paragraph report tells the order of the main ideas and supporting details for the report. The outline may be written in complete sentences or in phrases.

Read the selection about young spiders and the interview. Make notes and an outline for a two-paragraph report on young spiders.

A young spider or *spiderling* hatches inside a tiny bag of silk. Most spiders lay about 100 eggs in one bag. A few lay only one egg, but large spiders lay 2,000 eggs.

Most spiders leave the bag in a web or on a plant. The spiderlings hatch by themselves in warm months. Some spiders guard their eggs. An example is the wolf spider. This spider even carries her many young on her back for several days.

Q: What do spiderlings do during their first few days?

A: A spiderling's first task is to leave the silk bag. It tears a small hole in the bag and crawls out. It spins silk right away. It knows how to build a web. Many spiderlings travel by air. They sail in the wind on silk threads. I have seen spiders drifting two hundred miles at sea.

Independent Writing: Writing a Two-Paragraph Report page 285

Prewriting You will write a two-paragraph report on spiderlings. Use the notes and the outline you made to plan your report. Plan a clear topic sentence for each of the two paragraphs. List details in the outline for use in detail sentences.

Writing Write a two-paragraph report on spiderlings. In the first paragraph tell your readers what spiderlings are. Give details about how many of them hatch. In the second paragraph tell how spiderlings may travel. Give two examples of how they may travel.

Editing Use the check questions on page 284 and editing symbols to edit your report.

Reviewing Compound Subjects and Predicates pages 296-297

The **subject part** of a sentence names whom or what the sentence is about. A **simple subject** is the main word in the subject part. A **compound subject** has two or more simple subjects that have the same predicate. The subjects are joined by *and*.

simple subjects

Patrice, Lynn, and Jana jump rope together.

The **predicate part** of a sentence tells what action the subject does. A **simple predicate** is the main word or group of words in the predicate part. A **compound predicate** is a predicate that has two or more verbs that have the same subject. The verbs are joined by *and*.

verbs

They invent tricks and practice them.

Write each sentence. If the predicate is compound, underline it and write **compound predicate.** If the subject is compound, underline it and write **compound subject.** If the sentence has no compound predicate or compound subjects, write **not compound.**

1. Double Dutch is a jump-rope game.
2. Players enter and jump between the arcs of two ropes.
3. The two ropes whirl in opposite directions and slap the cement underfoot.
4. Double Dutch came from the Netherlands and became popular in America.
5. English settlers named the game and enjoyed it.
6. Rhythm, strength, and endurance are required for this sport.
7. Mike Williams and David Walker started a Double Dutch contest in 1973.
8. Players meet and display their skills every year.
9. Patrice, Lynn, and Jana formed a team.
10. They exercise and work on their form every day.
11. Speed and grace are important.
12. The girls invent and perfect original stunts for the contest.

Compound Sentences pages 298-299

A **compound sentence** is a sentence that contains two simple sentences joined by **and** or **but.** A comma is placed before a conjunction that joins the two ideas in a compound sentence.

Edgar Allan Poe was an American author, and he wrote some fascinating stories.

Write these sentences. Leave space between them. Circle each *and* or *but* that joins two simple sentences into a compound sentence. Write **not a compound** for each sentence that is not a compound sentence.

1. Edgar Allan Poe spent his first few years in Boston, but his family took him to England in 1815.
2. Poe was a good student in the private schools near London.
3. He sometimes attended the theater in England, and he read many books during his boyhood.
4. At age 11 Poe returned to the United States with his family and many experiences of the Old World.
5. In 1826 he became a student at the University of Virginia, and Poe continued his studies for another year.
6. Problems with money soon brought an end to Poe's schoolwork.
7. Poe had a chance to study law, but he decided on a writing career.
8. He spent two years in the United States Army, and he rose to the rank of sergeant-major.
9. Poe left the Army in 1829 with hopes for a career as a poet and storyteller.
10. After four more years of work Poe's books were published, but they did not become very popular.
11. Poe wrote reviews and articles for several magazines of the day in Baltimore, Maryland.
12. His work improved rapidly during these years, but he earned very little money from his best poems and stories.
13. In 1844 this writer achieved some success with a collection of 25 strange and haunting stories.

Building Compound Sentences pages 300-301

You can make **compound sentences** by joining two simple sentences with *and* or *but*. Use *and* when the sentences offer additional information. Use a comma just before the conjunction.

Denton likes vegetables, and broccoli is his favorite vegetable.

Denton likes vegetables. Broccoli is his favorite vegetable.

Use *but* when the ideas are contrasting or opposite.

Caroline likes potatoes, but she dislikes cauliflower.

Caroline likes potatoes. She dislikes cauliflower.

Write each pair of sentences as a compound sentence.

1. Potatoes have great historical value. Few people realize their importance.
2. Thomas Hughes was a fifth grade teacher in Belgium. He started the world's only potato museum.
3. His students collected information. They displayed their work in the classroom.
4. Newspapers described the museum. People from all over Europe visited.
5. People sent many things to the museum. Soon the display filled three classrooms.
6. Thomas Hughes tasted many fancy potato dishes. His favorite one remained a plain boiled potato.
7. Hughes was the only potato expert in the world. He became an object of curiosity.
8. His students study the potato. They only want the eyes for good luck.
9. The museum taught visitors about the value of potatoes. Many people felt better about its high price.
10. Belgium is an unlikely place for a potato museum. Potatoes are one of its leading crops.
11. People take potatoes for granted. They are one of the leading food crops in the world.
12. The Irish promoted potatoes in America. Colonists grew them in the 1600s.
13. Idaho grows the most potatoes in the country. Colorado grows the least.

Prepositions and Prepositional Phrases pages 304-305

A **preposition** is a word that relates a noun or a pronoun to another word.

Some prepositions are	about	after	for	of
	above	at	from	on
	across	by	in	without

A **prepositional phrase** is a group of words that begin with a preposition and end with a noun or pronoun.

A huge gray whale crashes through the waves.

A. Read the paragraph. Write numbers **1** through **8** on your paper. Beside each number write the prepositional phrase in each sentence.

1. The huge whale dives below the foam.
2. People on the boat cheer.
3. Twenty whale watchers crowd on the small deck.
4. Their boats follow the big animals at a safe distance.
5. Two more whales heave to the surface.
6. An old whale does a "skyhop" near the boat.
7. The whale stands on its tail.
8. The huge sea creature peers at the whale watchers.

B. Write each sentence below. Complete each one by putting one of the prepositional phrases in the box into the blank.

during the long swim	for the long ocean	of tiny shrimp-like animals
before the journey	off Baja, California	in the cold Bering Sea
of miles		

9. Gray whales swim thousands ____ each year.
10. These whales start out ____.
11. Gray whales head ____.
12. The long swim ends somewhere ____.
13. The whales feed hungrily ____.
14. The whales swallow tons ____.
15. Then the gray whales eat nothing ____.

Parts of Speech in Sentences pages 306-307

Words can be divided into groups according to the roles they play in sentences. These groups are called **parts of speech.** *Nouns, pronouns, adjectives, verbs,* and *adverbs* are five parts of speech.

A **noun** is a word that names a person, place, thing or idea.
A **pronoun** is a word that takes the place of a noun.
An **adjective** is a word that describes a noun or a pronoun.
A **verb** is a word that names an action.
An **adverb** is a word that describes an action.

A. Write each sentence. Then write the part of speech above each underlined word.

(1) More than a million beetles live on earth. **(2)** Beetles live almost everywhere. **(3)** They live in fresh water. **(4)** They live in swift streams. **(5)** Beetles also live on plants.

(6) Their hard front wings cover their backs. **(7)** The hard shell protects them. **(8)** Most beetles walk slowly. **(9)** They move like little trucks in low gear.

B. Write each pair of sentences. Then write how each underlined word is used.

1. I visited an insect zoo. The bee is my favorite insect.
2. We looked through the clean glass. Worker bees clean the hive.
3. A spider swung down on its web. Its body was covered with down.

C. Write each sentence. In each blank write a word that is the part of speech in parentheses.

1. You do not need a license for a ____. (noun)
2. John rides his bicycle ____. (adverb)
3. The police ____ you when ride down the street. (verb)
4. It is a ____ day for a trip by boat. (adjective)
5. His bicycle is ____. (adjective)
6. I run with ____. (pronoun)
7. A ____ is faster than a train. (noun)
8. We stopped ____ on the street. (pronoun)

Reviewing Commas, pages 308-309

Use a **comma (,)** to set off words such as *yes, no,* and *well* when they begin a sentence. Use a **comma (,)** to set off the name of a person who is spoken to directly in a sentence.

Use a **comma (,)** to separate the name of the day from the date, and the date from the year. Use a **comma (,)** after the year when it appears with the date in the middle of a sentence.

Use a **comma (,)** to separate the name of a city and state. Use a **comma (,)** after the name of a state when it appears with a city name in the middle of a sentence.

Use a **comma (,)** to separate each noun or verb in a series of three or more nouns or verbs.

Use a **comma (,)** before the conjunctions *and* or *but* in a compound sentence.

When writing conversation, use a **comma (,)** to separate the spoken words from the person who is saying them. Place the comma before the quotation marks. If the speaker asks a question, use a question mark **(?)** instead of a comma before the end quotation marks. If the speaker's name comes in the middle of the spoken words, use commas **(,)** to separate the spoken words from the speaker's name.

Write each sentence. Add commas where they are needed.

(1) Terri Sheila and I drove to Brewster New York and we visited the Hillside Outdoor Education Center. **(2)** Visitors gathered listened to a guide and learned about maple syrup. **(3)** The sights sounds and smells in the sugaring shed were wonderful. **(4)** A huge fire flickered and the syrup boiled.

(5) On Saturday March 6 1982 Sue was our guide. **(6)** "Well" she said "it's a special time of year." **(7)** Winter is over but it is too early for most other farm work" Terri added. **(8)** "Some farmers use electric drills vacuum the sap from the trees and store it in tanks" Sue explained.

Review Using the Dictionary pages 314-315

A dictionary is an alphabetical list of *entry words. Guide words* at the top of each page show the first and last entry words on that page. An entry word is divided into *syllables.* The letters and symbols in parentheses show the *pronunciation* of the word. The *part of speech* for the word is indicated by an abbreviation. If a word has more than one *meaning*, the meanings are numbered. Sometimes a sample sentence or phrase shows how the word is used.

Use the sample dictionary page below to answer the questions.

moccasin / modest

moc•ca•sin (mak´ə sen) *n.* **1.** a soft leather shoe or boot **2.** water moccasin: a copperhead or other snake resembling a moccasin.

mock (mok) *v.* **1.** to treat with scorn or disrespect. **2.** to challenge **3.** to imitate, or copy. *The dancers mock each gesture perfectly.*

mock (mok) *n.* **1.** an act of scorn **2.** an object of scorn. *He made a mock of his opponent.* **3.** an act of imitation **4.** a false copy or counterfeit

mod•ern (mod´ərn) *adj.* characteristic of the present, or recent past.

Pronunciation Key
at; āges; fäther; car; daring; end; mē; term; it; tiger; souvenir; hot; ōld; ôff; oil; fôrk; out; up; full; trüly; mūsic; sing; thin; zh in treasure; ə in lemon, ago, pencil, taken, circus; ər in letter, honor, dollar.

1. Which entry word has a verb and a noun form?
2. Which entry word is an adjective?
3. Which entry word has three syllables?
4. Where are the guide words located?
5. What are the guide words for the sample page?
6. What sentence under *mock* applies to the meaning an object of scorn?
7. Which entry word has only one meaning?

Independent Writing: Writing a Story page 319

A story has different parts. The *plot* describes the action in the story. The plot has a *beginning,* a *middle,* and an *end.* The *setting* tells where and when the story takes place. The *characters* are the people or animals in the story.

Prewriting Suppose that your class is writing stories to send to a story contest sponsored by a magazine for boys and girls. Remember that a story has three parts.

1. The **beginning** describes the characters and tells where and when the story takes place.
2. The **middle** tells what problem the characters must solve.
3. The **ending** tells how the characters solved their problem.

Choose a character, a setting, and a problem from the box below, or choose your own. Then make notes on each one.

Characters	*Settings*	*Problems*
a detective	an abandoned house	escaping from captivity
an inventor	a cellar	finding a lost person/animal
a boy	a shopping mall	returning home
a girl	a restaurant	finding a missing object
a pet animal	a hiking trail	surviving a storm
an extraterrestrial	a laboratory	discovering a secret

Writing Write an adventure story based on your notes. Use your own experiences to enrich your descriptions.

Editing Use the check questions on page 319 and the editing symbols to edit your story.

Index

Abbreviations, 48-49, 54, 66, 351, 361
  in addresses, 48, 49, 146
  chart of common, 48, 351
  of dates, 48-49, 146
  after dictionary entry word, 314
  in letters, 48, 49
  of proper names, 48, 49, 146
  of time, 49
Action verbs, 72-73, 147, 331, 334, 339, 362, 376
  definition of, 72, 226
  and linking verbs, difference between, 226-227, 234, 252
Action words, 63, 64, 82, 106; *see also* Action verbs
Addresses
  abbreviations in, 48, 49, 146
  in business letter, 102, 103, 104
  on envelope, 48-49
  friendly letter, 62, 64, 354
Adjectives, 192-207, 216-217, 333, 335
  comparative, 194-197, 198, 200, 206, 216
  definition of, 192-193, 198, 228, 306, 344, 368, 376
  with *-er* or *-est*, 194-195, 198, 200-206, 216, 332, 335, 344, 350, 369
  forming adverbs from, 264-265, 267, 286, 335
  after linking verbs, 228-229, 234, 252, 334
  with *more* and *most*, 196-197, 198-199, 216, 335, 343, 369
  predicate, 228, 229, 234, 252, 334
  prefixes before, 202-203, 206, 217
  proper, 201, 206, 216, 343, 369
  suffixes after, 202-203, 206, 217, 352
  synonyms, 204-205, 206, 217
Ads. *See* Advertisements
Adverbs, 260-267, 286, 334, 335
  comparison of, 262-263, 266, 286
  definition of, 260-261, 306, 343, 372, 376
  with *-er*, 262, 263, 266, 286, 335, 343, 350, 373
  with *-est*, 262, 263, 266, 286, 335, 343, 350, 373
  forming, from adjectives, 264-265, 267, 286, 335
  with *-ly*, 261, 262, 263, 264, 265, 286, 335, 343, 350, 373
  with *more*, 262, 263, 266, 286, 335, 343, 373
  with *most*, 262, 263, 266, 286, 335, 343, 373
  questions answered by, 260-261
  in Tom Swifty sentences, 267
Advertisement, 130, 131
  help-wanted, answering, 105
Agreement
  compound subject verb, 164-165
  pronoun-verb, 124, 125, 128-129, 141
  subject verb, 164, 165, 230, 234-235, 252
Almanac, 96, 97, 208, 209
  definition of, 96
  using for fact paragraph, 100
Alphabetical order
  of biographies in library, 96, 97
  in dictionary, 314
  of fiction books in library, 96, 97
Anderson, Marian, 218-223
Antonyms
  definition of, 230, 352, 371
  verb, 232-233, 235, 252
Apostrophe
  in contractions, 238, 239, 242, 253, 334, 347, 372
  in possessives, 50, 238, 239, 242, 253, 334, 347, 372
Atlas, 208, 209
Author card, 97, 208
Ballad, 254-257
  definition of, 254
  writing, 257
Be
  past tense forms of, 226, 235, 252, 334, 341, 360
  present tense forms of, 226, 234-235, 252, 334, 341, 360
  in progressive tenses, 236, 237, 242, 252, 340, 362, 365, 367, 370, 371
Biography, 218-223
  definition of, 218
  location of, in library, 96, 97
Body language, 119
Book
  parts of, 18-19
  titles of, 268, 269, 276, 287, 345, 373
Book report, 320-321, 355-356
  editing, 321
  steps in writing, 320
Braille, 163
Building sentences
  by adding phrases, 12-13
  combining and expanding sentences, 166-167
  with compound subjects, 166-167
  to form compound sentences, 298-301
Business letter
  address in, 102, 103, 104
  editing, 105
  fact paragraph in, 102-105
  indenting paragraphs in, 104
  parts of, 102-103, 107, 355
    body of, 102, 103, 104
    closing of, 102, 103, 104
    greeting in, 102, 103, 104
    heading in, 102, 103, 104
    signature of, 102, 103, 104

"Call It Courage," 324-329
Capitalization
beginning sentences with, 6, 9, 28, 268, 269, 276, 287, 345, 358, 373
in conversation writing, 170-171, 348, 368
of dates, 268, 269, 345, 373
of initials, 268, 269, 345, 373
of proper nouns, 46, 47, 66, 268, 269, 276, 287, 345, 373
in quotations, 171, 348, 368
of titles of books, 268, 269, 276, 287, 345, 373
Card catalog, 96-97, 208
Careers
accountant, 83
aerospace engineers, 277
author, 9
bookkeeper, 83
business owner, 83
clerk, 83
engineering, 277
firefighter, 243
journalist, 129
police officer, 243
sanitation engineer, 45
sanitation worker, 45
stock clerk, 83
"Casey Jones," 254-257
Closing
of business letter, 102, 103, 104, 385
of friendly letter, 62, 63, 64
Collage, 149
Commas, 14-15, 17, 29, 168-169, 172-173, 183, 308-309, 312-313, 322
in address of business letter, 102, 103
in business letter closings, 103
and cities and states, 14, 15, 168, 169, 308, 346, 368, 376
in compound sentences, 297, 300, 301, 303, 346, 376
before conjunctions, 308
in conversation writing, 170, 171, 308, 346-347, 368, 376
in dates, 14, 15, 168, 169, 308, 346, 368, 376
and nouns in a series, 168, 169, 308, 346, 368, 376
setting off personal names, 14, 15, 168, 169, 308, 346, 348, 368, 376
with verbs in series, 168, 169, 308, 309, 347, 368, 376
after *yes*, *no*, *well*, 14, 15, 168, 169, 308, 346, 368, 376
Common nouns, 46-47, 54, 147, 339, 361
definition of, 46
Comparison
with adjectives, 194-197, 198, 200, 206, 216
of adverbs, 262-263, 286, 334, 335
with metaphor, 58-59, 67, 353
with personification, 58, 59, 67, 353
with simile, 59, 67, 353
Complete sentences, 12, 211
Composition
of book report, 320-321
of business letter with fact paragraph, 102-105
of conversation writing, 178-181
of descriptive paragraphs, 60-65
editing, 26-27
of editorial with persuasive paragraph, 136-137
of exposition, 100-105, 214, 246-251, 284
of fact paragraph, 100-105
of friendly letter, 62-65, 66
of interviews, 212-213
of narration, 22-25, 316-319
of news report, 284
outlines for, 280-281, 282-283
of persuasive paragraphs, 134-139, 141
proofreading, 26-27
sensory images and figurative langauge in, 58-59, 67
of story, 316-319
of summary paragraphs, 214
surveys and, 212-213
of time-order paragraphs, 22-25
two-paragraph reports, 246-251
of weather report, 215
Compound nouns, 42-43, 45, 66, 146-147, 351, 361
definition of, 42
Compound predicate, 182, 296-297, 332, 333, 335
building sentences with, 166, 167
conjunction in, 160
definition of, 160, 297
verb tense in, 160-161
Compound sentences, 298-301, 335, 338, 375
building, 300-301
commas in, 297, 300, 303, 346, 376
conjunction in, 246, 300, 301
definition of, 298
Compound subjects, 158-159, 182, 296-297, 302, 322, 332, 335, 361, 367
agreement of verbs with, 164-165
building sentences with, 166, 167
conjunction in, 158-159
definition of, 158, 296
predicate of, 158
pronouns in, 158-159
Conjunctions
commas before, 308
in compound predicate, 160, 297
in compound sentences, 298, 300, 301
in compound subject, 158-159
definition of, 298, 345, 376
Context clues, 272-273, 276-277, 287

Contractions
apostrophe in, 238, 239, 242, 253, 334, 347, 472
definition of, 238
it's, 126, 127, 129, 141
of pronouns and verbs, 238, 239, 242, 253
they're, 126, 127, 129, 141
verb, 238-239, 242, 253
you're, 126, 127, 129, 141
Conversation writing, 178-181
editing, 181
punctuation in, 170-171, 173, 183, 308, 346-347, 348, 368, 376
Copyright page, of book, 18, 19
Creative expression
ballad, 257
biography, 218-223
fable, 30-33
haiku, 68-69
letter, 108-109
photo essay, 142-145
play, 184-189
short story, 324-329
true story, 288-293
Creative writing
ballad, 257
biography, 223
collage, 149
comparison writing, 293
fable, 33
friendly letter, 109
haiku, 69
interviewing, 149, 293
news article, 257
photo essay, 145
play, 189
story, 329
tanka, 69

Dates
abbreviations of, 48-49, 147
in business letter, 102, 103, 104
capitalization of, 268, 269, 345, 373
commas in, 14, 15, 168, 169, 308, 346, 368, 376
"Dear Ranger Rick," 108-109
Declarative sentence, 4, 5, 7, 28, 146, 330, 338, 358
definition of, 4
Description
action words and, 60
with adjectives, 192-207, 216-217
detail sentences for, 210, 211, 217
dictionary and, 60
in friendly letter, 62-65, 109
metaphor in, 58-59, 67, 353
sensory words and, 60
simile in, 58, 59, 67, 353
Descriptive paragraphs, 60-65, 210, 211, 217
action words in, 60
detail sentences in, 61, 210, 211, 217
friendly letter with, 62-65
synonyms, 61
topic sentence in, 61
Descriptive words, 58-60, 67
adding, to sentences, 12-13, 29
Detail sentences
in business letter, 103
for description, 61, 210, 211, 217
in editorial, 136, 137, 138
in fact paragraph, 100, 101, 104, 210, 211, 217
in persuasive paragraphs, 134, 135, 141
reasons in, 210, 211, 217
time order, 22, 23, 24, 25, 29, 210, 211, 217
in two-paragraph report, 247, 249, 251, 253
Diagraming, 357
Dialogue, in play, 184
Dictionary, 56-57
abbreviations in, 314
alphabetical order in, 314
entry word, 56, 57, 314
guide words, 56, 57, 314
pronunciation key, 314
sample page of, 56, 314
Table of English Spellings, 315
word meanings in, 314

Editing, 26-27
book report, 321
business letter, 105
conversation writing, 181
editorials, 139
friendly letter, 65
historical reports, 285
story, 319
summary paragraph, 215
two-paragraph report, 251
Editing questions, 26, 65, 105, 139, 181, 215, 251, 284, 319
Editing symbols, 26, 65, 105, 139, 181, 215, 251, 284, 319
Editorial(s), 130
concluding sentence of, 136, 137
detail sentences in, 136, 137, 138
editing, 139
fact paragraphs in, 136, 137
opinions in, 132, 136, 137
persuasive paragraphs in, 136-137
radio, 136
T.V., 136, 138
Editorial page, 136
Encyclopedia, 96, 97, 109, 208, 209
definition of, 96
using for fact paragraph, 100
using for outline, 282
English Spellings, Table of, 315
Entertainment section of newspaper, 130, 131
Entry word, dictionary, 56, 57, 314
abbreviations after, 314
information after, 314
meanings, 57

Exclamation marks, 5
after interjections, 6, 7
ending sentences, 6, 7, 28, 346, 358
Exclamatory sentences, 5, 7, 28, 146, 330, 338, 358
definition of, 5
Expanding Sentences. *See* Building sentences
Exploring language
changing word meanings, 17
expressions, origins of, 313
irregular and regular verb forms, 95
job titles, 235, 243
month and day names, origins of, 55
sesquipeds, 199
"Think Pink," 207
Tom Swifty sentences, 267
word origins, 163, 173, 303
words no longer used, 121
Exposition
biography writing, 223
book reports, 320-321
business letters, 102-105
friendly letters, 62-65, 108-109
historical report, 285
interviews, 212-215
news article, 284
paragraph of facts, 100
photo essay, 145
summary paragraph, 208-214
two-paragraph reports, 246-251

Fable, 30-33
writing, 33
Fact and opinion, difference between, 132-133
in persuasive paragraph, 134
Fact paragraphs, 100-105, 210, 211, 217
in business letters, 102-105
definition of, 132
detail sentence in, 100, 101, 104, 210, 211, 217
in editorials, 136, 137
questions answered in, 100, 101, 104
topic sentence in, 100, 104
using reference works for, 100
Fiction books, locating in library, 96-97
Figurative language, 58-59, 67
metaphor, 58-59, 67, 353
personification, 58, 59, 67, 353
simile, 58, 59, 67, 353
Films, using for reports, 248
Filmstrips, using for reports, 248
Friendly letter, 62-65, 67, 354
address, 62, 64, 354
detail sentences in, 62-65, 109
editing, 65
parts of, 62-63, 67, 354
topic sentence of, 63, 64
"Fulton's Folly," 184-188
Future tense
definition of, 77
form of, 77, 148, 331

Graphs
reading, 98-99
survey, 212
Greeting
in business letter, 102, 103, 104, 355
in friendly letter, 62, 63, 64
Guide words, dictionary, 56, 57, 314

Haiku, 68-69
Handbook, of book, 19
Heading
in business letter, 102, 103, 104, 355
in friendly letter, 62, 63, 64, 67
Headline, 130
Helping verbs
in future tense, 76
in progressive tenses, 236-237, 242, 252
Help-wanted ad, answering, 105
Historical report, 285
Homographs, 270-271, 276, 287, 352, 374
Homonyms, 126-127, 129, 141
definition of, 126, 352, 365

Imperative sentence, 5, 7, 28, 146, 330, 338, 358
definition of, 4
subject part of, 11
Indenting, 22, 24, 64, 104
in conversation writing, 170, 171
Independent writing
conversation writing, 181
descriptive paragraph, 56, 60
factual paragraph in business letter, 105
friendly letter, 65
persuasive paragraph, 139
story, 319
time-order paragraph, 27
two-paragraph report, 251
Index
book, 19
encyclopedia, 96
Indo-European language, 310
Initials
capitalization of, 268, 269, 345, 373
periods after, 268, 269
Interjections, 5, 345, 358
Interrogative sentence, 4-5, 7, 28, 146, 330, 338, 358
definition of, 4
Interviews, 212-213
for biography, 223
of family, 293
preparing for, 212
for reports, 248-249
summary paragraph of, 214
using for outline, 282
Interview notes, 212, 213, 214, 215

Interview Notes (Continued)
and outlines, 282, 283
for two-paragraph report, 249, 250
Interview questions, 212, 213, 214
and outlines, 282
for two-paragraph report, 249, 250
Irregular verbs, 88-91
past tense, special forms of, 88, 90, 94, 106-107
past tense with *have* of, special forms of, 88, 90, 94, 106-107
Italics, and titles of books, 268, 287
Its and *it's*, 126, 127, 129, 141

Job titles, 235
changing, 243

Language
history of, 310-311
levels of usage, 274-275
Letters, 108-109
abbreviations in, 48, 49
business, 102-105, 107, 355
friendly, 108-109
"Letters to the Editor," 130, 136
opinions in, 132
Library, 96-97
almanacs in, 96, 97
biographies in, 96, 97
card catalog in, 96-97
encyclopedias in, 96, 97
fiction books in, 96, 97
reference books in, 96, 97, 208-209
Library notes
for two-paragraph reports, 248, 250
using for outline, 282, 283
Library organization chart, 209
Linguists, 310
Linking verbs, 226-231, 234-235, 252, 334, 340-341, 362, 363, 365, 367, 370, 371
adjectives after, 228-229, 234, 252, 334
be, 226, 227, 234-235, 252
definition of, 226-227
nouns after, 228-229, 234, 252, 334
in present tense, using, 230, 234-235, 252
subject-verb agreement and, 230, 234-235, 252
Listening skills, 176-177
Literature
"Call It Courage," 324-329
"Casey Jones," 254-257
"Dear Ranger Rick," 108-109
"Fulton's Folly," 184-188
haiku, 68-69
"Marian Anderson," 218-223
"Prairie Blizzard," 288-293
"Rumors," 30
"Voyager I Visits Saturn," 142-145

Magazines, 208, 209
using for reports, 248
Main idea. *See* Topic sentence
Main verb
in future tense, 76
in progressive tenses, 236-237, 242
Maps, 208
"Marian Anderson," 218-223
"Maria's Slippers," 316-317
Metaphor, 58-59, 67, 353
definition of, 58
Middle English, 310, 311
Months, capitalization of, 268, 269, 276
Names, personal
capitalization of, 268, 276, 287
commas and, in direct quotations, 14, 15, 168, 169, 308, 346, 348, 368, 376
Narration
story, 314, 316, 324
time-order paragraph, 18, 25
Narrative poems, 254. *See* Ballads
News articles, 130, 136, 284
detail sentences in, 284
editing, 284
facts in, 132
steps in preparing, 284
topic sentence in, 284
writing, 257, 284
Newspapers, 208, 209
parts of, 130-131
No, commas after, 14, 15, 168, 169, 308, 346, 368, 376
Nonfiction books, 96, 97
Note-taking, 244-245
for oral reports, 285
phrase, 244, 245
sentence, 244, 245
steps in, 244
Nouns, 36-55, 112, 330-331, 335, 338, 360, 376
common, 46-47, 54, 66, 147, 339, 361
compound, 42-43, 45, 66, 146-147, 351, 361
definition of, 36-37, 228, 306
after linking verbs, 228, 229, 234, 252
plural, 38-41, 44, 66, 147, 238, 239, 242, 253, 331, 339, 349, 360
possessive, 50-51, 55, 67, 147, 238, 239, 242, 253, 331, 339, 361
predicate, 228-229, 234, 252, 334
proper, 46-47, 48-49, 54, 66, 147, 268, 269, 276, 287, 339, 345, 361, 373

Nouns (Continued)
in series, 168, 169, 308, 346, 368, 376
singular, 38-39, 44, 238, 239, 242, 253, 338, 360
suffixes, 52-53, 55, 67

Object(s)
of preposition, 304, 322
of verbs, 74-75, 82, 106, 116-117, 147, 337, 339, 362
Object pronouns, 116-117, 120-121, 140, 149, 332
definition of, 116-117
list of, 118
using, 118-119, 140
Old English, 310
Opinion
definition of, 132
in editorials, 132, 136, 137
and fact, difference between, 132-133
forming, 132
in persuasive paragraph, 132
in reviews of television programs, 139
Oral report, steps in giving, 285
Outline(s)
capitalization in, 278
and interview notes, 282, 283
interview questions and, 282
library notes for, 282, 283
main headings of, 278, 279, 280, 281
main idea of, 280
and oral reports, 285
parts of, 278, 356
periods in, 278
phrases in, 278, 279
review of, 287
Roman numerals in, 278, 280
sentences in, 278, 279
subheadings of, 278, 279, 280, 281
title, 278, 279, 280
two-part, 278-279, 280-281
writing, 282-283

Paragraphs, 20-28, 60-66, 210-215, 217, 246-251
descriptive, 60-66, 210, 211, 217
detail sentences in, 20, 21, 29, 210, 217
expository. *See* Fact, Summary
fact, 210, 211, 217
indenting, 22, 24, 64, 104
interview, 212-213
narrative, 22-25
opinion, 210, 211, 217
reasons. *See* Persuasive
reviewing, 210-211, 217
structure, 20-21
summary, 214-215
survey, 212-213
time-order in, 22-25, 29, 210, 211, 217
topic sentence of, 20, 21, 22, 23, 29, 210
two-paragraph reports, 246-251
Parts of speech, 306-307, 312, 322
Past tense
of action verbs, 76, 77, 80-81, 339, 362
of *be*, 226, 235, 252, 334, 341, 360
definition of, 76
forming, 80-81, 148, 331, 332, 349-350, 362
of irregular verbs, 88-89, 90-91, 94, 106-107, 342, 363
review of, 83, 106
using, 80-81
Past tense with *has* or *have*
forms of, 86-87, 148, 332, 340, 363
of irregular verbs, 88-89, 90-91, 94, 106-107
review of, 94, 106
Periodicals, 208, 209
Periods
in coversation writing, 171, 348, 368
ending sentences, 6, 7, 28, 346-358
after initials in personal names, 268, 269
in outlines, 278
Personification, 58, 59, 67, 353
definition of, 58
Persuasion, 134-139, 141
detail sentences in, 134, 135, 141
in editorials, 136-138
facts and, 134
opinion and, 134
reasons and, 134-135
in television reviews, 139
Photo essay, 142-145
caption, 142
definition of, 142
Phrase notes, 244, 245
Phrases, in outlines, 278, 279
Plays, 184-189
dialogue in, 184
stage directions for, 184
Plot, 316
Plural nouns, 38-41, 66
definition of, 38
forming, 38-41, 66, 147, 331, 349, 360
Poetry
ballads, 254-257
haiku, 68-69
narrative, 254
tanka, 69
Possessive nouns, 50-51, 67, 147, 331
apostrophe in, 50, 238, 239, 242, 253, 334, 347, 372
plural forms of, 50-51
singular form of, 50, 51
Possessive pronouns, 122-123, 149, 332, 343, 364
definition of, 122
homonyms sounding like, 126-127, 129, 141

Possessive pronouns (Continued)
kinds of, 122-123
review of, 128, 140
usage
alone, 122, 123
in front of nouns, 122, 123
"Prairie Blizzard," 288-293
Predicate, 10-11, 72, 152-153, 306-307, 330, 337, 359, 366. *See also* Verbs
adding descriptive words to, 12-13, 16, 29
compound, 160-161, 163, 182, 296-297, 332, 333, 334, 335
definition of, 10, 152
review of, 16, 29, 162
simple, 156-157, 162, 182, 332, 337, 366
Predicate adjectives, 228, 229, 234, 252, 334
Predicate nouns, 228, 229, 234, 252, 334
Prefixes, 92-93, 95, 107
definition of, 202, 351, 363, 370
mis-, 92, 351
pre-, 92, 351
re-, 92, 351
un-, 92, 202, 203, 206, 217, 351
Prepositional phrases, 304-305, 312, 322
definition of, 304, 345, 376
Prepositions, 304-305, 312, 322
chart of commonly used, 304
definition of, 304, 345, 376
Present perfect tense, 86-91
forms of, 86-87
Present tense, 172, 183
agreement with subject, 165
agreement with subject pronouns, 124, 125, 128-129, 141
of *be*, 226, 234-235, 252, 334, 341, 360
definition of, 76
forming, 77, 78, 331, 332, 349, 362
of *have*, 84-85, 106
review of, 82-83, 106
using, 78-79
Progressive tense, 236-237, 242, 252, 340, 362, 365, 367, 370, 371
Pronouns, 112-129, 140-141, 149, 332, 335
in compound subject, 158-159
contractions of, and verbs, 238, 239, 242, 253
definition of, 112, 307, 343, 364, 367
list of common, 112, 343, 365
as objects, 116-117, 120-121, 140, 149, 332, 343, 364
possessive, 122-123, 128, 140, 149, 332, 343, 365
as subjects, 114-115, 120, 121, 140, 147, 332, 343, 364
Pronoun-verb agreement, 124-125, 128-129, 141
rules for, 124
Pronunciation key, dictionary, 314
Proofreading. *See* Editing
Proper adjectives, 201, 206, 216
capitalization of, 201
definition of, 201, 343, 369
forming, 201
Proper nouns, 46-47, 54, 66, 147
abbreviations of, 48-49, 147
capitalization of, 46, 47, 66, 268, 269, 276, 287, 345, 373
definition of, 46
as proper adjectives, 200
Proverb, 30
Punctuation marks. *See* Commas, Exlamation mark, Period, Question mark, Quotation mark
Question mark
in conversation writing, 170, 171, 309, 346, 348, 368, 376
ending sentences, 6, 7, 28, 346, 358
Question sentence. *See* Interrogative sentences
Quotation(s), 170-171
commas in, 308, 347, 368, 376
Quotation marks
in conversation writing, 170, 348, 368
and titles of poems, 268
and titles of short stories, 268

Reasons
in editorials, 136, 137, 138
and opinions in paragraphs, 210, 211, 217
Records, using for reports, 248
Reference works, 96, 97
using, 208-209
for fact paragraphs, 100
for outline, 282
for reports, 248
Relief map, 208
Reports
historical, 285
news, 284. *See also* News articles
oral, 285
outlining, 280-281
planning, 280
two-paragraph, 246-251
weather, 215
Reviews, of television programs, 139
Road map, 208
Roman numerals, in outlines, 278, 280
"Rumors," 30-33

Sensory images, 58-59, 67
Sensory words, 58-59, 60

Sentence notes, 244, 245
Sentences, 2-12, 146, 152-173, 330
capitalization of first word of, 6-7, 9, 28, 146, 268, 269, 276, 287, 345, 358, 373
combining, 172, 298-299
complete, 12, 211
compound, 298-301, 303, 335, 338, 346, 375, 376
declarative, 4, 5, 7, 28, 146, 330, 338, 358
definition of, 2-3, 152, 337
end punctuation in, 6-7, 9, 28
exclamatory, 5, 7, 28, 146, 330, 338, 358
expanding. *See* Building sentences
imperative, 4-5, 7, 11, 28, 146, 330, 338, 358
interrogative, 4-5, 7, 28, 146, 330, 338, 358
kinds of, 4-5, 8, 28, 146, 330, 338
in outlines, 278, 279
parts of, 2
predicate, 10-11, 29, 72, 146, 152-153, 330, 337
subject, 10-11, 28, 72, 146, 152-153, 330, 337
review of, 8-9, 28-29
simple, 298, 338, 375
Tom Swifty, 267
Sesquipeds, 199
Setting, 316
Short story, 325-329
characters of, 324
parts of, 324
plot of, 324
setting of, 324
Signature
in business letter, 102, 103, 104, 355
in friendly letter, 62, 63, 64, 67
Simile, 58, 59, 67, 353
definition of, 58
Simple predicate, 156-157, 182, 296
definition of, 156
review of, 162
Simple sentences, 298, 338, 375
Simple subject, 152-153, 182, 296
definition of, 152
review of, 162
Singular nouns, 38-39, 44, 238, 239, 242, 253, 338, 360
definition of, 38
Speaking skills, 176-177
oral report, 285
Spelling rules
for adjectives ending with *-er* or *-est*, 200, 206, 216, 350, 369
forming adverbs from adjectives, 264-265, 286, 350, 373
for forming plural nouns, 38-41, 66, 349, 360
homonyms, 126-127, 129, 141
for prefixes, 203-204, 206, 217
for suffixes, 203-204, 206, 217
for verbs, 79-81, 349-350, 362
Stage directions, 184
Story, 316-319
characters, 316, 318
editing, 319
main character of, 317, 319
parts of, 316, 318
planning, 318
plot of, 316, 318
review of, 323
setting, 316, 318
writing, 319
Study and reference skills
book, parts of, 18-19
dictionary usage, 56-57, 314-315
fact and opinion, 132-133
graphs and tables, 98-99
library usage, 96-97
listening skills, 176-177
newspaper, 130-131
note-taking, 244-245
paragraph structure, 20-21
reference works, 208-209
test-taking, 174-175
two-part outline, 278-279
Subject, 10-11, 72, 152-153, 306, 330, 337, 359, 366
adding descriptive words to, 12-13, 16, 29
agreement with verb, 164, 165
agreement of verbs with, 164-165
compound, 158-159, 163, 182, 302, 322, 332, 335, 337, 366, 367
definition of, 10, 337, 358
in imperative sentence, 11
review of, 16, 28
simple, 154-155, 162, 182, 332, 337, 366
Subject card, 97, 208
definition of, 152
review of, 162
Subject pronouns, 114-115, 149, 332
agreement with verb, 124-125
in compound subject, 158-159
definition of, 114
list of, 118
review of, 120, 121, 140
using, 118-119, 140
correctly, 114
Subject-verb agreement, 164, 165
linking verbs, 230, 234-235, 252
Suffixes
definition of, 52, 202, 352, 361, 370
-er, 52, 53, 67, 352
-ful, 202, 203, 206, 217, 352
-less, 52, 53, 67, 202, 203, 206, 217, 352
-ness, 52, 53, 67, 352
noun, 52-53, 55, 67
-or, 52, 53, 67
-y, 202, 203, 206, 217, 352
Summary paragraph
editing, 215
of interview, 214
Surveys, 212-213
Synonyms
adjective, 204-205, 206, 217

Synonyms (Continued)
definition of, 204, 240, 352, 370, 372
in descriptive paragraphs, 61
verb, 240-241, 243, 253

Table of contents, of book, 18, 19
Tables
reading, 98-99
survey, 212
Tanka, 69
Telling sentences. *See* Declarative sentence
Television reviews, 139
Tense of a verb. *See* Verb tenses
Test-taking skills, 174-175
Their, they're, and *there,* 126-127, 129, 141
Time-order paragraphs, 22-25, 29, 210, 211, 217
detail sentences in, 22, 23, 24, 25, 29, 210, 211, 217
editing, 26-27
topic sentence in, 24, 25, 29
writing, 25, 27
Time-order words, 20, 21, 22, 23
Title(s)
book
capitalization of, 268, 269, 276, 287, 345, 373
italization of, 268, 287
of outlines, 278, 279, 280
poems, quotations around, 268
short stories, quotations around, 268
of two-paragraph report, 247, 249, 251
Title card, 97, 208
Title page, of book, 18, 19
Tom Swifty sentences, 267
Topic sentences
in business letter, 103, 104
definition, 22
in descriptive paragraph, 56, 60
in editorial, 136, 137, 138
in fact paragraph, 100, 104
in friendly letter, 63, 64
in paragraph, 210, 211
in persuasive paragraph, 134, 135, 141
in summary paragraph, 214
in time-order paragraph, 22
in two-paragraph report, 246-247, 249, 251, 253
True story, 288-293
Two-paragraph reports, 246-251
detail sentences in, 247, 249, 251, 253
editing, 251
historical, 285
information, gathering for, 248-249
main idea of, 248, 249
news report, 284
outline for, 278-279, 280-281
review of, 253
title for, 247, 249, 251
topic sentences in, 246-247, 249, 251, 253
writing, 248-249, 251, 253

Usage, levels of, 274-275

Verb(s), 72-95, 147-148, 226-243, 331-332, 335. *See also* Predicate
action, 72-73, 147, 226-227, 234, 252, 331, 334, 339, 362, 376
antonyms, 232-233, 335, 352
contractions of pronouns and, 238-239, 242, 253
definition of, 306
ending in *-ing*, 236-237, 242, 252
helping, 86, 88, 90, 340, 363
irregular, 88-91, 342-343, 363
linking, 226-231, 234-235, 252, 334, 340, 370, 371
with no objects, 74
object of, 72-75, 82, 106, 116-117, 339, 362
review of, 234-235, 242-243, 252-253
in series, 168, 169, 308, 309, 347, 368, 376
synonyms, 240-241, 243, 253
Verb tenses, 76-81, 148, 331-332, 334, 339-343
in compound predicate, 160-161
future, 77, 339, 362
past, 76, 86, 90, 339, 340, 342-343, 349-350, 362, 363
past progressive, 236-237, 242, 252, 340, 371
present, 76, 78, 84, 164, 172, 183, 339, 340, 341, 349, 362, 363, 365, 367
present progressive, 236-237, 242, 252, 340, 371
review of, 82-83, 106
"Voyager I Visits Saturn," 142-145

Weather report, 215
in newspaper, 130, 131
Well, commas after, 14, 15, 168, 169, 308, 346, 368, 376
Word bank, 25, 104, 138, 181
Word meanings
changing, 17
from context clues, 272-273, 287
Word origins, 310, 311
Word usage, levels of, 274-275
World atlas, 208

Yes, commas after, 14, 15, 168, 169, 308, 346, 368, 376
You're and *your*, 126, 127, 129, 141

ZIP code, 64, 103